# SUPERMAN

# SUPERMA

## secret identity

# kurt busiek
writer

# stuart immonen
### artist, colorist,
### original covers

## todd klein letterer

## superman created by
## jerry siegel and
## joe shuster

Joey Cavalieri
EDITOR-ORIGINAL SERIES

Harvey Richards
ASSISTANT EDITOR-ORIGINAL SERIES

Robert Greenberger
SENIOR EDITOR-COLLECTED EDITION

Robbin Brosterman
DESIGN DIRECTOR – BOOKS

Amie Brockway-Metcalf
PUBLICATION DESIGN

Bob Harras
VP – EDITOR-IN-CHIEF

Diane Nelson
PRESIDENT

Dan DiDio and Jim Lee
CO-PUBLISHERS

Geoff Johns
CHIEF CREATIVE OFFICER

John Rood
EXECUTIVE VP – SALES, MARKETING AND
BUSINESS DEVELOPMENT

Amy Genkins
SENIOR VP – BUSINESS AND LEGAL AFFAIRS

Nairi Gardiner
SENIOR VP – FINANCE

Jeff Boison
VP – PUBLISHING OPERATIONS

Mark Chiarello
VP – ART DIRECTION AND DESIGN

John Cunningham
VP – MARKETING

Terri Cunningham
VP – TALENT RELATIONS AND SERVICES

Alison Gill
SENIOR VP – MANUFACTURING AND OPERATIONS

Hank Kanalz
SENIOR VP – DIGITAL

Jay Kogan
VP – BUSINESS AND LEGAL AFFAIRS,
PUBLISHING

Jack Mahan
VP – BUSINESS AFFAIRS, TALENT

Nick Napolitano
VP – MANUFACTURING ADMINISTRATION

Sue Pohja
VP – BOOK SALES

Courtney Simmons
SENIOR VP – PUBLICITY

Bob Wayne
SENIOR VP – SALES

## SUPERMAN: SECRET IDENTITY

DC Comics, 1700 Broadway, New York, NY 10019
A Warner Bros. Entertainment Company
Printed by RR Donnelley, Salem, VA, USA.  3/1/13
Third Printing.
ISBN:978-1-4012-0451-8

Cover illustration by Stuart Immonen

Library of Congress Cataloging-in-Publication Data

Busiek, Kurt.
Superman : Secret Identity / Kurt Busiek, Stuart Immonen.
p. cm.
"Originally published in single magazine form in Superman: Secret Identity 1-4."
ISBN 978-1-4012-0451-8
1. Graphic novels. I. Immonen, Stuart, illustrator. II. Title. III. Title: Secret Identity.
PN6728.S9B87 2013
741.5'973–dc23
2012046013

for **elliot s! maggin**, **curt swan** and **julius schwartz**

# secret origins

Sometimes you just know. You have an idea, and it just clicks. You know it's going to work.

Sometimes you don't, of course. And sometimes, the idea sneaks up on you…

Here's the part that didn't go into the proposal, when I was pitching this series:

It was 1985. I'd been working as a professional comics writer for about three years, off and on — too often off for my tastes, but that's a whole 'nother story. DC was in the throes of CRISIS ON INFINITE EARTHS, which would shake up their history in a major, never-been-anything-fully-like-it-before-or-since way. And in the midst of all this, a comic book came out: DC COMICS PRESENTS #87, written by Elliot S. Maggin, pencilled by Curt Swan, edited by the legendary Julius Schwartz. This series was and is dedicated to them, and with good reason.

To them, it may have been just another assignment, another way to feed the hungry maw of monthly publication. I've never spoken to any of them about it, and Curt and Julie are no longer with us to ask, but I think of it that way: a clever idea to fill the pages of the latest issue, an opportunity afforded by the event that was CRISIS to do something that would surprise a few readers and have a few unusual twists. Something to do your best on, sure, as the job demands, but not a career highlight or anything. Just another monthly issue, another clever idea in a medium that demands a constant flow of them.

To me, though, it was something else entirely.

It was the story of the Superboy of Earth-Prime. The young Clark Kent of one of DC's alternate Earths — the one that is supposed to be the "real world," with no super-heroes or aliens or monsters (with a minor exception or two here and there). In this world, the DC heroes were all known as comic-book characters.

And young Clark, growing up in Maine or New Hampshire — I confess, I don't recall the details, I haven't read the issue in some years and can't find the new copy I bought awhile ago — has lived his whole life with the taunts of his schoolmates for having the same name as the famous super-hero. All the worse, because he looks like the Clark of the comics, too. I knew how this could be — not simply because we all know the nature of childhood cruelty, but because my sisters and I had a babysitter named Kent Clarke when I was a kid, and I saw some of what he dealt with.

But then young Clark discovers he has Superman's powers, too, and the sense of freedom, of release that this gave him was a wonderful thing. That's the part that resonated with me most. There's a delicious irony in the concept of being teased for something that everyone knows isn't true, but turns out to be true after all — your inner strength, your magical secret that the world doesn't know. And it fit perfectly with the classic underpinnings of Superman as a character, the nerdy exterior masking the powerful secret identity. I was immediately hooked by the character, and saw possibilities in him — a terrific tension between exterior expectations and his inner secret, a context that was different from any other Superman series, because in this guy's world, Superman is a trademark, a pop-culture icon. The taunts become worse and more engagingly specific. *Look*, the world around him teases. *Look at what you're not, what you can never hope to be.* Isn't it funny how far you are from this ideal? But no — you *are* that ideal. And only you know it.

I wanted to see a monthly series about this kid. Heck, I wanted to write it.

And then, as I had to know was coming, our young hero has an adventure with Superman (that was the concept of DC COMICS PRESENTS, Superman team-up stories), and heads off at the end into the Great Crisis, where he survives to go off into a misty Valhalla of sorts, but his world is wiped out, destroyed along the way to a theoretically more streamlined DC universe.

And I knew it had to happen and I knew the character would never have

been created without knowing there wasn't going to be any more, but I was still disappointed. It didn't matter that he lived through it — it was the world that made him special, the world that thought of Superman as a comic-book hero, not knowing that this one put-upon kid really had the goods. That was the part that was cool, the part I wanted to see explored — or better yet, the part I wanted to get to explore myself.

On the other hand, there was no point in pitching anyone at DC the idea. "Hey, I know — I'll do a regular series about a one-shot character who lived on an Earth you just destroyed. Bring it all back just for me!" They'd have looked at me like I had cats in my skull. One-issue wonders who didn't make a splash didn't get their own series, even if it didn't involve reversing the biggest sales splash the company had had in years.

But the idea didn't go away. Every now and then, I'd find myself thinking about that kid, about the great little idea that was never able to go anywhere, and wish I could do something with it. Still, it clearly wasn't going to happen. If nothing else, characters from *years-old* one-shot stories didn't get their own series either.

Jump ahead to fifteen years later, or something close to it. By now, I've made something of a name for myself on series such as *Marvels* and ASTRO CITY, and I have a reputation as a guy who can take a different angle on super-heroes, look at what they say about humanity as much as — or in some cases instead of — their high-flying adventures. And DC, in the era after CRISIS, had gone through a number of continuity upheavals. Along the way, we'd seen the classic Superboy erased from history, a "pocket universe" Superboy briefly in existence, a comic based on a TV version of Superboy, a brand-new Superboy with a different history and powers and very likely more.

But they still weren't going to let me do a series about a near-forgotten one-issue wonder from a long-destroyed setting, no matter how much I liked him. So I kept shoving the idea away, knowing I'd never get to explore it.

Still, I found myself thinking and

talking about the nature of super-hero stories a lot, part of exploring the genre in different ways that I was doing with ASTRO CITY. One point I made a lot was that people think of the super-hero genre as inherently adolescent, all about a youngster's wish-fulfillment dreams of power, of being able to do everything he couldn't as a powerless, marginalized child. And nowhere was this more evident than in Superman. Clark Kent was the shy adolescent (or stand-in for same), seen as meek and spineless, unattractive to Lois Lane, his romantic avatar, and incapable of winning respect. But as fast as a teenager's voice cracks, he could become the über-adult, Superman, powerful, respected, the target of Lois's romantic dreams, able literally to move mountains and famous the world over. It was the adolescent transformation from boy to man writ large.

But while most people who'd bring this up did so as an example of the limitations of the super-hero genre, I argued, I could see it as an indication of the power of it. Here was a very human, very personal thing, something large audiences could easily identify with emotionally, played out as metaphor, as a sweeping larger-than-life tale. Well, if super-heroes could do that, couldn't they do it for other things, too? What about female adolescence? Or maturity? Old age? If Captain America can be America-as-wartime-power writ large, could you build a super-hero around other abstract ideas? The self-image of emerging African nations? The fall of Communism? The punk movement, the Jazz Age, whatever? It seemed to me the possibilities were endless.

I was aided in this, in part, by the fact that I knew it could be done because it had been — notably in *Superfolks*, a wonderful satirical novel by Robert Mayer (currently available in reissue from About Comics, and soon to get another new edition from St. Martin's Press), which recast Superman as a super-hero facing the downward slope of middle age and the long slide to retirement. *Superfolks* proved, at least to me, that the power of the super-hero genre could reach further than people thought.

And at some point, in telling tales of super-heroes that centered on different ideas, different emotional conflicts, that damned Superboy of Earth-Prime slipped back into my head.

The concept was simple. Instead of seeing the adolescent in Superman and roving to other characters to see other things, why not just stay with the big blue guy? If he can embody adolescence, can he embody adulthood? Fatherhood? Old age? Why not? And if that core idea — that sense of I-may-look-like-a-boy-but-there's-a-man-within that defines the stumbling self-discovery of adolescence — works so well, why not the others? At every stage in life, there's a difference between how the world sees us and who we think we are, who our secret self is, down deep inside. Why not look at other stages of that?

And hey, wouldn't that be an intriguing way to use that character who's been nagging at me all these years?

So when editor Joey Cavalieri asked me if I had any ideas for Superman special projects, well, there it was, lying in wait. The project I knew I'd never be able to do.

And he liked it.

Now, as noted, I didn't mention DC COMICS PRESENTS #87. Not until quite a bit later. I didn't want anyone thinking of this as an obscure continuity revival of a character few people remembered. So I spun images of archetypes and the power of metaphor, and probably something about Gail Sheehy's *Passages*, suggesting a story that uses the familiar iconography of Superman to look at a life, to explore the conflicts we all face, not just as adolescents, but as young adults, as romantic partners, as parents and more. A story that takes the concept of the secret identity and uses it as a metaphor for our own inner selves, the part of us that most of the world doesn't get to see, that we share with few others across a lifetime.

"Sure," he said. "Let me see a pitch on that."

At this point, I should say something about Stuart Immonen, whose artwork on this project is both stunning and perfect for the story and the characters. I'd been working with Stuart on a couple of other projects, and I was regularly impressed not only with Stuart's amazing versatility — he can draw anything and make it look good — but with his facility for and interest in human drama. Stuart's a terrific storyteller and a skilled draftsman, but first and foremost he's an ideal example of the idea that to truly achieve a sense of wonder in the fantastic stuff of comics, you first need to believe in the people. If you can believe in the guy standing on the sidewalk, you'll believe it when he sees another man fly overhead. And Stuart can make you believe in that guy on the sidewalk like nobody's business.

I don't actually remember whether I first broached the idea that became SUPERMAN: SECRET IDENTITY to Joey or to Stuart. I remember spinning it out to Stuart as a chance to do something more open than the often-crowded plots I'd given him on our other work — a chance to contrast the scenes of human drama with vistas of moonlit flights, of tranquil mountain peaks, of glorying in the wonder of superpowers more than the violence. After a while, he started to get impatient — sure, fine, sounded good to him. I could stop trying to sell him on it.

Stuart sounded good to Joey, too.

The pitch went in, the outline got written and revised, and we eventually got an okay on the project, which took longer than just breezing through it like that suggests, but wasn't all that interesting a process. And then we were good to go.

That's the point where I could let people know about the other reason I wanted to do it — the fanboy itch to finally write that cool character I'd glimpsed so briefly, so long ago. It was too late, now -- they liked the story, they liked the approach, so we'd gotten past the point where "You want to bring back *who*?!" was going to be a problem.

Ironically, that's also the point where the project stopped being about the Superboy of Earth-Prime, too.

See, what I would have liked about writing the Superboy of Earth-Prime was all the texture, all the little explorations of his situation. What I had in my head was an ongoing adventure series, where you'd see relationships develop slowly, a supporting cast get built up over time — and probably a rogues gallery of threats, too -- and the fun would be in the day-to-day management of his secret. How does it affect his first date, when he's trying to be suave and confident, but there's a four-alarm fire raging in the next town over and he's got to ditch his date? What's it like to be able to fly to Patagonia during study hall, but fail your driver's test? How does he handle the growing-but-uncertain suspicion of his parents — or does he tell them — or of a friend at school?

There'd be ongoing subplots, lots of intrigue and adventure, and probably a lot of knockabout super-hero action.

Not anymore, though.

Because there's a difference between a series and a story — and what we'd worked SECRET IDENTITY out to be was four stories, all set in

different time-periods of our Clark's life. In a series, you can wander around, explore side-alleys, look at the same situation from different angles, indulge in slow development. That's what a sitcom is on TV, after all — exploring a particular situation over and over again, delving into the characters more and more, until you've exhausted what you can do with them or the audience has abandoned you. A single story, though, is more like a movie — you've got one structure, one arc, one run through the situation, so you've got to do all the important stuff, make your point, deliver on your theme, and then you're done. No wandering around, no slow, ongoing growth. You simply don't have the time, or the room.

Plus, since we'd decided on a world where Clark was a secret, he couldn't have big splashy battles with super-villains anyway.

No, instead of wandering around wringing every last opportunity out of a teenaged Clark, we had an idea to serve, the idea of adolescence, of figuring out who you *want* to be as your adult self is emerging, letting you know what you *can* be. And then we had to move on to the next idea, the next stage.

I expect it made for a better — or at the very least, less conventional — story, and I don't regret tackling it this way at all. I'm just noting that we went off in our own direction, starting from the same point as what Elliot, Curt and Julie had done, but heading off over the horizon almost instantly, getting one dramatic structure out of their setup and then plunging ten years into the future to see what major life issues Clark could tangle with next.

And Stuart decided he wanted to take a different approach to the art — instead of doing a traditional pencil job and handing it over to an inker and colorist to bring through, he wanted to keep control of it himself, all the way through. He did a tight, illustrative pencil rendering on each page, then scanned it into the computer and digitally colored it, using a palette inspired by 1950s advertising art. The result was striking, unusual, and rich in mood and atmosphere, enhancing the emotion of the character stuff and the splendor of the fantasy. Just check out the double-page spread of Clark's first flight, and see if you don't agree. By the time we finished the first issue, I knew this was really Stuart's book, and my job as writer was to try to make the scripts good enough to stand with that glorious artwork.

The end result was something of a surprise, judging from the reviews and from reader feedback. Nobody really knew what to expect from a project with such an oddball premise — hey, wasn't there a DC COMICS PRESENTS something like this, years ago? — but those who gave it a try got swept up in it, and we got some of the best reviews I've received in my entire career.

And it didn't turn out to be the series I was itching to do back in 1985, but I'm grateful to Elliot, Curt and Julie for their work on that story, without which this one couldn't possibly have existed. And I'm proud to have worked with Stuart on it — and with Joey, who shepherded it through the production process with patience and care, and Todd Klein and Amie Brockway-Metcalf, who did such a restrained and elegant job with lettering and publication design, respectively.

It was one of those ideas that sneaks up on you when you're not looking, and turns out to be something almost entirely other than what you thought it was going to be when you first spotted it. But sometimes, those are the best ideas — they take you places you didn't think you could go, and teach you things you didn't know you knew.

I think this was one of those — and I hope, once you've read it, you agree.

And hey, guys, if anyone's up for a SUPERBOY OF EARTH-PRIME monthly...

**—KURT BUSIEK**
AUGUST 2004

# chapter one **smallville**

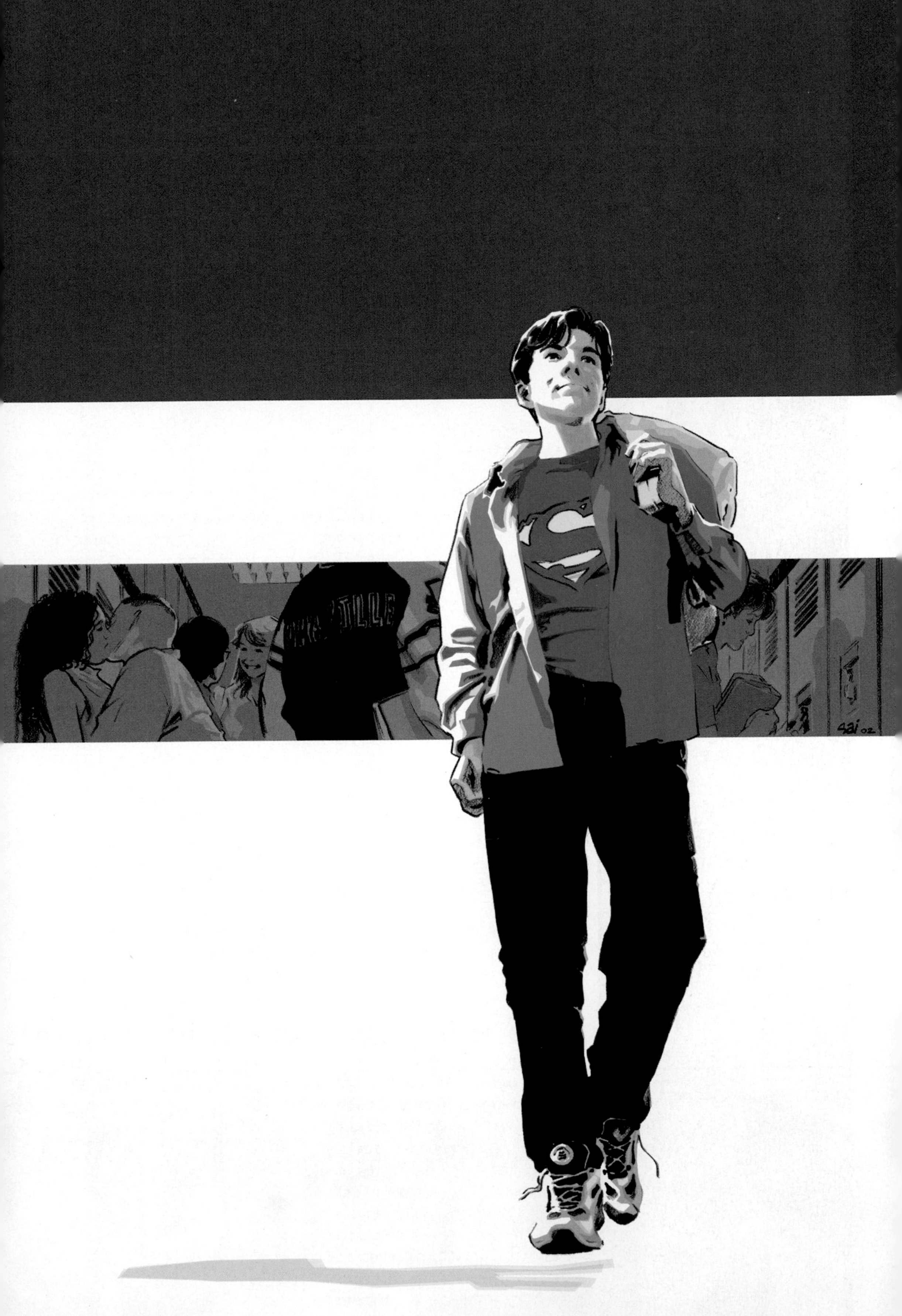

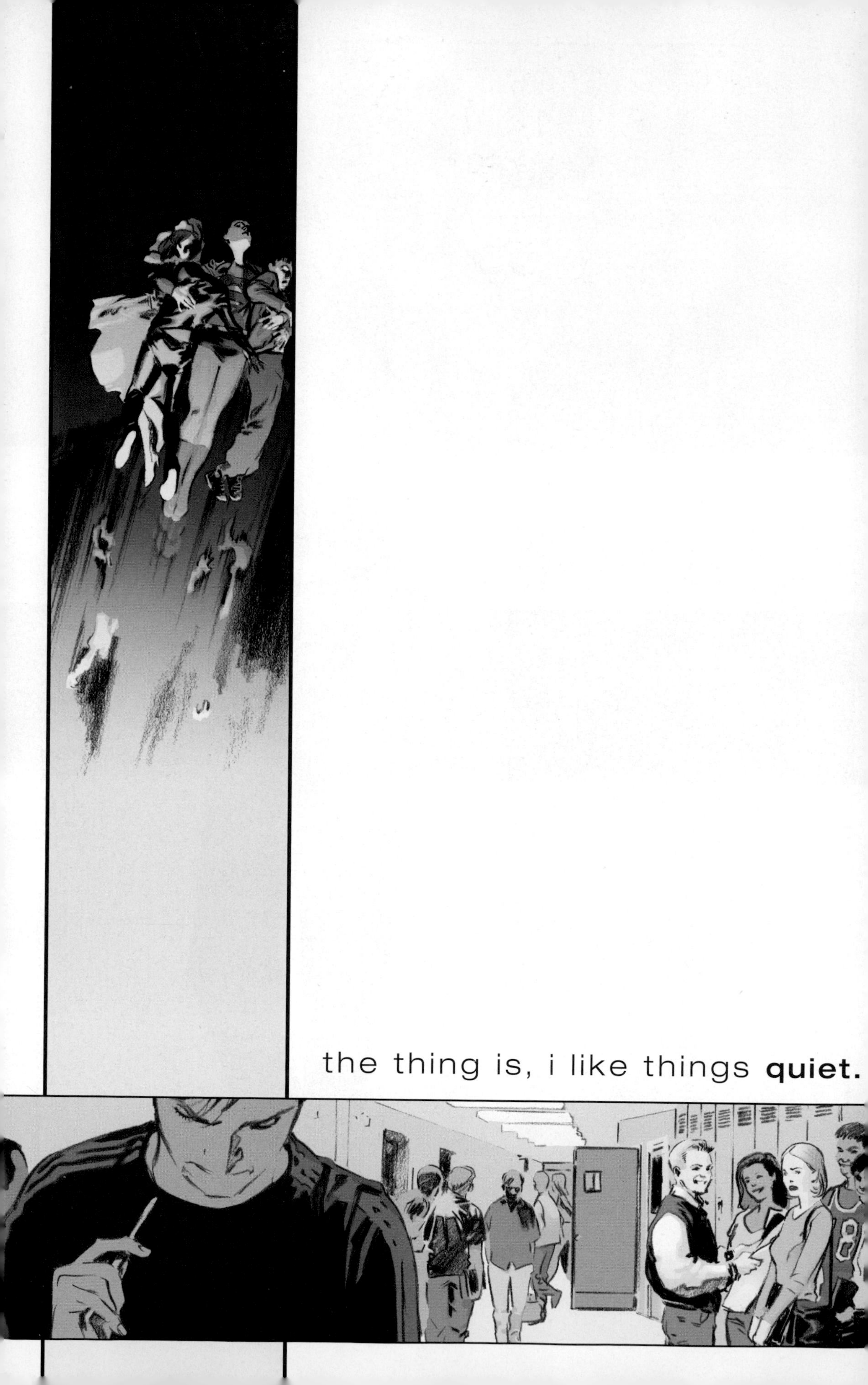
the thing is, i like things **quiet.**

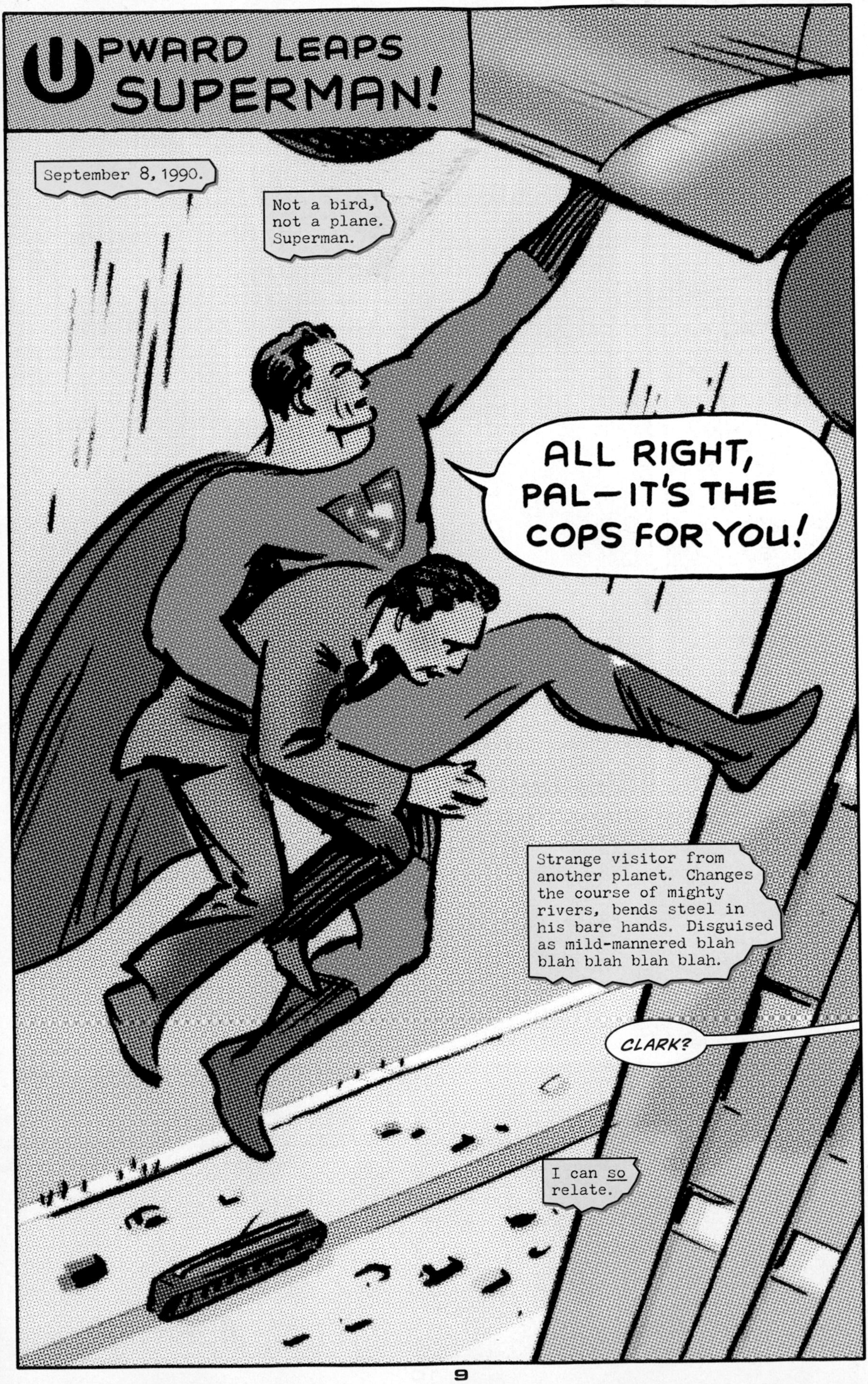
UPWARD LEAPS SUPERMAN!
September 8, 1990.
Not a bird, not a plane. Superman.
ALL RIGHT, PAL—IT'S THE COPS FOR YOU!
Strange visitor from another planet. Changes the course of mighty rivers, bends steel in his bare hands. Disguised as mild-mannered blah blah blah blah blah.
CLARK?
I can so relate.

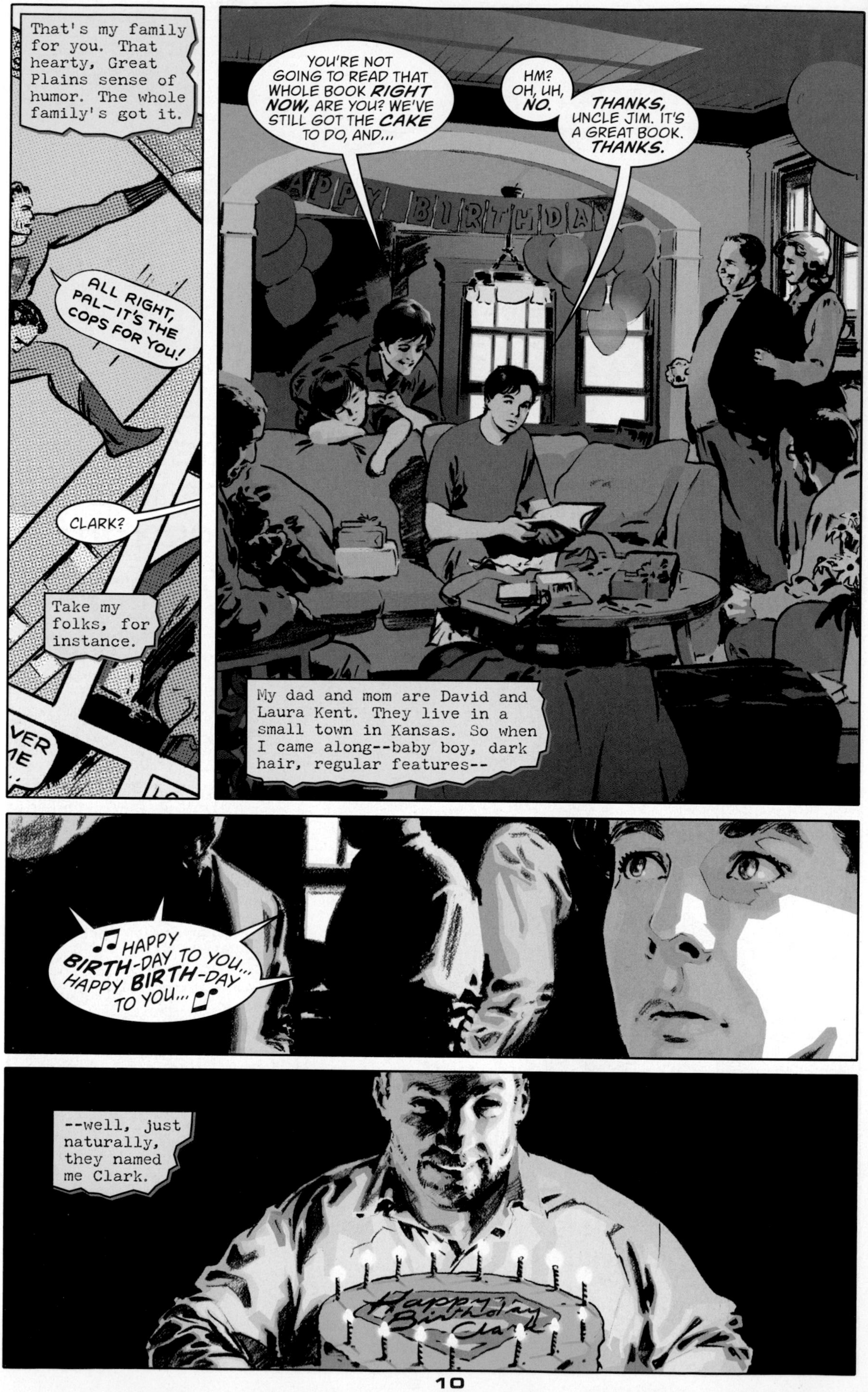
That's my family for you. That hearty, Great Plains sense of humor. The whole family's got it.
ALL RIGHT, PAL—IT'S THE COPS FOR YOU!
CLARK?
Take my folks, for instance.
YOU'RE NOT GOING TO READ THAT WHOLE BOOK RIGHT NOW, ARE YOU? WE'VE STILL GOT THE CAKE TO DO, AND...
HM? OH, UH, NO.
THANKS, UNCLE JIM. IT'S A GREAT BOOK. THANKS.
My dad and mom are David and Laura Kent. They live in a small town in Kansas. So when I came along--baby boy, dark hair, regular features--
♫ HAPPY BIRTH-DAY TO YOU... HAPPY BIRTH-DAY TO YOU... ♫
--well, just naturally, they named me Clark.
Happy Birthday Clark

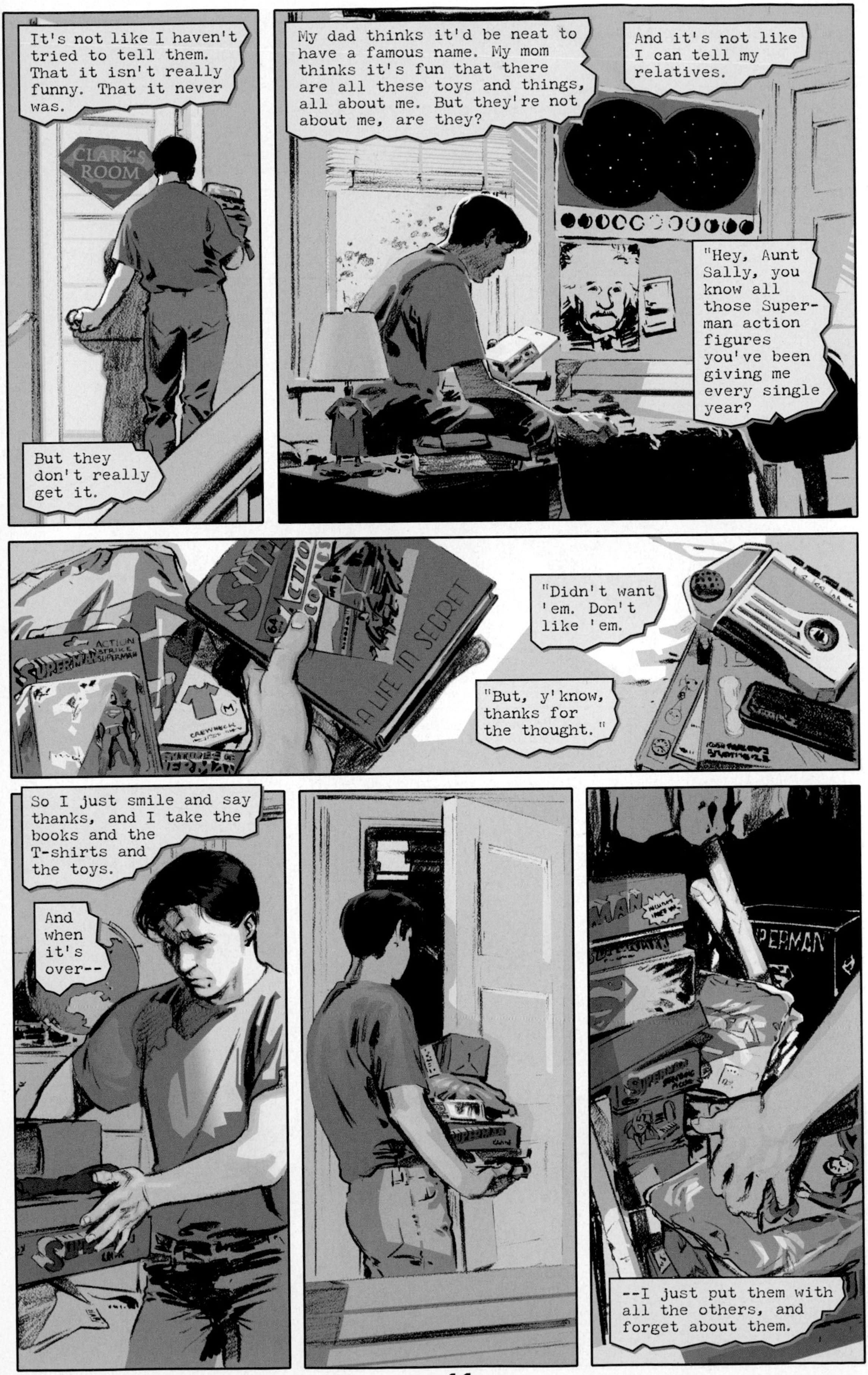
It's not like I haven't tried to tell them. That it isn't really funny. That it never was.
CLARK'S ROOM
But they don't really get it.
My dad thinks it'd be neat to have a famous name. My mom thinks it's fun that there are all these toys and things, all about me. But they're not about me, are they?
And it's not like I can tell my relatives.
"Hey, Aunt Sally, you know all those Superman action figures you've been giving me every single year?
"Didn't want 'em. Don't like 'em.
"But, y'know, thanks for the thought."
A LIFE IN SECRET
SUPERMAN
So I just smile and say thanks, and I take the books and the T-shirts and the toys.
And when it's over--
--I just put them with all the others, and forget about them.

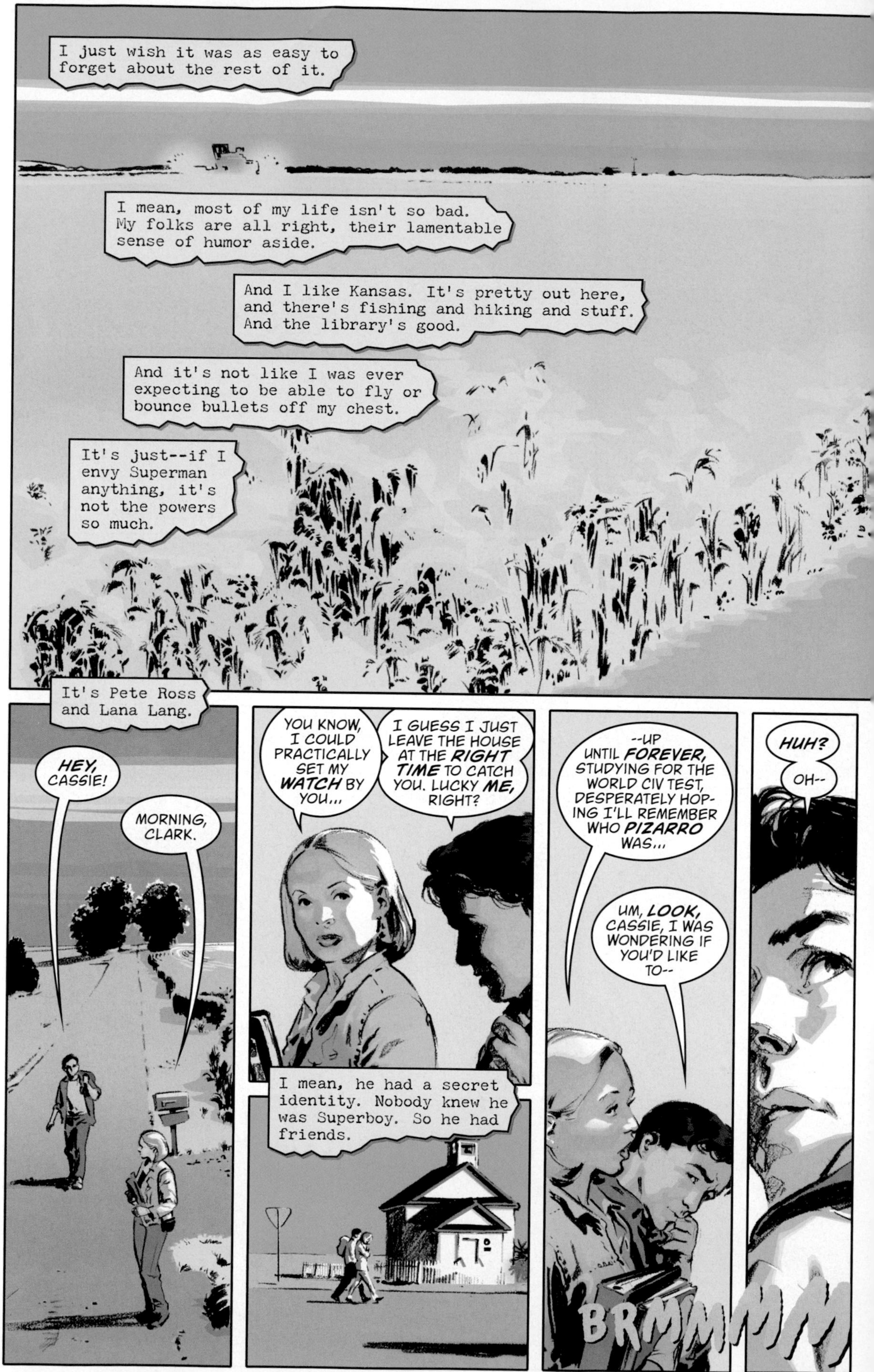
I just wish it was as easy to forget about the rest of it.
I mean, most of my life isn't so bad. My folks are all right, their lamentable sense of humor aside.
And I like Kansas. It's pretty out here, and there's fishing and hiking and stuff. And the library's good.
And it's not like I was ever expecting to be able to fly or bounce bullets off my chest.
It's just--if I envy Superman anything, it's not the powers so much.
It's Pete Ross and Lana Lang.
HEY, CASSIE!
MORNING, CLARK.
YOU KNOW, I COULD PRACTICALLY SET MY WATCH BY YOU...
I GUESS I JUST LEAVE THE HOUSE AT THE RIGHT TIME TO CATCH YOU. LUCKY ME, RIGHT?
I mean, he had a secret identity. Nobody knew he was Superboy. So he had friends.
--UP UNTIL FOREVER, STUDYING FOR THE WORLD CIV TEST, DESPERATELY HOPING I'LL REMEMBER WHO PIZARRO WAS...
UM, LOOK, CASSIE, I WAS WONDERING IF YOU'D LIKE TO--
HUH?
OH--
BRMMMMM

--NO!

HA HA HA HA HA HA HA HA HA HA HA

Nobody messed with Superboy for being called Clark Kent. Why would they?

WHAT'CHA GOT *HERE*, SUPERBOY? LUTHOR'S *SECRET PLANS*? SCHEMATICS FOR *METALLO*?

*C'MON*, KENT-- COME TAKE 'EM *BACK*! OR WHAT'SA MATTER? CAN'T *FLY* TODAY?

NO PROB--

--YOU CAN JUST PICK IT ALL UP AT *SUPER-SPEED*!

HAHAHAHAH HA HA HA HA HA HAHAHA HA

So mostly I just envy him being able to have a normal life.

But sometimes, just sometimes...

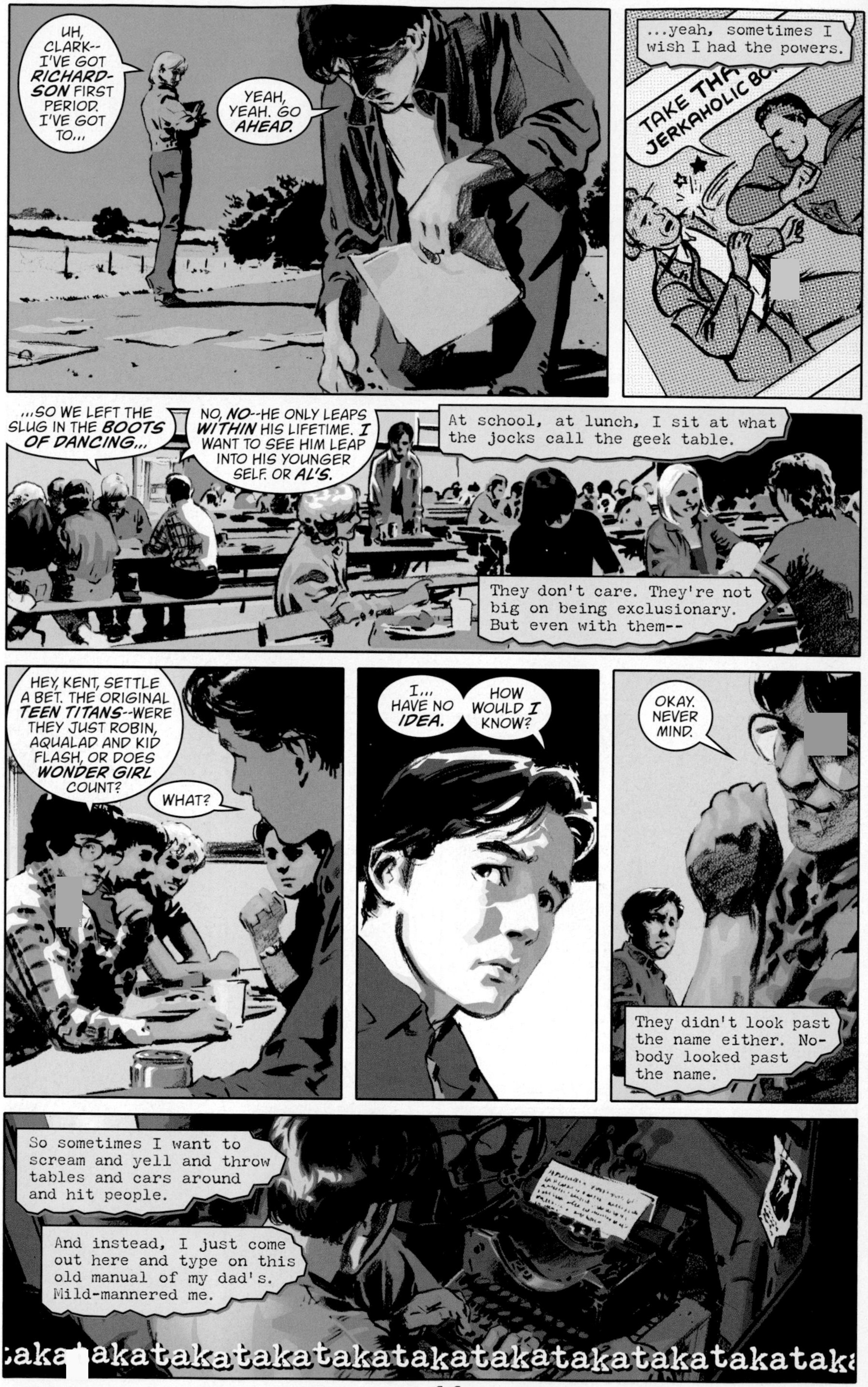
UH, CLARK-- I'VE GOT RICHARDSON FIRST PERIOD. I'VE GOT TO...
YEAH, YEAH. GO AHEAD.
...yeah, sometimes I wish I had the powers.
TAKE THA
JERKAHOLIC BO
...SO WE LEFT THE SLUG IN THE BOOTS OF DANCING...
NO, NO--HE ONLY LEAPS WITHIN HIS LIFETIME. I WANT TO SEE HIM LEAP INTO HIS YOUNGER SELF. OR AL'S.
At school, at lunch, I sit at what the jocks call the geek table.
They don't care. They're not big on being exclusionary. But even with them--
HEY, KENT, SETTLE A BET. THE ORIGINAL TEEN TITANS--WERE THEY JUST ROBIN, AQUALAD AND KID FLASH, OR DOES WONDER GIRL COUNT?
WHAT?
I... HAVE NO IDEA.
HOW WOULD I KNOW?
OKAY. NEVER MIND.
They didn't look past the name either. Nobody looked past the name.
So sometimes I want to scream and yell and throw tables and cars around and hit people.
And instead, I just come out here and type on this old manual of my dad's. Mild-mannered me.
takatakatakatakatakatakatakatakatakataka

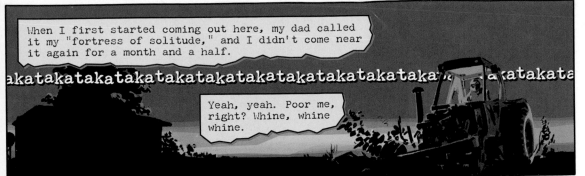

When I first started coming out here, my dad called it my "fortress of solitude," and I didn't come near it again for a month and a half.

akatakatakatakatakatakatakatakatakatakatakatakatakata...akatakata

Yeah, yeah. Poor me, right? Whine, whine whine.

Still, I'm not going to grow up to be Holden Caulfield or anything. Can't see that happening. I'm just not the type.

So when I get too fed up with it, I take off for the Smoky Hills and spend the weekend hiking.

It's close enough to bicycle to, and far enough away to leave everything else behind.

So it's just me. I don't even bring this typewriter, or even a notebook.

And it's good.

Just me. Alone.

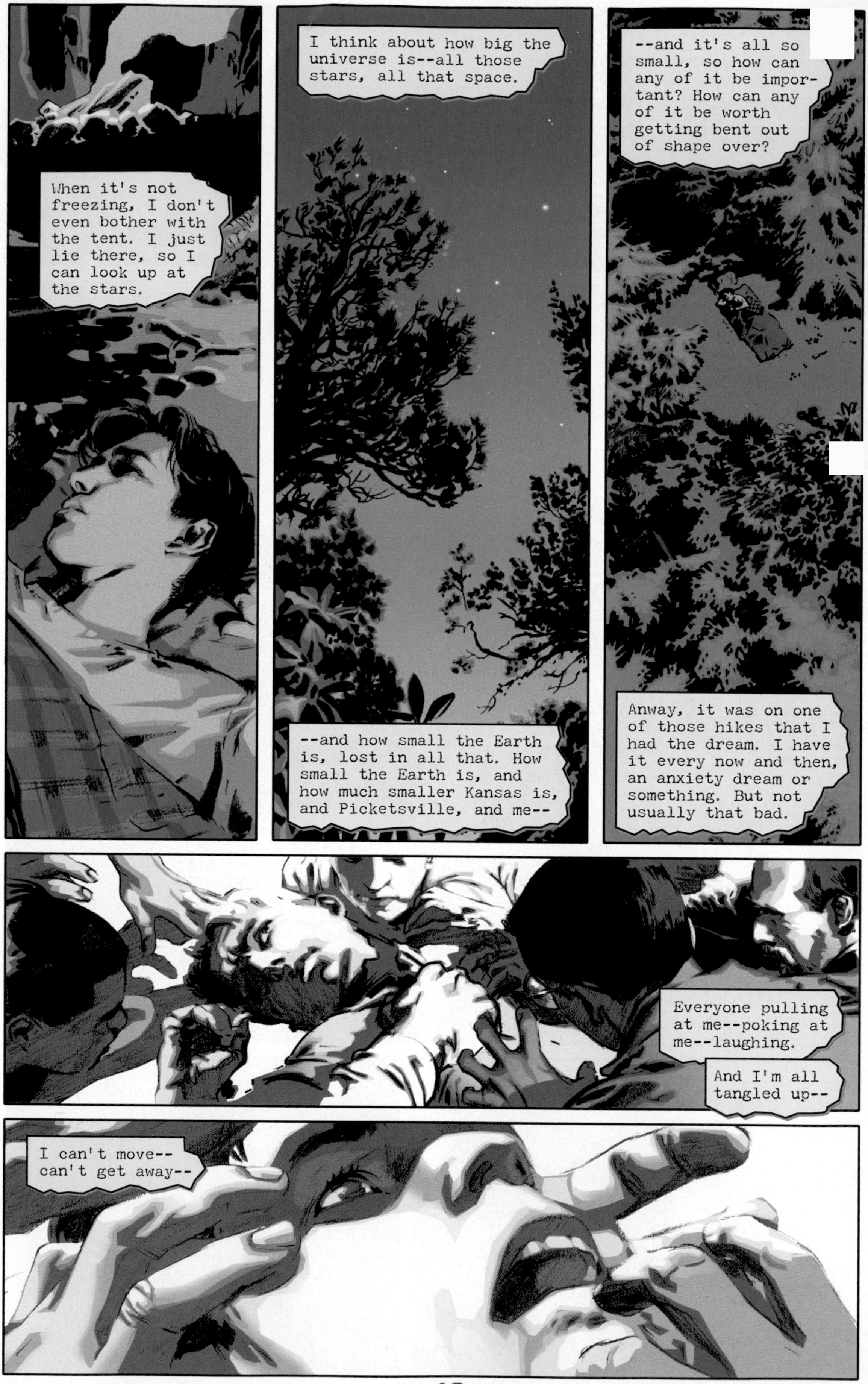
When it's not freezing, I don't even bother with the tent. I just lie there, so I can look up at the stars.
I think about how big the universe is--all those stars, all that space.
--and how small the Earth is, lost in all that. How small the Earth is, and how much smaller Kansas is, and Picketsville, and me--
--and it's all so small, so how can any of it be impor-tant? How can any of it be worth getting bent out of shape over?
Anway, it was on one of those hikes that I had the dream. I have it every now and then, an anxiety dream or something. But not usually that bad.
Everyone pulling at me--poking at me--laughing.
And I'm all tangled up--
I can't move--can't get away--

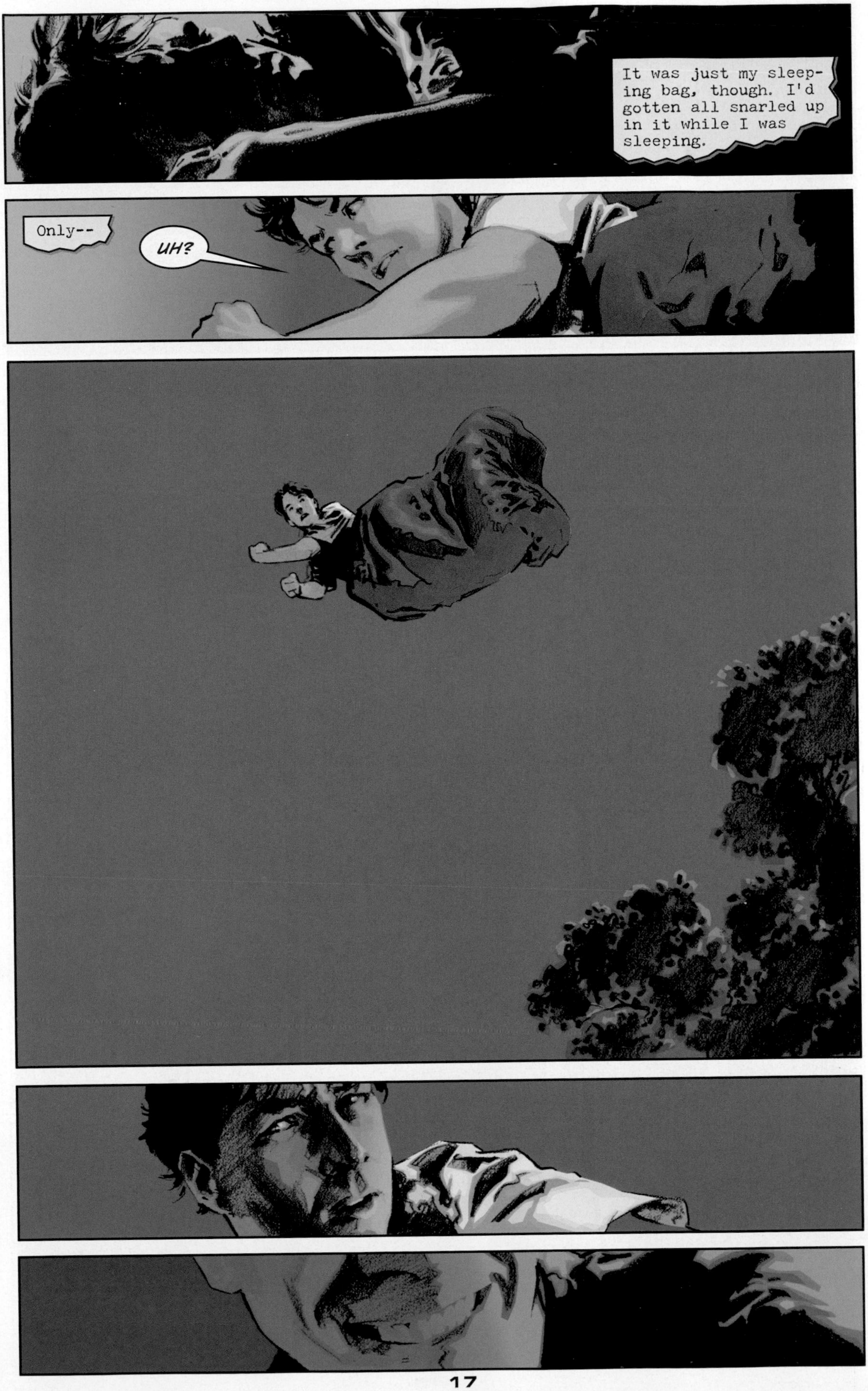
It was just my sleeping bag, though. I'd gotten all snarled up in it while I was sleeping.
Only--
UH?

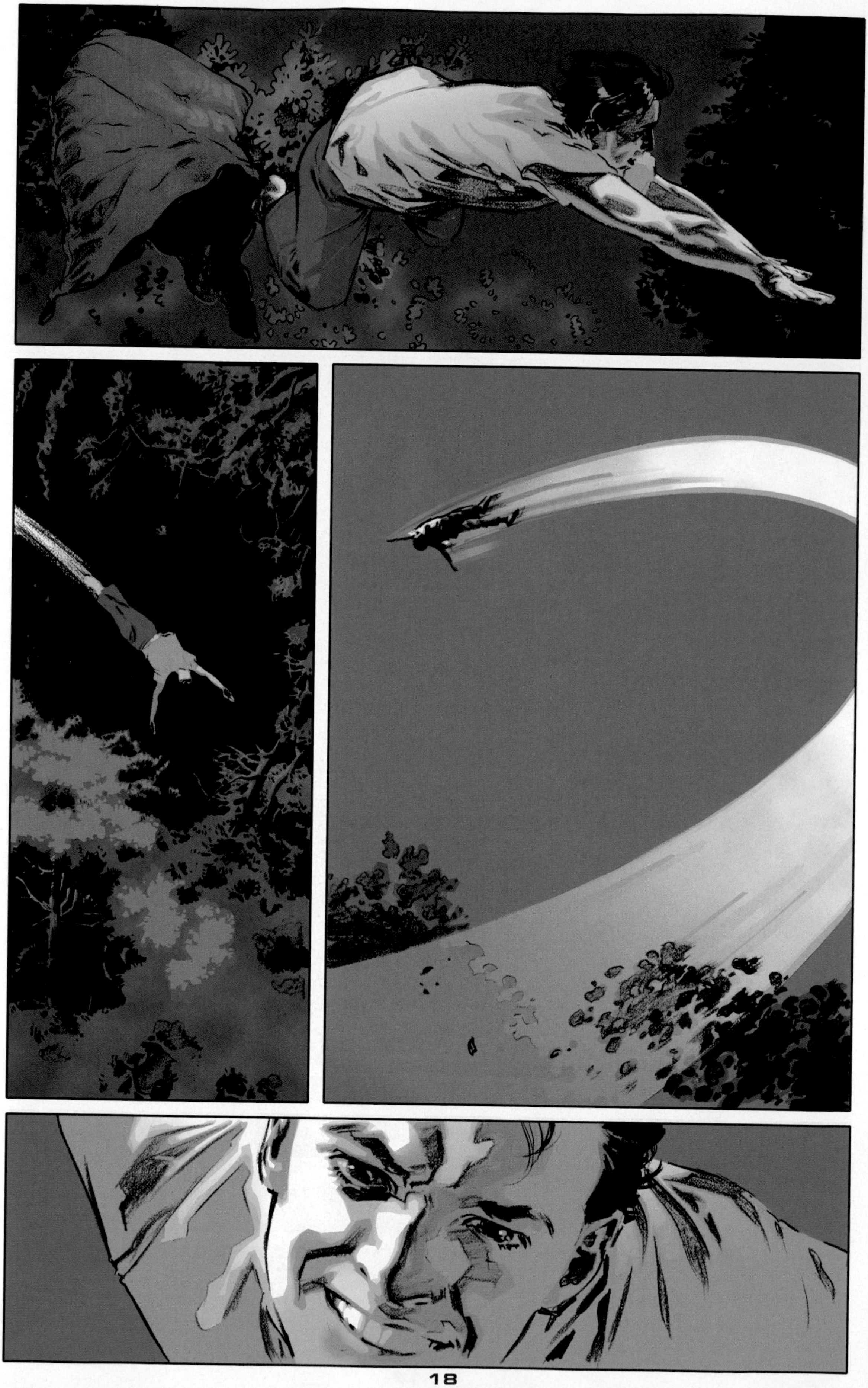

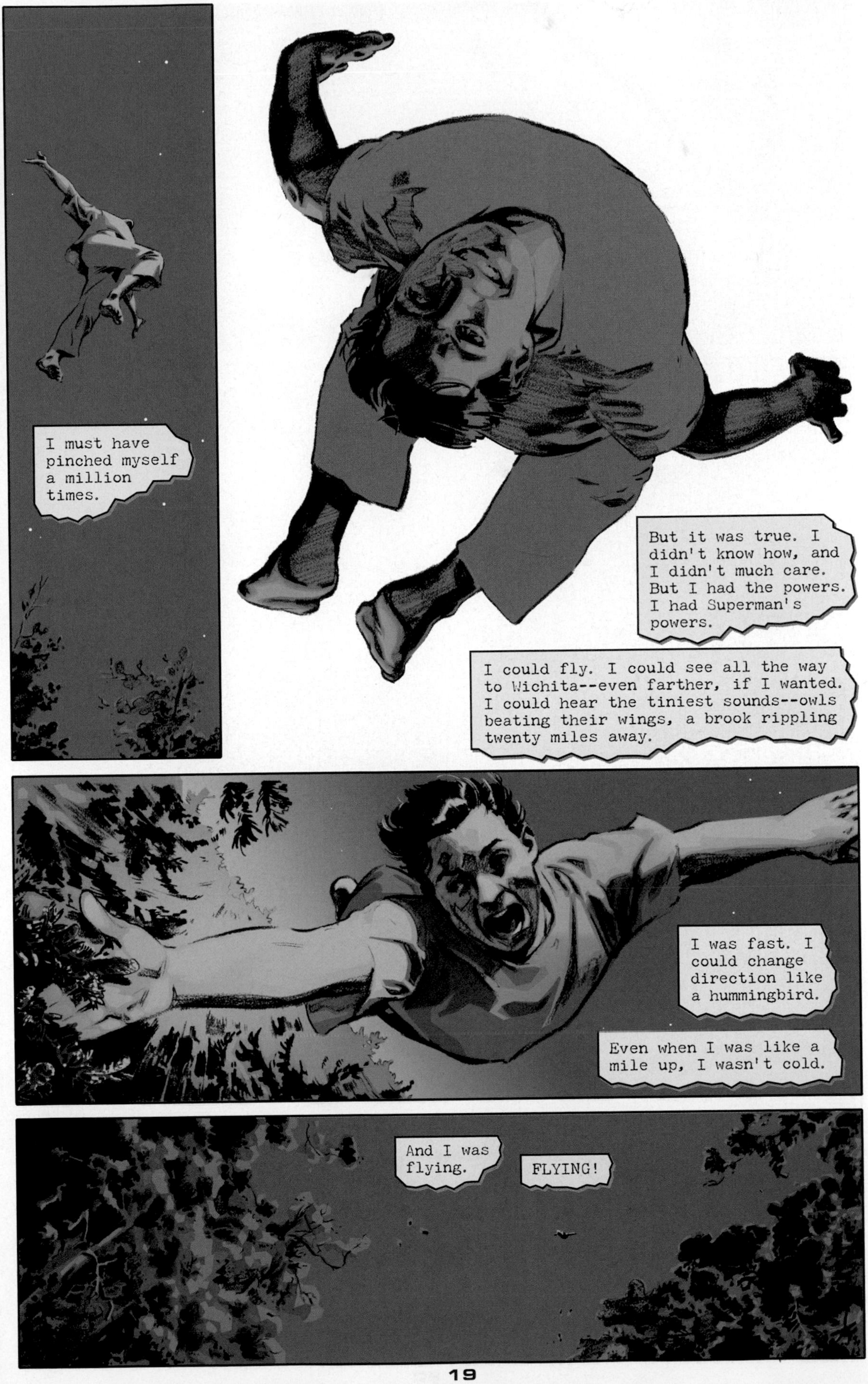
I must have pinched myself a million times.
But it was true. I didn't know how, and I didn't much care. But I had the powers. I had Superman's powers.
I could fly. I could see all the way to Wichita--even farther, if I wanted. I could hear the tiniest sounds--owls beating their wings, a brook rippling twenty miles away.
I was fast. I could change direction like a hummingbird.
Even when I was like a mile up, I wasn't cold.
And I was flying.
FLYING!

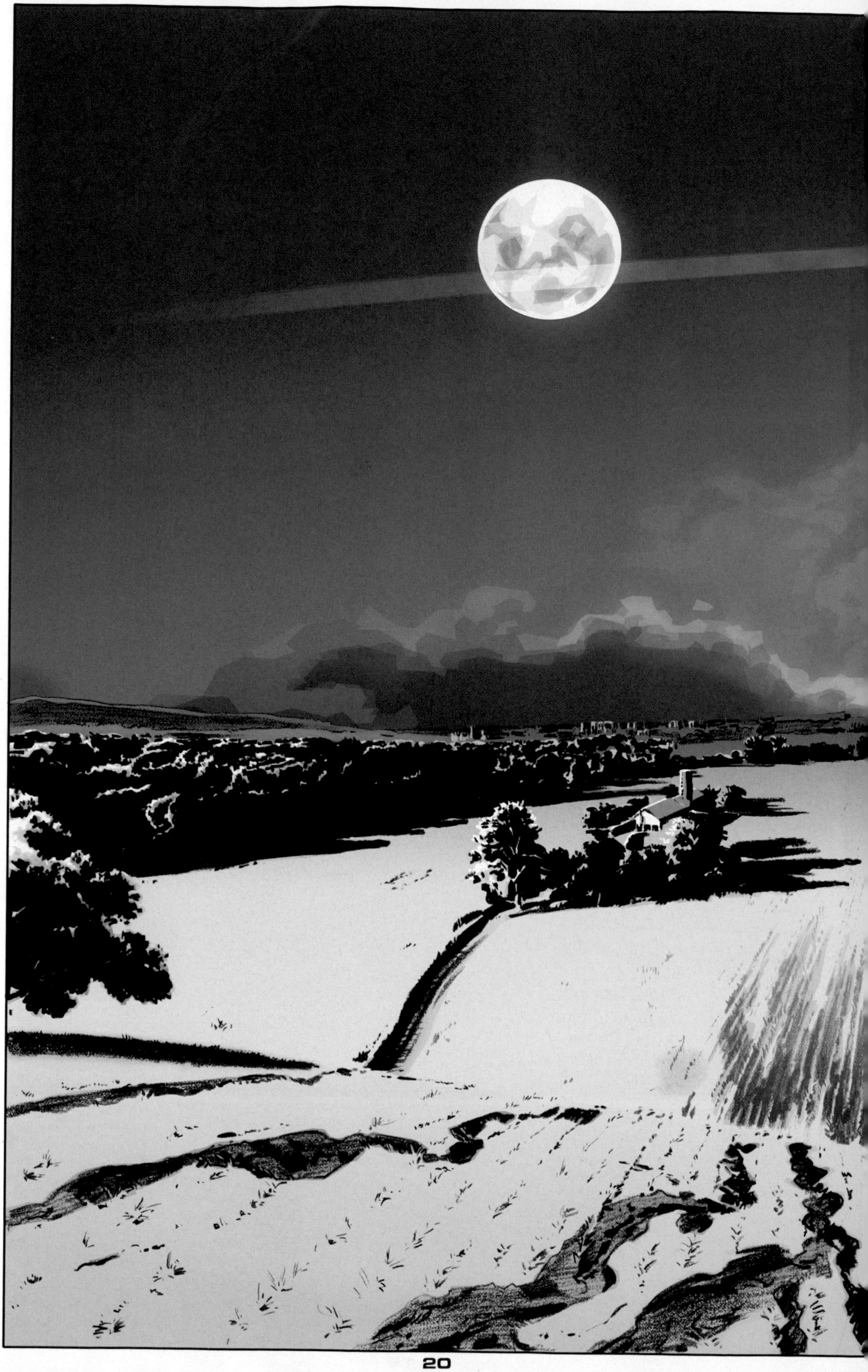

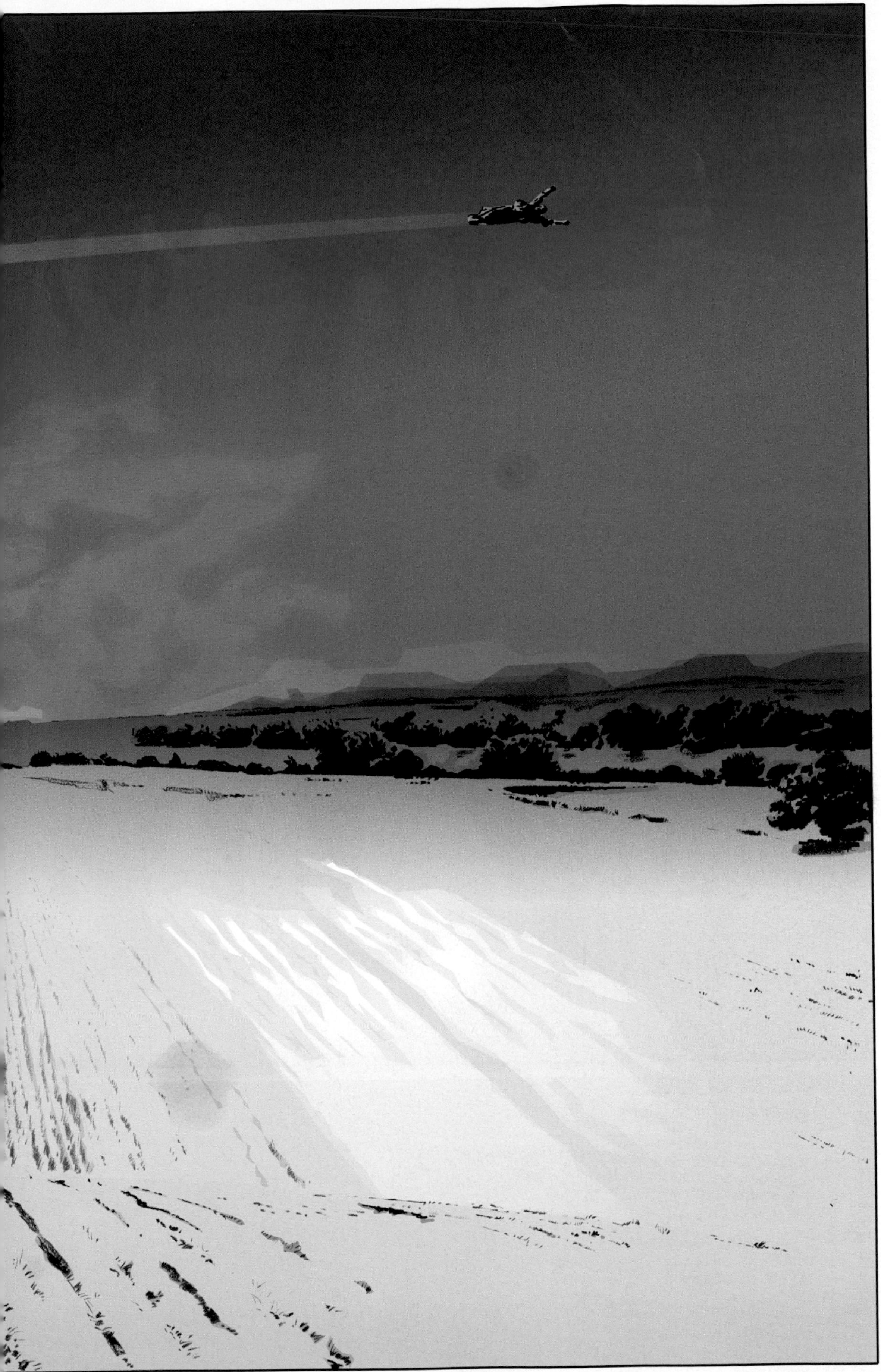

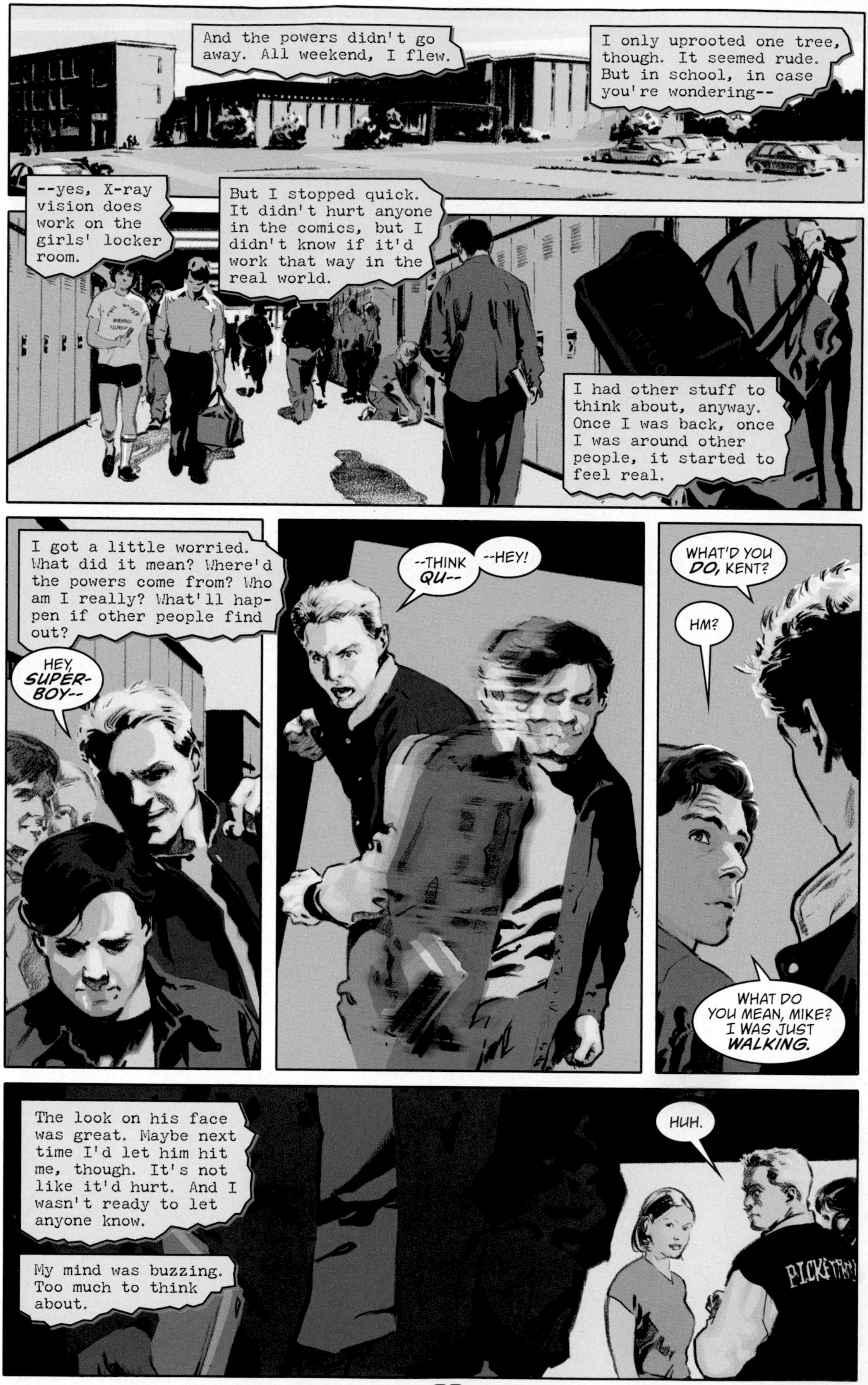
And the powers didn't go away. All weekend, I flew.
I only uprooted one tree, though. It seemed rude. But in school, in case you're wondering--
--yes, X-ray vision does work on the girls' locker room.
But I stopped quick. It didn't hurt anyone in the comics, but I didn't know if it'd work that way in the real world.
I had other stuff to think about, anyway. Once I was back, once I was around other people, it started to feel real.
I got a little worried. What did it mean? Where'd the powers come from? Who am I really? What'll happen if other people find out?
HEY, SUPER-BOY--
--THINK QU--
--HEY!
WHAT'D YOU DO, KENT?
HM?
WHAT DO YOU MEAN, MIKE? I WAS JUST WALKING.
The look on his face was great. Maybe next time I'd let him hit me, though. It's not like it'd hurt. And I wasn't ready to let anyone know.
My mind was buzzing. Too much to think about.
HUH.

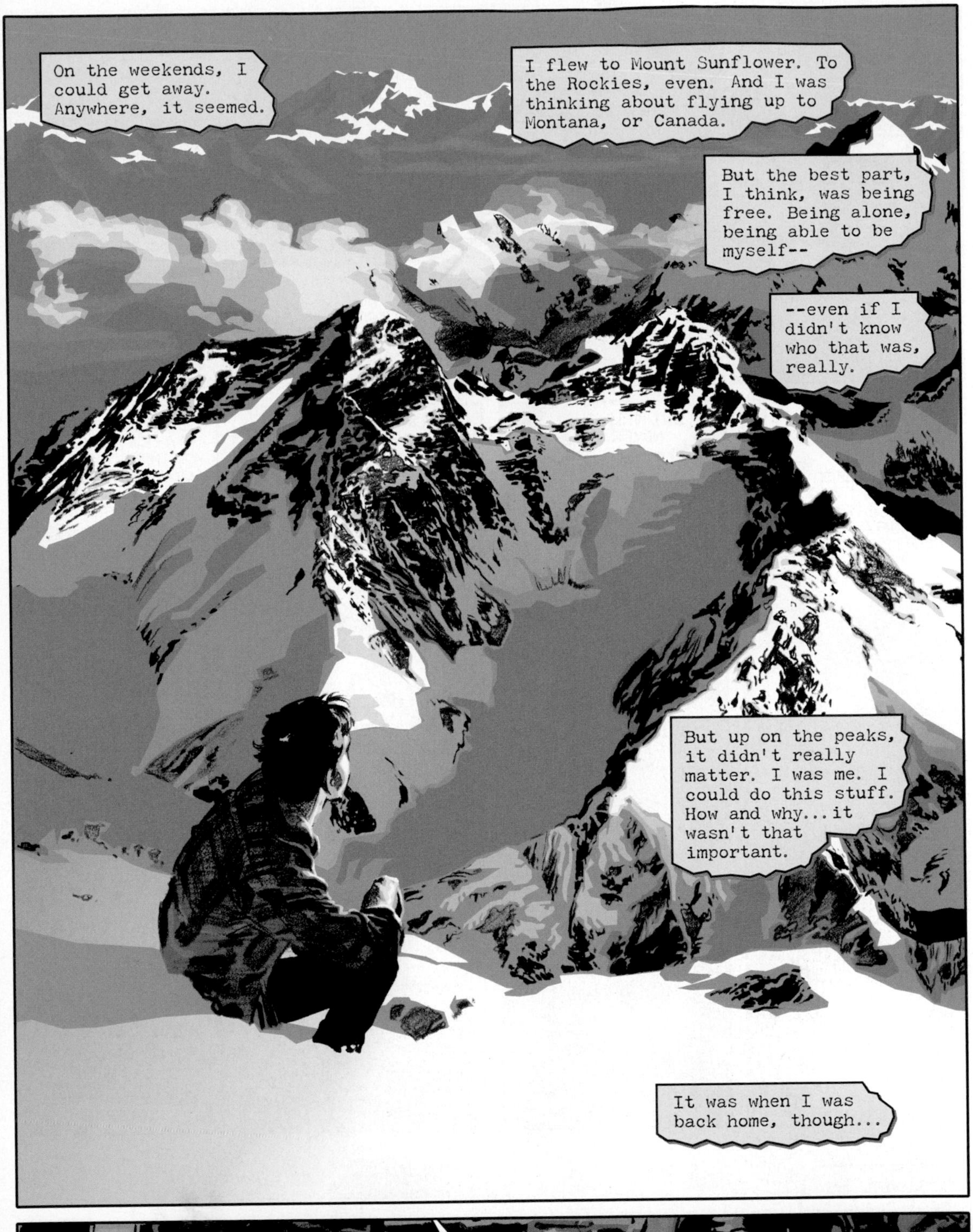
On the weekends, I could get away. Anywhere, it seemed.
I flew to Mount Sunflower. To the Rockies, even. And I was thinking about flying up to Montana, or Canada.
But the best part, I think, was being free. Being alone, being able to be myself--
--even if I didn't know who that was, really.
But up on the peaks, it didn't really matter. I was me. I could do this stuff. How and why...it wasn't that important.
It was when I was back home, though...

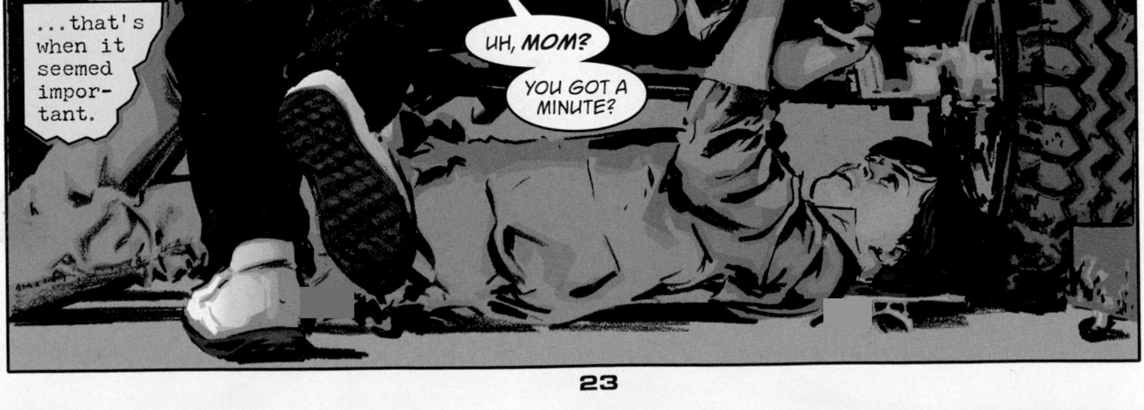
...that's when it seemed impor- tant.
UH, MOM?
YOU GOT A MINUTE?

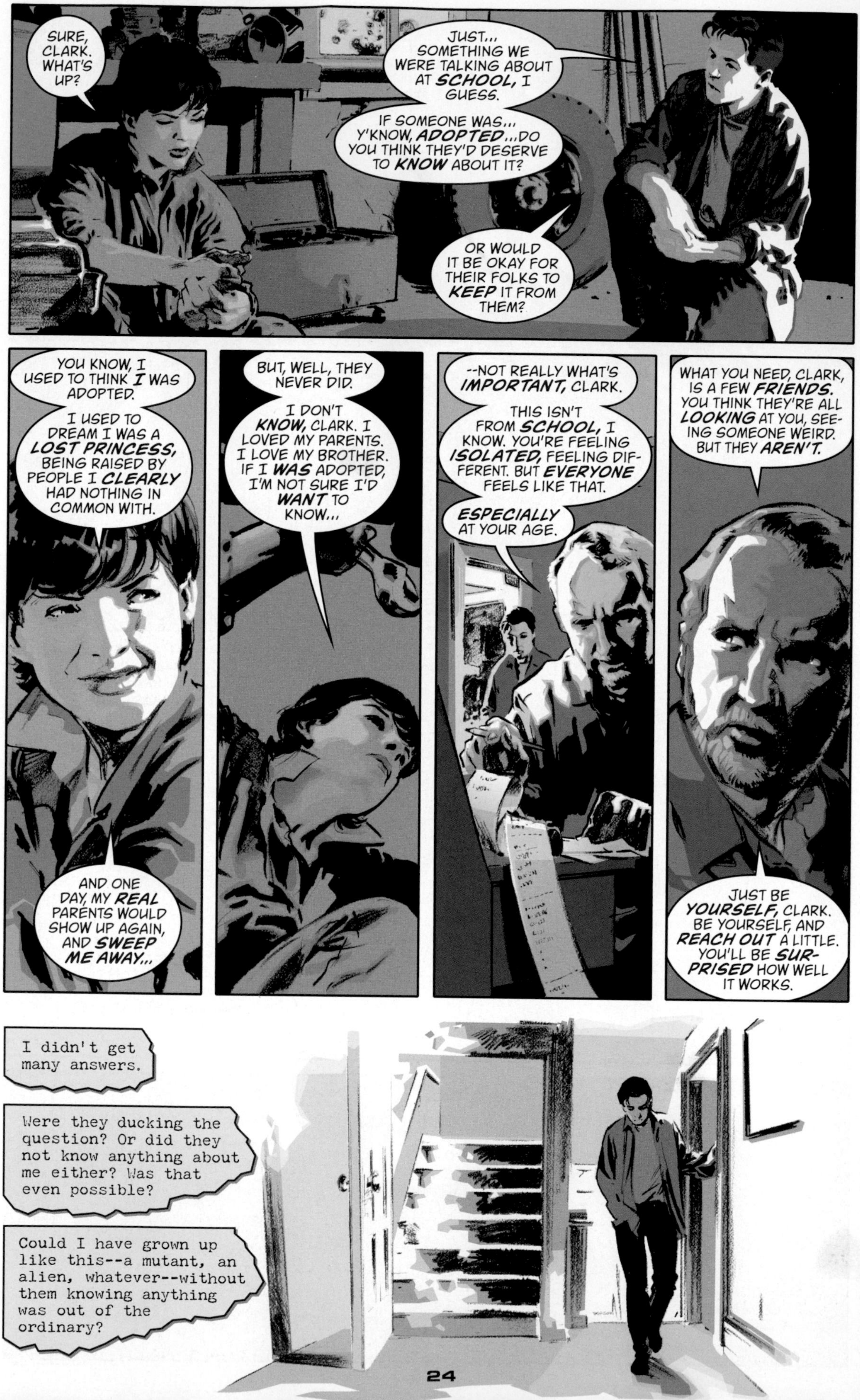
SURE, CLARK. WHAT'S UP?
JUST... SOMETHING WE WERE TALKING ABOUT AT SCHOOL, I GUESS.
IF SOMEONE WAS... Y'KNOW, ADOPTED...DO YOU THINK THEY'D DESERVE TO KNOW ABOUT IT?
OR WOULD IT BE OKAY FOR THEIR FOLKS TO KEEP IT FROM THEM?
YOU KNOW, I USED TO THINK I WAS ADOPTED.
I USED TO DREAM I WAS A LOST PRINCESS, BEING RAISED BY PEOPLE I CLEARLY HAD NOTHING IN COMMON WITH.
AND ONE DAY, MY REAL PARENTS WOULD SHOW UP AGAIN, AND SWEEP ME AWAY...
BUT, WELL, THEY NEVER DID.
I DON'T KNOW, CLARK. I LOVED MY PARENTS. I LOVE MY BROTHER. IF I WAS ADOPTED, I'M NOT SURE I'D WANT TO KNOW...
--NOT REALLY WHAT'S IMPORTANT, CLARK.
THIS ISN'T FROM SCHOOL, I KNOW. YOU'RE FEELING ISOLATED, FEELING DIF-FERENT. BUT EVERYONE FEELS LIKE THAT.
ESPECIALLY AT YOUR AGE.
WHAT YOU NEED, CLARK, IS A FEW FRIENDS. YOU THINK THEY'RE ALL LOOKING AT YOU, SEE-ING SOMEONE WEIRD. BUT THEY AREN'T.
JUST BE YOURSELF, CLARK. BE YOURSELF, AND REACH OUT A LITTLE. YOU'LL BE SUR-PRISED HOW WELL IT WORKS.
I didn't get many answers.
Were they ducking the question? Or did they not know anything about me either? Was that even possible?
Could I have grown up like this--a mutant, an alien, whatever--without them knowing anything was out of the ordinary?

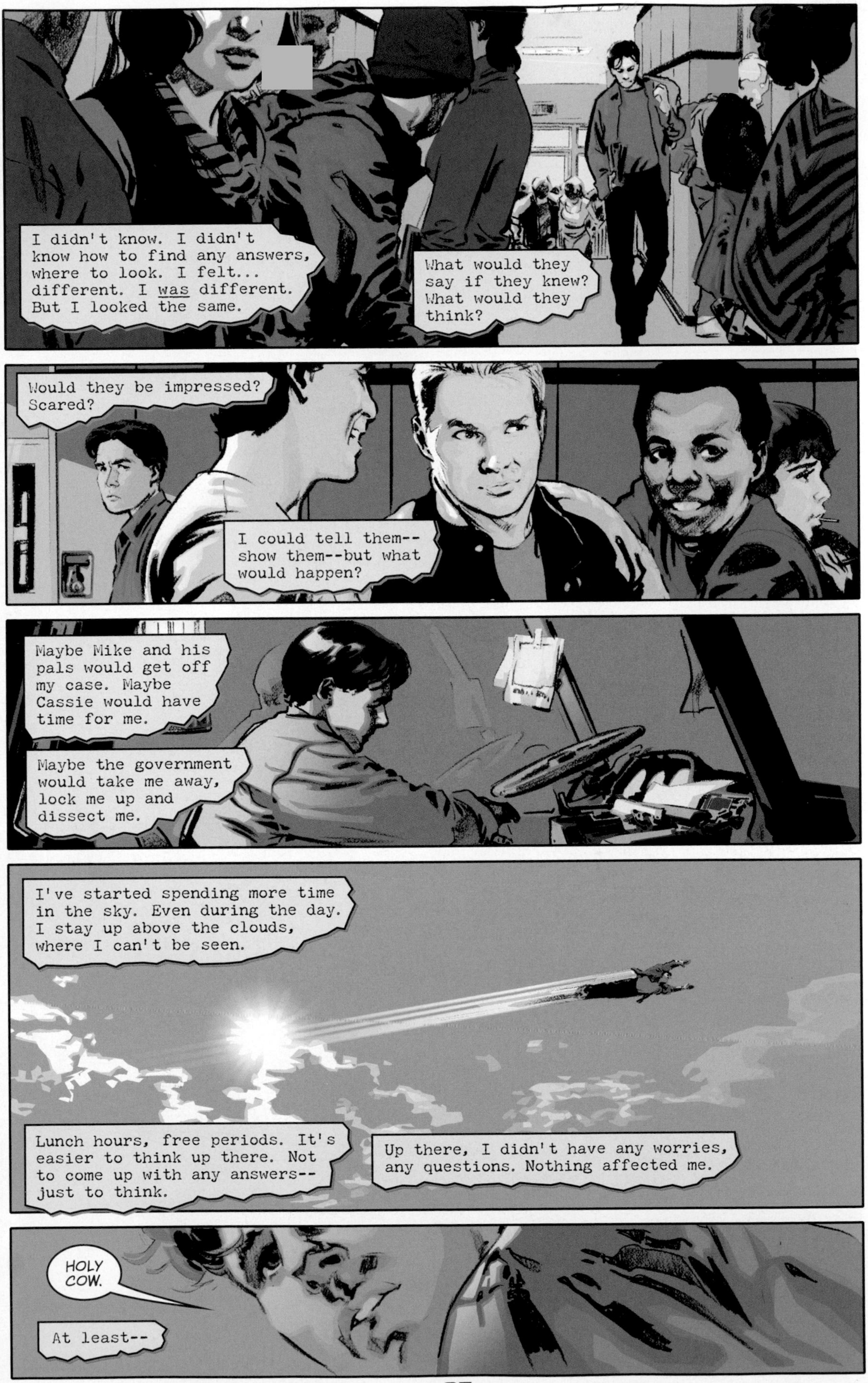

I didn't know. I didn't know how to find any answers, where to look. I felt... different. I was different. But I looked the same.
What would they say if they knew? What would they think?
Would they be impressed? Scared?
I could tell them--show them--but what would happen?
Maybe Mike and his pals would get off my case. Maybe Cassie would have time for me.
Maybe the government would take me away, lock me up and dissect me.
I've started spending more time in the sky. Even during the day. I stay up above the clouds, where I can't be seen.
Lunch hours, free periods. It's easier to think up there. Not to come up with any answers--just to think.
Up there, I didn't have any worries, any questions. Nothing affected me.
HOLY COW.
At least--

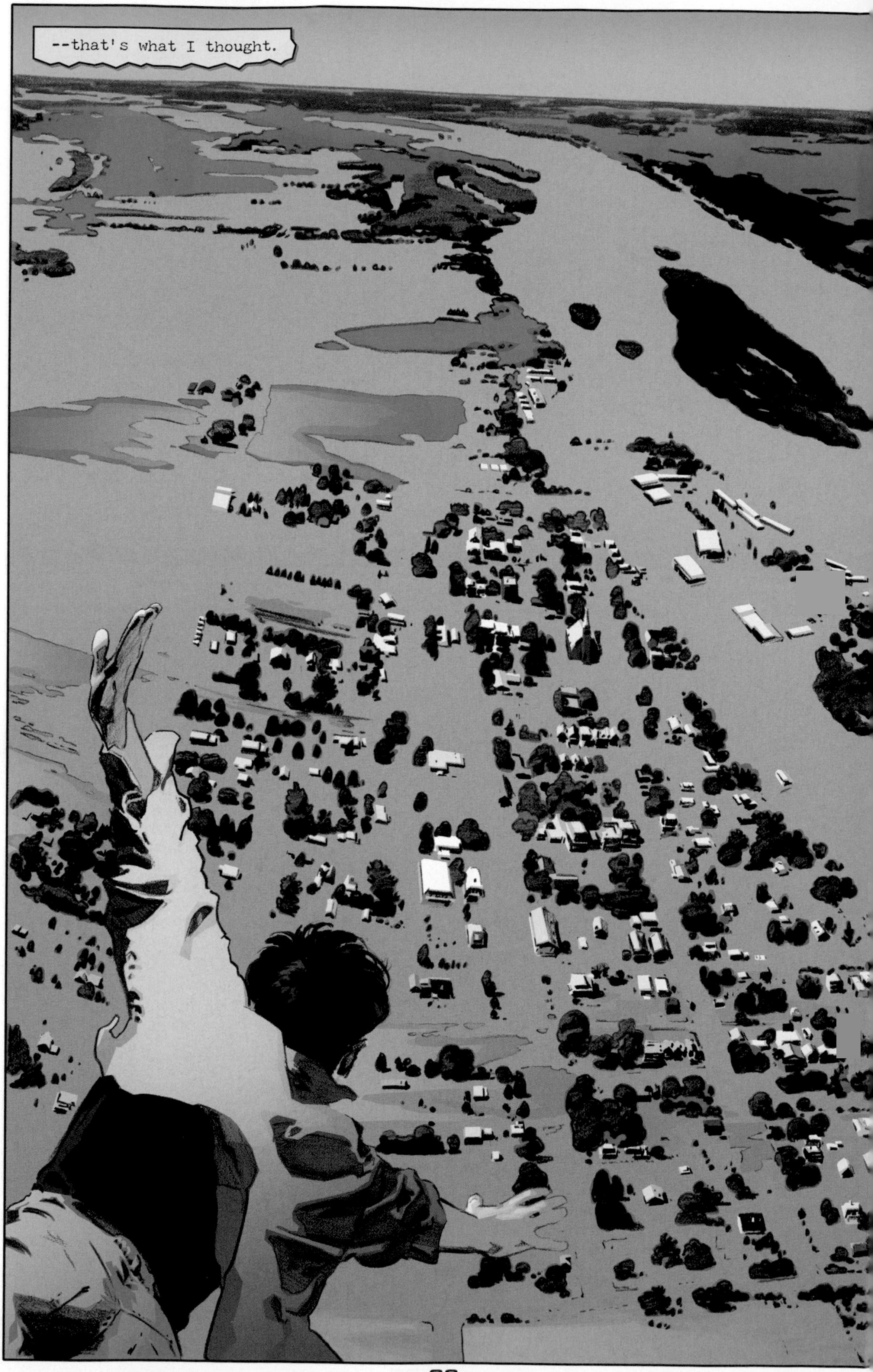
--that's what I thought.

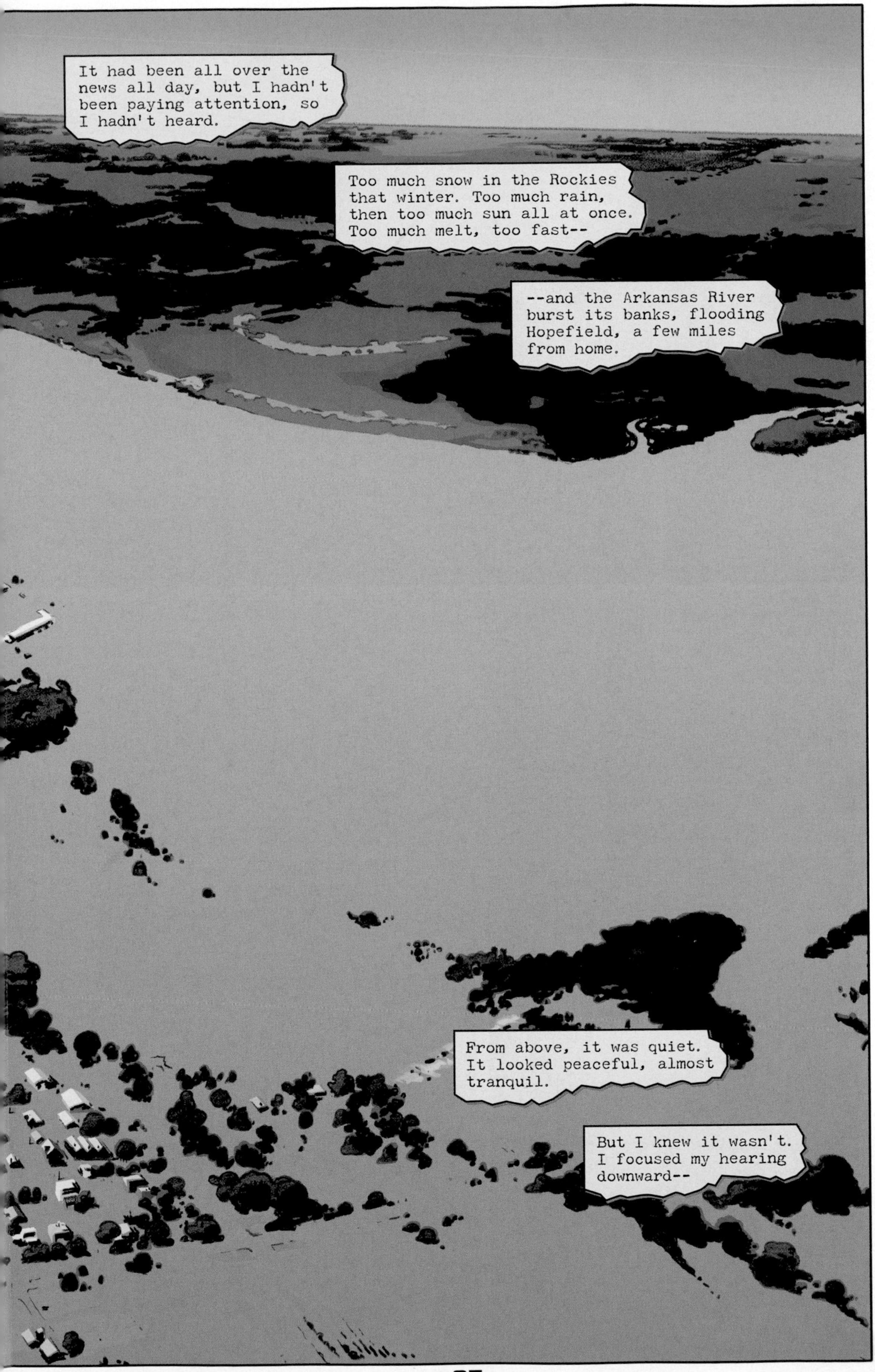
It had been all over the news all day, but I hadn't been paying attention, so I hadn't heard.
Too much snow in the Rockies that winter. Too much rain, then too much sun all at once. Too much melt, too fast--
--and the Arkansas River burst its banks, flooding Hopefield, a few miles from home.
From above, it was quiet. It looked peaceful, almost tranquil.
But I knew it wasn't. I focused my hearing downward--

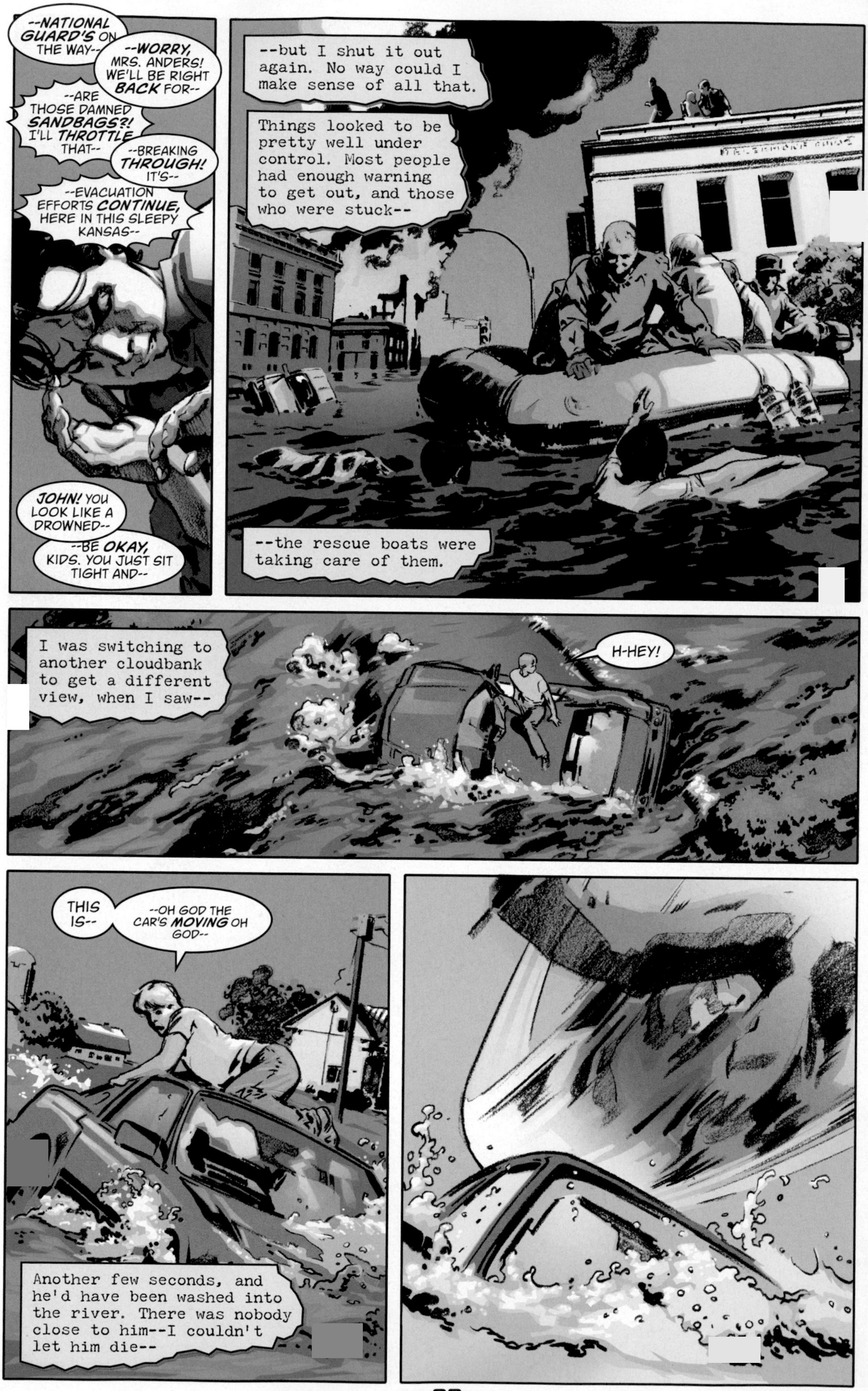
--NATIONAL GUARD'S ON THE WAY--
--WORRY, MRS. ANDERS! WE'LL BE RIGHT BACK FOR--
--ARE THOSE DAMNED SANDBAGS?! I'LL THROTTLE THAT--
--BREAKING THROUGH! IT'S--
--EVACUATION EFFORTS CONTINUE, HERE IN THIS SLEEPY KANSAS--
JOHN! YOU LOOK LIKE A DROWNED--
--BE OKAY, KIDS. YOU JUST SIT TIGHT AND--
--but I shut it out again. No way could I make sense of all that.
Things looked to be pretty well under control. Most people had enough warning to get out, and those who were stuck--
--the rescue boats were taking care of them.
I was switching to another cloudbank to get a different view, when I saw--
H-HEY!
THIS IS--
--OH GOD THE CAR'S MOVING OH GOD--
Another few seconds, and he'd have been washed into the river. There was nobody close to him--I couldn't let him die--

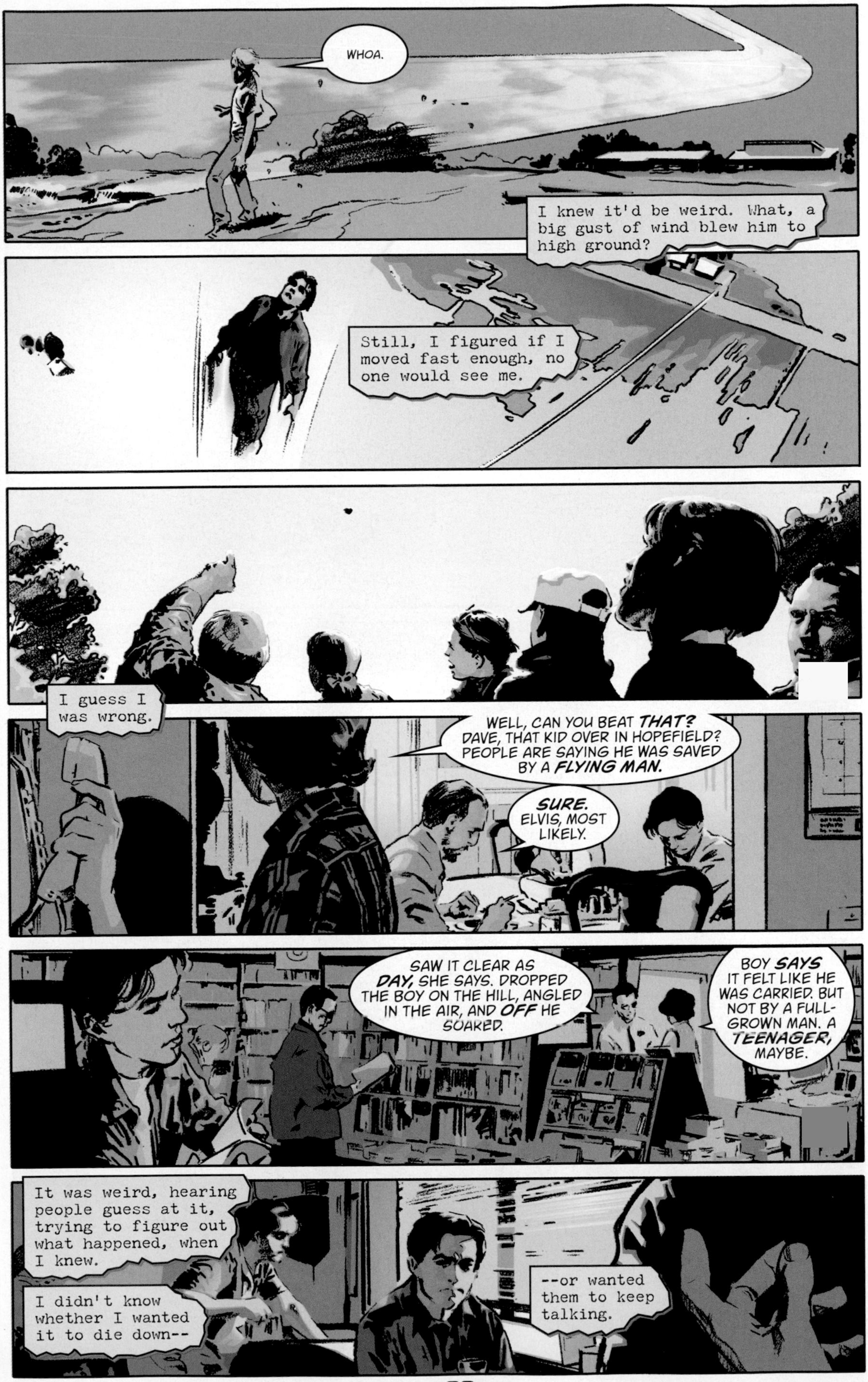
WHOA.
I knew it'd be weird. What, a big gust of wind blew him to high ground?
Still, I figured if I moved fast enough, no one would see me.
I guess I was wrong.
WELL, CAN YOU BEAT THAT? DAVE, THAT KID OVER IN HOPEFIELD? PEOPLE ARE SAYING HE WAS SAVED BY A FLYING MAN.
SURE. ELVIS, MOST LIKELY.
SAW IT CLEAR AS DAY, SHE SAYS. DROPPED THE BOY ON THE HILL, ANGLED IN THE AIR, AND OFF HE SOARED.
BOY SAYS IT FELT LIKE HE WAS CARRIED. BUT NOT BY A FULL-GROWN MAN. A TEENAGER, MAYBE.
It was weird, hearing people guess at it, trying to figure out what happened, when I knew.
I didn't know whether I wanted it to die down--
--or wanted them to keep talking.

And then they really started talking.

Friday October 5, 1990

# The HOPEFIELD CLARION

WEATHER
TODAY: Clearing H 66
TONIGHT: L 50
TUES. Ptly. Cloudy H 62
EDITORIAL PAGE A 14

# FLYING BOY!

## Is Flood Rescue Only Latest Sighting?

by Wendy Case
Special to the Clarion

HOPEFIELD – Area residents are talking, and not just about last week's flood. Spurred on by the apparently miraculous rescue of Todd Sullivan from Tuesday's floodwaters, they're discussing a topic that they'd previously thought to be just a hallucination on the part of a few locals, or perhaps a daydream. But as more and more come forward, we have to ask: Is Nowlan County home to a flying boy?

Sullivan, 15, was trapped atop a stranded car during the flood, when the currents became so strong that the car was swept into the swollen Arkansas River. "I'd have been a goner too," he asserts, "but just as it _____ over, someone _____

me, picked me up an_____ carried me to the oppos_____ bank. Carried me rig_____ through the air!"

Sullivan is not alon_____ claiming what he d_____ either. "We were out o_____ north bank, watching _____ rescue efforts," _____ Margerie Robinson. _____ saw Todd. He just _____ of…appeared. He _____ dropped off, by a blu_____ then we saw it--th_____ paused, and it was _____ teenager. He just _____ off, heading south."

One bystander s_____ photograph, but _____ considerable disa_____ over what it s_____ could be a flying _____ Klaus Varhaus, p_____ of the Clarion. _____ the Loch Ness M_____ Or Bigfoot, flu_____ the air by a c_____ money, he say_____ on the object _____ or even an i_____ the negative.

...ible flying boy over Hopefield?

Apparently, I'd been spotted a few times.

A reporter--a stringer for the Topeka Herald-Gazette--had been hearing stories about a flying kid.

After the flood, she put 'em all together. There was a picture, too, but even I couldn't swear it wasn't a bird.

Anyway, that's all it took to bring the circus to Hopefield, and every other town in the area.

Newspapers, TV, radio, paranormal experts, debunkers. Even some people--

--I couldn't tell what their game was.

They talked to everyone. Some people did their best--

--WAS WATERING MY GARDEN A MONTH OR SO BACK, AND I *SAW* IT--TOO SMALL TO BE A *PLANE*, AND IT DIDN'T HAVE *WINGS*--

--some just liked the attention--

--*COURSE* WE KNOW HIM, BUT WE RESPECT PEOPLE'S PRIVACY AROUND HERE.

BUT I COULD TELL YOU *STORIES*. I TAUGHT HIM HOW TO *STEER*, YOU KNOW. BACK WHEN HE WAS A TOT, HE COULDN'T GO BUT *STRAIGHT*, AND--

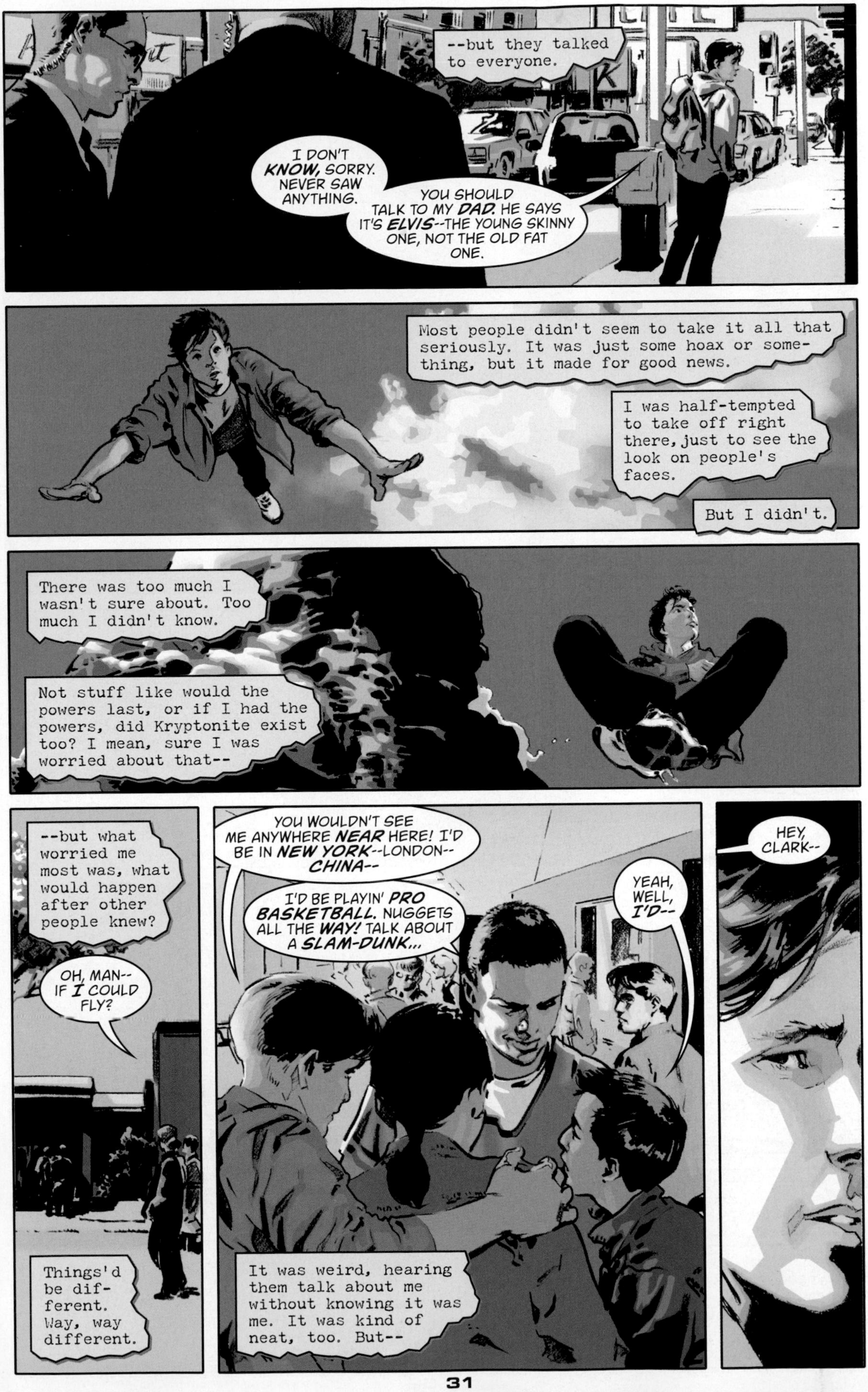
--but they talked to everyone.
I DON'T KNOW, SORRY. NEVER SAW ANYTHING.
YOU SHOULD TALK TO MY DAD. HE SAYS IT'S ELVIS--THE YOUNG SKINNY ONE, NOT THE OLD FAT ONE.
Most people didn't seem to take it all that seriously. It was just some hoax or something, but it made for good news.
I was half-tempted to take off right there, just to see the look on people's faces.
But I didn't.
There was too much I wasn't sure about. Too much I didn't know.
Not stuff like would the powers last, or if I had the powers, did Kryptonite exist too? I mean, sure I was worried about that--
--but what worried me most was, what would happen after other people knew?
OH, MAN-- IF I COULD FLY?
Things'd be different. Way, way different.
YOU WOULDN'T SEE ME ANYWHERE NEAR HERE! I'D BE IN NEW YORK--LONDON--CHINA--
I'D BE PLAYIN' PRO BASKETBALL. NUGGETS ALL THE WAY! TALK ABOUT A SLAM-DUNK...
YEAH, WELL, I'D--
It was weird, hearing them talk about me without knowing it was me. It was kind of neat, too. But--
HEY, CLARK--

--LOOKS LIKE YOU GOT SOME COMPETITION, HUH?

I guess it made sense. With a real "super-boy" in the news, it made having me around--

--that much funnier.

OOPS! WHERE'RE THOSE SUPER-REFLEXES, KENT?

A real laugh riot.

HEY, ALMOST FLEW THAT TIME! YOU'RE GETTIN' THERE!

I rolled with it, though.

It's not like it hurt me, right? I'm invulnerable--

--they can't hurt me at all.

CLARK, ARE YOU--?

I'M FINE-- FINE!

She felt sorry for me. Sorry! All the stuff I can do, the powers I have, and she--

akatakatakatakatakatakatak     katakataka

But she doesn't know about that. None of them do. I don't stand up for myself, don't tell them, because I'm too--too--

I'm too scared. I just don't know what I'm scared of.

God, I need some answers! I need to know what I am, need to know what it means! I need to KNOW!!

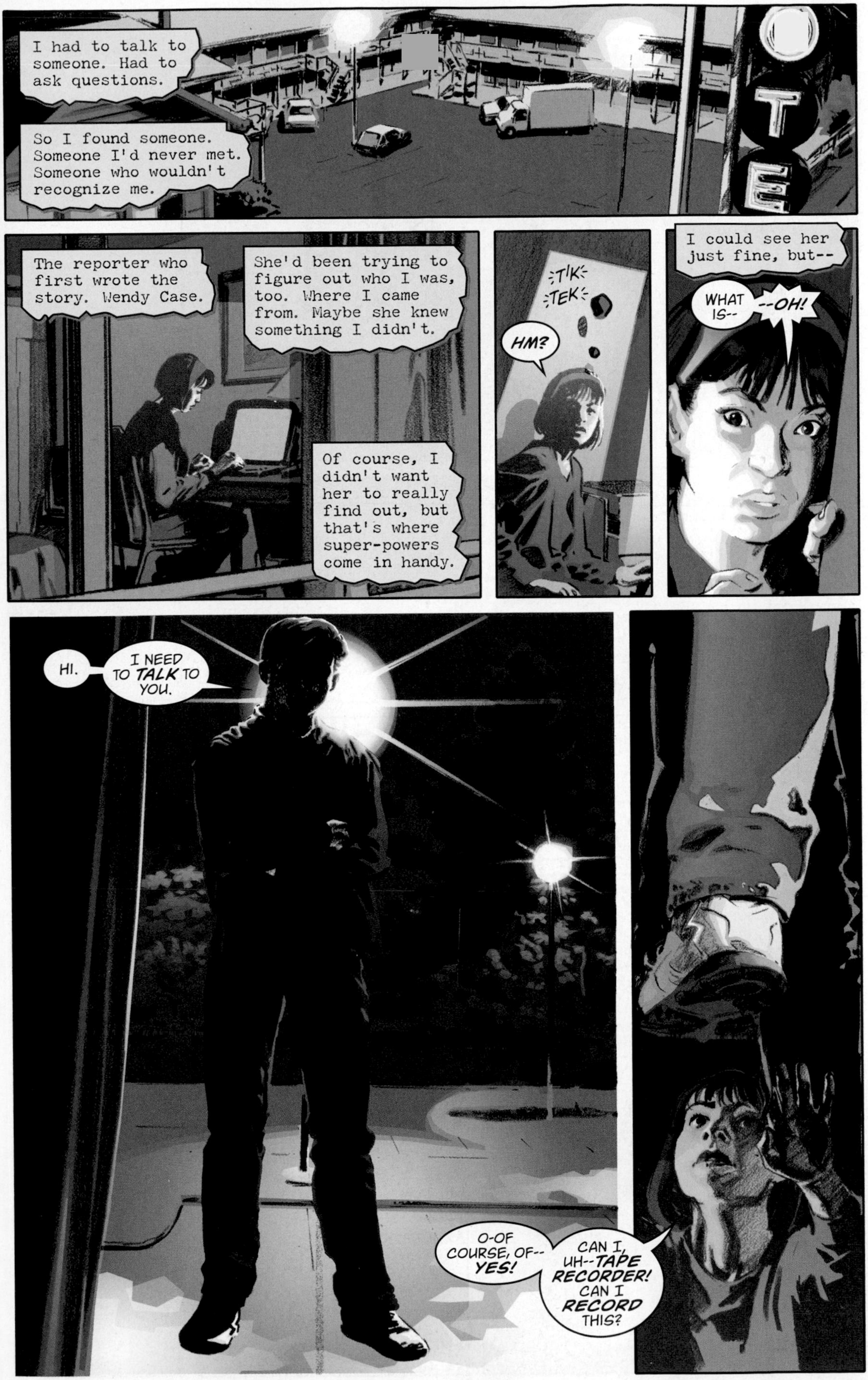

I had to talk to someone. Had to ask questions.
So I found someone. Someone I'd never met. Someone who wouldn't recognize me.
The reporter who first wrote the story. Wendy Case.
She'd been trying to figure out who I was, too. Where I came from. Maybe she knew something I didn't.
Of course, I didn't want her to really find out, but that's where super-powers come in handy.
TIK
TEK
HM?
I could see her just fine, but--
WHAT IS--
--OH!
HI.
I NEED TO TALK TO YOU.
O-OF COURSE, OF-- YES!
CAN I, UH--TAPE RECORDER! CAN I RECORD THIS?

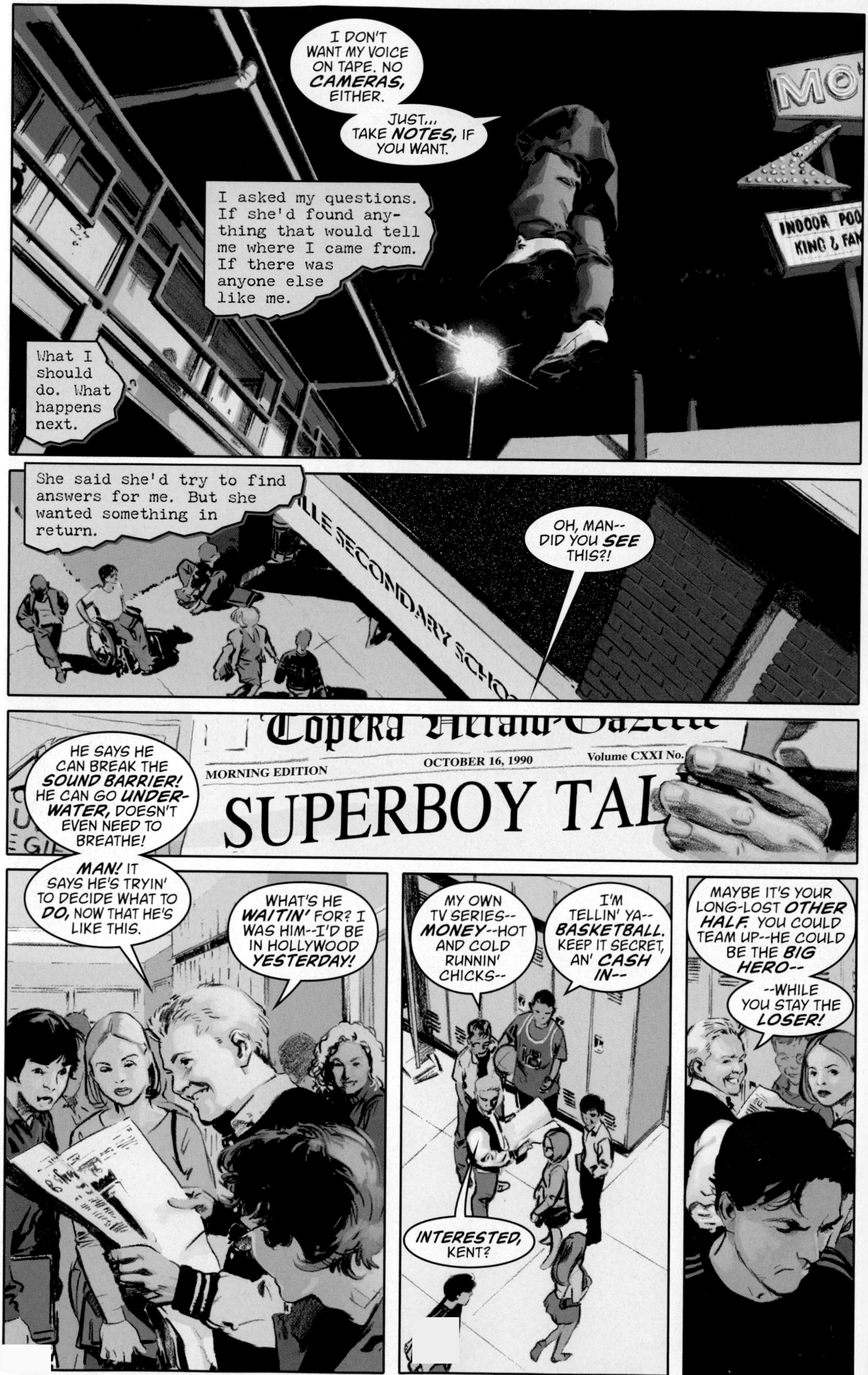
I DON'T WANT MY VOICE ON TAPE. NO CAMERAS, EITHER.
JUST... TAKE NOTES, IF YOU WANT.
MO
INDOOR POO
KING & FAN
I asked my questions. If she'd found anything that would tell me where I came from. If there was anyone else like me.
What I should do. What happens next.
She said she'd try to find answers for me. But she wanted something in return.
LLE SECONDARY SCHO
OH, MAN-- DID YOU SEE THIS?!
Topeka Herald-Gazette
MORNING EDITION
OCTOBER 16, 1990
Volume CXXI No.
SUPERBOY TAL
HE SAYS HE CAN BREAK THE SOUND BARRIER! HE CAN GO UNDERWATER, DOESN'T EVEN NEED TO BREATHE!
MAN! IT SAYS HE'S TRYIN' TO DECIDE WHAT TO DO, NOW THAT HE'S LIKE THIS.
WHAT'S HE WAITIN' FOR? I WAS HIM--I'D BE IN HOLLYWOOD YESTERDAY!
MY OWN TV SERIES-- MONEY--HOT AND COLD RUNNIN' CHICKS--
I'M TELLIN' YA-- BASKETBALL. KEEP IT SECRET, AN' CASH IN--
INTERESTED, KENT?
MAYBE IT'S YOUR LONG-LOST OTHER HALF. YOU COULD TEAM UP--HE COULD BE THE BIG HERO--
--WHILE YOU STAY THE LOSER!

HAHAHAHAHAHAHAHAHA HAHA

YEAH, MIKE, WHATEVER. **WHATEVER.**

He doesn't bother me as much anymore. Well, he tries-- but I don't care.

And I'm not spending so much time on mountaintops any- more. Not now--

--not when I might have answers soon--

*...GETTING* SOMEWHERE, BUT IT'S HARD, NOT BEING ABLE TO TALK TO YOUR *FAMILY,* CHECK YOUR *HISTORY,* LIKE THAT.

MY PAPER WOULD LIKE TO MAKE AN *OFFER:* WE'LL HANDLE YOUR ANNOUNCEMENT, YOUR *DEBUT*--WE'LL PRE- SENT YOU TO THE WORLD.

WE'LL TAKE CARE OF *EVERY- THING*--ALL THE *ARRANGEMENTS,* SECURITY, HANDLING THE REST OF THE *PRESS*--

JUST FROM THE *BOOK DEALS* AND *TALK SHOWS* ALONE, YOU'D BE SET FOR LIFE.

WOULDN'T YOU LIKE TO BUY YOUR FOLKS THEIR *DREAM HOUSE?* DRIVE THE COOLEST CAR? YOU COULD EVEN MEET THE *PRESIDENT.*

AND THEN WE'LL BE BETTER ABLE TO *HELP* YOU-- DO SOME REAL, *IN- FORMED* RESEARCH-- FIND OUT WHO YOU ARE--

I didn't say yes. But I'm thinking about it.

Buying Mom and Dad a house. That'd be cool. And maybe the other kids were right.

MANN DRUGS
Walton Avenue
ICE CREAM

Maybe not Bryan, maybe, with the dopey basket- ball thing, but who wouldn't want to be on TV? Be rich and famous...

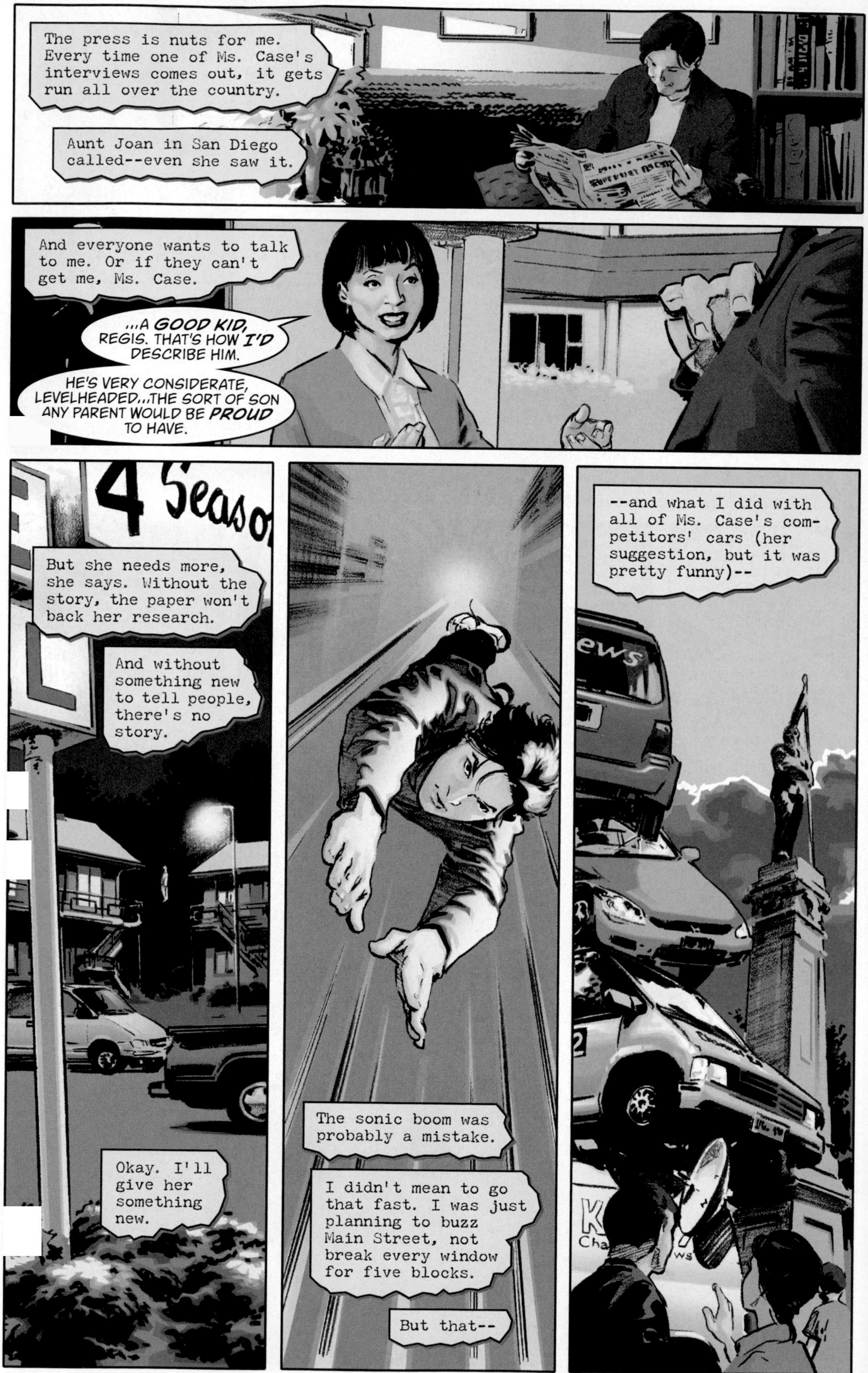
The press is nuts for me. Every time one of Ms. Case's interviews comes out, it gets run all over the country.
Aunt Joan in San Diego called--even she saw it.
And everyone wants to talk to me. Or if they can't get me, Ms. Case.
...A GOOD KID, REGIS. THAT'S HOW I'D DESCRIBE HIM.
HE'S VERY CONSIDERATE, LEVELHEADED...THE SORT OF SON ANY PARENT WOULD BE PROUD TO HAVE.
4 Season
But she needs more, she says. Without the story, the paper won't back her research.
And without something new to tell people, there's no story.
Okay. I'll give her something new.
The sonic boom was probably a mistake.
I didn't mean to go that fast. I was just planning to buzz Main Street, not break every window for five blocks.
But that--
--and what I did with all of Ms. Case's competitors' cars (her suggestion, but it was pretty funny)--

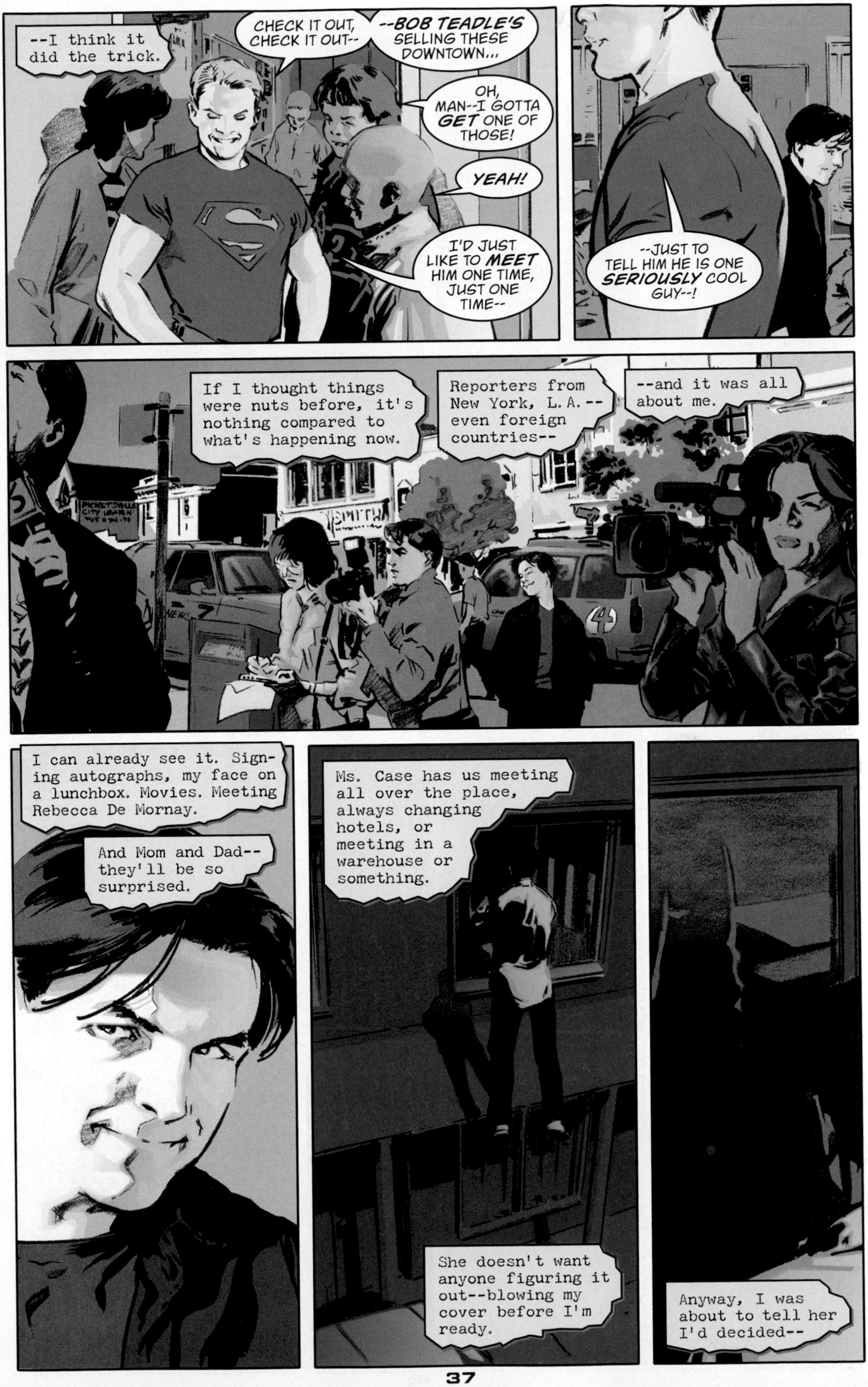
--I think it did the trick.
CHECK IT OUT, CHECK IT OUT--
--BOB TEADLE'S SELLING THESE DOWNTOWN...
OH, MAN--I GOTTA GET ONE OF THOSE!
YEAH!
I'D JUST LIKE TO MEET HIM ONE TIME, JUST ONE TIME--
--JUST TO TELL HIM HE IS ONE SERIOUSLY COOL GUY--!
If I thought things were nuts before, it's nothing compared to what's happening now.
Reporters from New York, L. A.--even foreign countries--
--and it was all about me.
I can already see it. Signing autographs, my face on a lunchbox. Movies. Meeting Rebecca De Mornay.
And Mom and Dad--they'll be so surprised.
Ms. Case has us meeting all over the place, always changing hotels, or meeting in a warehouse or something.
She doesn't want anyone figuring it out--blowing my cover before I'm ready.
Anyway, I was about to tell her I'd decided--

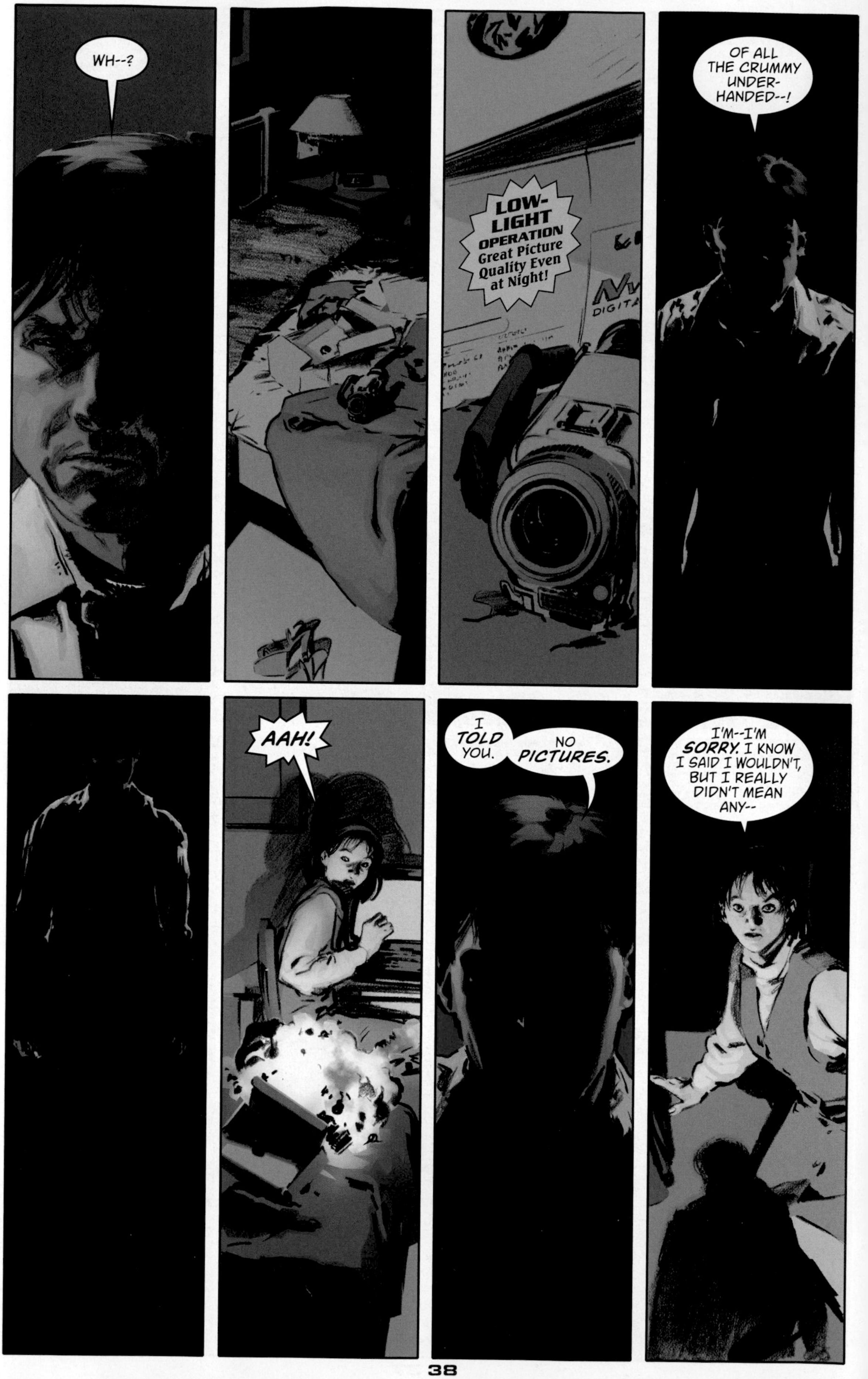
WH--?
LOW-LIGHT OPERATION Great Picture Quality Even at Night!
OF ALL THE CRUMMY UNDER-HANDED--!
AAH!
I TOLD YOU.
NO PICTURES.
I'M--I'M SORRY. I KNOW I SAID I WOULDN'T, BUT I REALLY DIDN'T MEAN ANY--

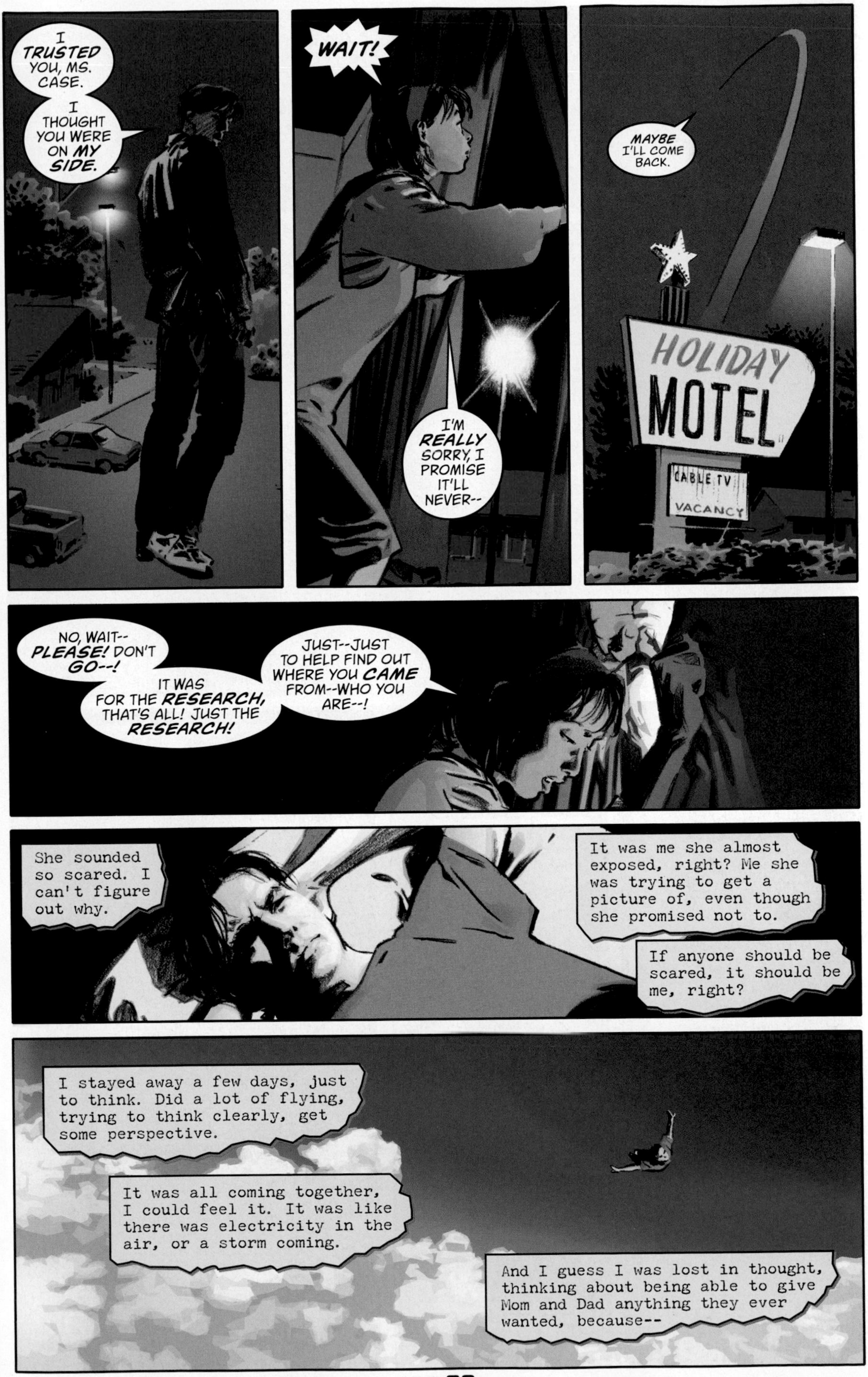
I TRUSTED YOU, MS. CASE.
I THOUGHT YOU WERE ON MY SIDE.
WAIT!
I'M REALLY SORRY, I PROMISE IT'LL NEVER--
MAYBE I'LL COME BACK.
HOLIDAY MOTEL
CABLE TV
VACANCY
NO, WAIT-- PLEASE! DON'T GO--!
IT WAS FOR THE RESEARCH, THAT'S ALL! JUST THE RESEARCH!
JUST--JUST TO HELP FIND OUT WHERE YOU CAME FROM--WHO YOU ARE--!
She sounded so scared. I can't figure out why.
It was me she almost exposed, right? Me she was trying to get a picture of, even though she promised not to.
If anyone should be scared, it should be me, right?
I stayed away a few days, just to think. Did a lot of flying, trying to think clearly, get some perspective.
It was all coming together, I could feel it. It was like there was electricity in the air, or a storm coming.
And I guess I was lost in thought, thinking about being able to give Mom and Dad anything they ever wanted, because--

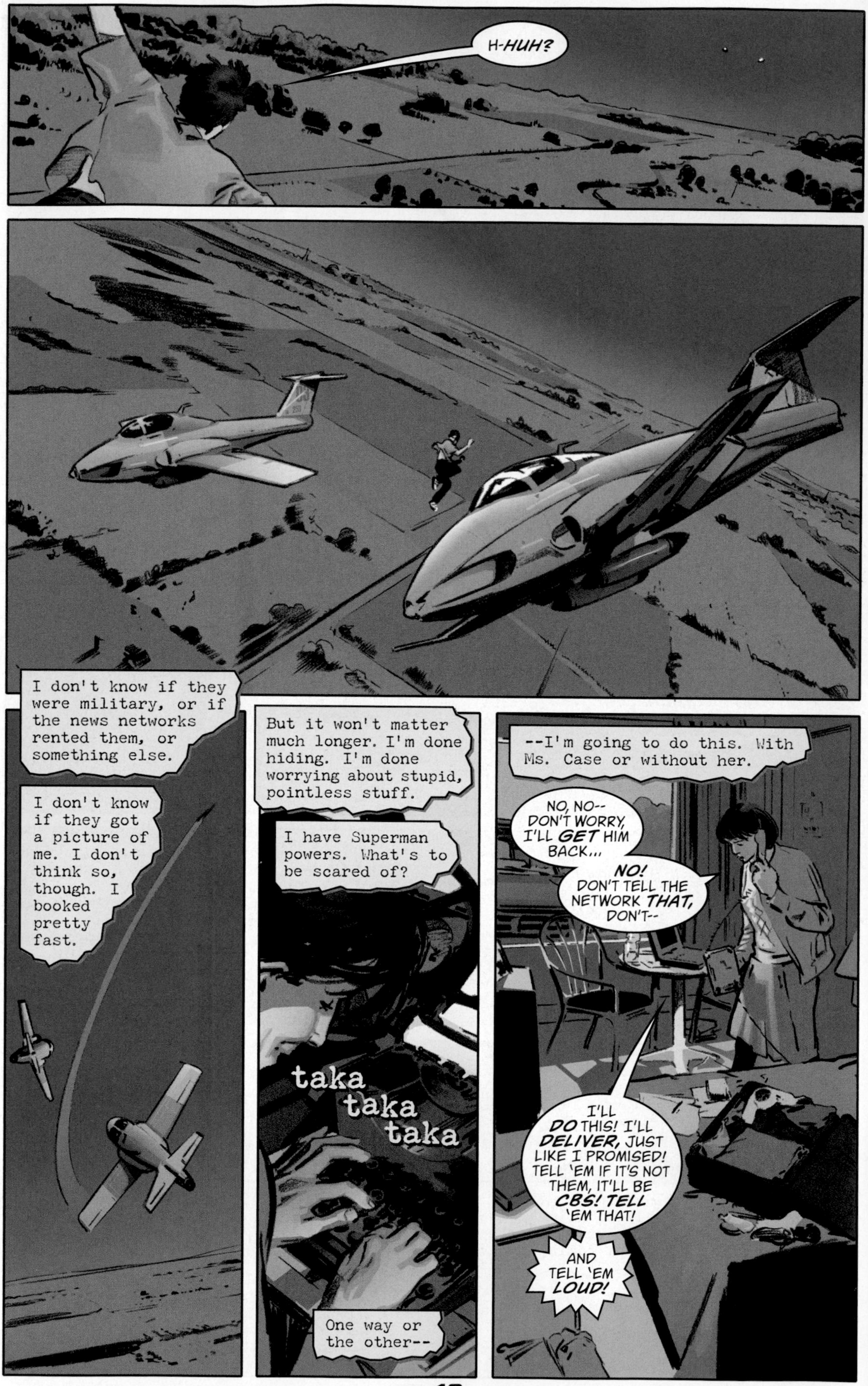
H-HUH?
I don't know if they were military, or if the news networks rented them, or something else.
I don't know if they got a picture of me. I don't think so, though. I booked pretty fast.
But it won't matter much longer. I'm done hiding. I'm done worrying about stupid, pointless stuff.
I have Superman powers. What's to be scared of?
taka taka taka
One way or the other--
--I'm going to do this. With Ms. Case or without her.
NO, NO-- DON'T WORRY, I'LL GET HIM BACK...
NO! DON'T TELL THE NETWORK THAT, DON'T--
I'LL DO THIS! I'LL DELIVER, JUST LIKE I PROMISED! TELL 'EM IF IT'S NOT THEM, IT'LL BE CBS! TELL 'EM THAT!
AND TELL 'EM LOUD!

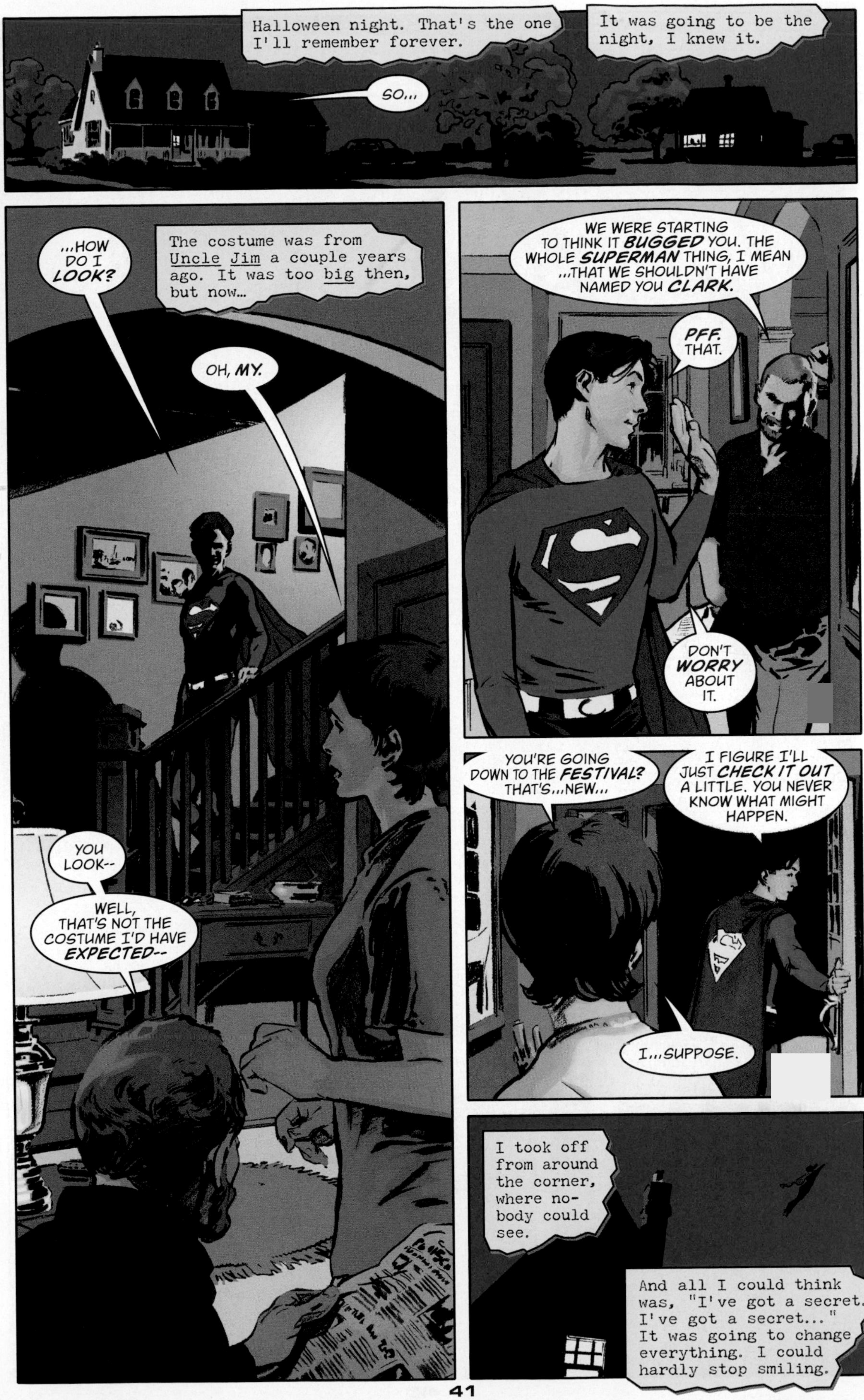
Halloween night. That's the one I'll remember forever.
It was going to be the night, I knew it.
SO...
...HOW DO I LOOK?
The costume was from Uncle Jim a couple years ago. It was too big then, but now...
OH, MY.
YOU LOOK--
WELL, THAT'S NOT THE COSTUME I'D HAVE EXPECTED--
WE WERE STARTING TO THINK IT BUGGED YOU. THE WHOLE SUPERMAN THING, I MEAN ...THAT WE SHOULDN'T HAVE NAMED YOU CLARK.
PFF. THAT.
DON'T WORRY ABOUT IT.
YOU'RE GOING DOWN TO THE FESTIVAL? THAT'S...NEW...
I FIGURE I'LL JUST CHECK IT OUT A LITTLE. YOU NEVER KNOW WHAT MIGHT HAPPEN.
I...SUPPOSE.
I took off from around the corner, where nobody could see.
And all I could think was, "I've got a secret. I've got a secret..." It was going to change everything. I could hardly stop smiling.

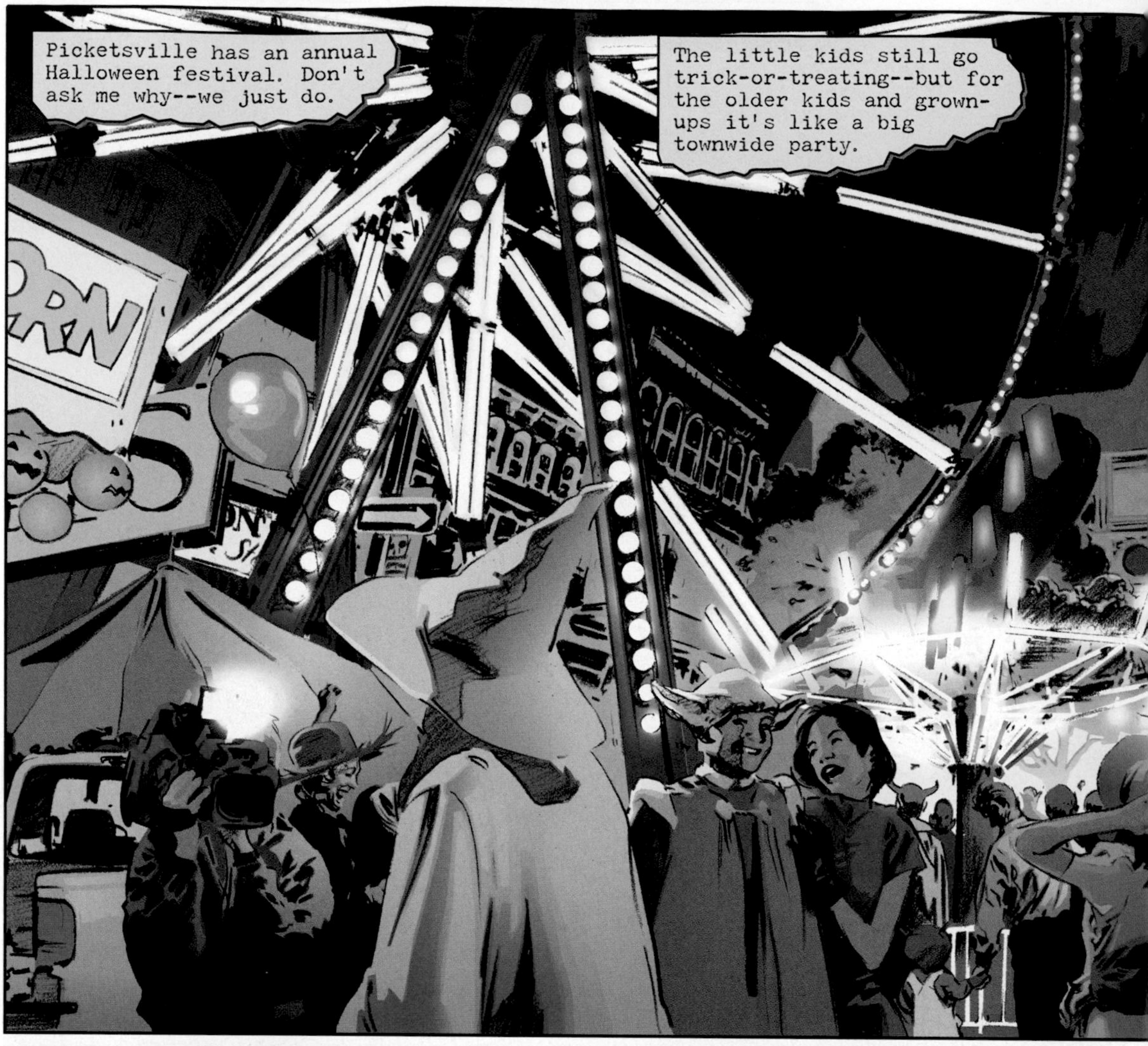
Picketsville has an annual Halloween festival. Don't ask me why--we just do.
The little kids still go trick-or-treating--but for the older kids and grown-ups it's like a big townwide party.

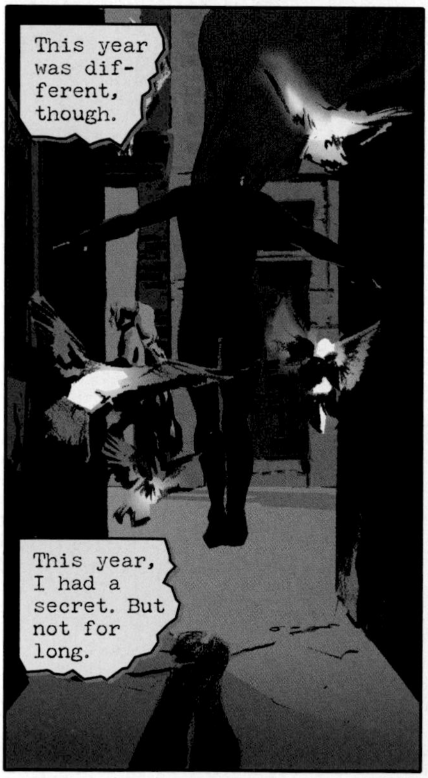
This year was dif-ferent, though.
This year, I had a secret. But not for long.

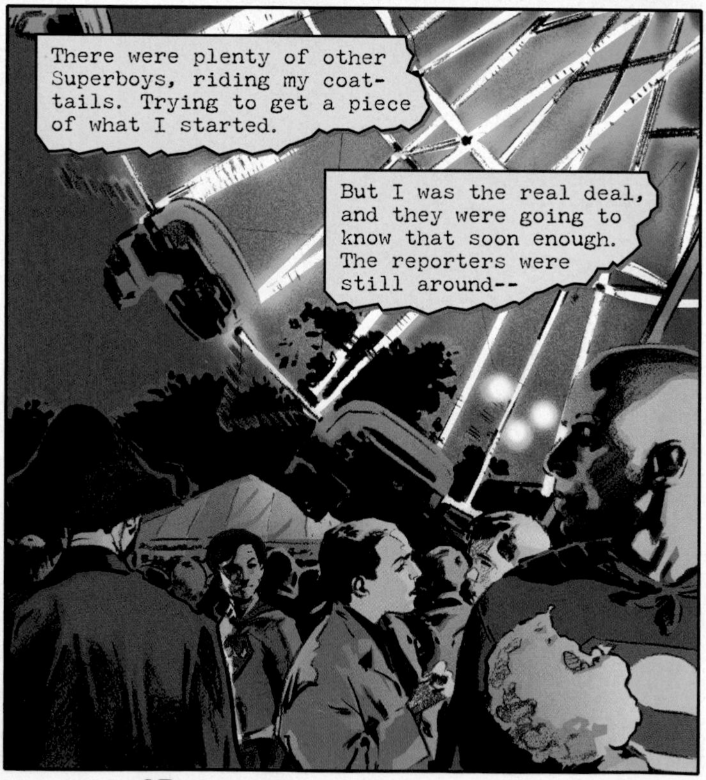
There were plenty of other Superboys, riding my coat-tails. Trying to get a piece of what I started.
But I was the real deal, and they were going to know that soon enough. The reporters were still around--

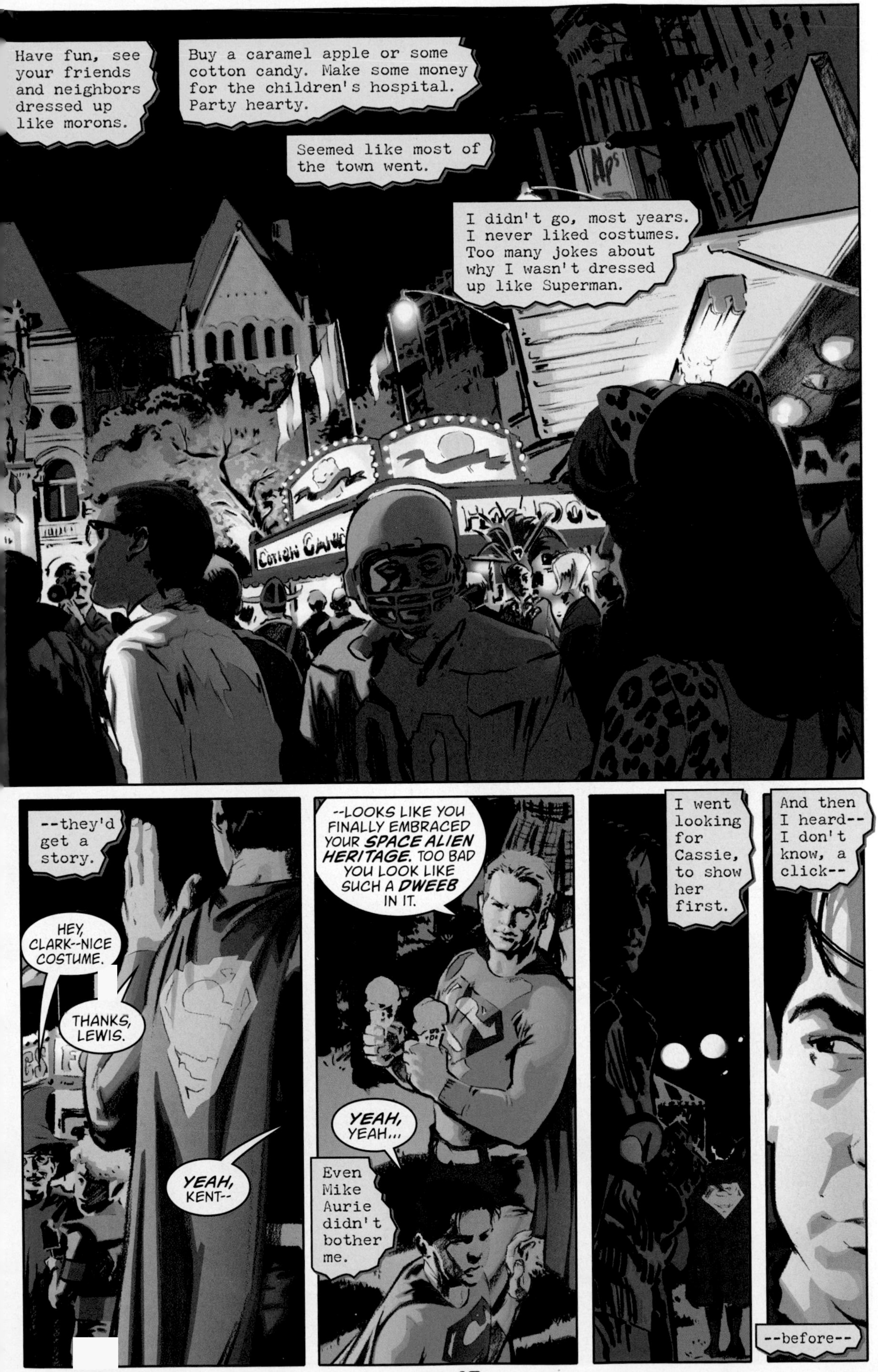
Have fun, see your friends and neighbors dressed up like morons.
Buy a caramel apple or some cotton candy. Make some money for the children's hospital. Party hearty.
Seemed like most of the town went.
I didn't go, most years. I never liked costumes. Too many jokes about why I wasn't dressed up like Superman.
--they'd get a story.
HEY, CLARK--NICE COSTUME.
THANKS, LEWIS.
YEAH, KENT--
--LOOKS LIKE YOU FINALLY EMBRACED YOUR SPACE ALIEN HERITAGE. TOO BAD YOU LOOK LIKE SUCH A DWEEB IN IT.
YEAH, YEAH...
Even Mike Aurie didn't bother me.
I went looking for Cassie, to show her first.
And then I heard-- I don't know, a click--
--before--

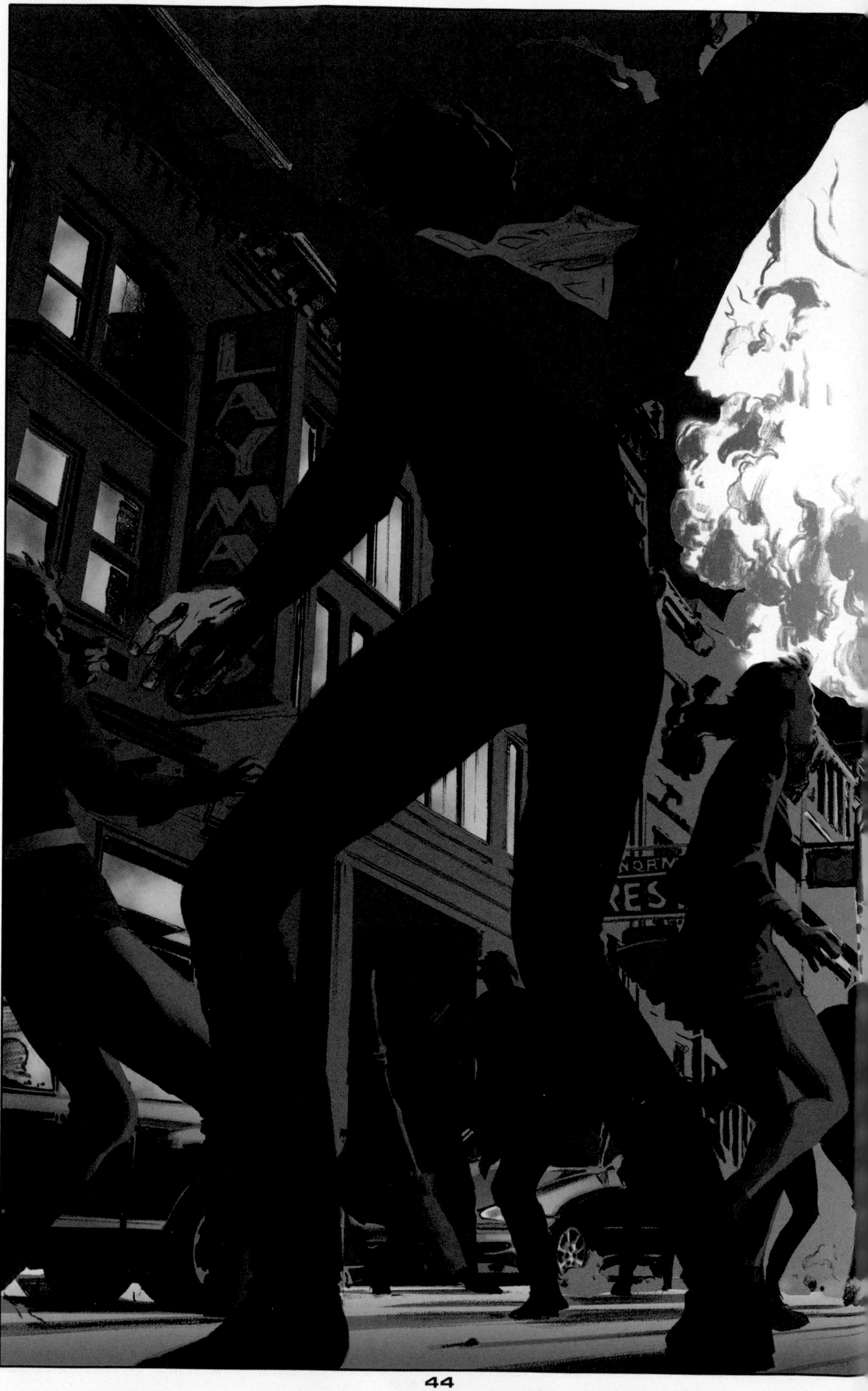

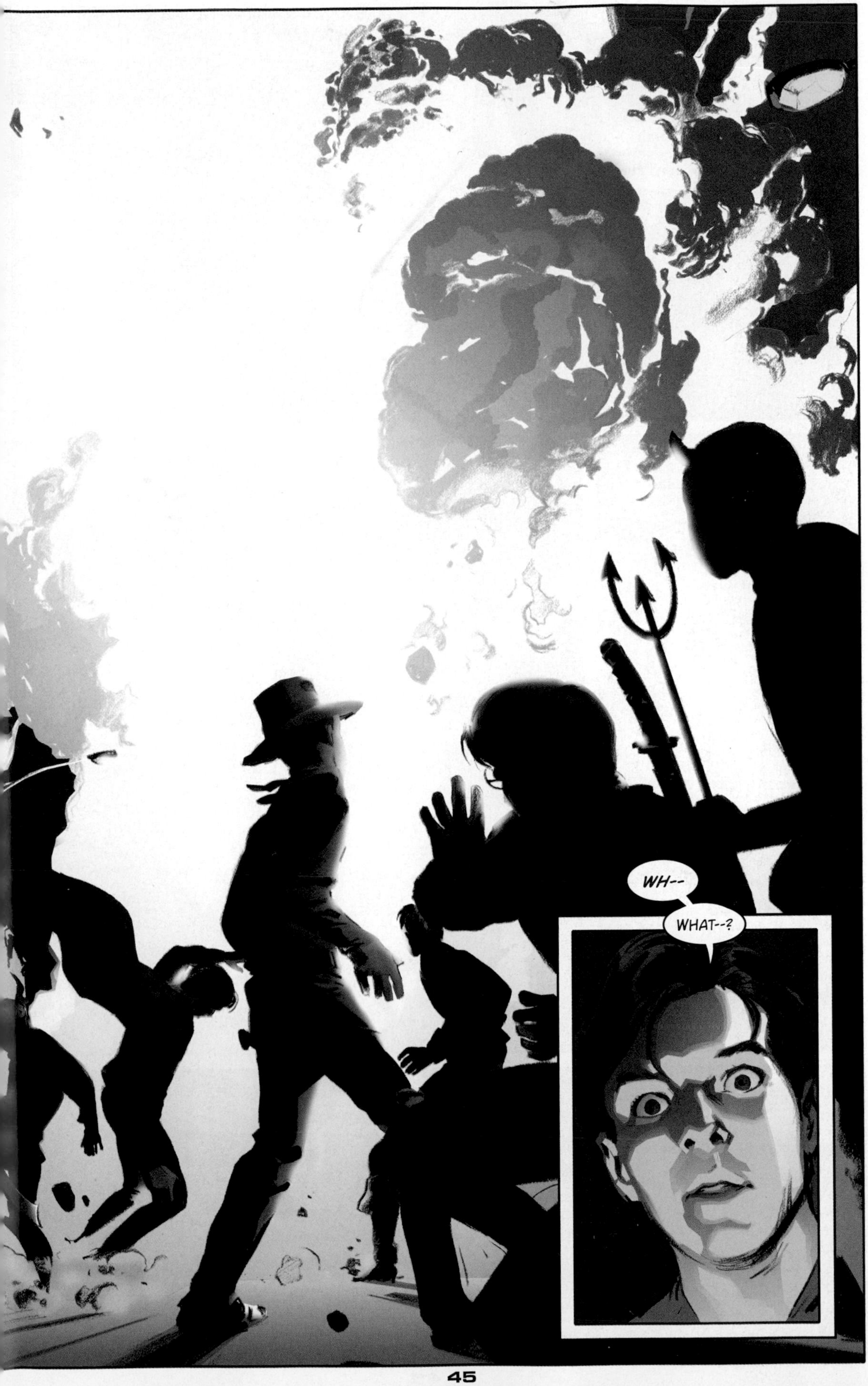
WH--
WHAT--?

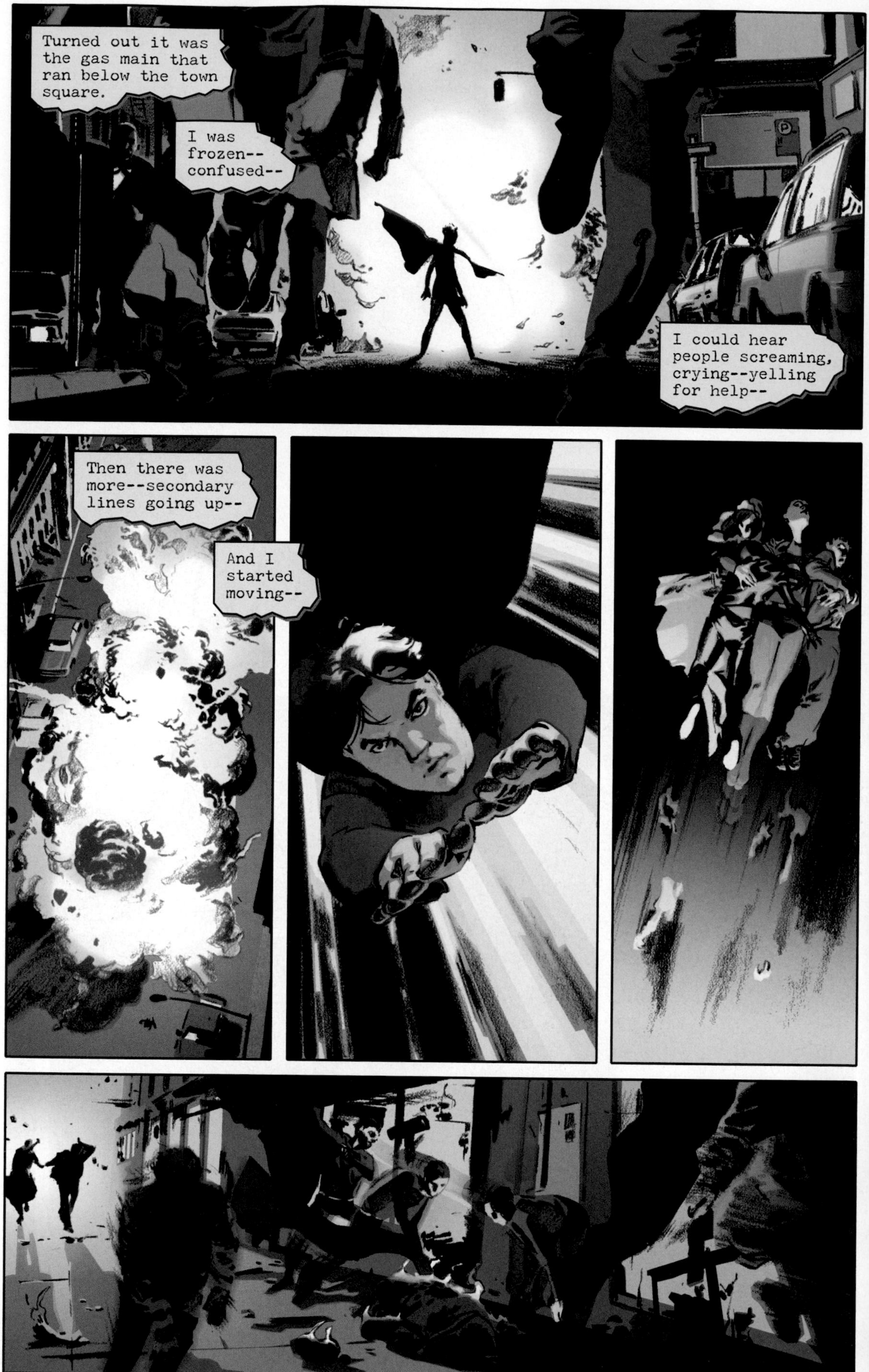
Turned out it was the gas main that ran below the town square.
I was frozen--confused--
I could hear people screaming, crying--yelling for help--
Then there was more--secondary lines going up--
And I started moving--

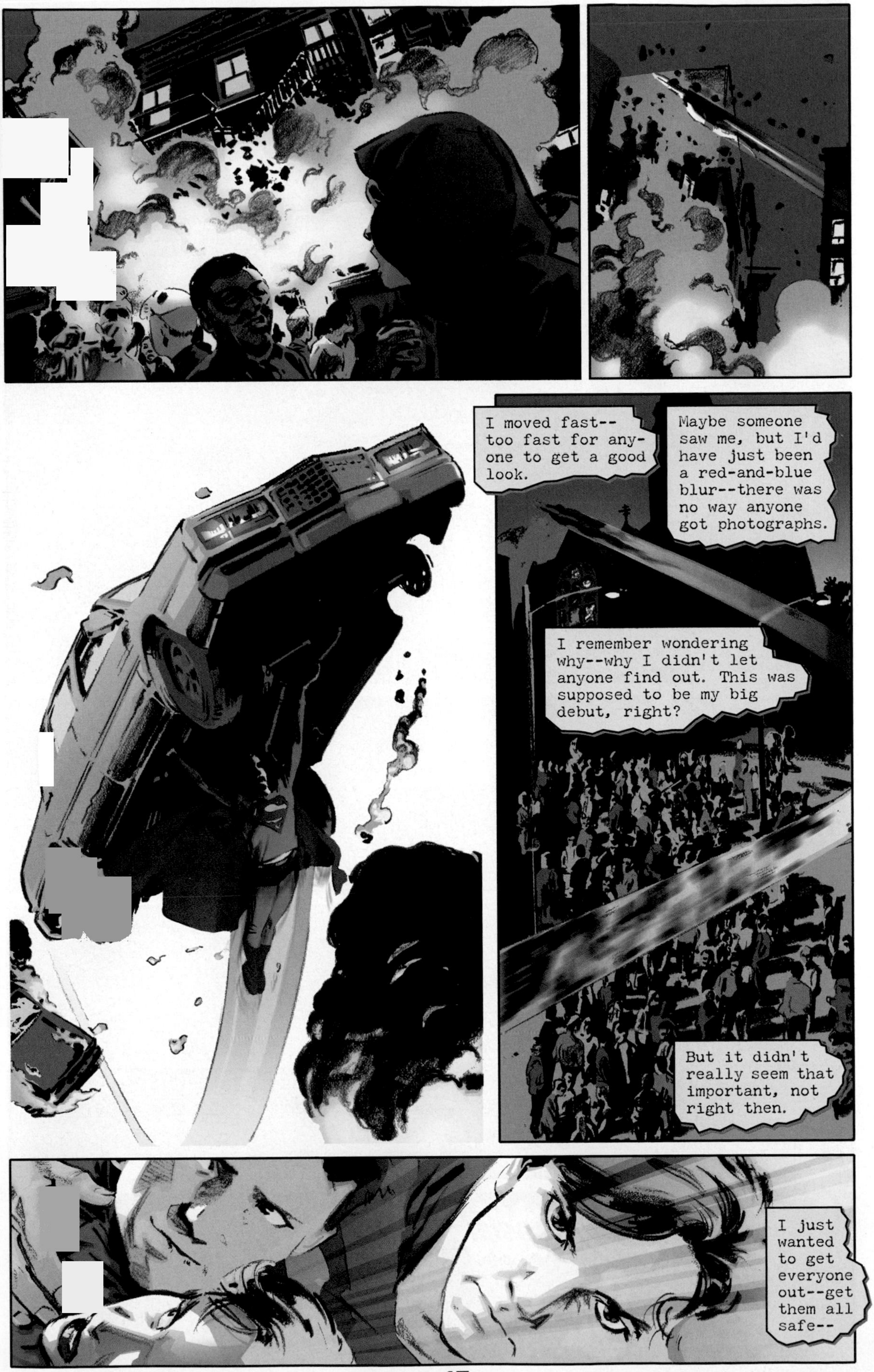
I moved fast--too fast for any-one to get a good look.
Maybe someone saw me, but I'd have just been a red-and-blue blur--there was no way anyone got photographs.
I remember wondering why--why I didn't let anyone find out. This was supposed to be my big debut, right?
But it didn't really seem that important, not right then.
I just wanted to get everyone out--get them all safe--

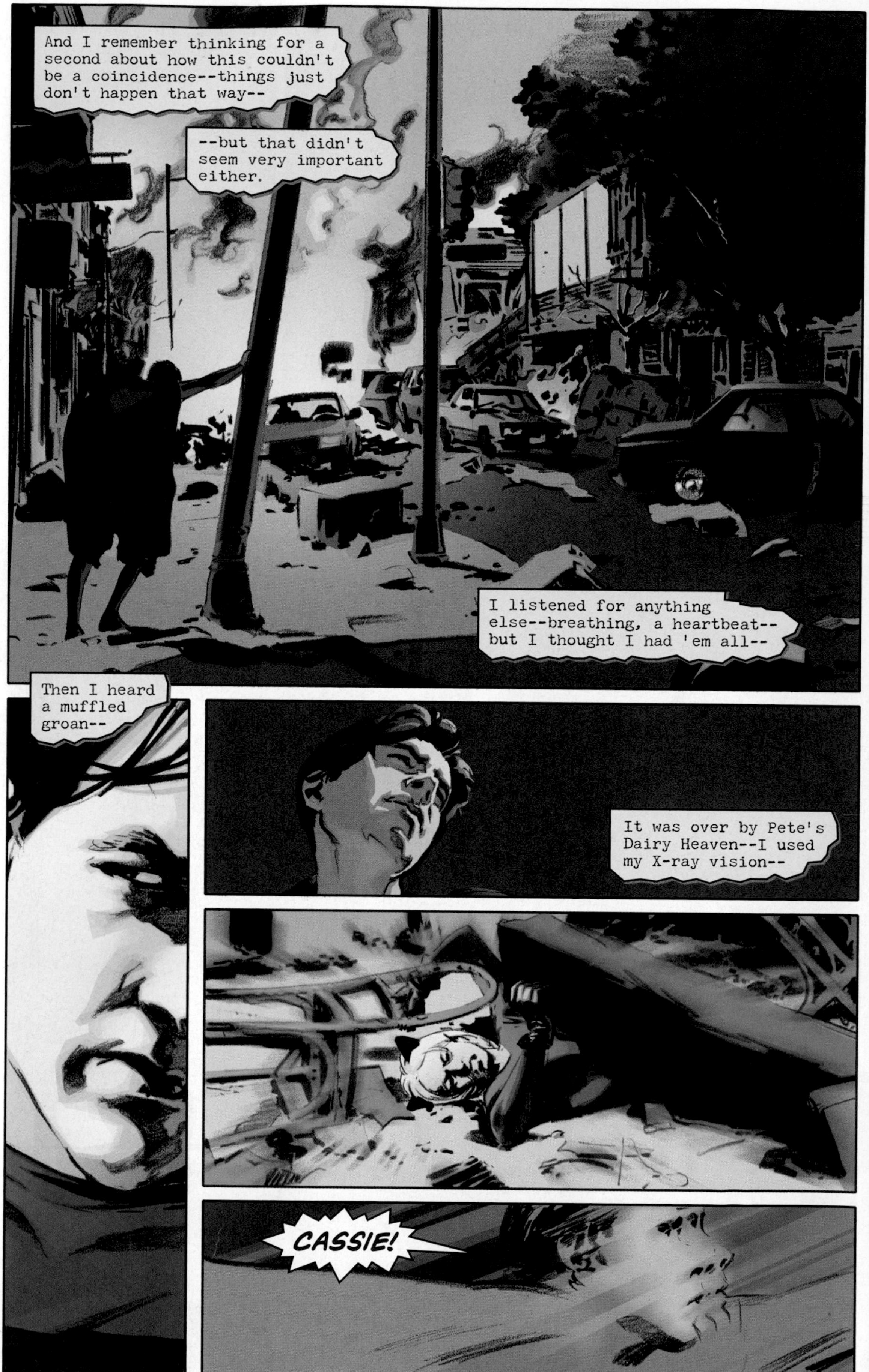
And I remember thinking for a second about how this couldn't be a coincidence--things just don't happen that way--
--but that didn't seem very important either.
I listened for anything else--breathing, a heartbeat--but I thought I had 'em all--
Then I heard a muffled groan--
It was over by Pete's Dairy Heaven--I used my X-ray vision--
CASSIE!

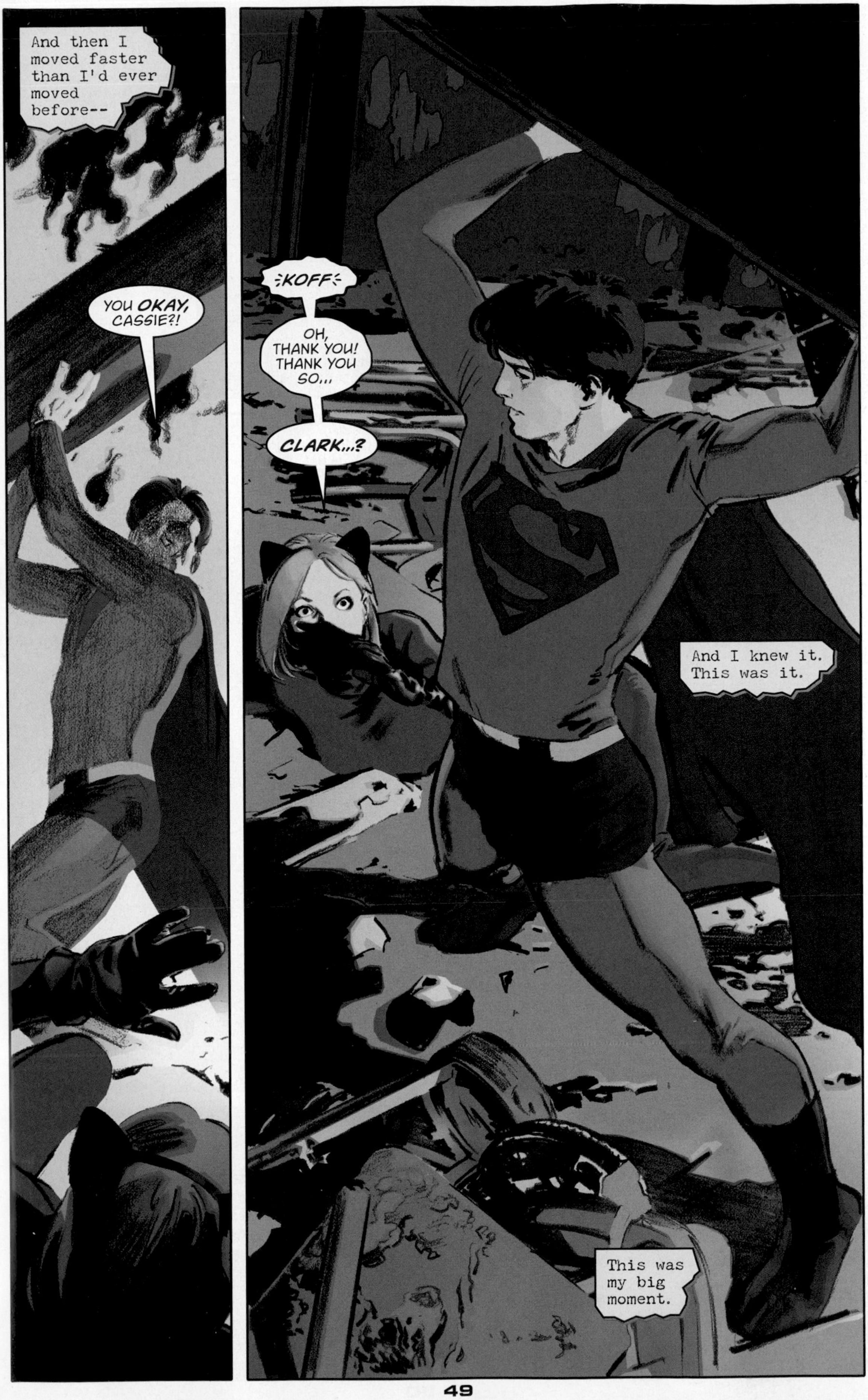
And then I moved faster than I'd ever moved before--
YOU OKAY, CASSIE?!
KOFF
OH, THANK YOU! THANK YOU SO...
CLARK...?
And I knew it. This was it.
This was my big moment.

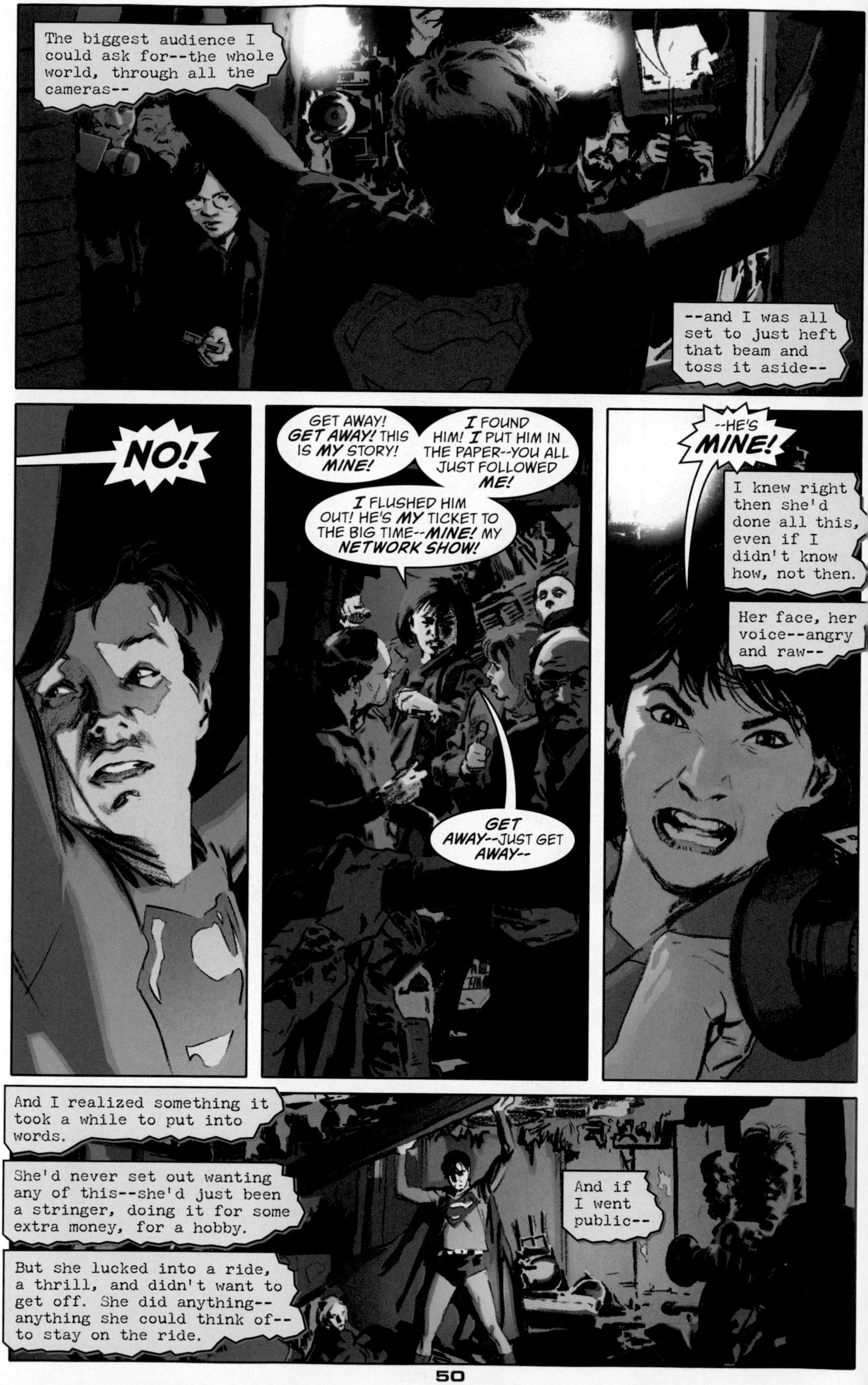
The biggest audience I could ask for--the whole world, through all the cameras--
--and I was all set to just heft that beam and toss it aside--
NO!
GET AWAY! GET AWAY! THIS IS MY STORY! MINE!
I FOUND HIM! I PUT HIM IN THE PAPER--YOU ALL JUST FOLLOWED ME!
I FLUSHED HIM OUT! HE'S MY TICKET TO THE BIG TIME--MINE! MY NETWORK SHOW!
GET AWAY--JUST GET AWAY--
--HE'S MINE!
I knew right then she'd done all this, even if I didn't know how, not then.
Her face, her voice--angry and raw--
And I realized something it took a while to put into words.
She'd never set out wanting any of this--she'd just been a stringer, doing it for some extra money, for a hobby.
But she lucked into a ride, a thrill, and didn't want to get off. She did anything--anything she could think of--to stay on the ride.
And if I went public--

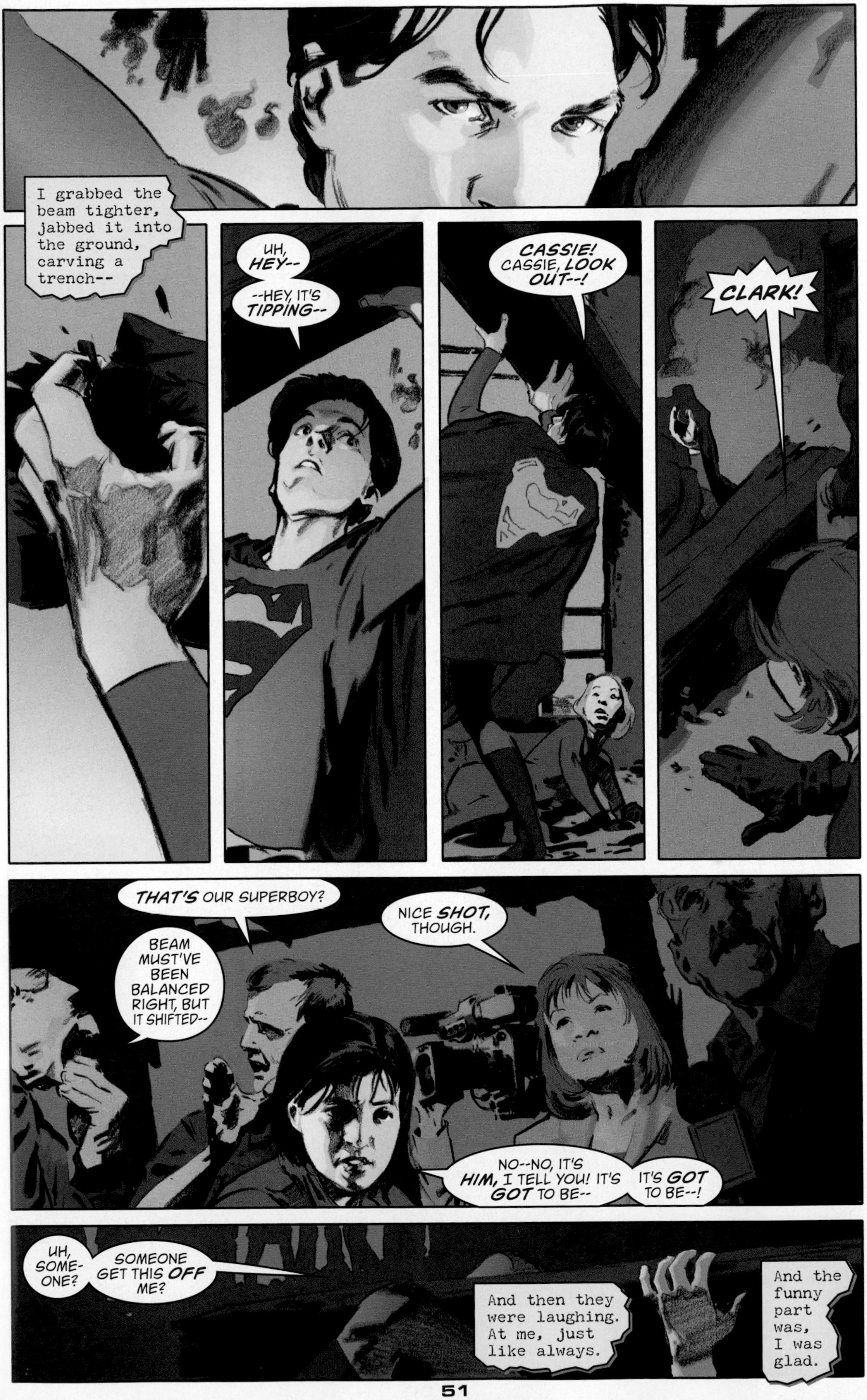
I grabbed the beam tighter, jabbed it into the ground, carving a trench--
UH, HEY--
--HEY, IT'S TIPPING--
CASSIE! CASSIE, LOOK OUT--!
CLARK!
THAT'S OUR SUPERBOY?
BEAM MUST'VE BEEN BALANCED RIGHT, BUT IT SHIFTED--
NICE SHOT, THOUGH.
NO--NO, IT'S HIM, I TELL YOU! IT'S GOT TO BE--
IT'S GOT TO BE--!
UH, SOME-ONE?
SOMEONE GET THIS OFF ME?
And then they were laughing. At me, just like always.
And the funny part was, I was glad.

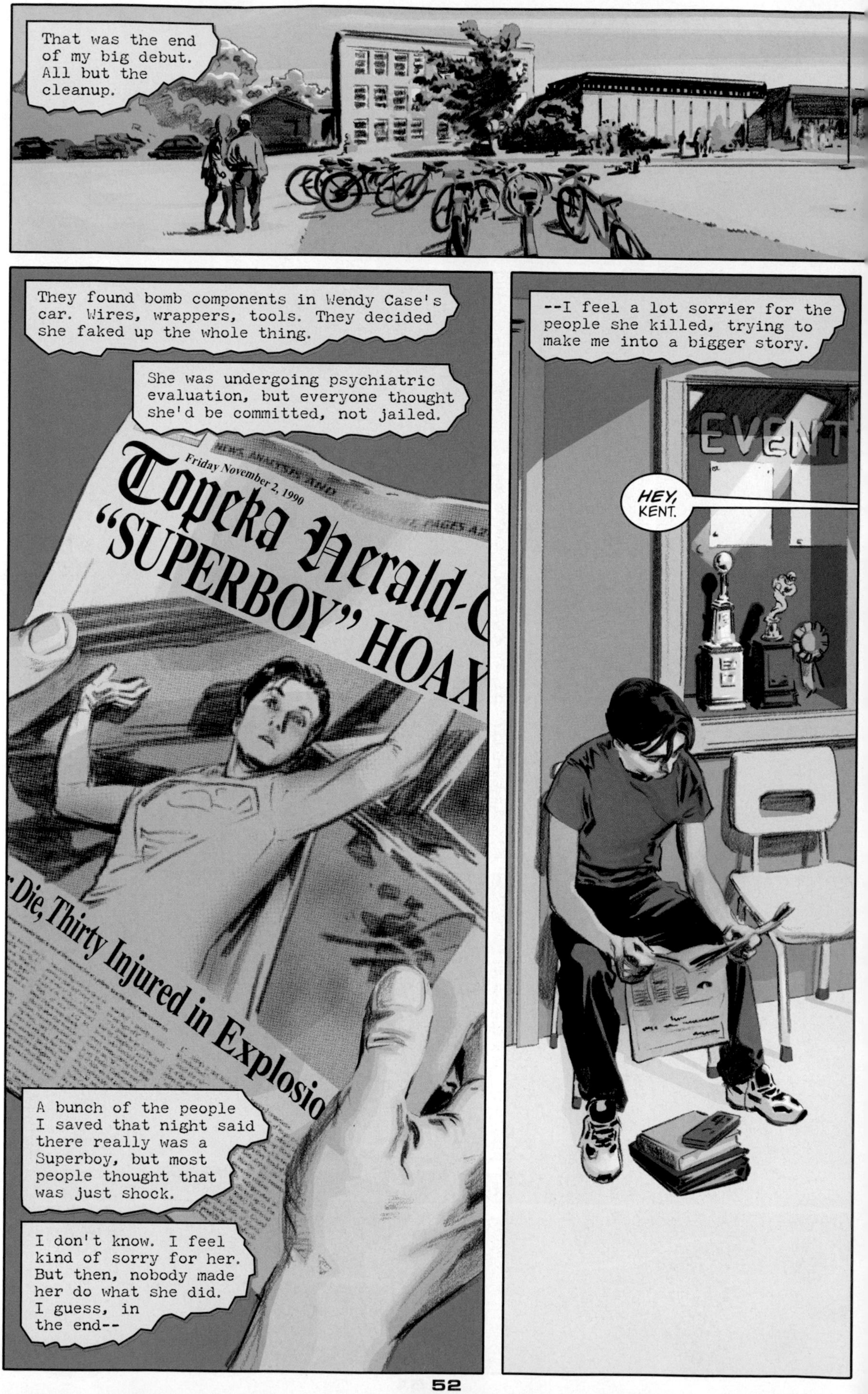
That was the end of my big debut. All but the cleanup.
They found bomb components in Wendy Case's car. Wires, wrappers, tools. They decided she faked up the whole thing.
She was undergoing psychiatric evaluation, but everyone thought she'd be committed, not jailed.
Topeka Herald-C
Friday November 2, 1990
"SUPERBOY" HOAX
r Die, Thirty Injured in Explosio
A bunch of the people I saved that night said there really was a Superboy, but most people thought that was just shock.
I don't know. I feel kind of sorry for her. But then, nobody made her do what she did. I guess, in the end--
--I feel a lot sorrier for the people she killed, trying to make me into a bigger story.
EVENT
HEY, KENT.

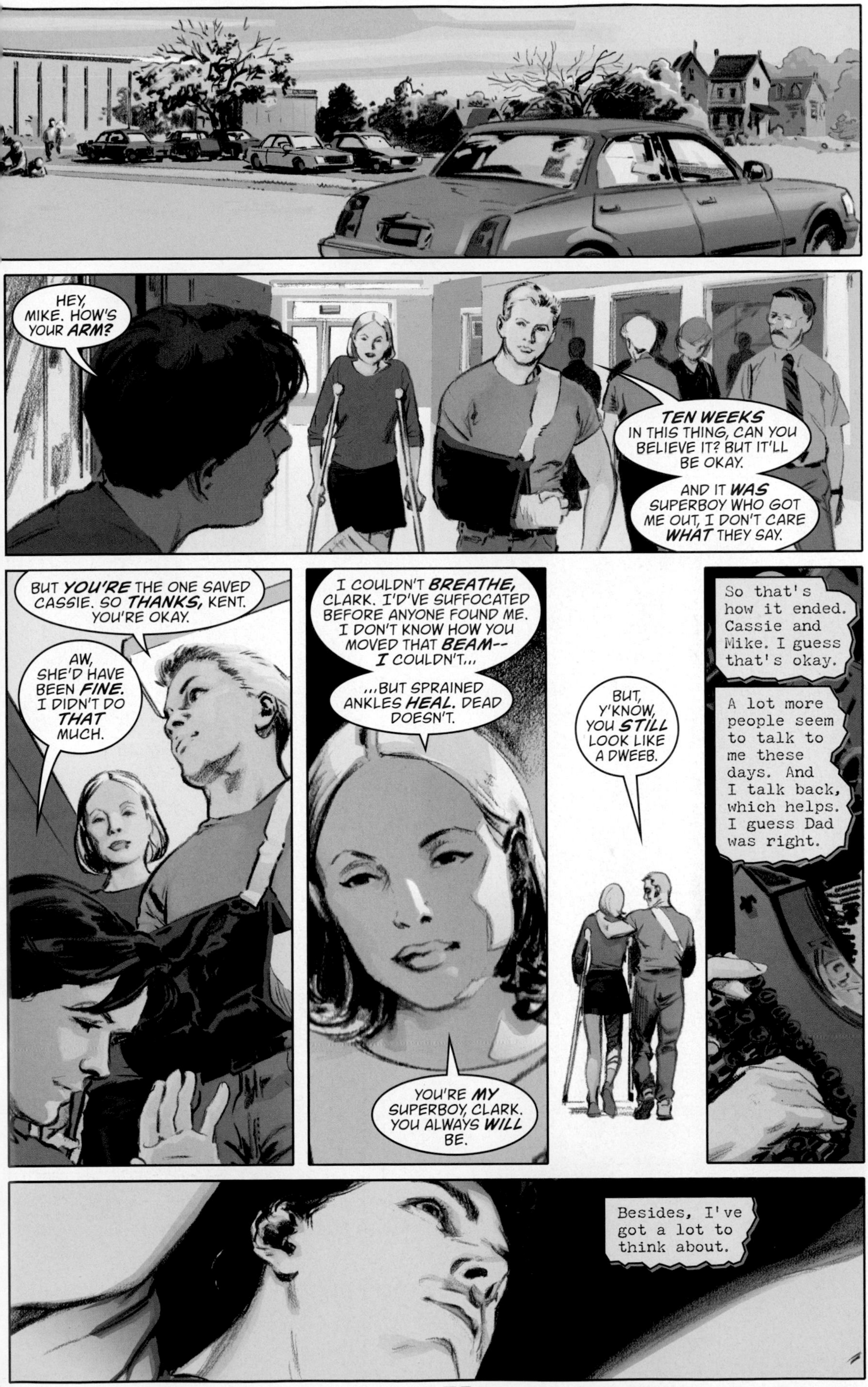
HEY, MIKE. HOW'S YOUR ARM?
TEN WEEKS IN THIS THING, CAN YOU BELIEVE IT? BUT IT'LL BE OKAY.
AND IT WAS SUPERBOY WHO GOT ME OUT, I DON'T CARE WHAT THEY SAY.
BUT YOU'RE THE ONE SAVED CASSIE. SO THANKS, KENT. YOU'RE OKAY.
AW, SHE'D HAVE BEEN FINE. I DIDN'T DO THAT MUCH.
I COULDN'T BREATHE, CLARK. I'D'VE SUFFOCATED BEFORE ANYONE FOUND ME. I DON'T KNOW HOW YOU MOVED THAT BEAM-- I COULDN'T...
...BUT SPRAINED ANKLES HEAL. DEAD DOESN'T.
YOU'RE MY SUPERBOY, CLARK. YOU ALWAYS WILL BE.
BUT, Y'KNOW, YOU STILL LOOK LIKE A DWEEB.
So that's how it ended. Cassie and Mike. I guess that's okay.
A lot more people seem to talk to me these days. And I talk back, which helps. I guess Dad was right.
Besides, I've got a lot to think about.

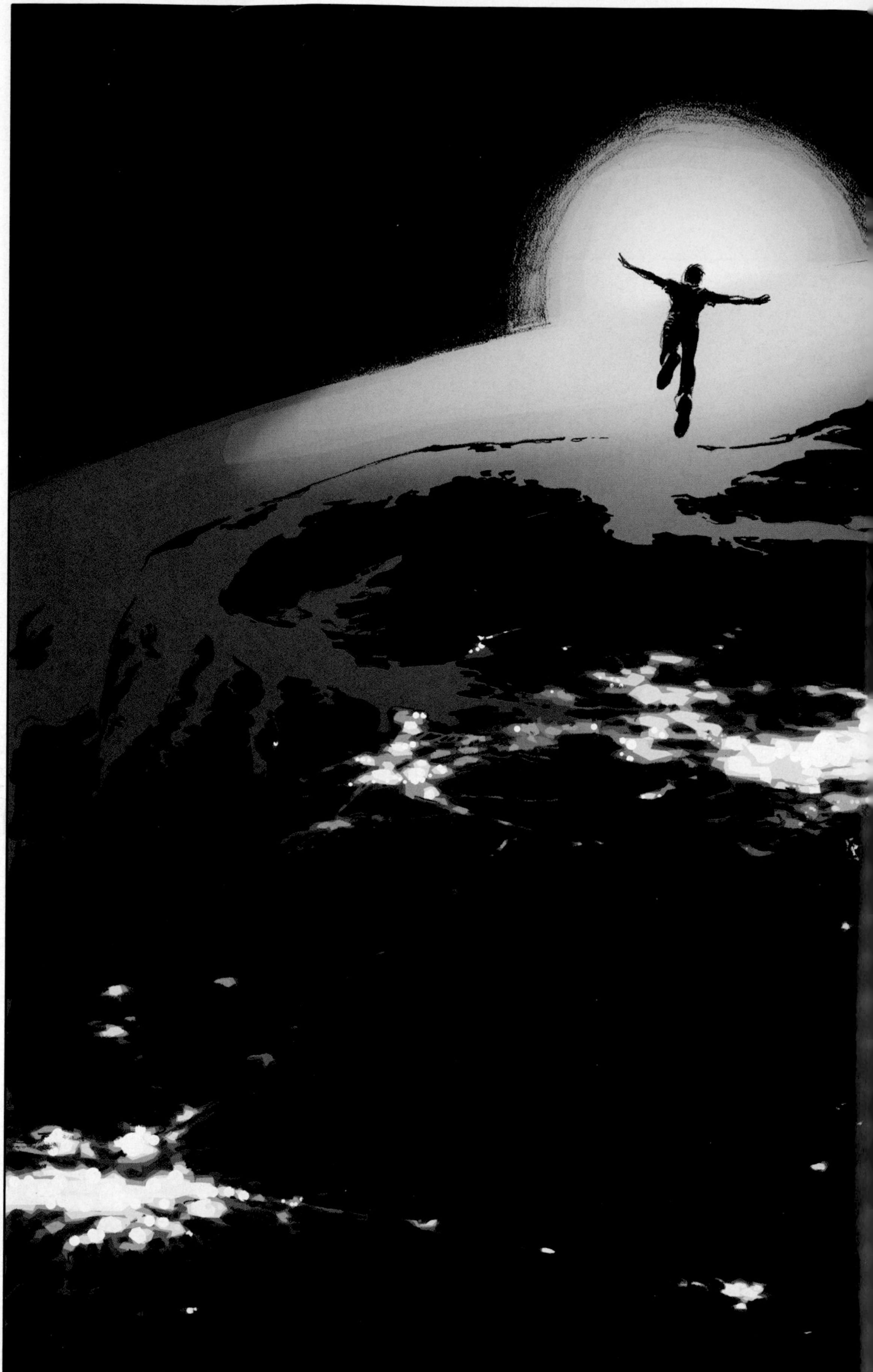

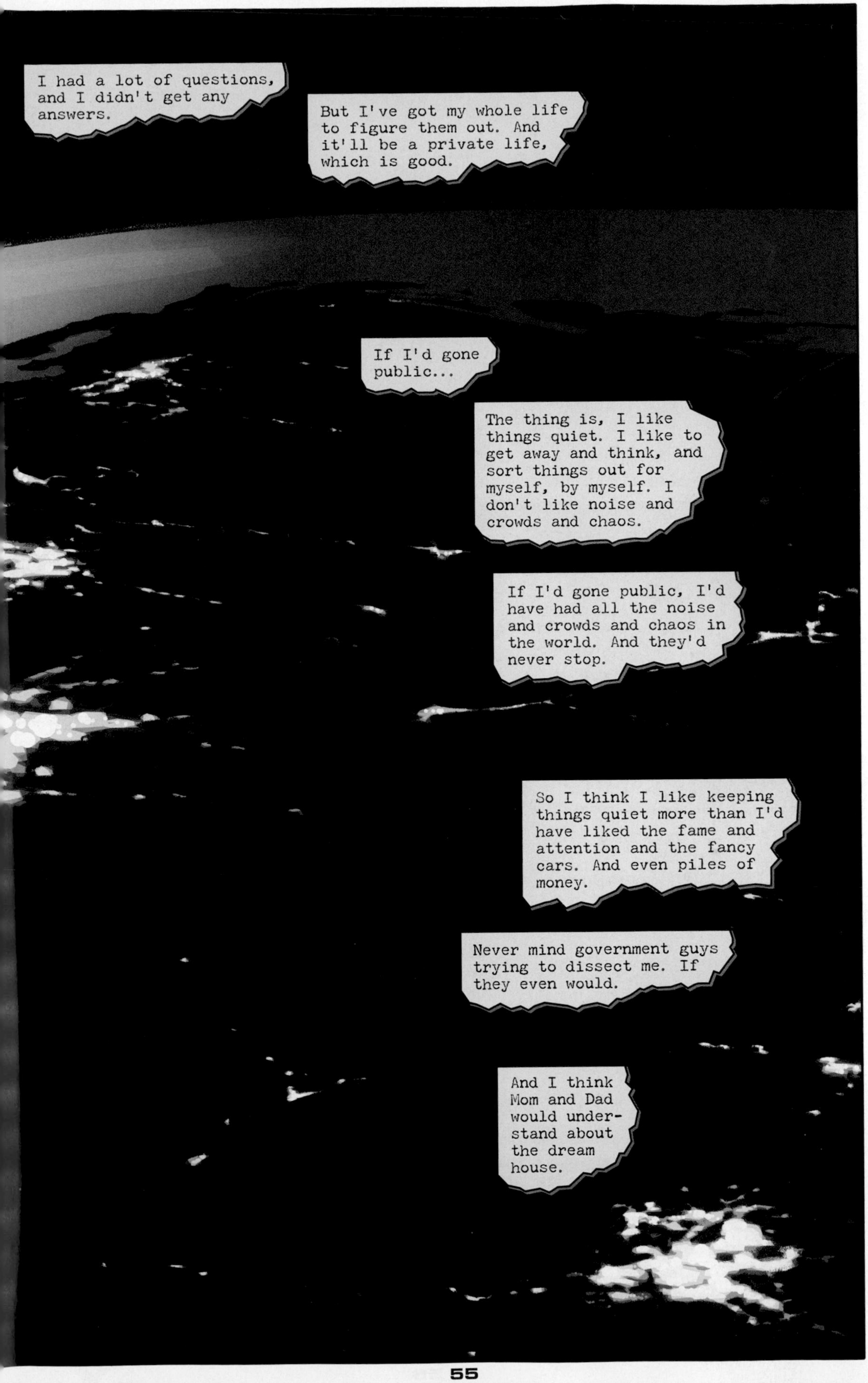
I had a lot of questions, and I didn't get any answers.
But I've got my whole life to figure them out. And it'll be a private life, which is good.
If I'd gone public...
The thing is, I like things quiet. I like to get away and think, and sort things out for myself, by myself. I don't like noise and crowds and chaos.
If I'd gone public, I'd have had all the noise and crowds and chaos in the world. And they'd never stop.
So I think I like keeping things quiet more than I'd have liked the fame and attention and the fancy cars. And even piles of money.
Never mind government guys trying to dissect me. If they even would.
And I think Mom and Dad would under-stand about the dream house.

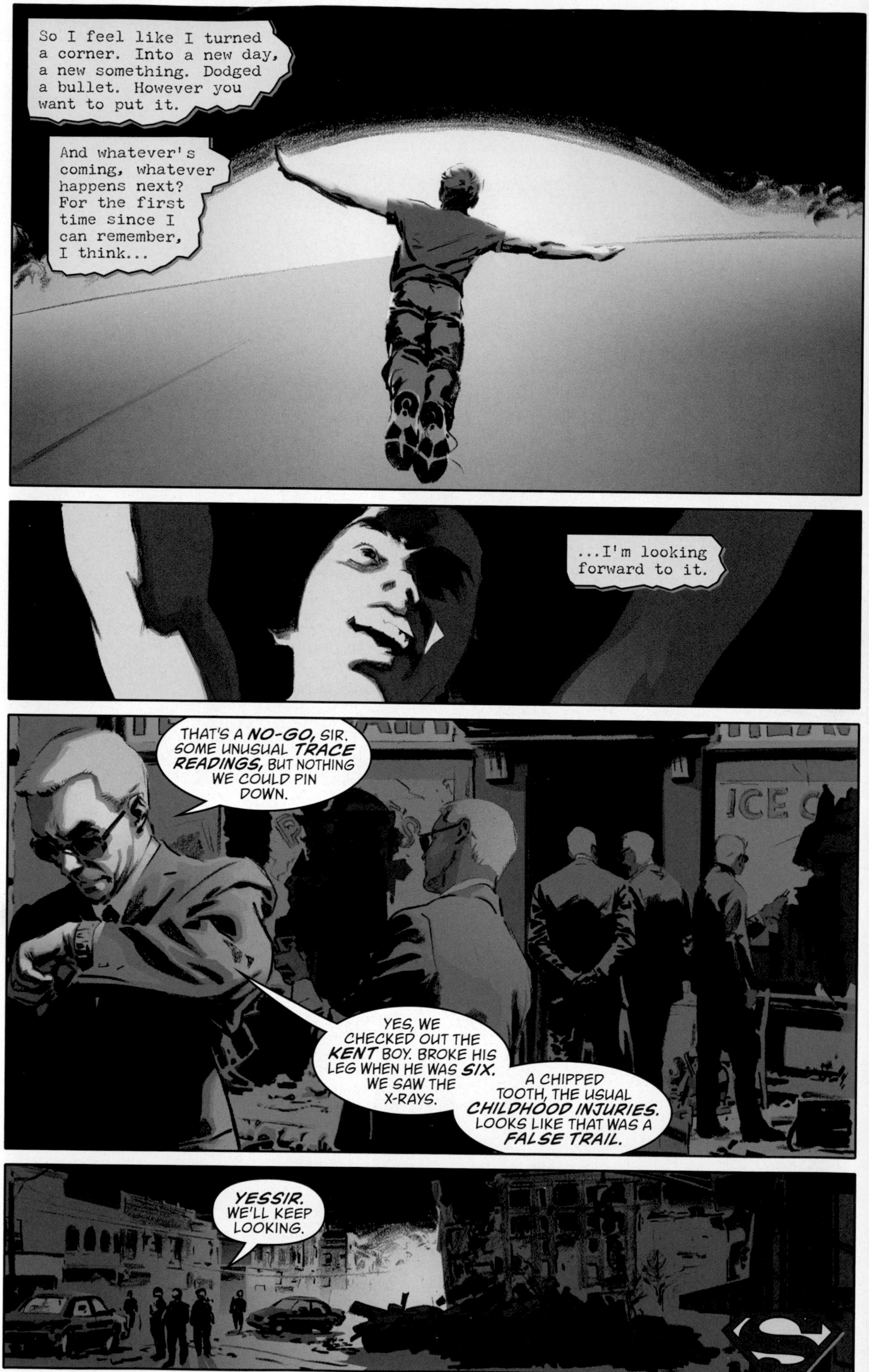
So I feel like I turned a corner. Into a new day, a new something. Dodged a bullet. However you want to put it.
And whatever's coming, whatever happens next? For the first time since I can remember, I think...
...I'm looking forward to it.
THAT'S A NO-GO, SIR. SOME UNUSUAL TRACE READINGS, BUT NOTHING WE COULD PIN DOWN.
ICE C
YES, WE CHECKED OUT THE KENT BOY. BROKE HIS LEG WHEN HE WAS SIX. WE SAW THE X-RAYS.
A CHIPPED TOOTH, THE USUAL CHILDHOOD INJURIES. LOOKS LIKE THAT WAS A FALSE TRAIL.
YESSIR. WE'LL KEEP LOOKING.

# chapter two **metropolis**

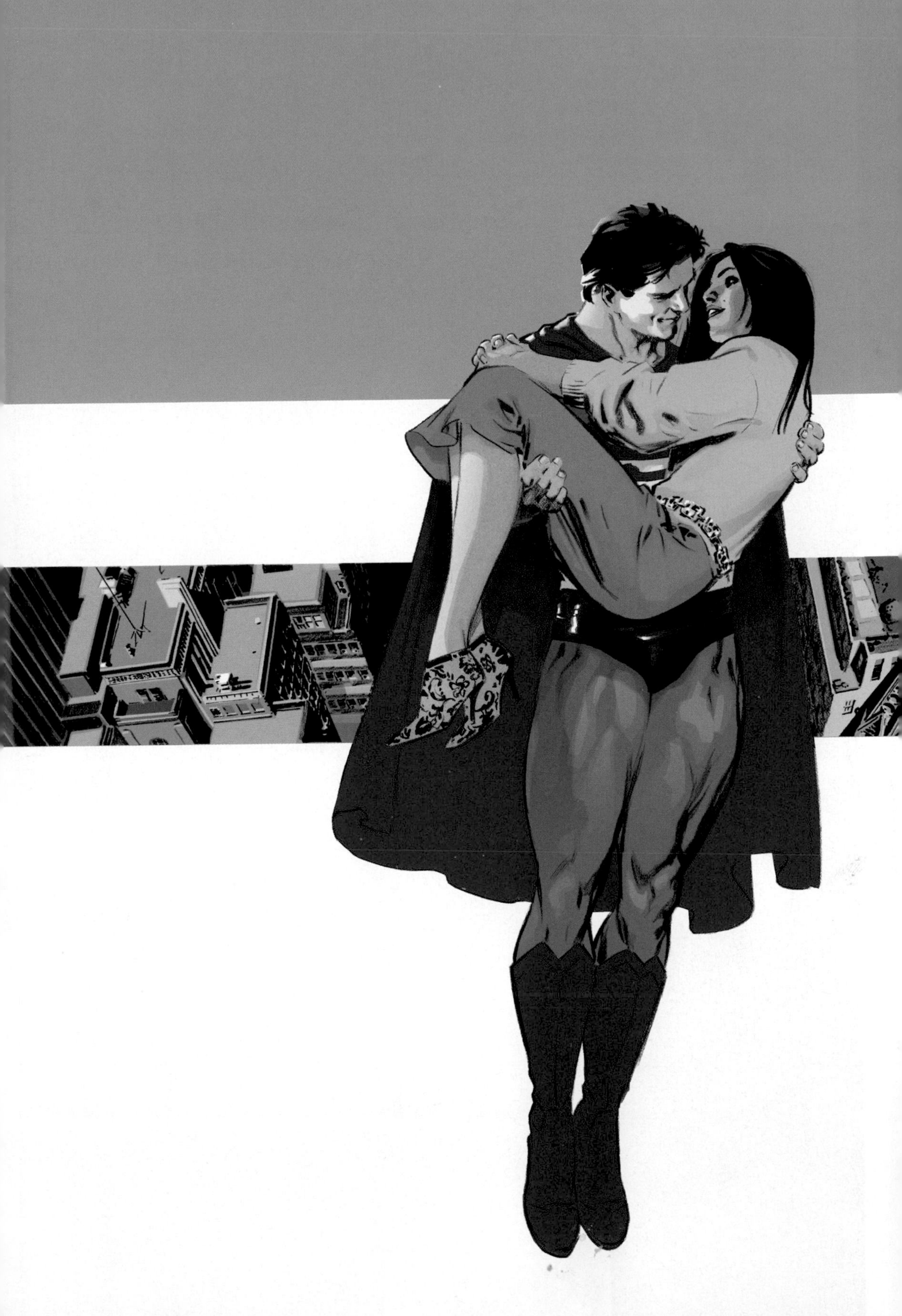

a secret **shared** is a secret **exposed**.

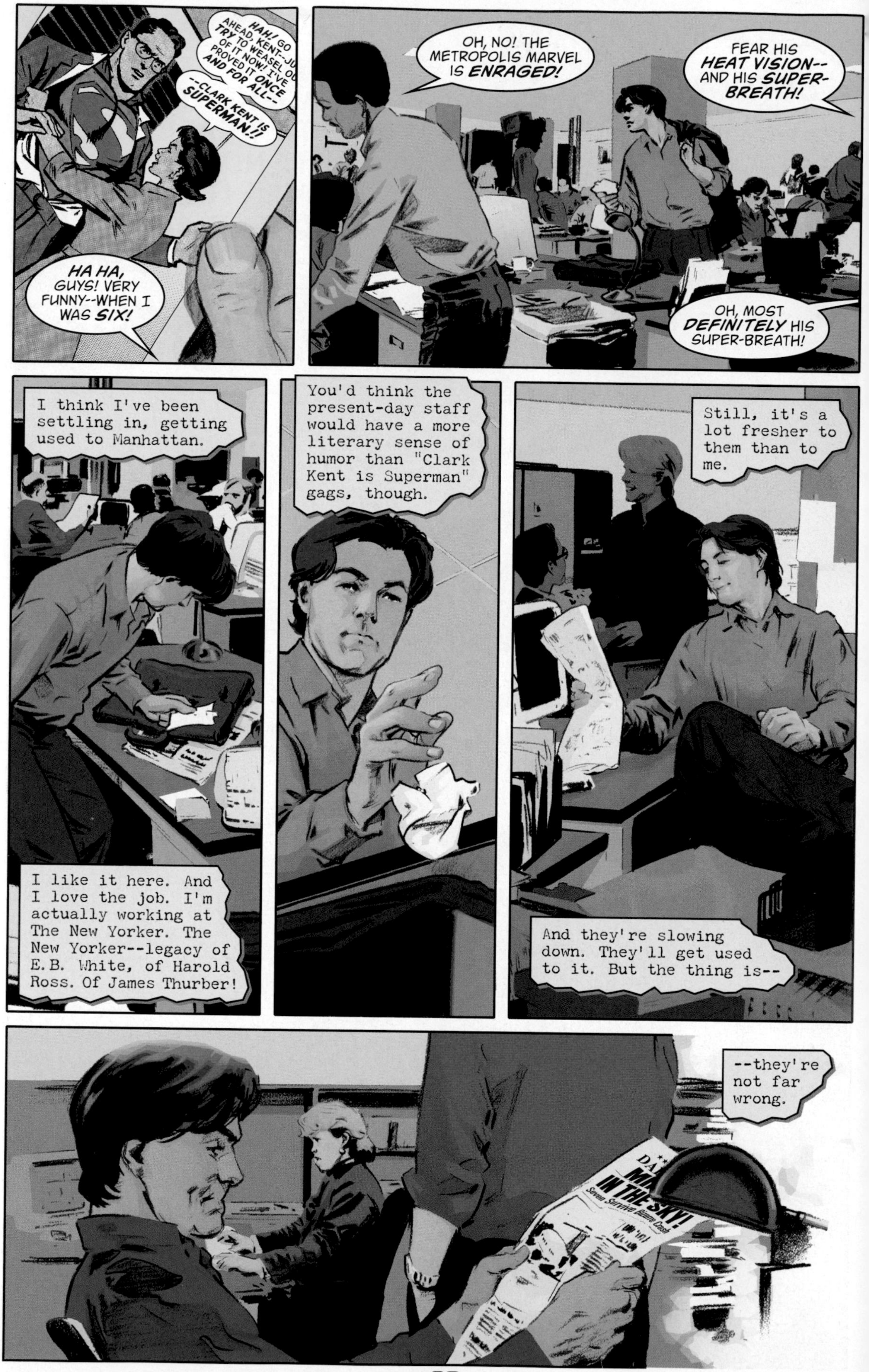
HAH! GO AHEAD, KENT-JU TRY TO WEASEL OU OF IT NOW! I'VE PROVED IT ONCE AND FOR ALL--
--CLARK KENT IS SUPERMAN!!
HA HA, GUYS! VERY FUNNY--WHEN I WAS SIX!
OH, NO! THE METROPOLIS MARVEL IS ENRAGED!
FEAR HIS HEAT VISION-- AND HIS SUPER-BREATH!
OH, MOST DEFINITELY HIS SUPER-BREATH!
I think I've been settling in, getting used to Manhattan.
I like it here. And I love the job. I'm actually working at The New Yorker. The New Yorker--legacy of E.B. White, of Harold Ross. Of James Thurber!
You'd think the present-day staff would have a more literary sense of humor than "Clark Kent is Superman" gags, though.
Still, it's a lot fresher to them than to me.
And they're slowing down. They'll get used to it. But the thing is--
--they're not far wrong.
IN THE SKY!
Seven Survive Bizarre Crash

It was just last night--

--the plane was a corporate jet-- an Airbus ACJ. The papers said it had been skating by with barely any maintenance checks.

They lost an engine. Hell, they practically lost a wing.

HOLD ON, PETE! FOR CHRISSAKES, HOLD ON! STRAIGHTEN HER OUT!

I C-CAN'T! I--

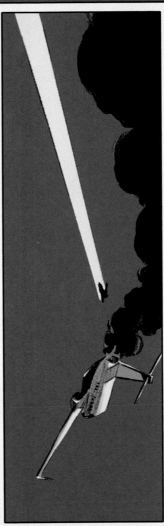

WH--?

YOU *DID* IT, PETE!

I *DIDN'T*, I COULDN'T POSSIBLY--

WHAT'S *OUT* THERE?

The airframe was damaged, coming apart. They had to get down to the ground. Fast.

And even then, they weren't going to stay in one piece.

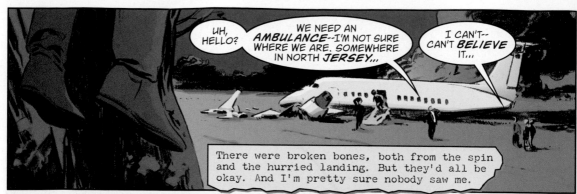

UH, HELLO?

WE NEED AN *AMBULANCE*--I'M NOT SURE WHERE WE ARE. SOMEWHERE IN NORTH *JERSEY*...

I CAN'T-- CAN'T *BELIEVE* IT...

There were broken bones, both from the spin and the hurried landing. But they'd all be okay. And I'm pretty sure nobody saw me.

Not that it'd matter if they did.

That's why I wear the costume. I learned years ago that if people knew about me, I'd have no peace. I'd be a freak, a curiosity. A monster, even.

People would go nuts-- wanting to know how I can do it, where the powers come from.

And I don't even know any of that myself.

But if someone sees me, what are they going to say?

"It was Superman, officer. He swooped out of the sky and saved me!"

Yeah, sure. Who's going to believe that? I've seen some stories on the Internet, stuff I've done. Everyone treats it as a joke.

No, as long as I don't get spotted right out in broad daylight, I'm safe.

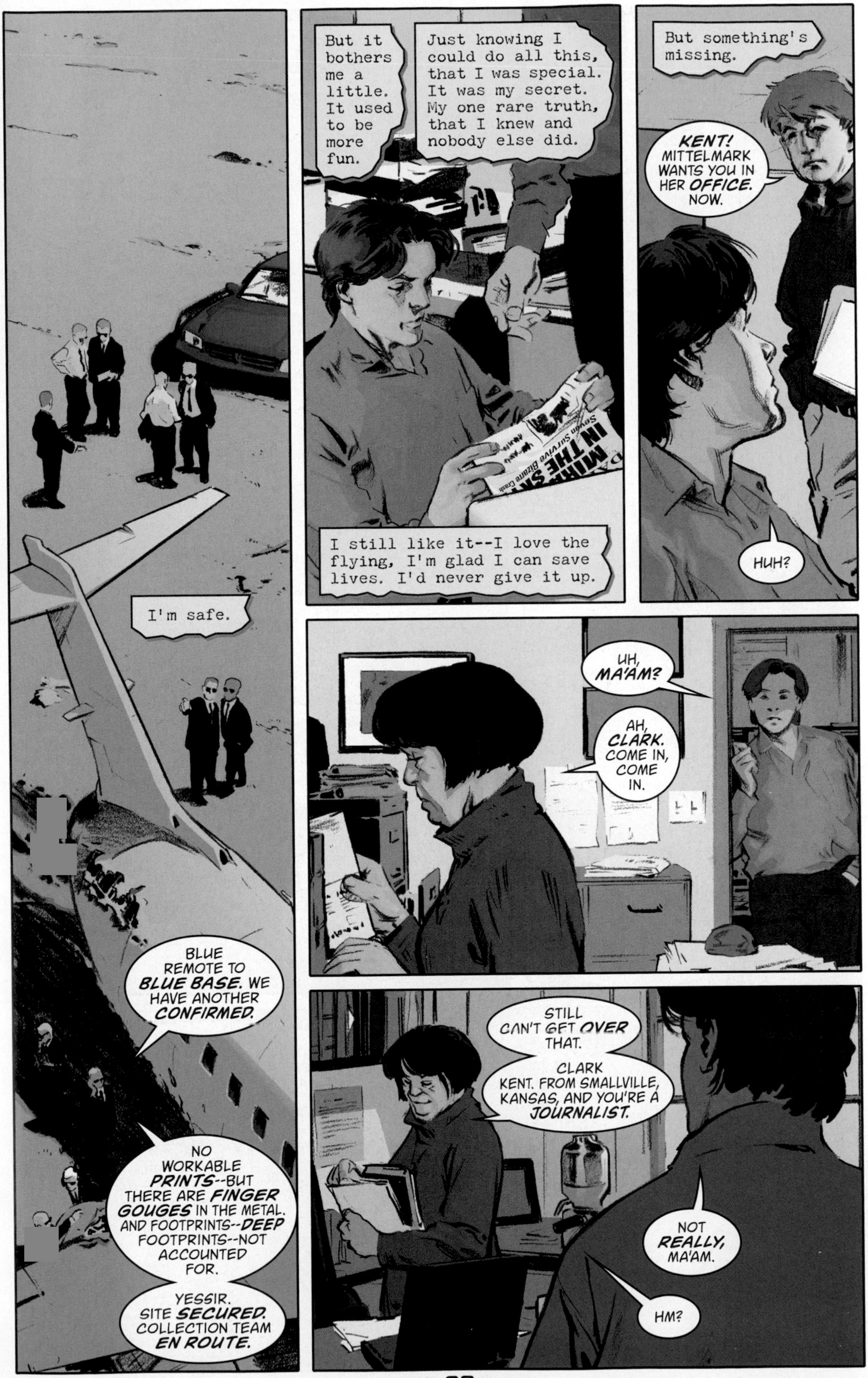

I'm safe.
BLUE REMOTE TO BLUE BASE. WE HAVE ANOTHER CONFIRMED.
NO WORKABLE PRINTS--BUT THERE ARE FINGER GOUGES IN THE METAL. AND FOOTPRINTS--DEEP FOOTPRINTS--NOT ACCOUNTED FOR.
YESSIR. SITE SECURED. COLLECTION TEAM EN ROUTE.
But it bothers me a little. It used to be more fun.
Just knowing I could do all this, that I was special. It was my secret. My one rare truth, that I knew and nobody else did.
I still like it--I love the flying, I'm glad I can save lives. I'd never give it up.
But something's missing.
KENT! MITTELMARK WANTS YOU IN HER OFFICE. NOW.
HUH?
UH, MA'AM?
AH, CLARK. COME IN, COME IN.
STILL CAN'T GET OVER THAT.
CLARK KENT. FROM SMALLVILLE, KANSAS, AND YOU'RE A JOURNALIST.
NOT REALLY, MA'AM.
HM?

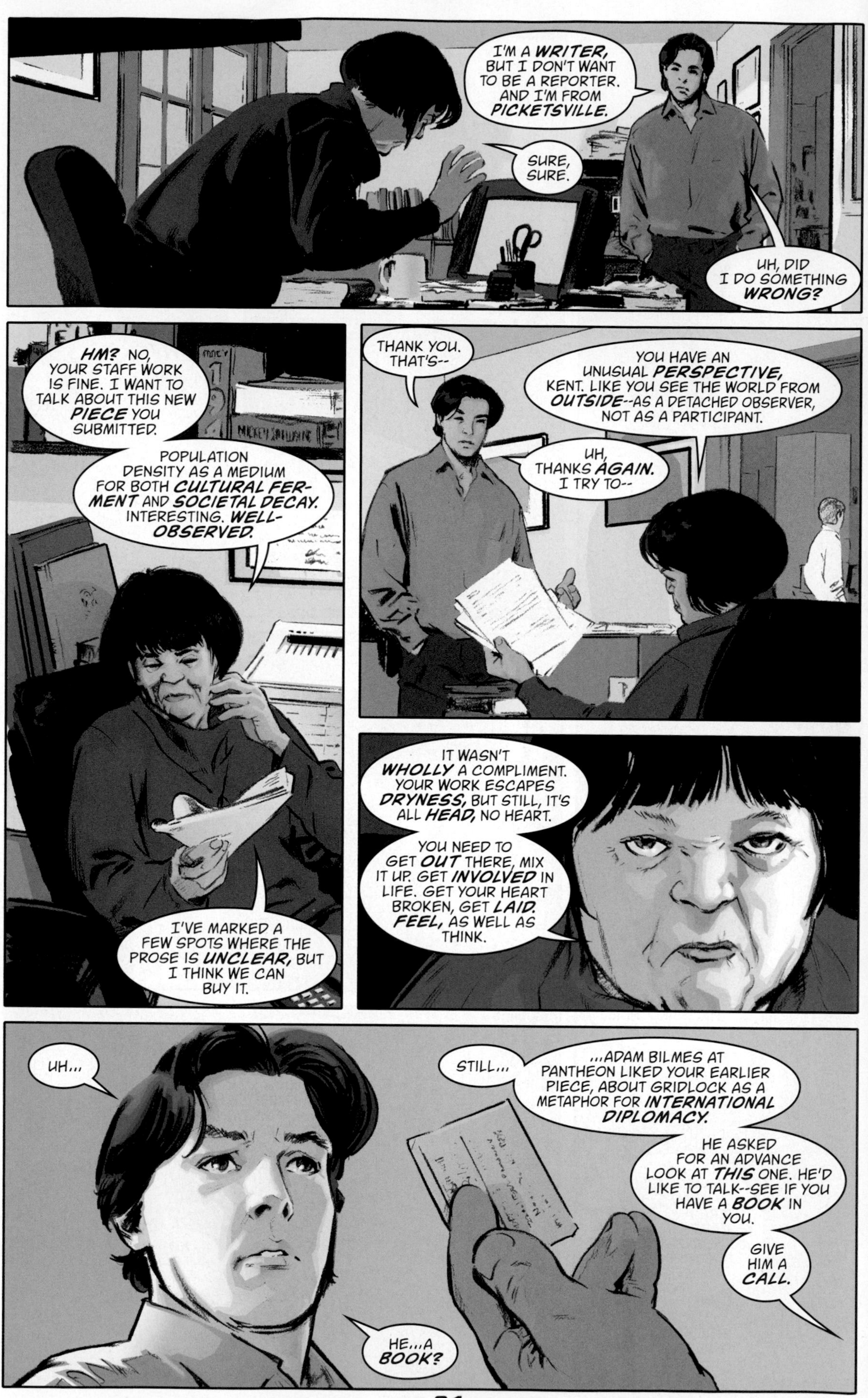
I'M A WRITER, BUT I DON'T WANT TO BE A REPORTER. AND I'M FROM PICKETSVILLE.
SURE, SURE.
UH, DID I DO SOMETHING WRONG?
HM? NO, YOUR STAFF WORK IS FINE. I WANT TO TALK ABOUT THIS NEW PIECE YOU SUBMITTED.
POPULATION DENSITY AS A MEDIUM FOR BOTH CULTURAL FERMENT AND SOCIETAL DECAY. INTERESTING. WELL-OBSERVED.
I'VE MARKED A FEW SPOTS WHERE THE PROSE IS UNCLEAR, BUT I THINK WE CAN BUY IT.
THANK YOU. THAT'S--
YOU HAVE AN UNUSUAL PERSPECTIVE, KENT. LIKE YOU SEE THE WORLD FROM OUTSIDE--AS A DETACHED OBSERVER, NOT AS A PARTICIPANT.
UH, THANKS AGAIN. I TRY TO--
IT WASN'T WHOLLY A COMPLIMENT. YOUR WORK ESCAPES DRYNESS, BUT STILL, IT'S ALL HEAD, NO HEART.
YOU NEED TO GET OUT THERE, MIX IT UP. GET INVOLVED IN LIFE. GET YOUR HEART BROKEN, GET LAID. FEEL, AS WELL AS THINK.
UH...
STILL...
...ADAM BILMES AT PANTHEON LIKED YOUR EARLIER PIECE, ABOUT GRIDLOCK AS A METAPHOR FOR INTERNATIONAL DIPLOMACY.
HE ASKED FOR AN ADVANCE LOOK AT THIS ONE. HE'D LIKE TO TALK--SEE IF YOU HAVE A BOOK IN YOU.
GIVE HIM A CALL.
HE...A BOOK?

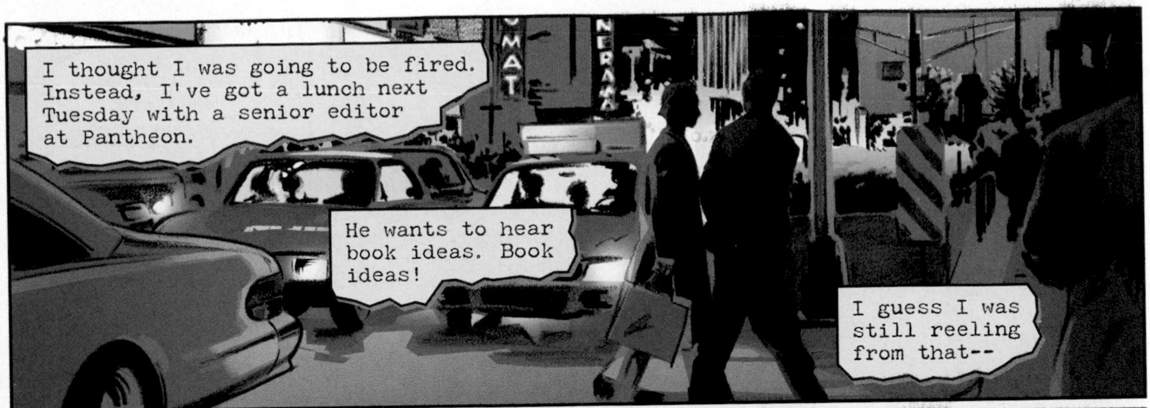
I thought I was going to be fired. Instead, I've got a lunch next Tuesday with a senior editor at Pantheon.
He wants to hear book ideas. Book ideas!
I guess I was still reeling from that--

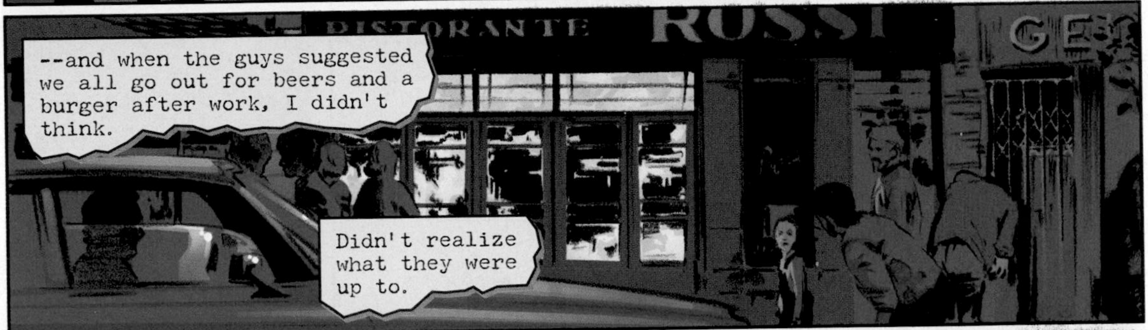
RISTORANTE ROSSI
--and when the guys suggested we all go out for beers and a burger after work, I didn't think.
Didn't realize what they were up to.

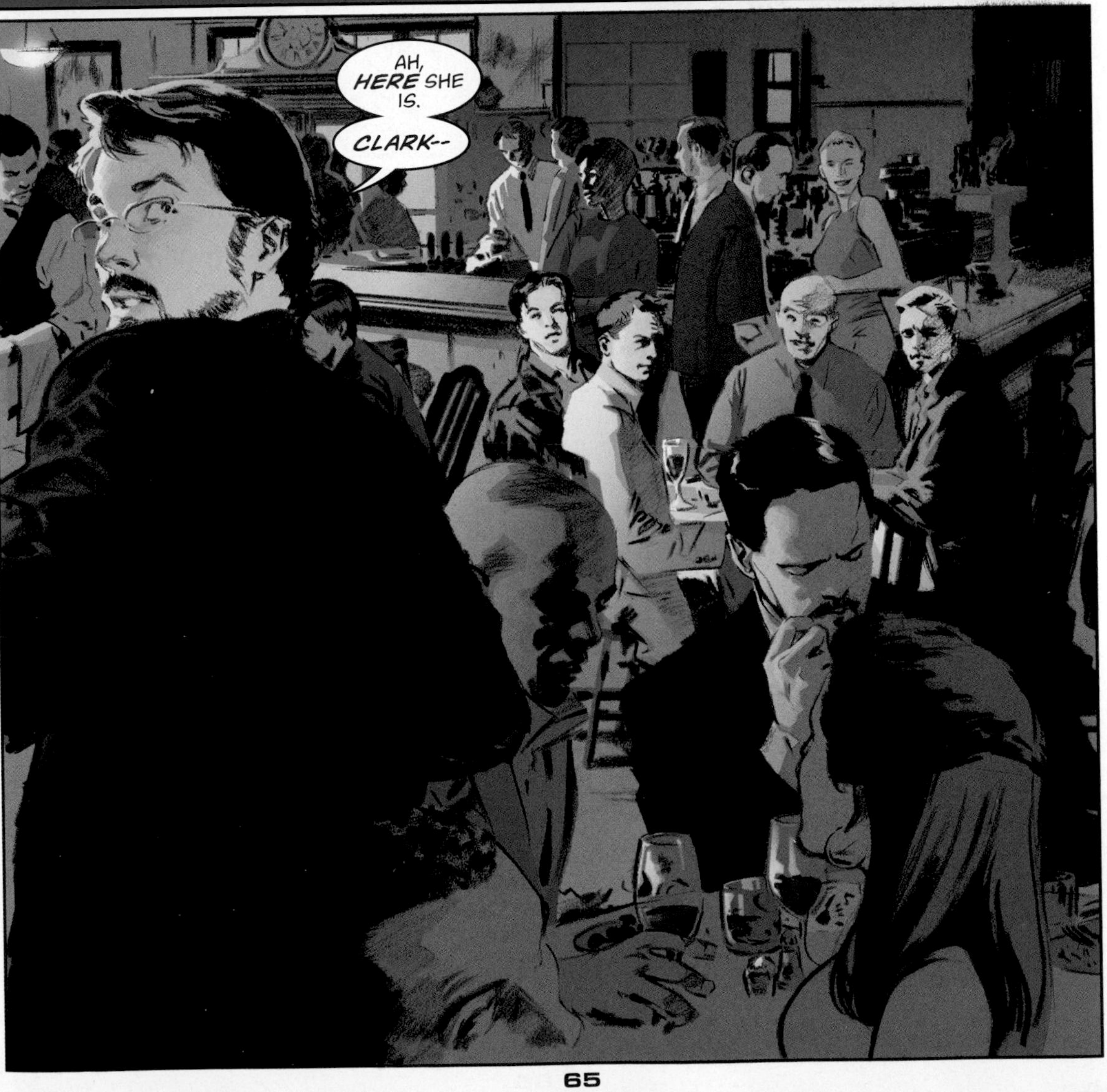
AH, HERE SHE IS.
CLARK--

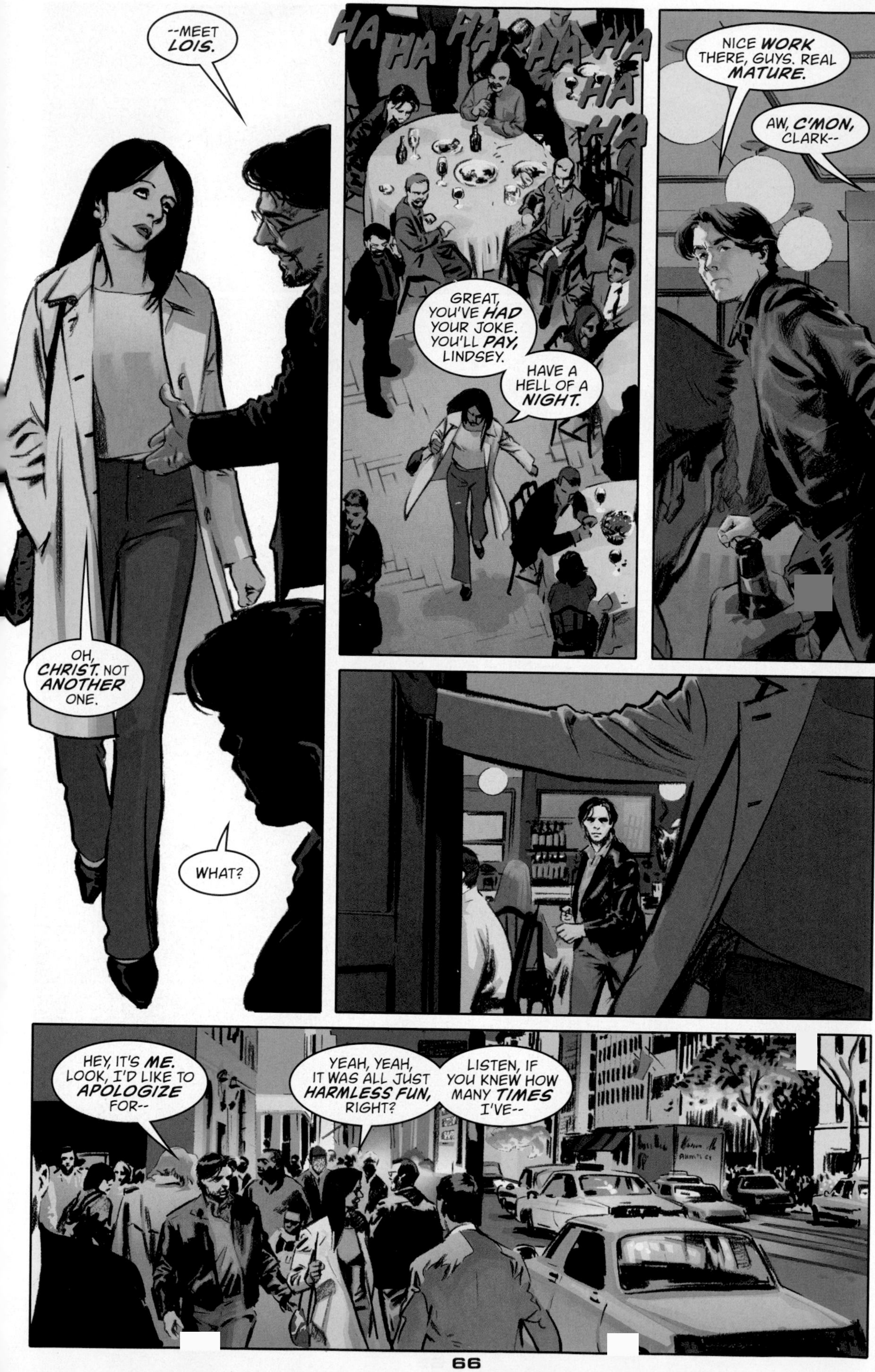
--MEET LOIS.
OH, CHRIST. NOT ANOTHER ONE.
WHAT?
HA HA HA HA HA HA HA HA HA
GREAT, YOU'VE HAD YOUR JOKE. YOU'LL PAY, LINDSEY.
HAVE A HELL OF A NIGHT.
NICE WORK THERE, GUYS. REAL MATURE.
AW, C'MON, CLARK--
HEY, IT'S ME. LOOK, I'D LIKE TO APOLOGIZE FOR--
YEAH, YEAH, IT WAS ALL JUST HARMLESS FUN, RIGHT?
LISTEN, IF YOU KNEW HOW MANY TIMES I'VE--

--NO, WAIT. YOU PROBABLY *DO*, HUH?

*PROBABLY.* I'M NOT JUST A *CLARK.* I'M A CLARK *KENT.*

I'VE BEEN SET UP WITH *EIGHTEEN* LOISES, *SEVEN* LANAS, AND A CAT GRANT.

CAT GRANT? IS THAT SOMEONE FROM *SUPERMAN?*

BEATS ME. MY COLLEGE ROOMMATE THOUGHT IT WAS *HYSTERICAL,* THOUGH, SO I GUESS SO.

SORRY IF I WAS *RUDE.*

NO PROBLEM. I'D DO THAT *MYSELF,* IF I HAD THE GUTS.

HI. CLARK KENT. BUT YOU *KNEW* THAT.

HI. *LOIS CHAUDHARI.*

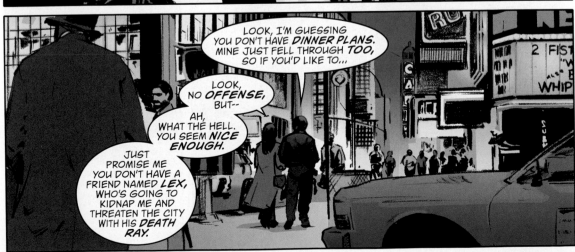

LOOK, I'M GUESSING YOU DON'T HAVE *DINNER PLANS.* MINE JUST FELL THROUGH *TOO,* SO IF YOU'D LIKE TO...

LOOK, NO *OFFENSE,* BUT--

AH, WHAT THE HELL. YOU SEEM *NICE ENOUGH.*

JUST PROMISE ME YOU DON'T HAVE A FRIEND NAMED *LEX,* WHO'S GOING TO KIDNAP ME AND THREATEN THE CITY WITH HIS *DEATH RAY.*

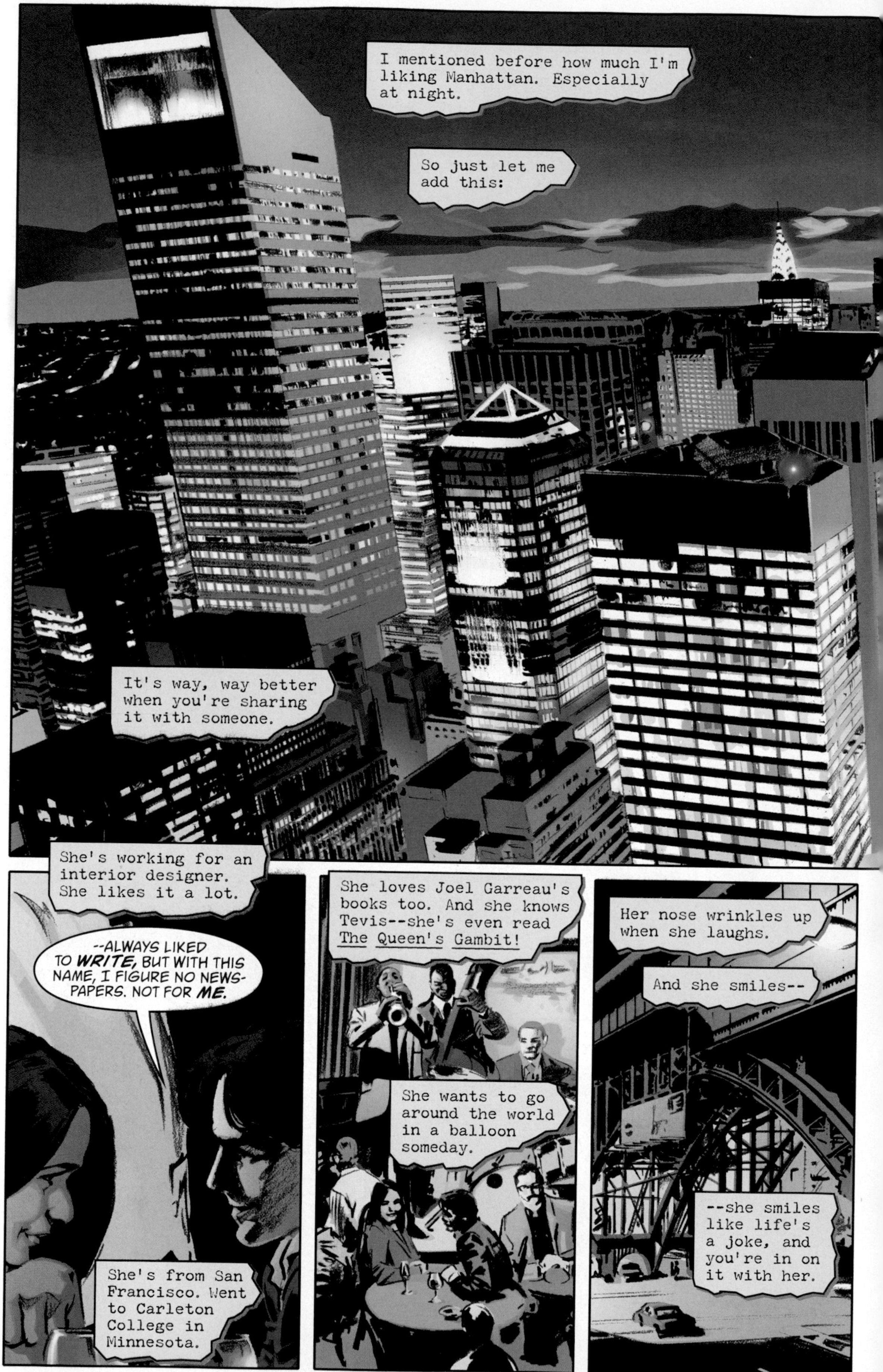
I mentioned before how much I'm liking Manhattan. Especially at night.
So just let me add this:
It's way, way better when you're sharing it with someone.
She's working for an interior designer. She likes it a lot.
--ALWAYS LIKED TO WRITE, BUT WITH THIS NAME, I FIGURE NO NEWSPAPERS. NOT FOR ME.
She's from San Francisco. Went to Carleton College in Minnesota.
She loves Joel Garreau's books too. And she knows Tevis--she's even read The Queen's Gambit!
She wants to go around the world in a balloon someday.
Her nose wrinkles up when she laughs.
And she smiles--
--she smiles like life's a joke, and you're in on it with her.

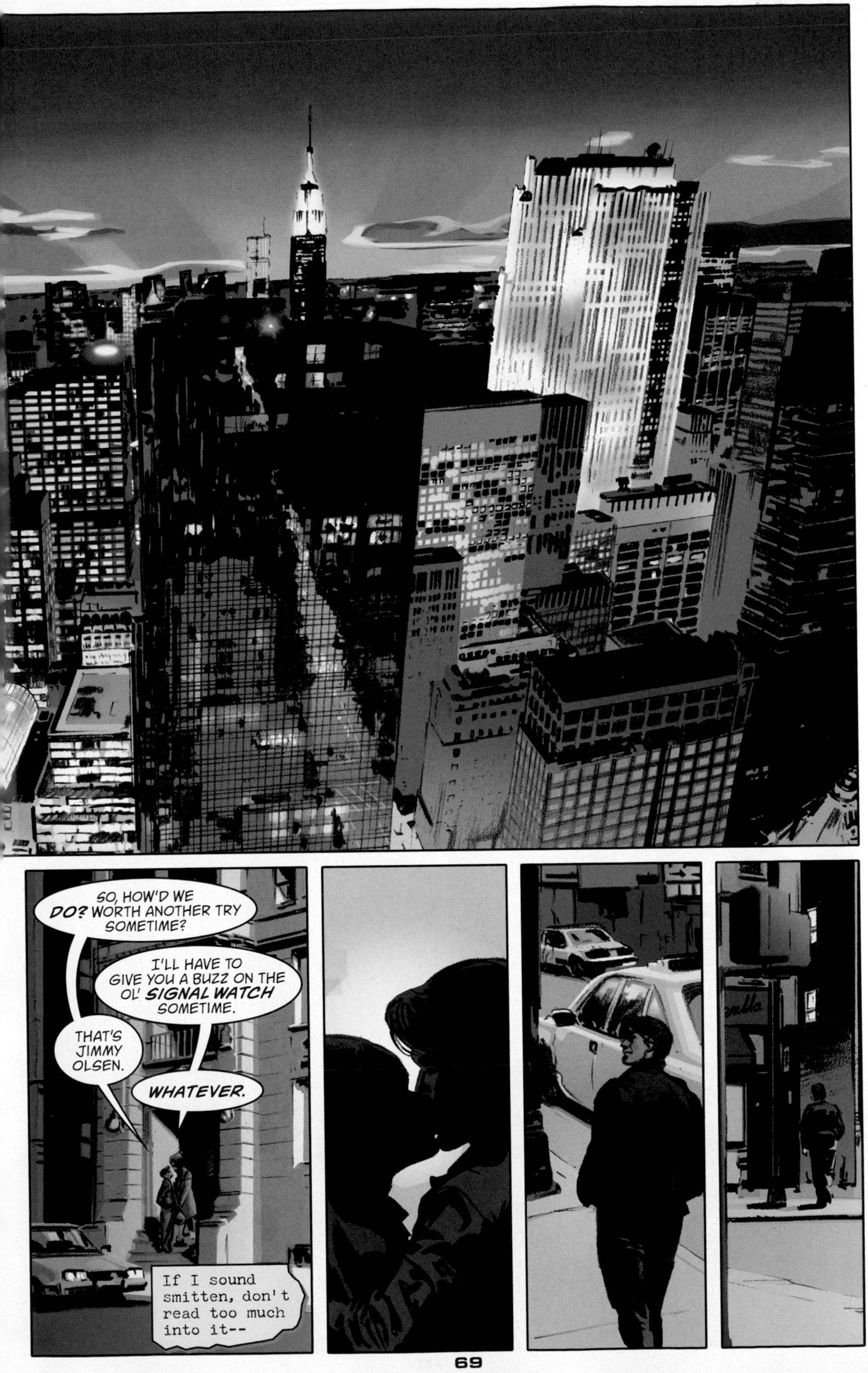
SO, HOW'D WE DO? WORTH ANOTHER TRY SOMETIME?
I'LL HAVE TO GIVE YOU A BUZZ ON THE OL' SIGNAL WATCH SOMETIME.
THAT'S JIMMY OLSEN.
WHATEVER.
If I sound smitten, don't read too much into it--

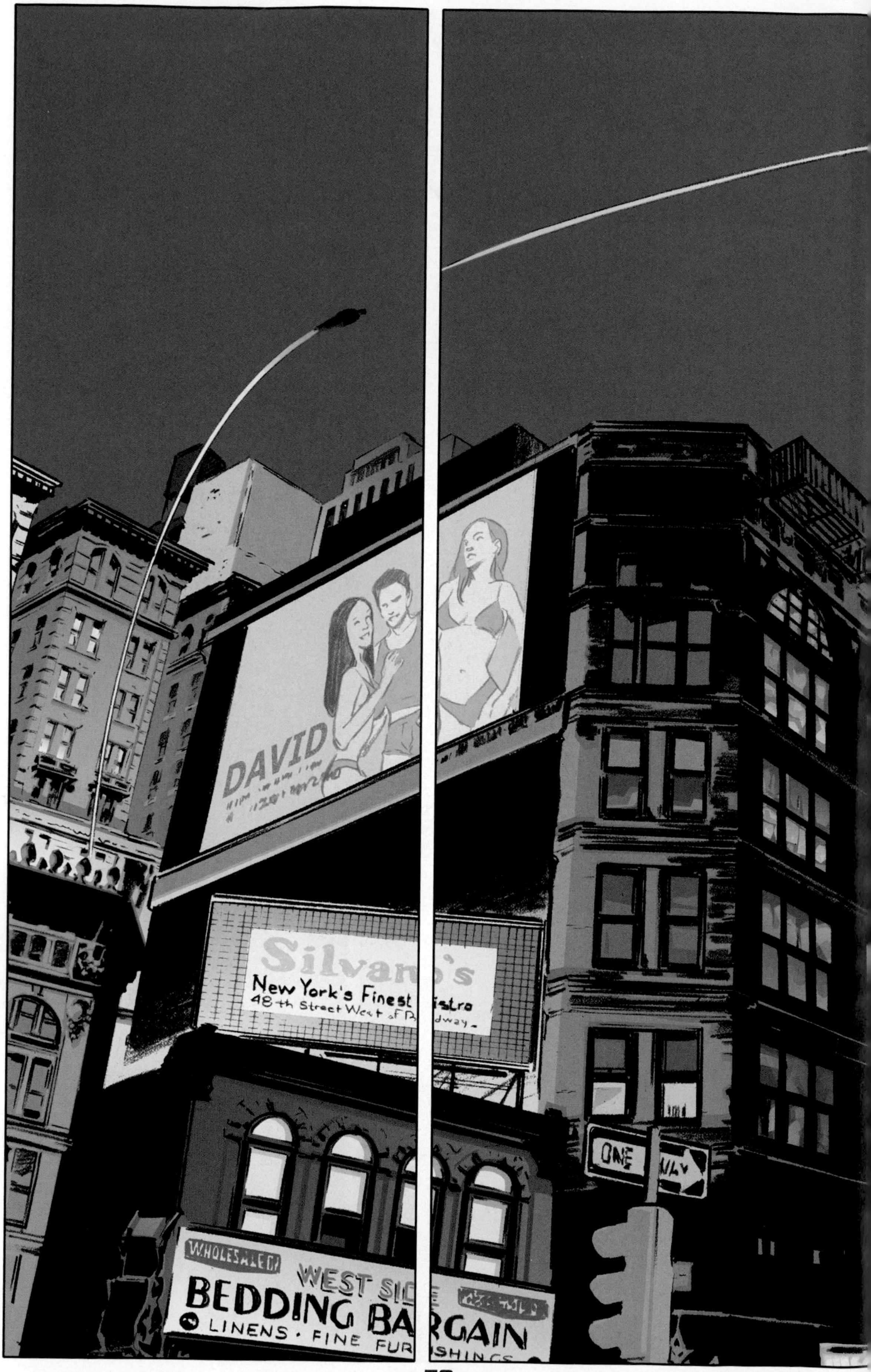
DAVID
Silvano's
New York's Finest istro
48th Street West of dway.
WHOLESALE
BEDDING BARGAIN
LINENS · FINE FUR

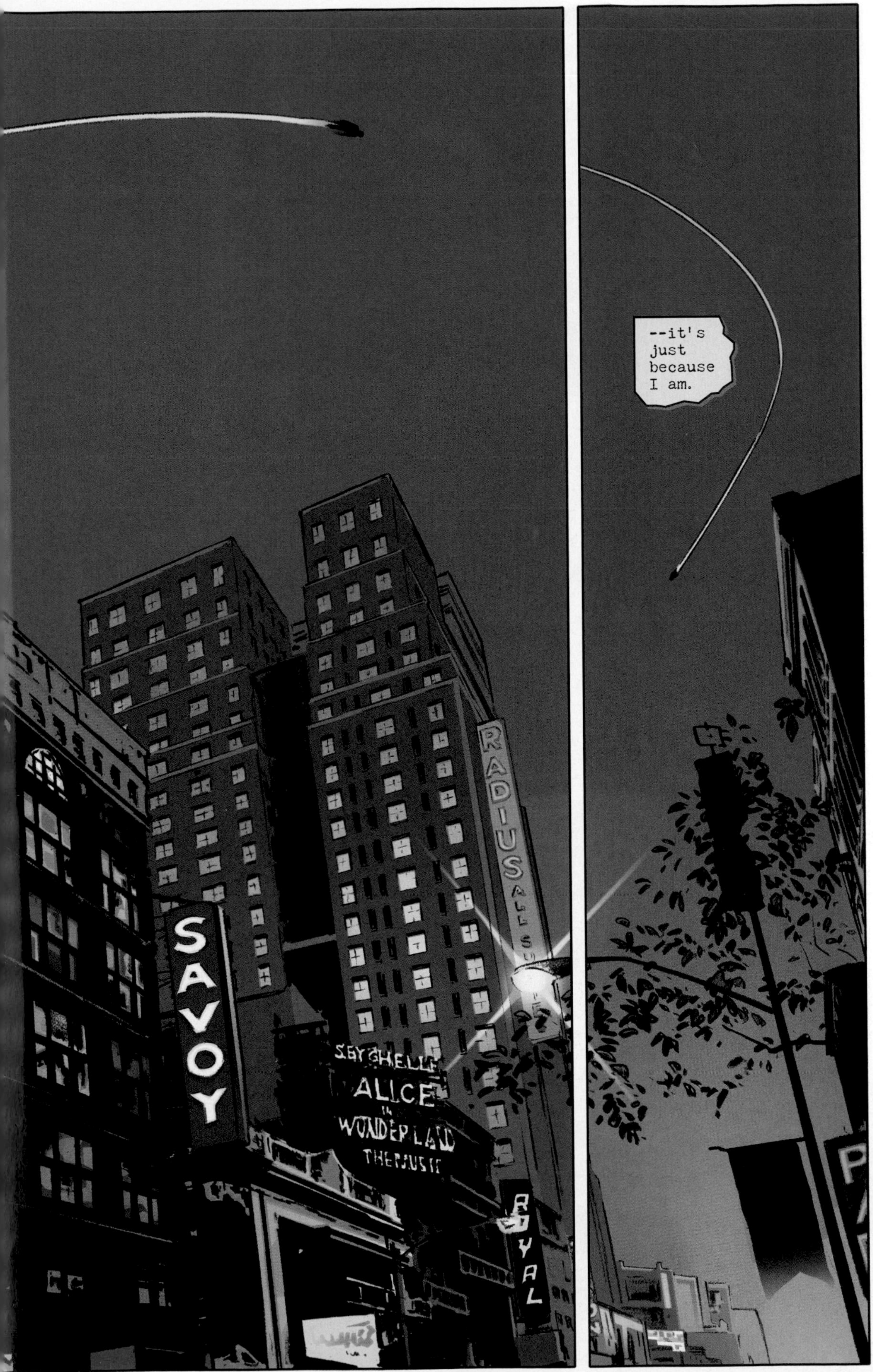
SAVOY
RADIUS
ALICE
IN
WONDERLAND
ROYAL
--it's just because I am.

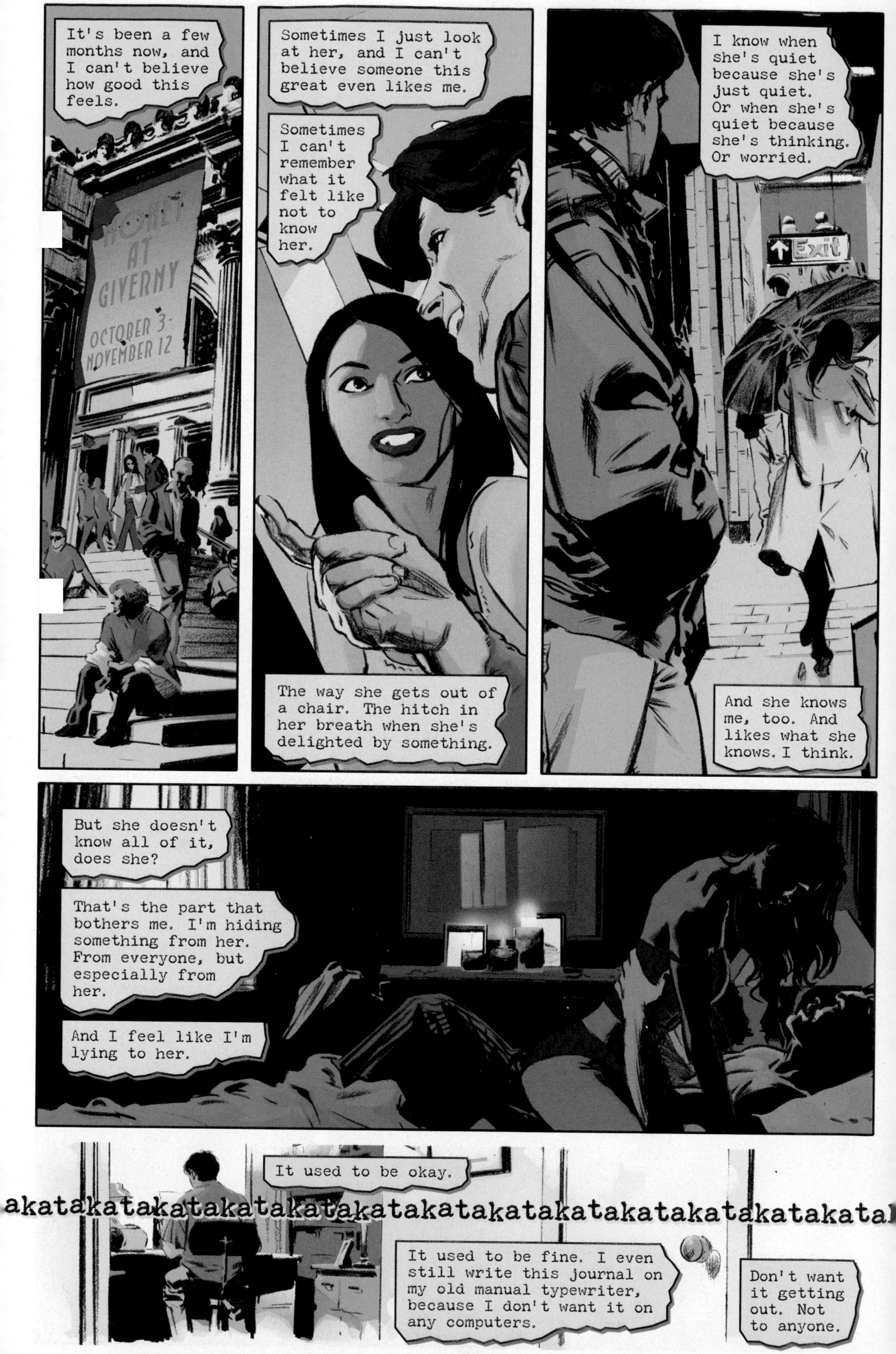
It's been a few months now, and I can't believe how good this feels.
MONET AT GIVERNY OCTOBER 3- NOVEMBER 12
Sometimes I just look at her, and I can't believe someone this great even likes me.
Sometimes I can't remember what it felt like not to know her.
The way she gets out of a chair. The hitch in her breath when she's delighted by something.
I know when she's quiet because she's just quiet. Or when she's quiet because she's thinking. Or worried.
Exit
And she knows me, too. And likes what she knows. I think.
But she doesn't know all of it, does she?
That's the part that bothers me. I'm hiding something from her. From everyone, but especially from her.
And I feel like I'm lying to her.
It used to be okay.
akatakatakatakatakatakatakatakatakatakatakatakata
It used to be fine. I even still write this journal on my old manual typewriter, because I don't want it on any computers.
Don't want it getting out. Not to anyone.

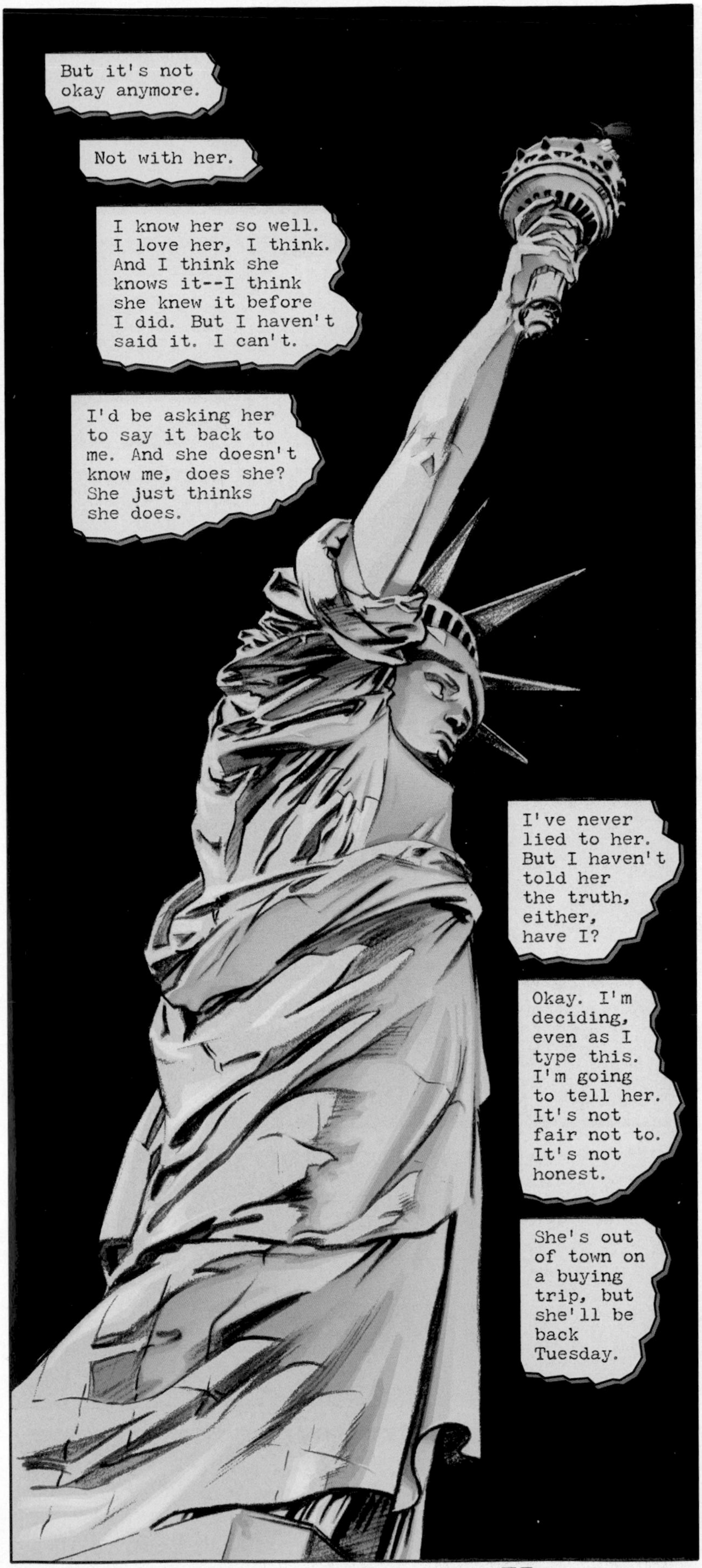
But it's not okay anymore.
Not with her.
I know her so well. I love her, I think. And I think she knows it--I think she knew it before I did. But I haven't said it. I can't.
I'd be asking her to say it back to me. And she doesn't know me, does she? She just thinks she does.
I've never lied to her. But I haven't told her the truth, either, have I?
Okay. I'm deciding, even as I type this. I'm going to tell her. It's not fair not to. It's not honest.
She's out of town on a buying trip, but she'll be back Tuesday.

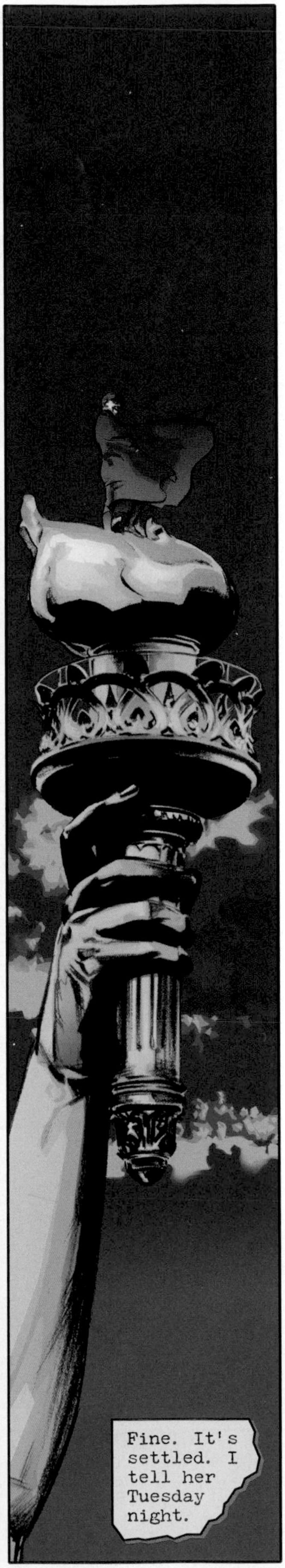
Fine. It's settled. I tell her Tuesday night.

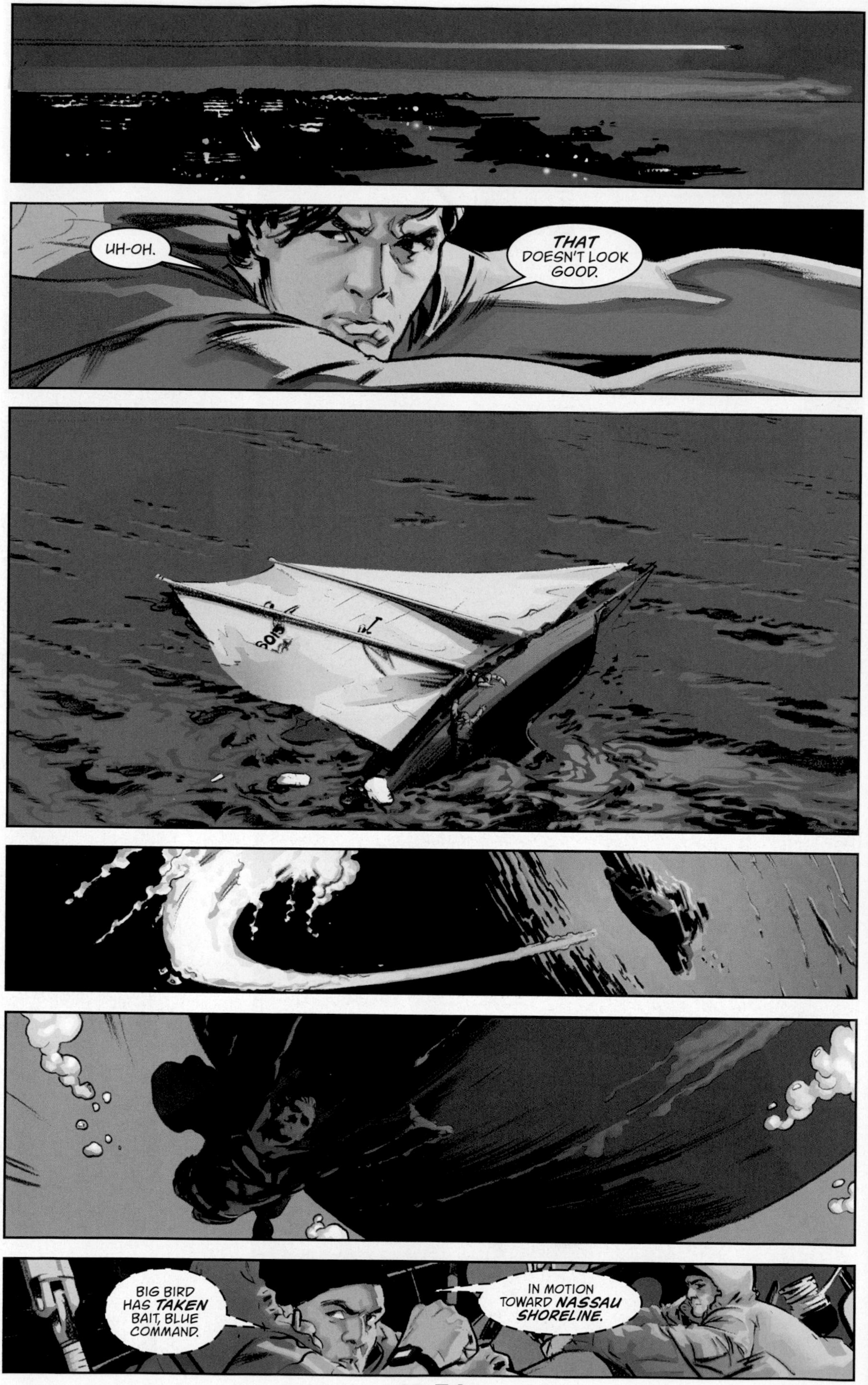
UH-OH.
THAT DOESN'T LOOK GOOD.
BIG BIRD HAS TAKEN BAIT, BLUE COMMAND.
IN MOTION TOWARD NASSAU SHORELINE.

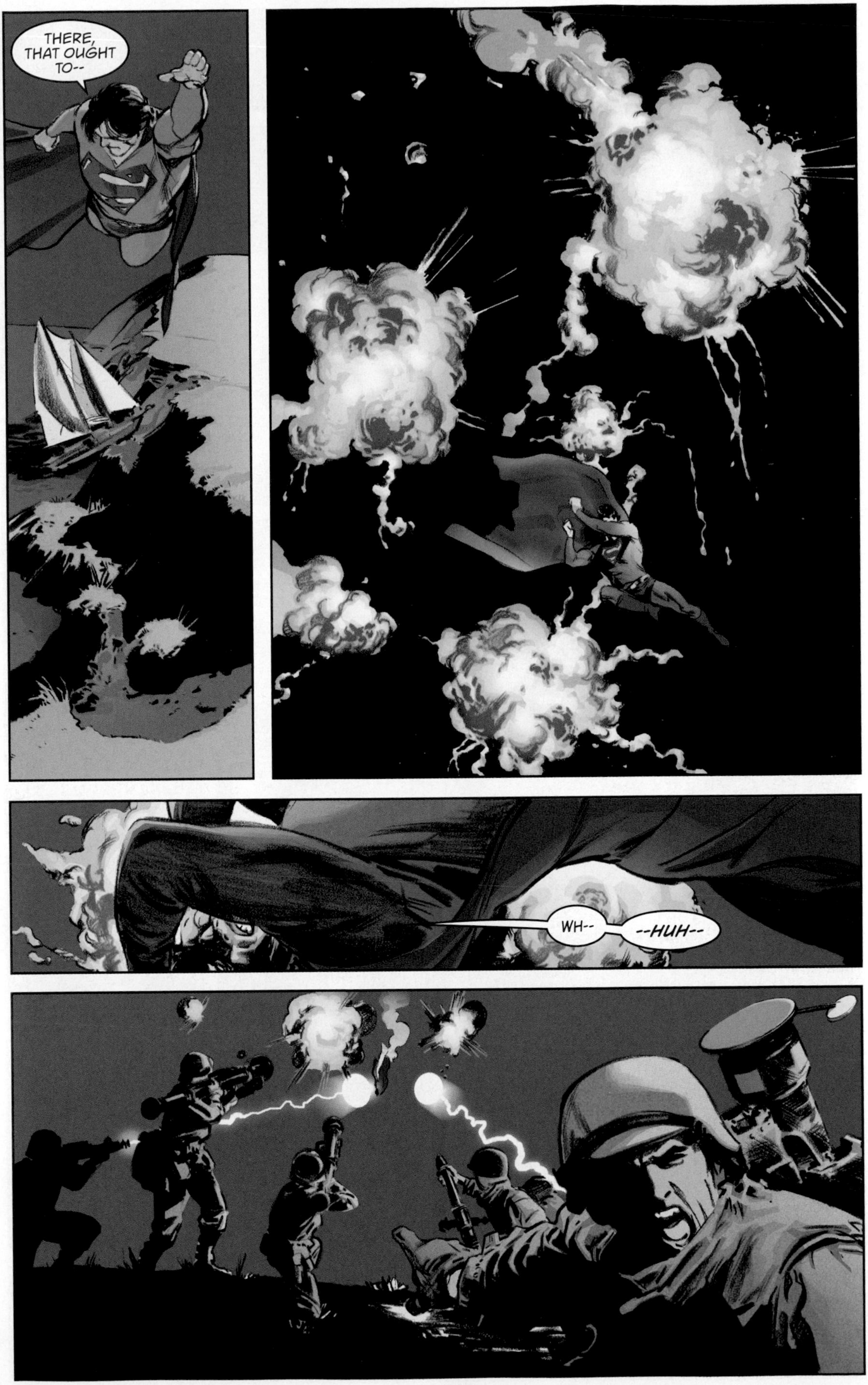
THERE, THAT OUGHT TO--
WH--
--HUH--

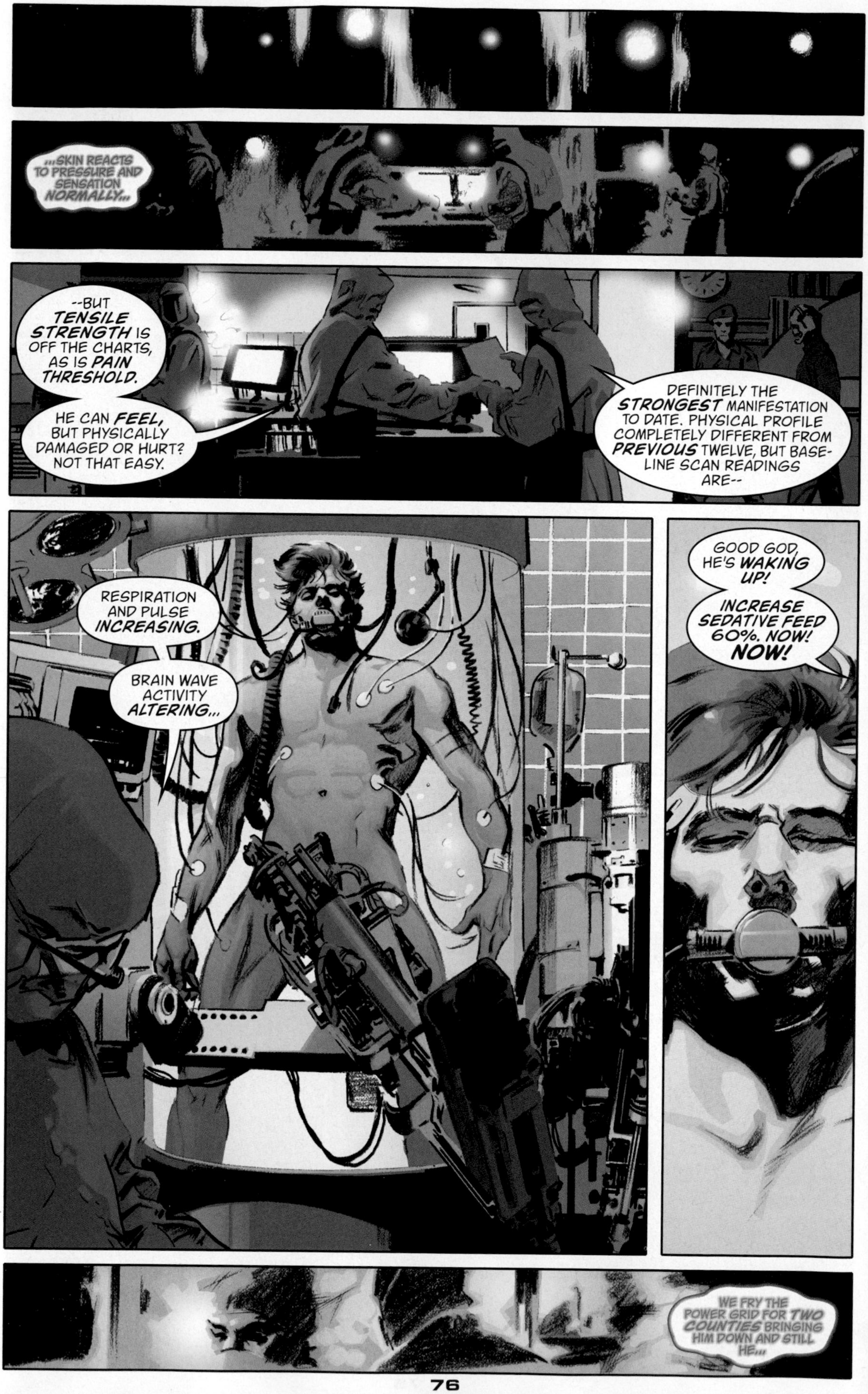
...SKIN REACTS TO PRESSURE AND SENSATION NORMALLY...
--BUT TENSILE STRENGTH IS OFF THE CHARTS, AS IS PAIN THRESHOLD.
HE CAN FEEL, BUT PHYSICALLY DAMAGED OR HURT? NOT THAT EASY.
DEFINITELY THE STRONGEST MANIFESTATION TO DATE. PHYSICAL PROFILE COMPLETELY DIFFERENT FROM PREVIOUS TWELVE, BUT BASE-LINE SCAN READINGS ARE--
RESPIRATION AND PULSE INCREASING.
BRAIN WAVE ACTIVITY ALTERING...
GOOD GOD, HE'S WAKING UP!
INCREASE SEDATIVE FEED 60%. NOW! NOW!
WE FRY THE POWER GRID FOR TWO COUNTIES BRINGING HIM DOWN AND STILL HE...

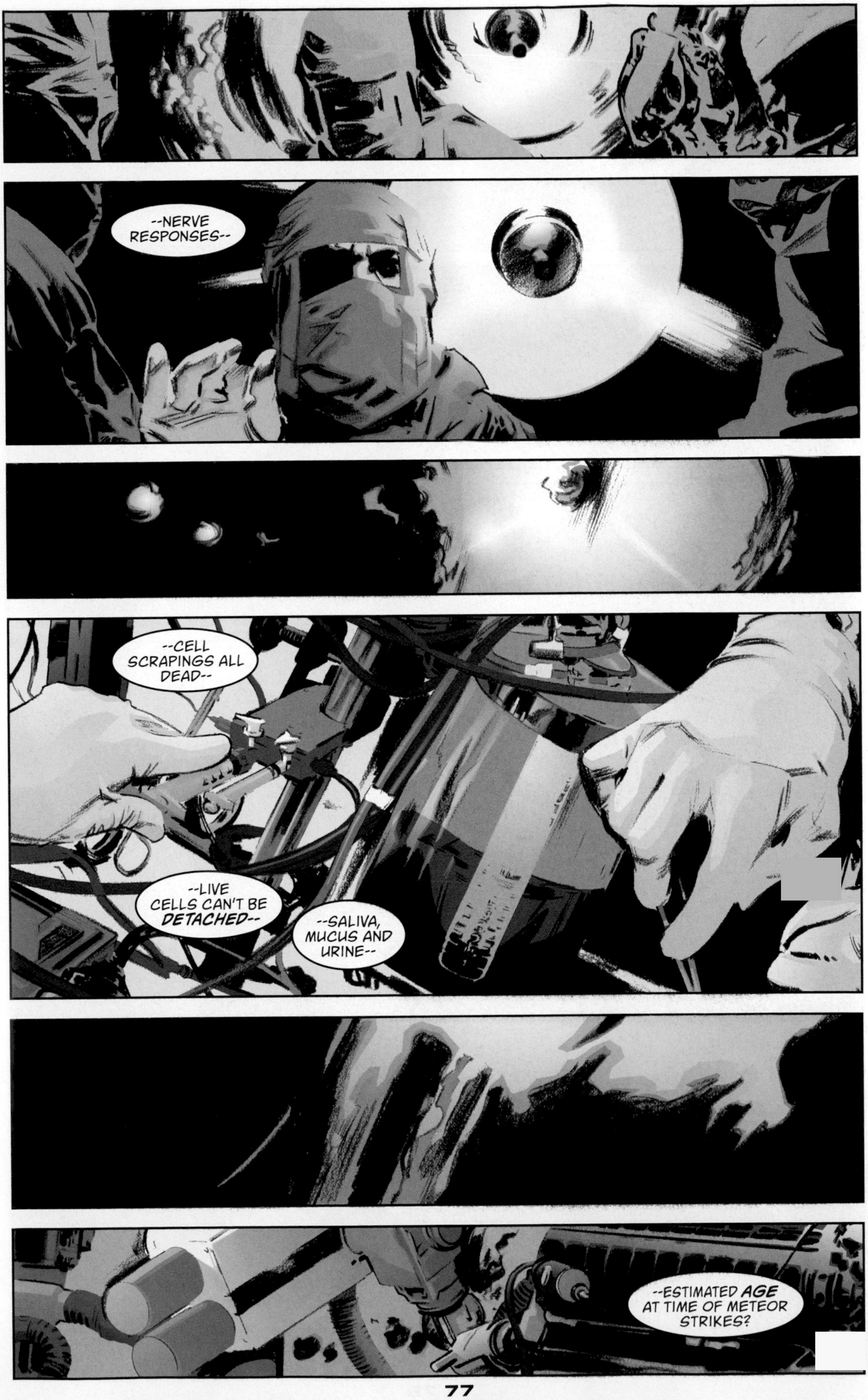
--NERVE RESPONSES--
--CELL SCRAPINGS ALL DEAD--
--LIVE CELLS CAN'T BE DETACHED--
--SALIVA, MUCUS AND URINE--
--ESTIMATED AGE AT TIME OF METEOR STRIKES?

HELPLESS, SUPERMAN--

--HELPLESS UNDER THE GLOW OF *RED SUN RADIATION!* YOU'LL REMAIN MY PRISONER FOR *ETERNITY!*

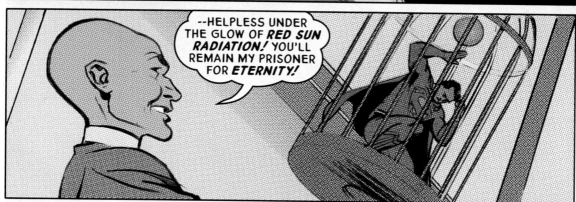

ETERNITY...

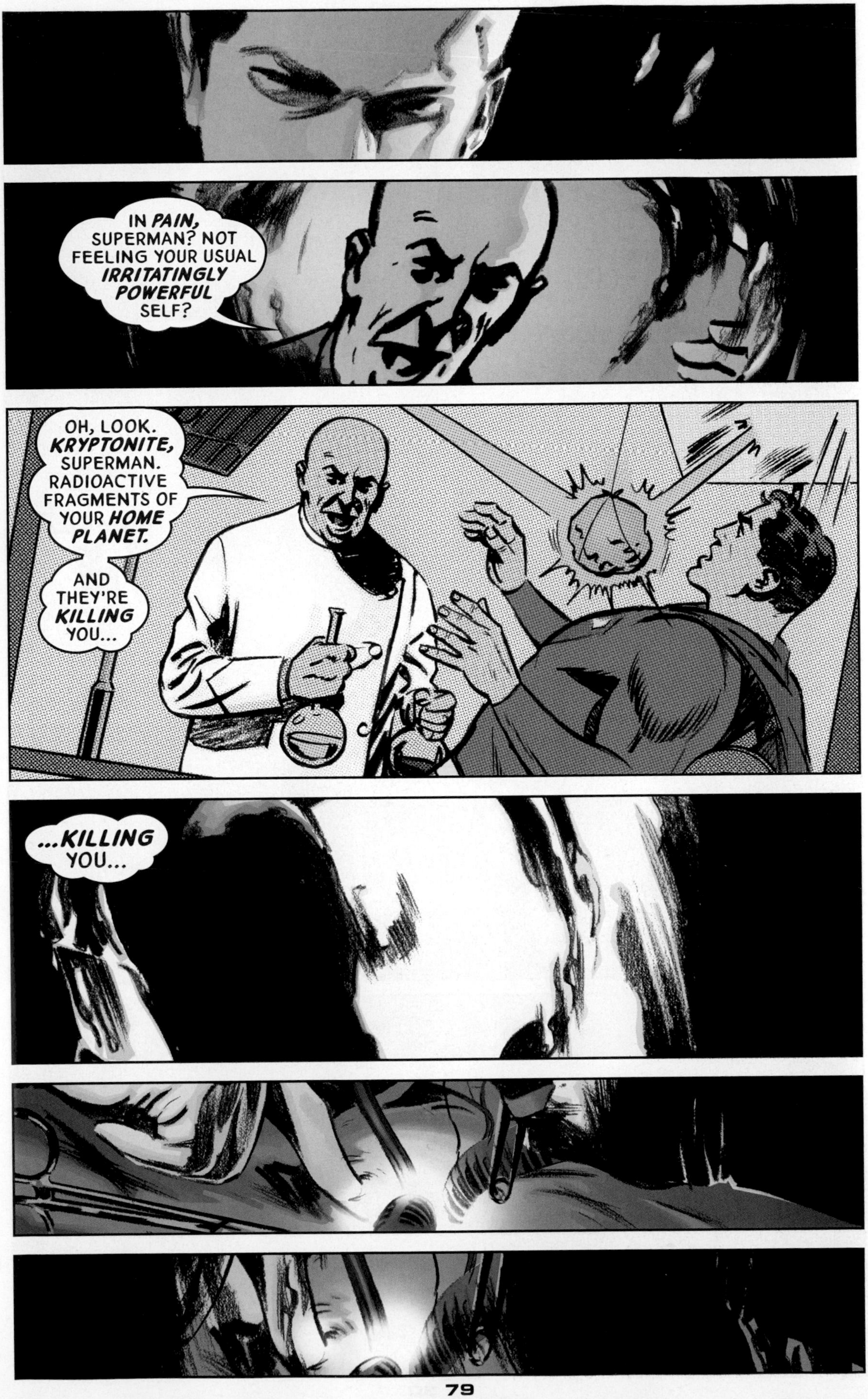

IN PAIN, SUPERMAN? NOT FEELING YOUR USUAL IRRITATINGLY POWERFUL SELF?
OH, LOOK. KRYPTONITE, SUPERMAN. RADIOACTIVE FRAGMENTS OF YOUR HOME PLANET.
AND THEY'RE KILLING YOU...
...KILLING YOU...

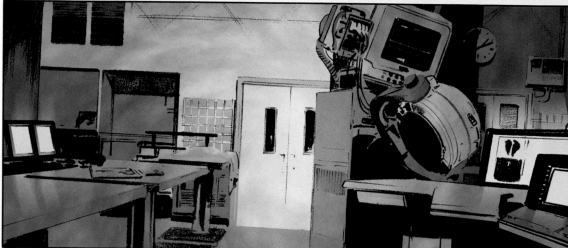

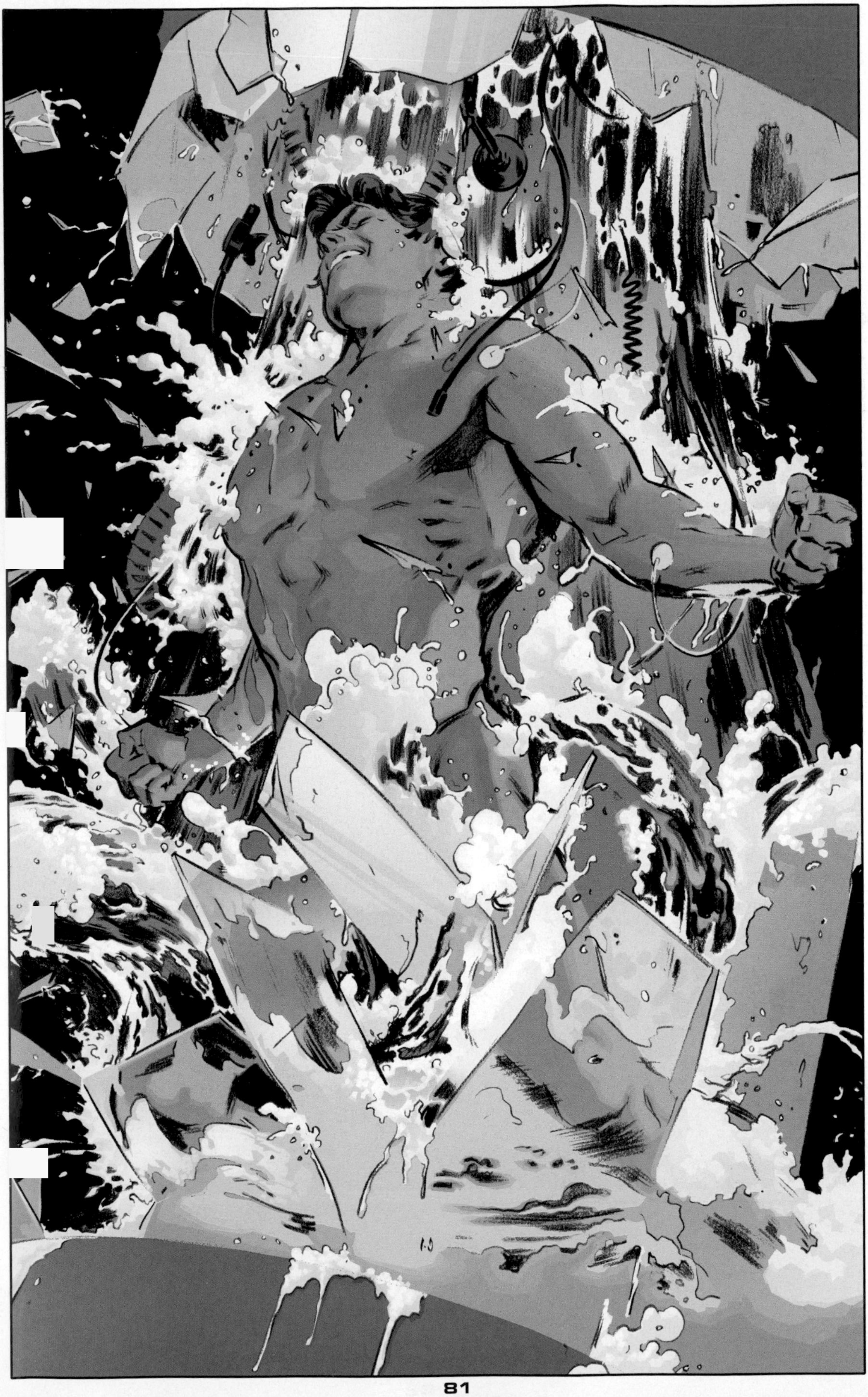

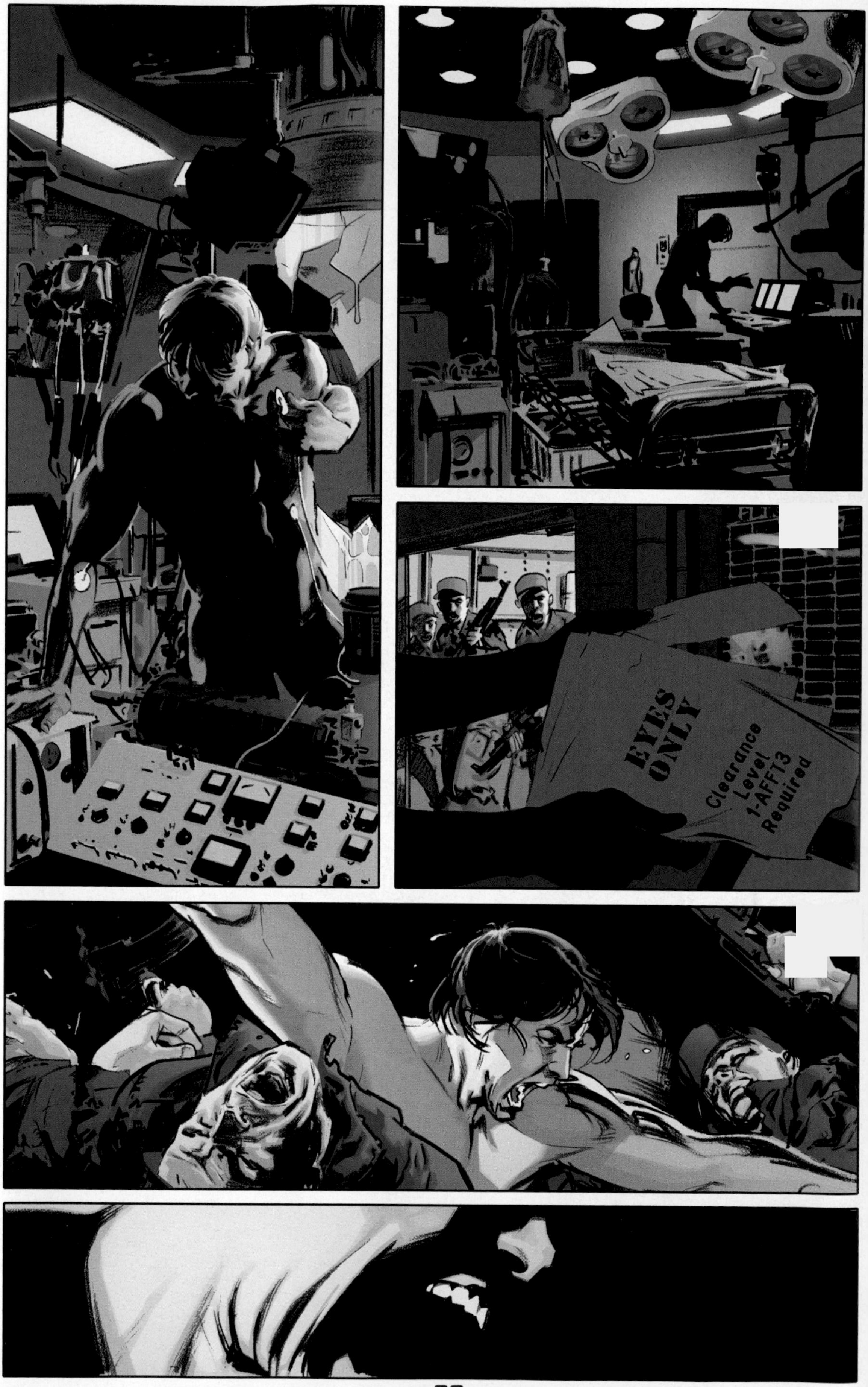
EYES ONLY
Clearance Level 1-AFFT3 Required

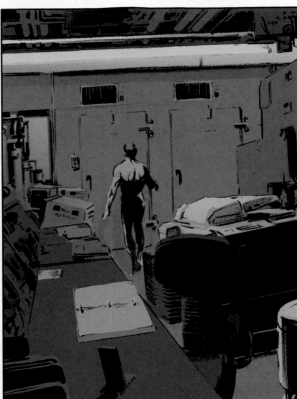

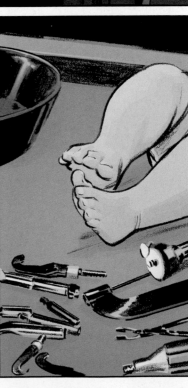

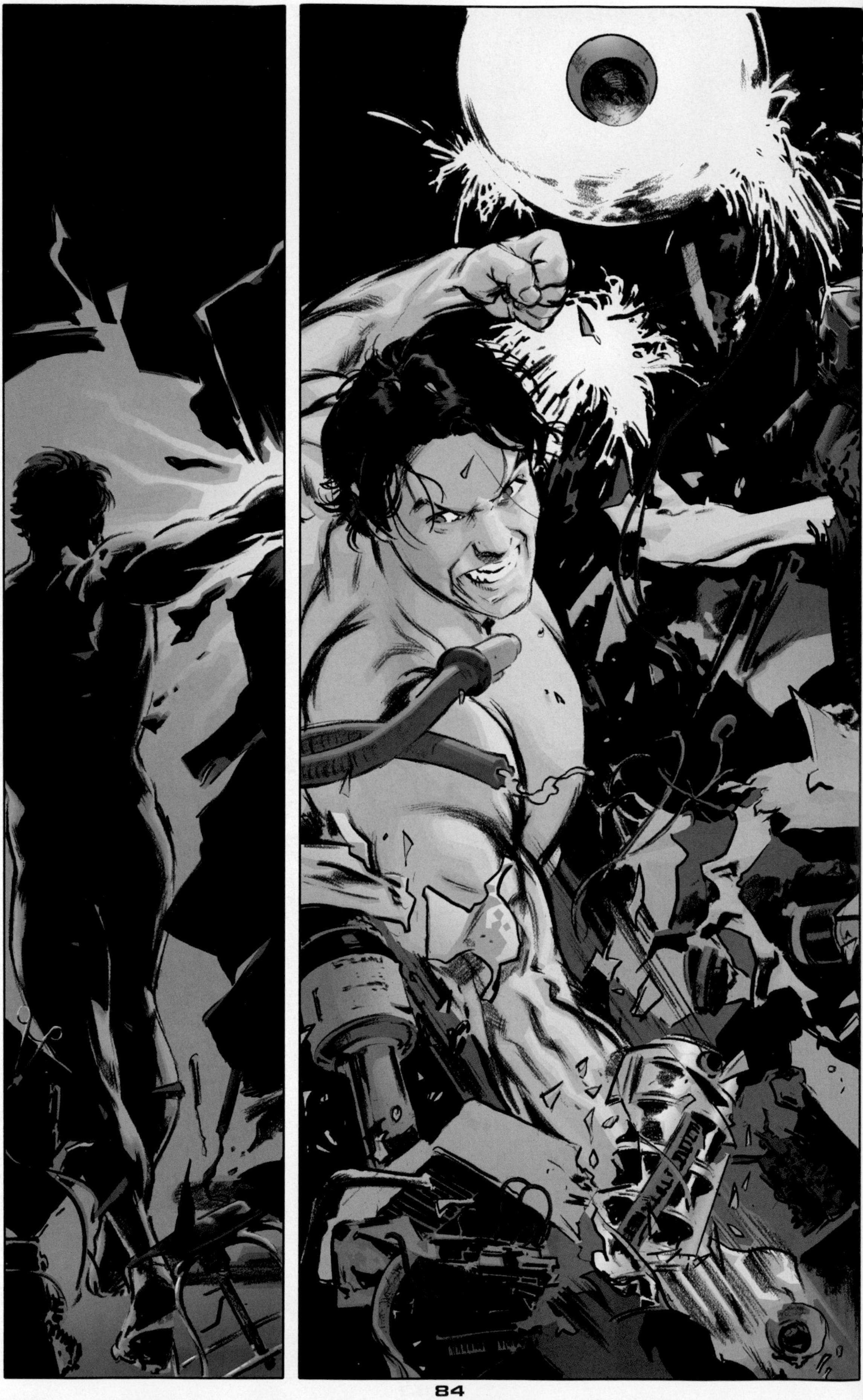

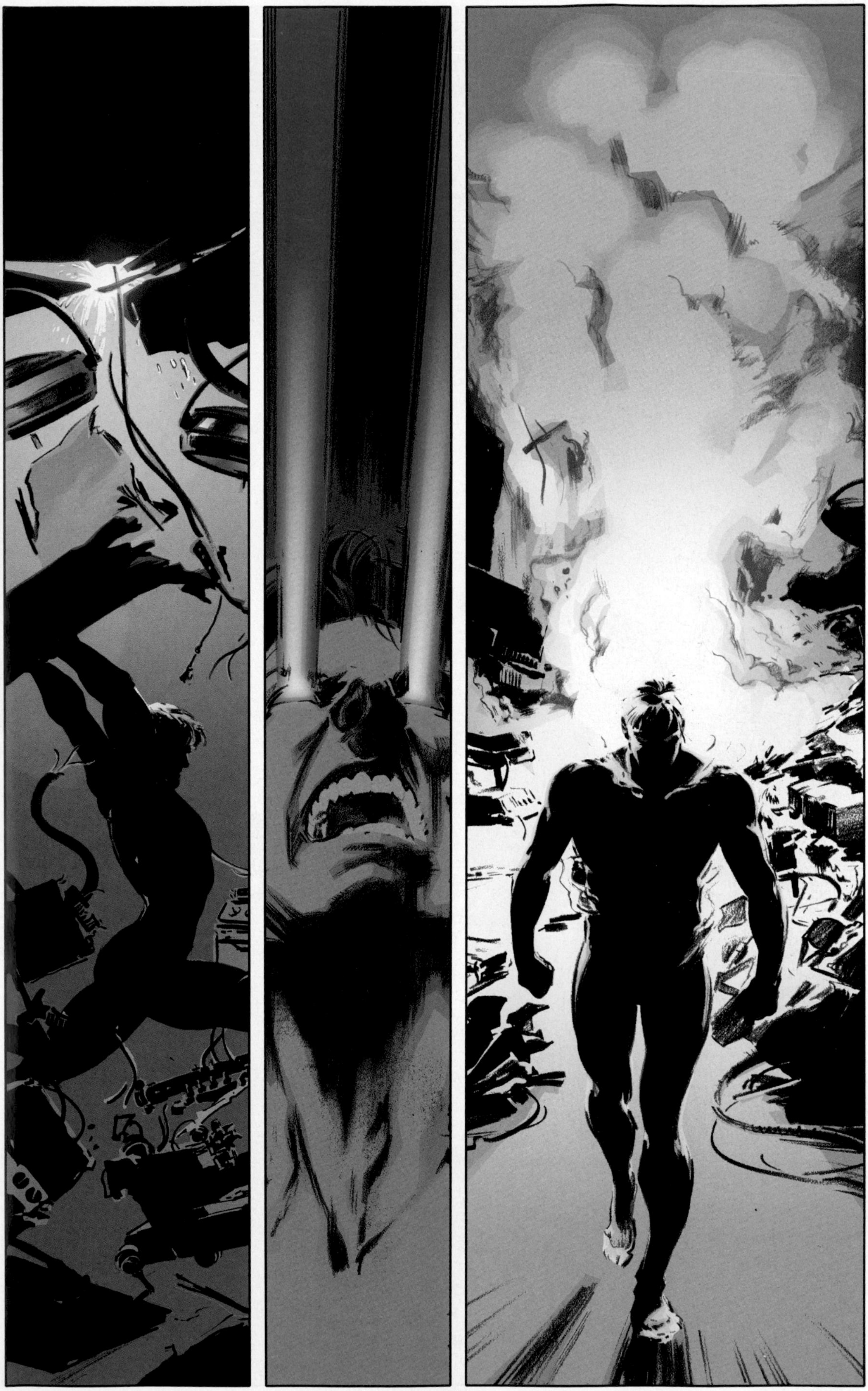

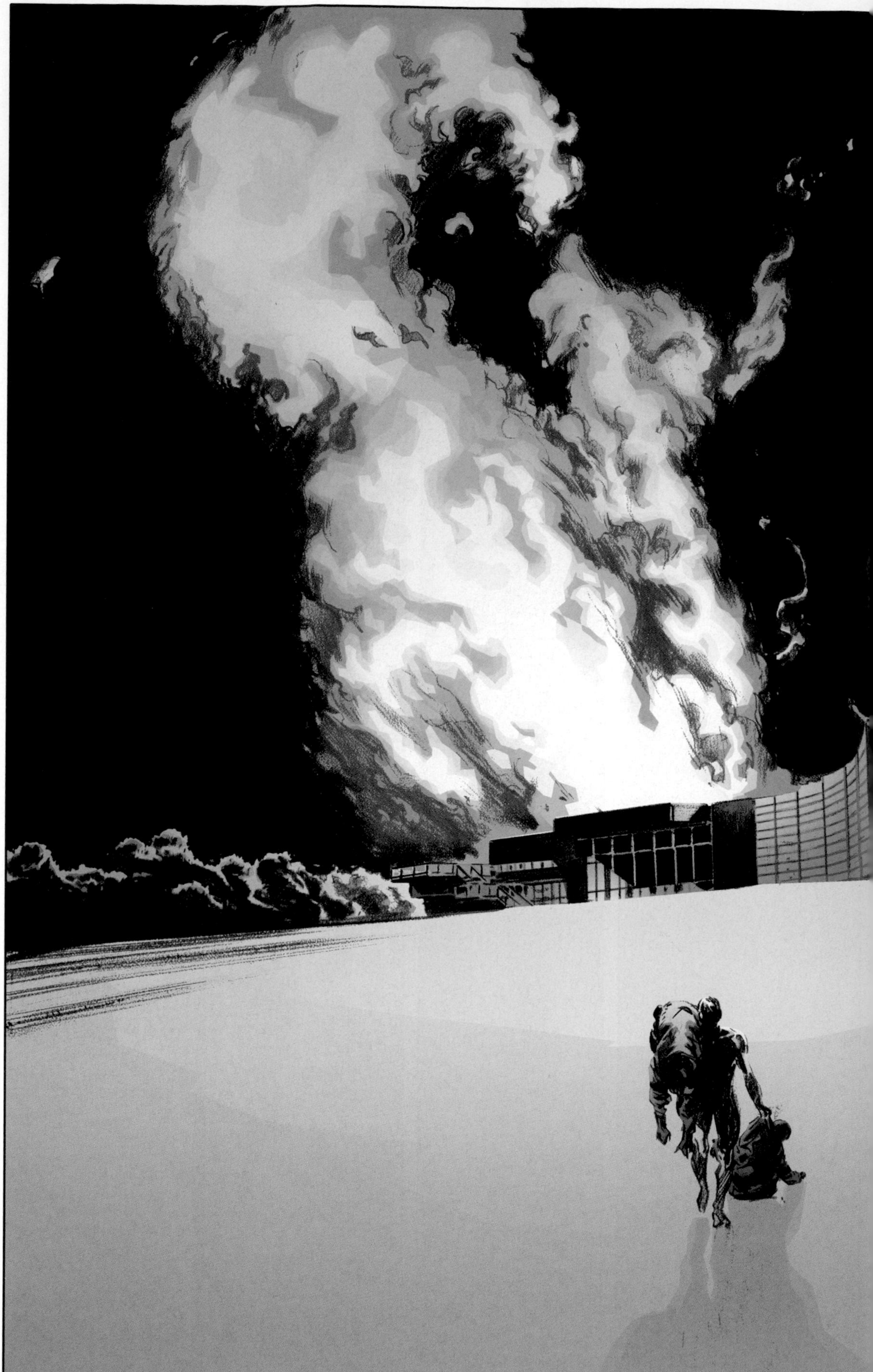

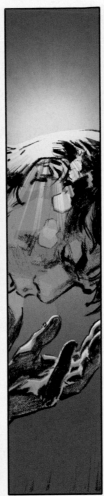

OH GOD--

OH, GOD--

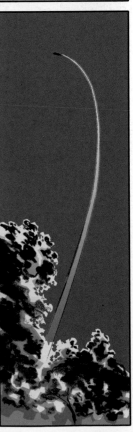

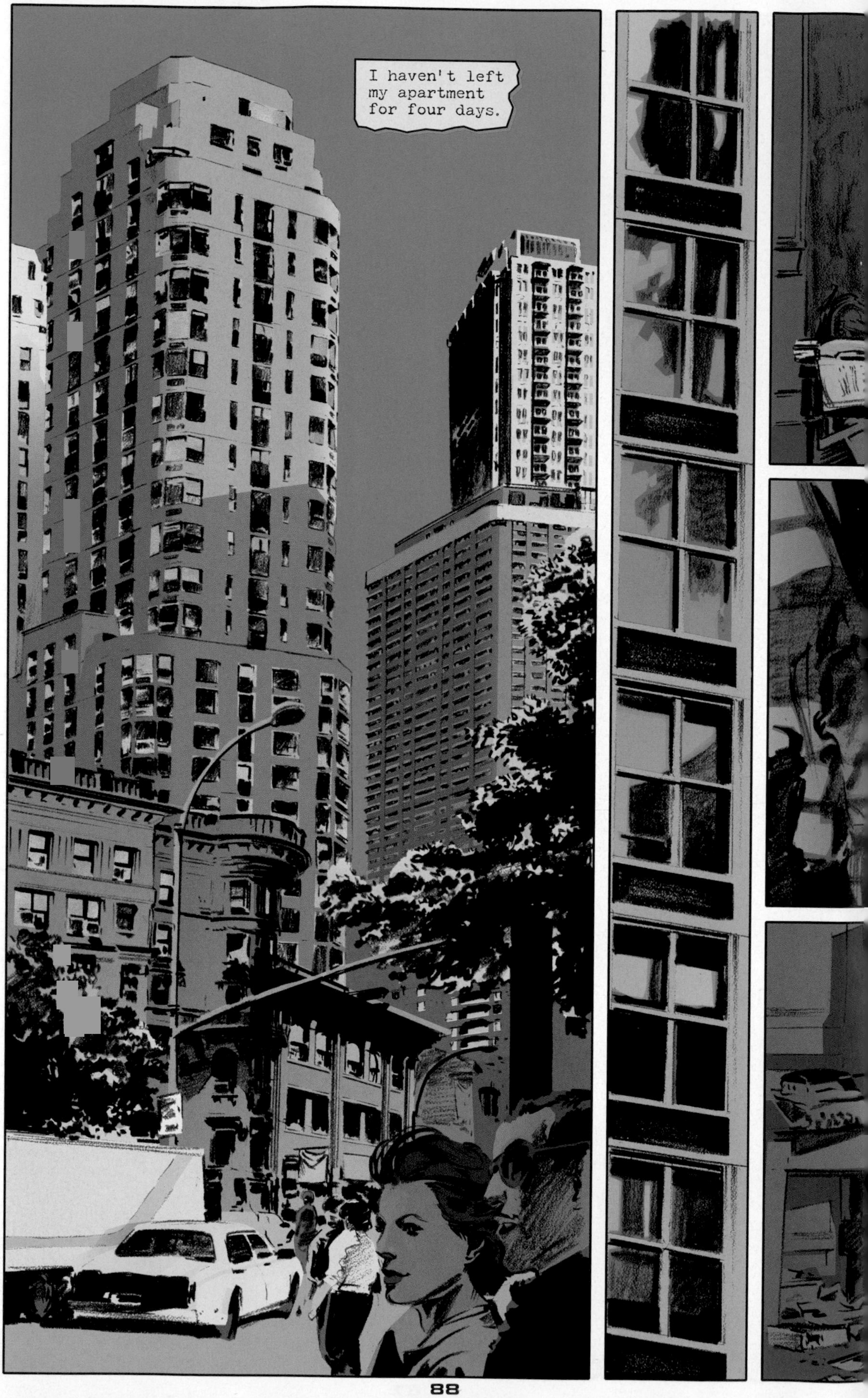
I haven't left my apartment for four days.

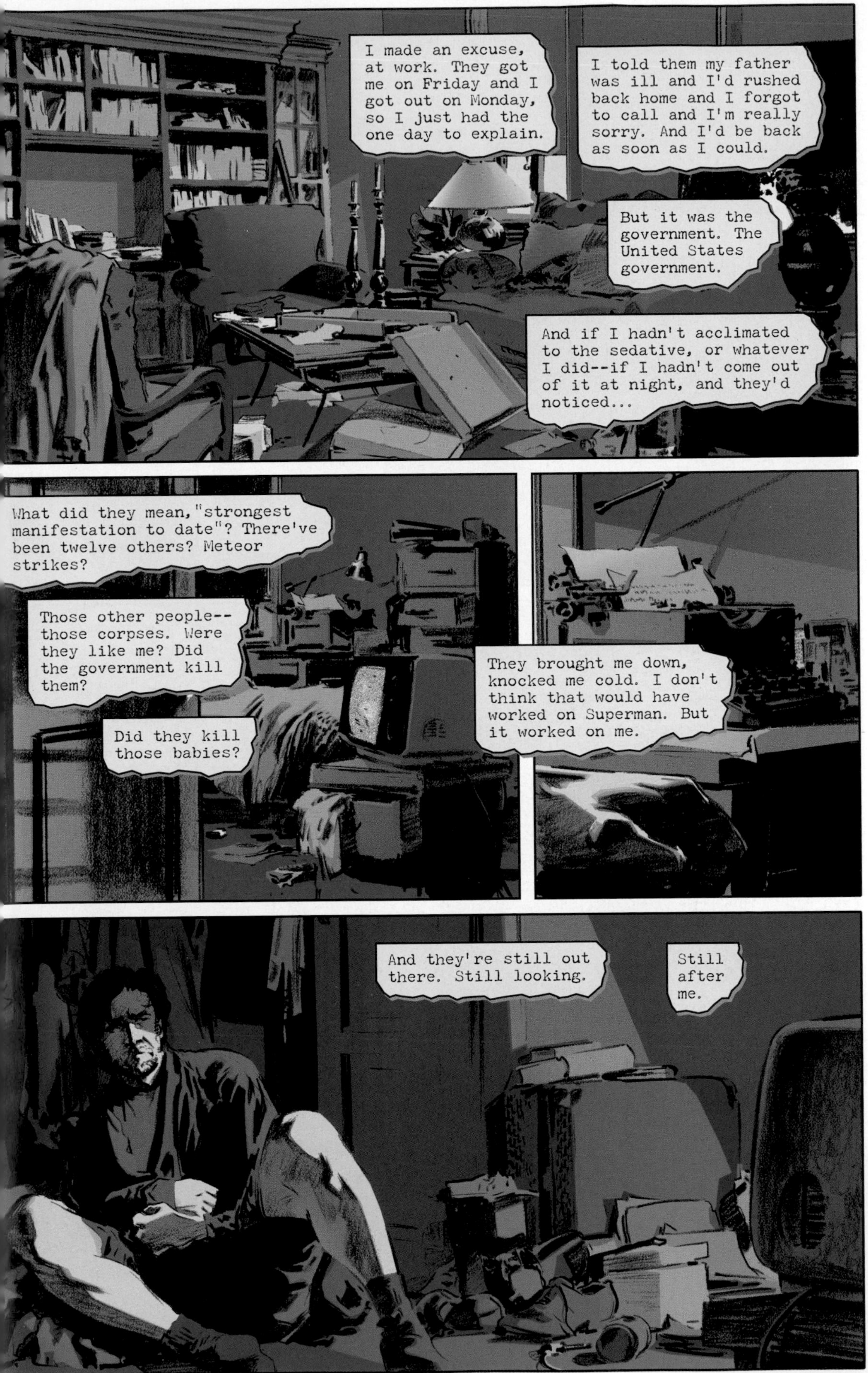
I made an excuse, at work. They got me on Friday and I got out on Monday, so I just had the one day to explain.
I told them my father was ill and I'd rushed back home and I forgot to call and I'm really sorry. And I'd be back as soon as I could.
But it was the government. The United States government.
And if I hadn't acclimated to the sedative, or whatever I did--if I hadn't come out of it at night, and they'd noticed...
What did they mean, "strongest manifestation to date"? There've been twelve others? Meteor strikes?
Those other people--those corpses. Were they like me? Did the government kill them?
Did they kill those babies?
They brought me down, knocked me cold. I don't think that would have worked on Superman. But it worked on me.
And they're still out there. Still looking.
Still after me.

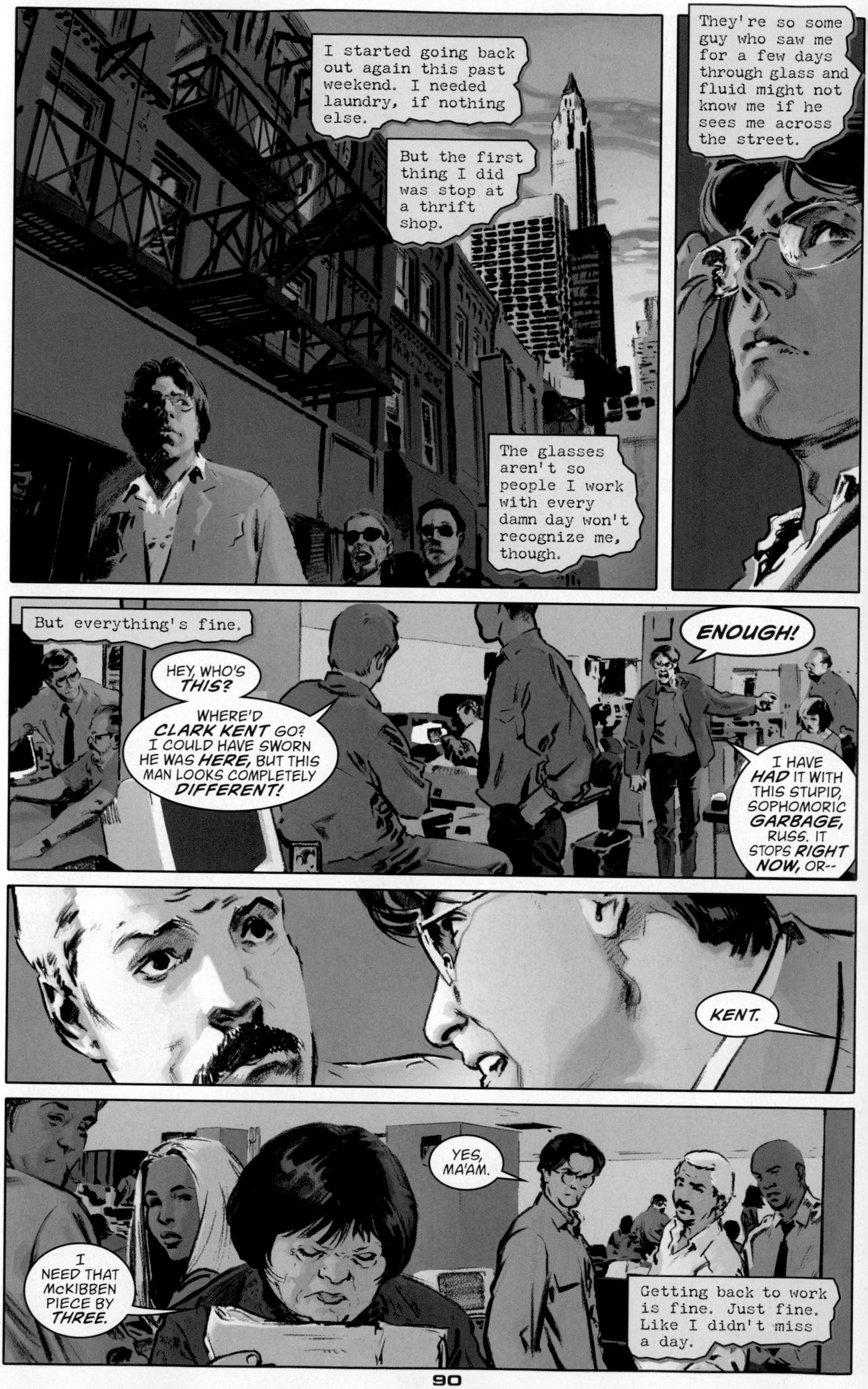

I started going back out again this past weekend. I needed laundry, if nothing else.
But the first thing I did was stop at a thrift shop.
The glasses aren't so people I work with every damn day won't recognize me, though.
They're so some guy who saw me for a few days through glass and fluid might not know me if he sees me across the street.
But everything's fine.
HEY, WHO'S THIS?
WHERE'D CLARK KENT GO? I COULD HAVE SWORN HE WAS HERE, BUT THIS MAN LOOKS COMPLETELY DIFFERENT!
ENOUGH!
I HAVE HAD IT WITH THIS STUPID, SOPHOMORIC GARBAGE, RUSS. IT STOPS RIGHT NOW, OR--
KENT.
YES, MA'AM.
I NEED THAT McKIBBEN PIECE BY THREE.
Getting back to work is fine. Just fine. Like I didn't miss a day.

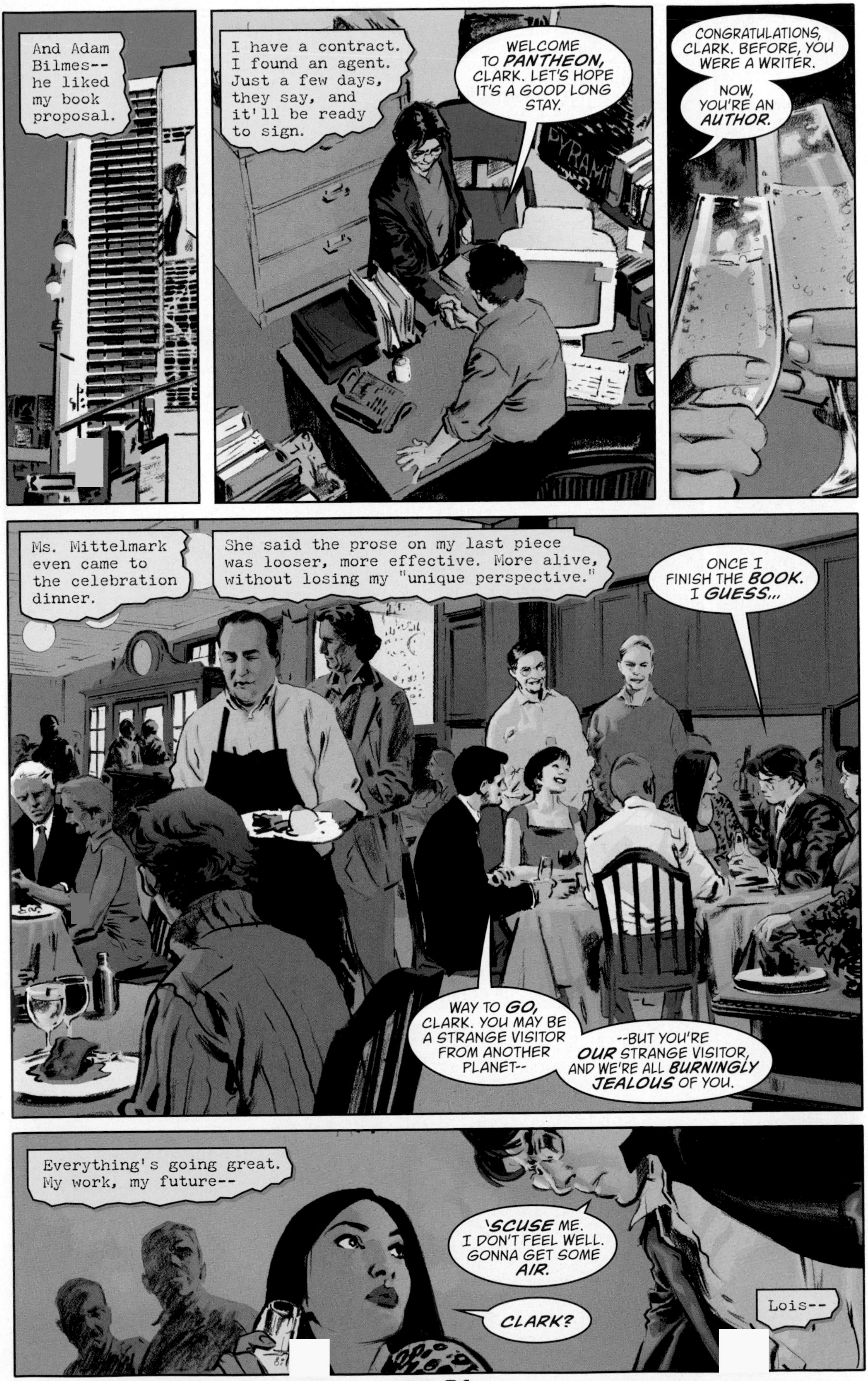
And Adam Bilmes--he liked my book proposal.
I have a contract. I found an agent. Just a few days, they say, and it'll be ready to sign.
WELCOME TO PANTHEON, CLARK. LET'S HOPE IT'S A GOOD LONG STAY.
CONGRATULATIONS, CLARK. BEFORE, YOU WERE A WRITER.
NOW, YOU'RE AN AUTHOR.
Ms. Mittelmark even came to the celebration dinner.
She said the prose on my last piece was looser, more effective. More alive, without losing my "unique perspective."
ONCE I FINISH THE BOOK. I GUESS...
WAY TO GO, CLARK. YOU MAY BE A STRANGE VISITOR FROM ANOTHER PLANET--
--BUT YOU'RE OUR STRANGE VISITOR, AND WE'RE ALL BURNINGLY JEALOUS OF YOU.
Everything's going great. My work, my future--
'SCUSE ME. I DON'T FEEL WELL. GONNA GET SOME AIR.
CLARK?
Lois--

THANKS FOR MAKING *COFFEE*, HON.

YOU WERE UP SO LATE WORKING ON THAT VIRTUAL MODEL FOR THE *RUSSELL OFFICES*...

CLARK, IS YOUR *FATHER* OKAY?

HM?

WELL, YOU SEEM *PREOCCUPIED*-- EVER SINCE YOUR DAD HAD THAT TROUBLE, YOU'VE BEEN DISTANT...

IT WAS *NOTHING.* A SCARE, BUT IT TURNED OUT TO BE A FOOD THING. HE DOESN'T EVEN LIKE US TO BRING IT UP.

I'M *FINE,* REALLY.

There've been some more stories about "Superman sightings" on the Internet.

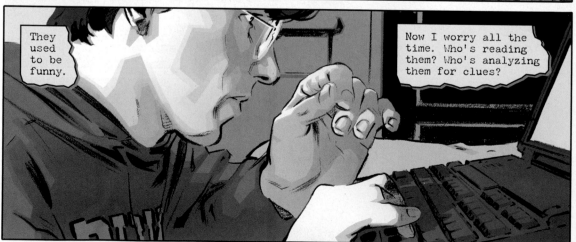

They used to be funny.

Now I worry all the time. Who's reading them? Who's analyzing them for clues?

92

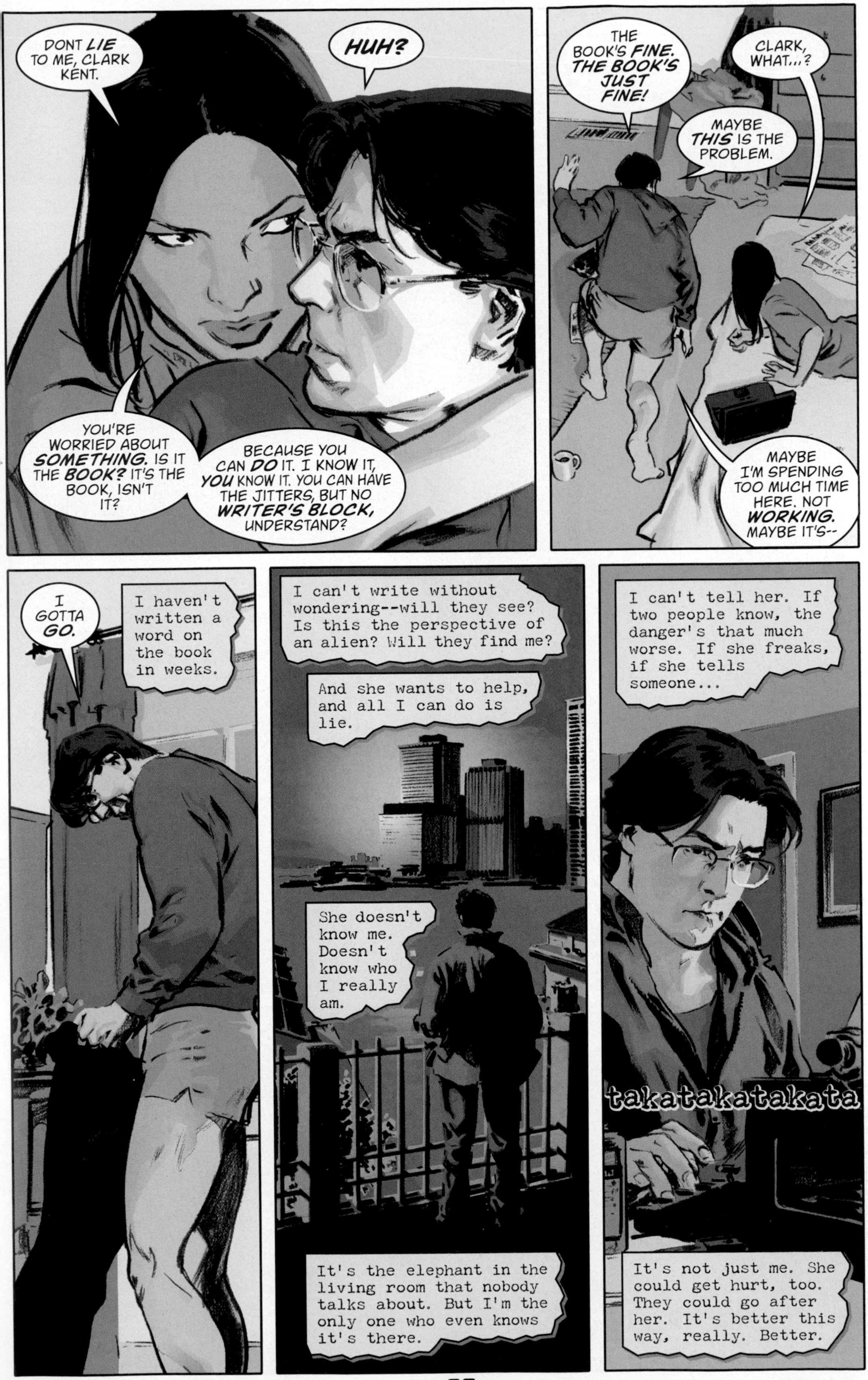
DONT LIE TO ME, CLARK KENT.
HUH?
YOU'RE WORRIED ABOUT SOMETHING. IS IT THE BOOK? IT'S THE BOOK, ISN'T IT?
BECAUSE YOU CAN DO IT. I KNOW IT, YOU KNOW IT. YOU CAN HAVE THE JITTERS, BUT NO WRITER'S BLOCK, UNDERSTAND?
THE BOOK'S FINE. THE BOOK'S JUST FINE!
CLARK, WHAT...?
MAYBE THIS IS THE PROBLEM.
MAYBE I'M SPENDING TOO MUCH TIME HERE. NOT WORKING. MAYBE IT'S--
I GOTTA GO.
I haven't written a word on the book in weeks.
I can't write without wondering--will they see? Is this the perspective of an alien? Will they find me?
And she wants to help, and all I can do is lie.
She doesn't know me. Doesn't know who I really am.
It's the elephant in the living room that nobody talks about. But I'm the only one who even knows it's there.
I can't tell her. If two people know, the danger's that much worse. If she freaks, if she tells someone...
takatakatakata
It's not just me. She could get hurt, too. They could go after her. It's better this way, really. Better.

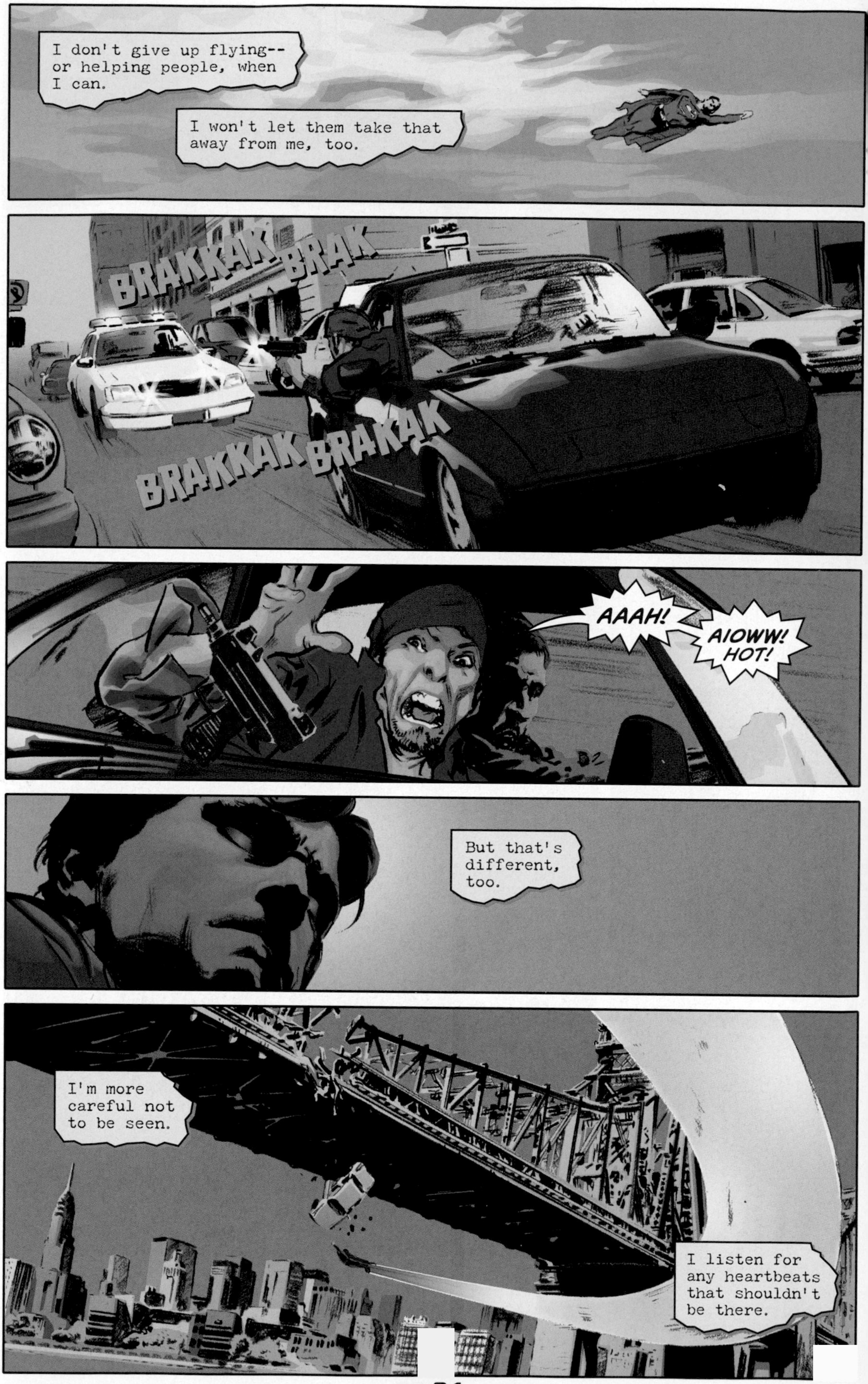

I don't give up flying--or helping people, when I can.
I won't let them take that away from me, too.
BRAKKAK BRAK
BRAKKAK BRAKAK
AAAH!
AIOWW! HOT!
But that's different, too.
I'm more careful not to be seen.
I listen for any heartbeats that shouldn't be there.

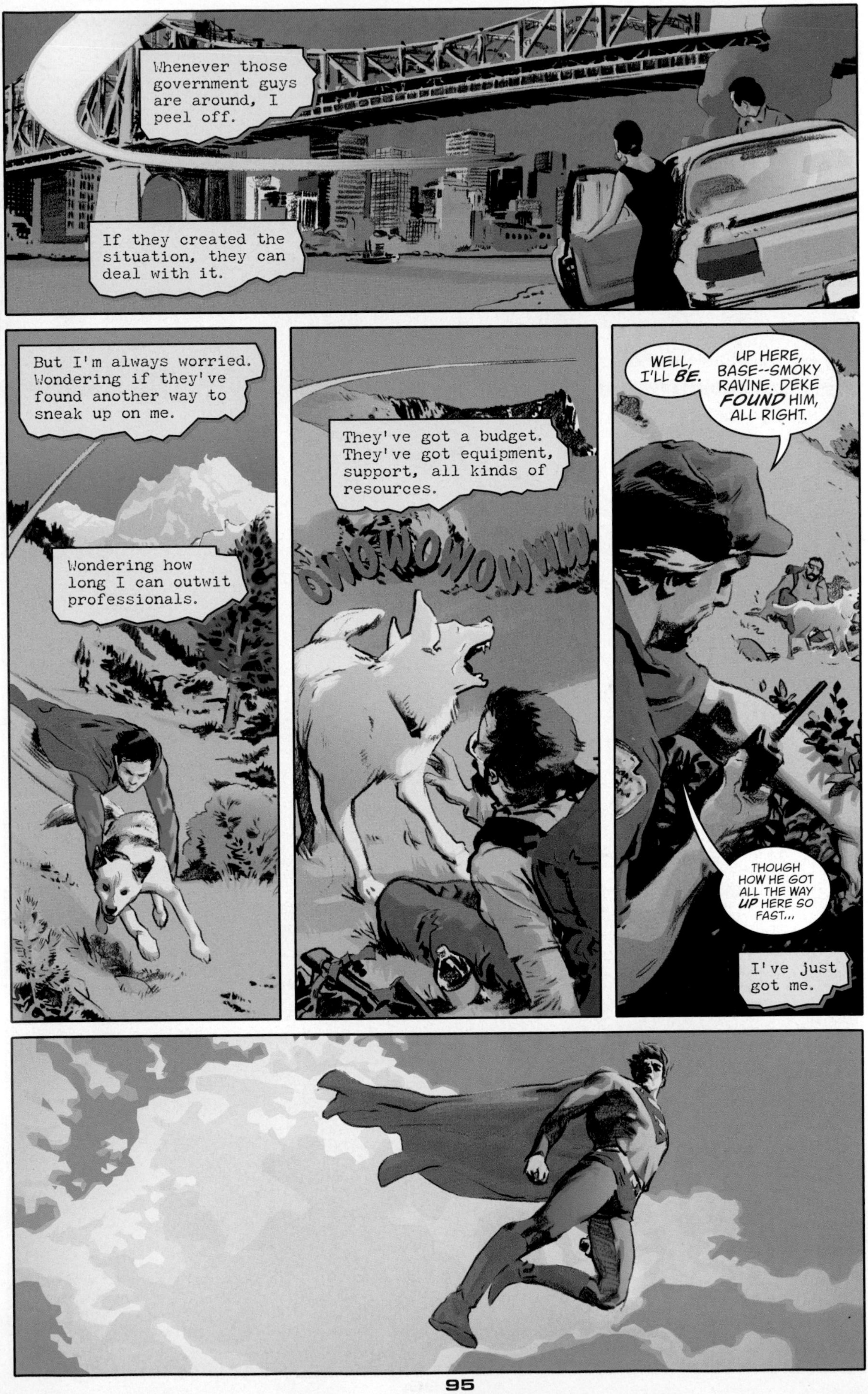

Whenever those government guys are around, I peel off.
If they created the situation, they can deal with it.
But I'm always worried. Wondering if they've found another way to sneak up on me.
Wondering how long I can outwit professionals.
They've got a budget. They've got equipment, support, all kinds of resources.
OWOWOWOWWW
WELL, I'LL *BE.*
UP HERE, BASE--SMOKY RAVINE. DEKE *FOUND* HIM, ALL RIGHT.
THOUGH HOW HE GOT ALL THE WAY *UP* HERE SO FAST...
I've just got me.

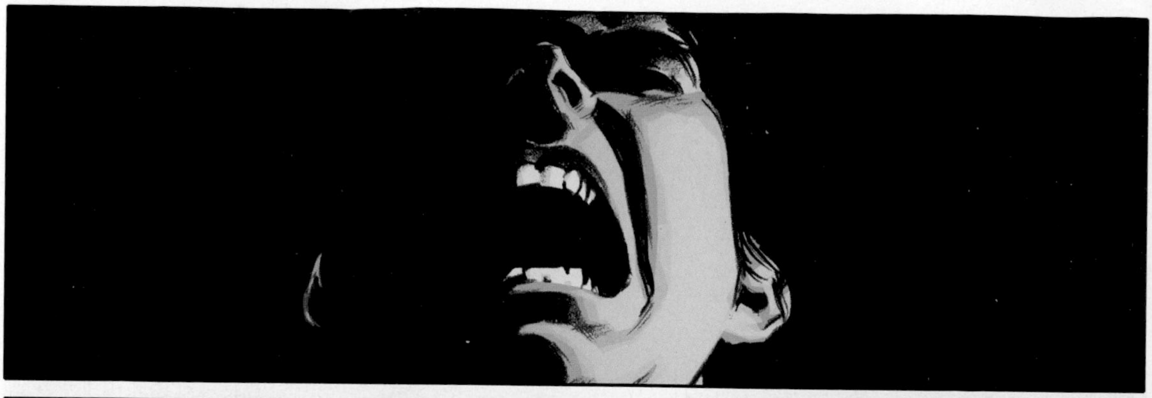

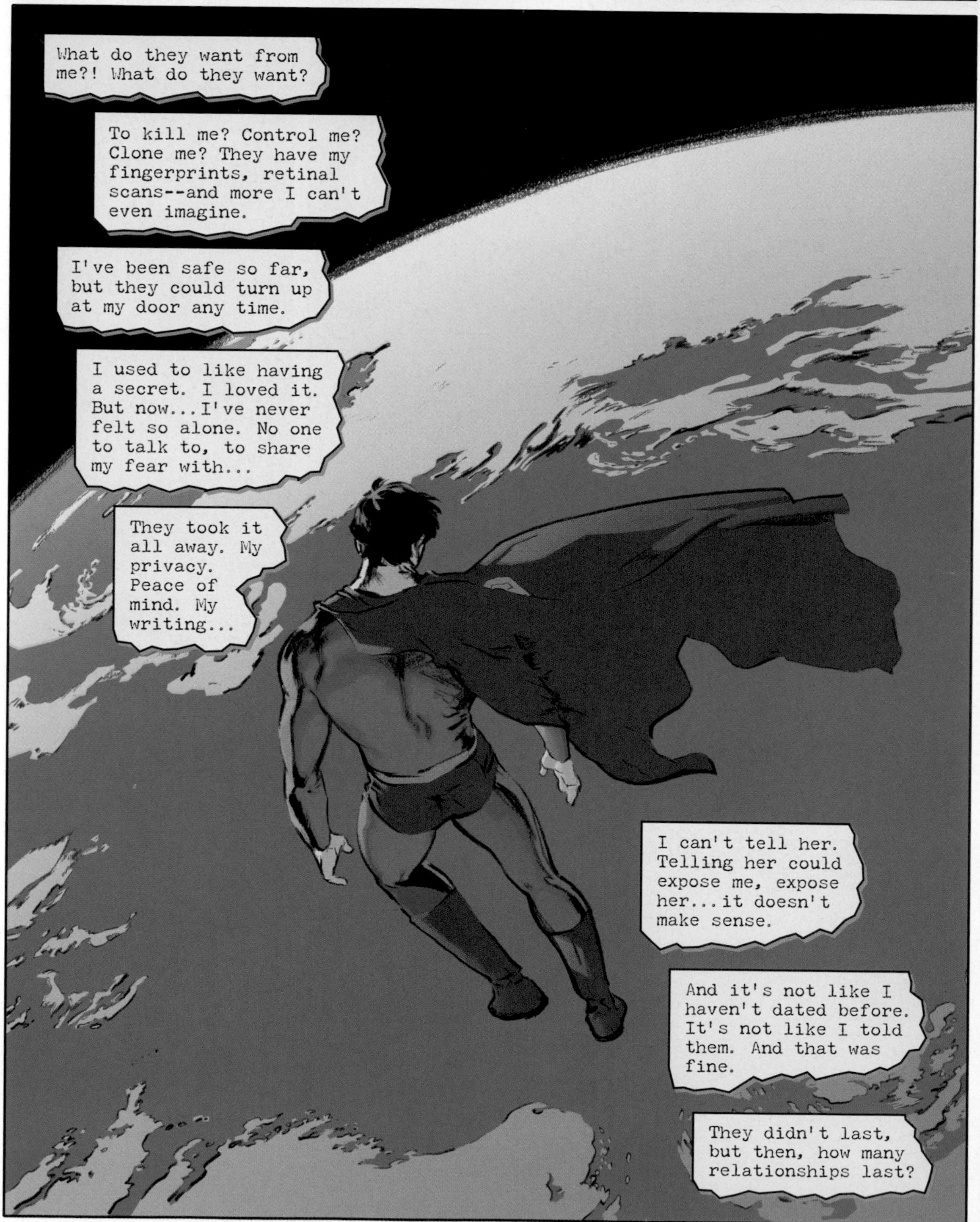

What do they want from me?! What do they want?
To kill me? Control me? Clone me? They have my fingerprints, retinal scans--and more I can't even imagine.
I've been safe so far, but they could turn up at my door any time.
I used to like having a secret. I loved it. But now...I've never felt so alone. No one to talk to, to share my fear with...
They took it all away. My privacy. Peace of mind. My writing...
I can't tell her. Telling her could expose me, expose her...it doesn't make sense.
And it's not like I haven't dated before. It's not like I told them. And that was fine.
They didn't last, but then, how many relationships last?

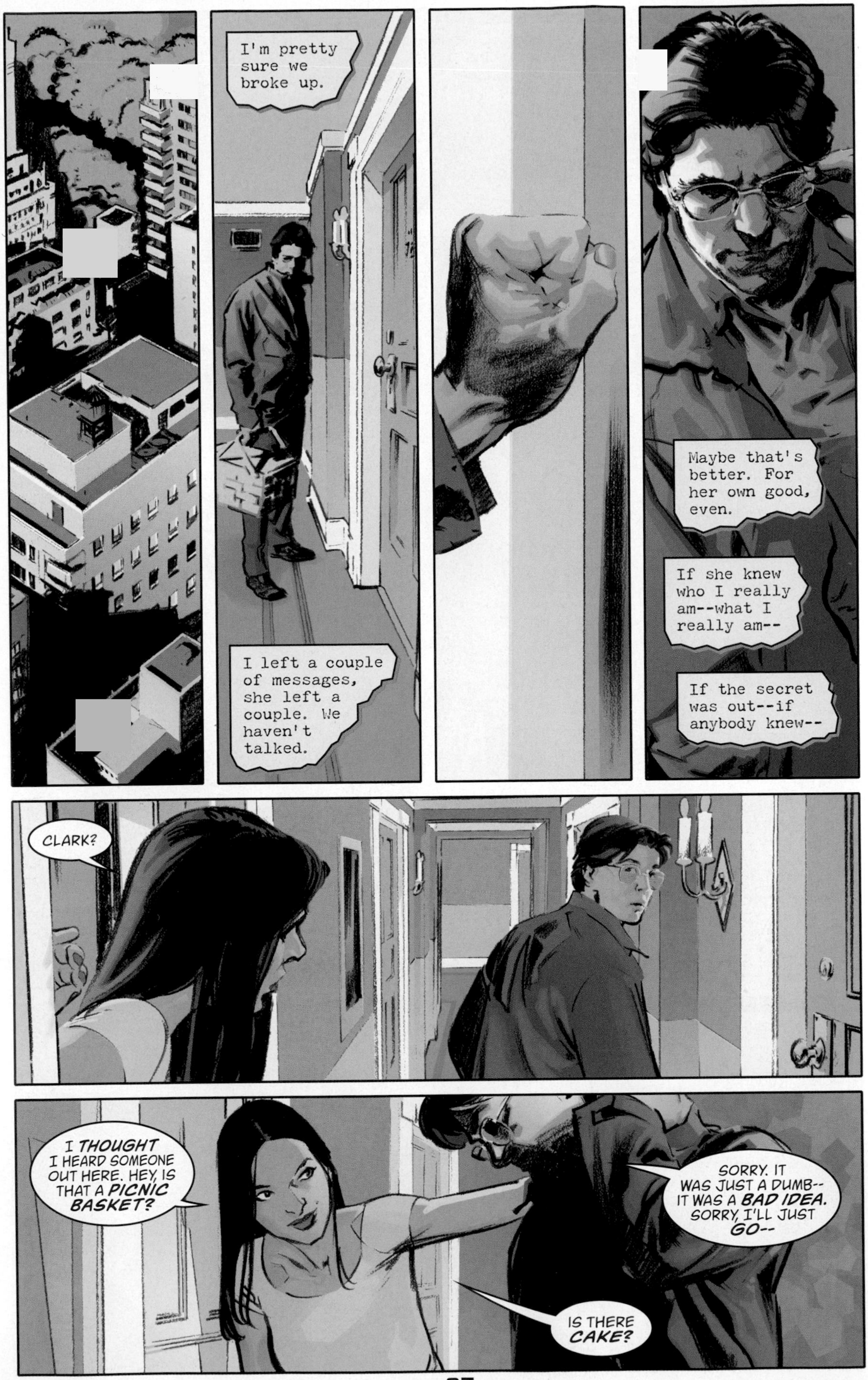
I'm pretty sure we broke up.
I left a couple of messages, she left a couple. We haven't talked.
Maybe that's better. For her own good, even.
If she knew who I really am--what I really am--
If the secret was out--if anybody knew--
CLARK?
I THOUGHT I HEARD SOMEONE OUT HERE. HEY, IS THAT A PICNIC BASKET?
SORRY. IT WAS JUST A DUMB-- IT WAS A BAD IDEA. SORRY, I'LL JUST GO--
IS THERE CAKE?

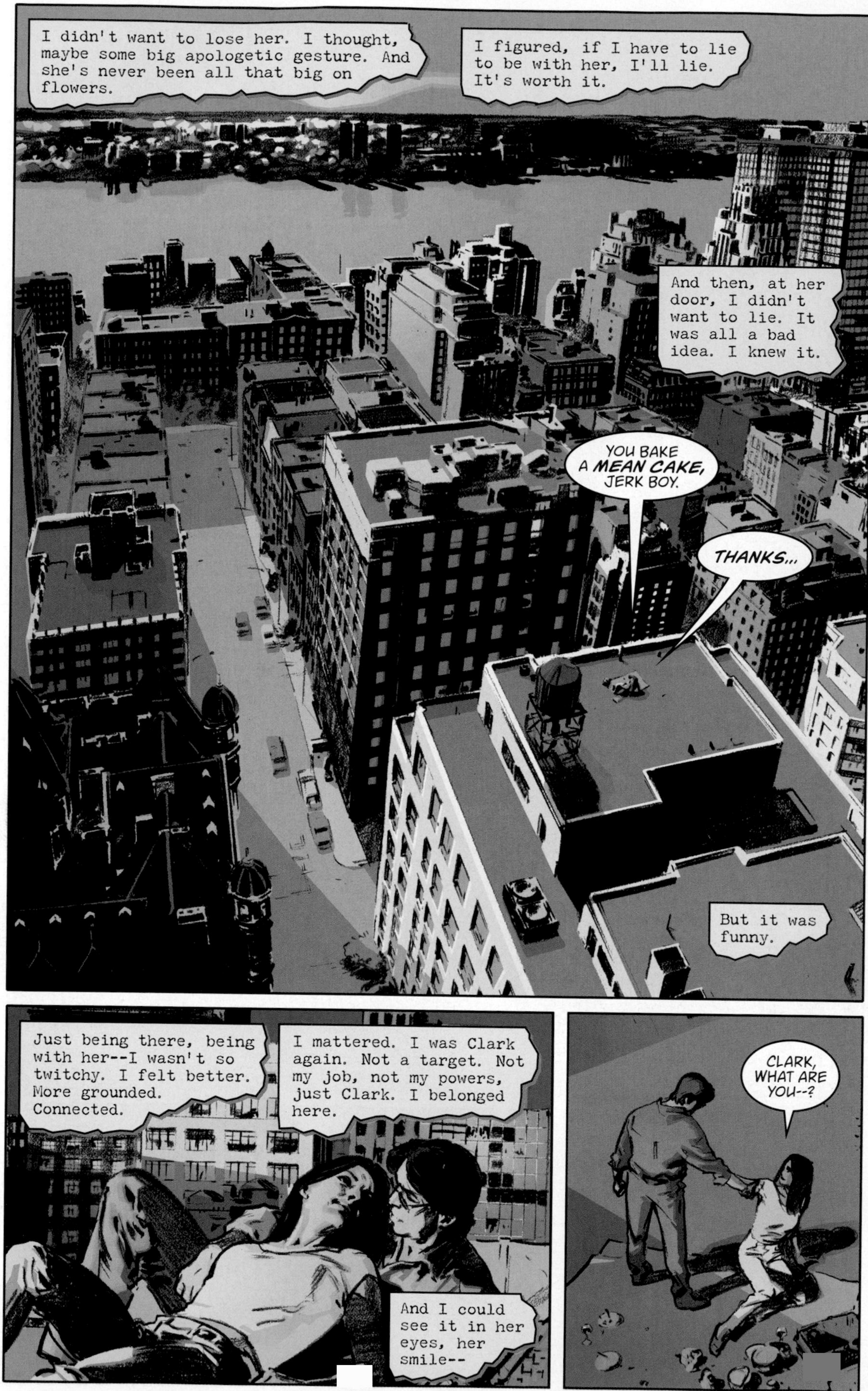
I didn't want to lose her. I thought, maybe some big apologetic gesture. And she's never been all that big on flowers.
I figured, if I have to lie to be with her, I'll lie. It's worth it.
And then, at her door, I didn't want to lie. It was all a bad idea. I knew it.
YOU BAKE A MEAN CAKE, JERK BOY.
THANKS...
But it was funny.
Just being there, being with her--I wasn't so twitchy. I felt better. More grounded. Connected.
I mattered. I was Clark again. Not a target. Not my job, not my powers, just Clark. I belonged here.
And I could see it in her eyes, her smile--
CLARK, WHAT ARE YOU--?

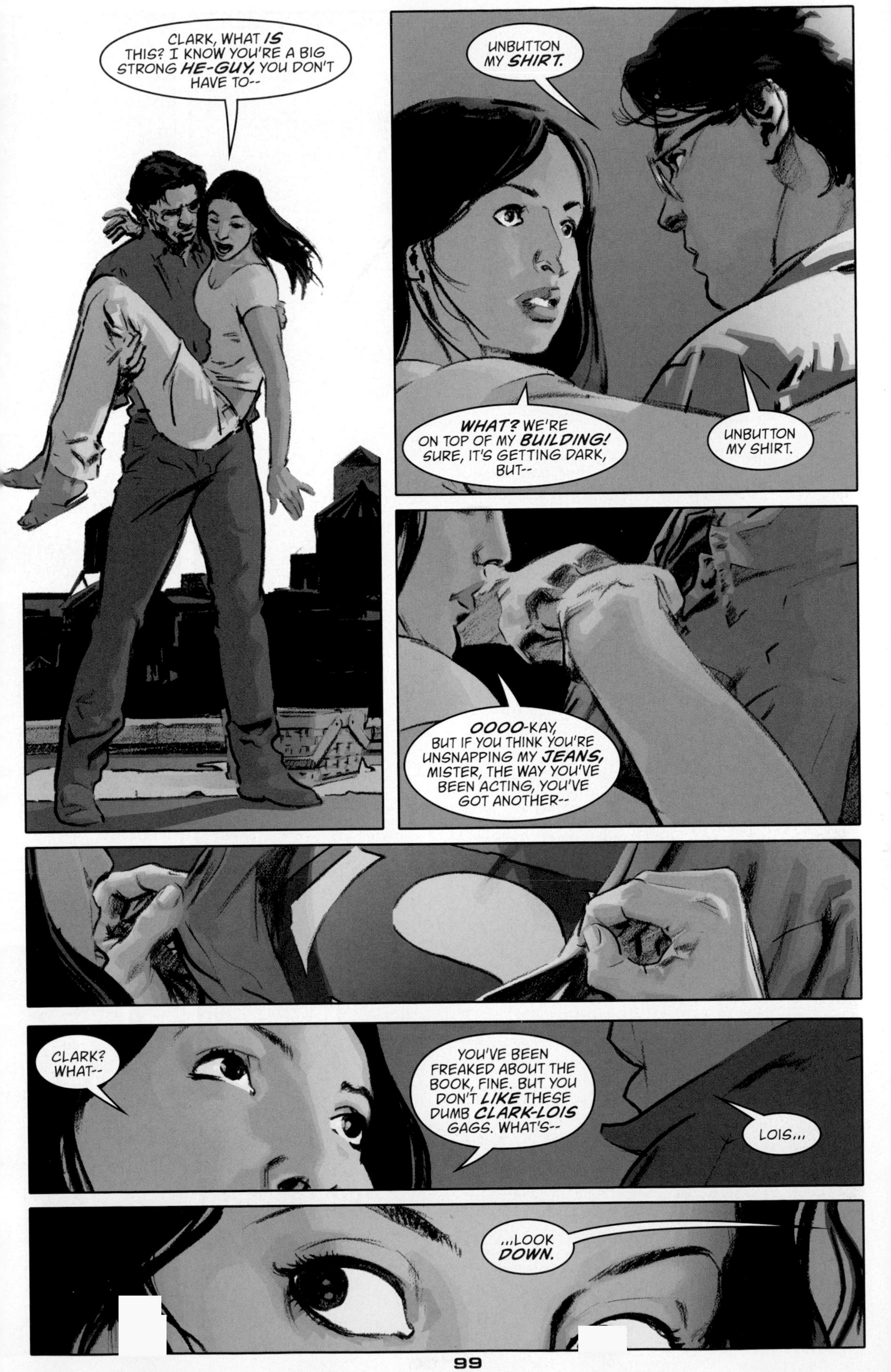
CLARK, WHAT IS THIS? I KNOW YOU'RE A BIG STRONG HE-GUY, YOU DON'T HAVE TO--
UNBUTTON MY SHIRT.
WHAT? WE'RE ON TOP OF MY BUILDING! SURE, IT'S GETTING DARK, BUT--
UNBUTTON MY SHIRT.
OOOO-KAY, BUT IF YOU THINK YOU'RE UNSNAPPING MY JEANS, MISTER, THE WAY YOU'VE BEEN ACTING, YOU'VE GOT ANOTHER--
CLARK? WHAT--
YOU'VE BEEN FREAKED ABOUT THE BOOK, FINE. BUT YOU DON'T LIKE THESE DUMB CLARK-LOIS GAGS. WHAT'S--
LOIS...
...LOOK DOWN.

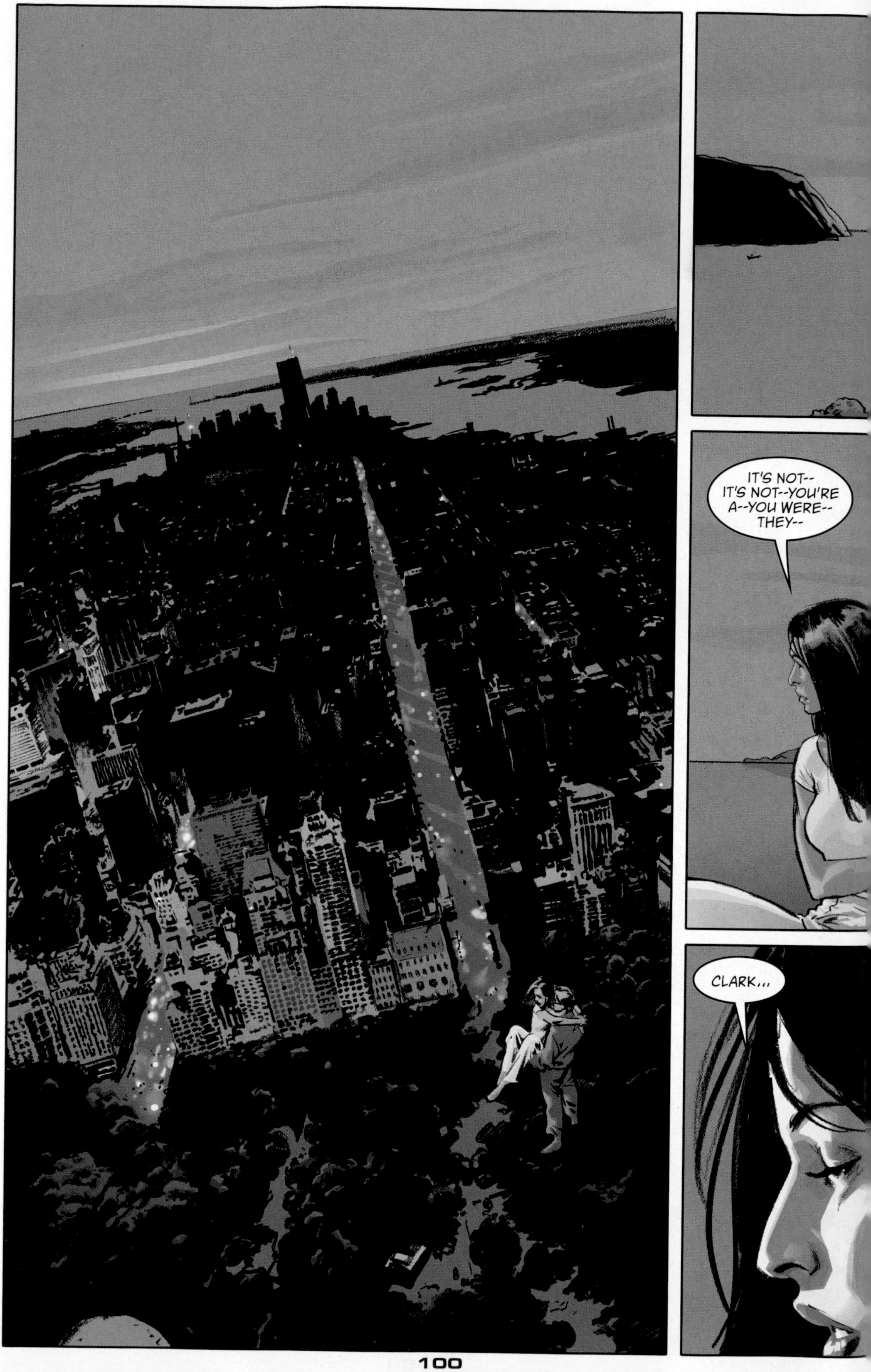
IT'S NOT--
IT'S NOT--YOU'RE A--YOU WERE--THEY--
CLARK...

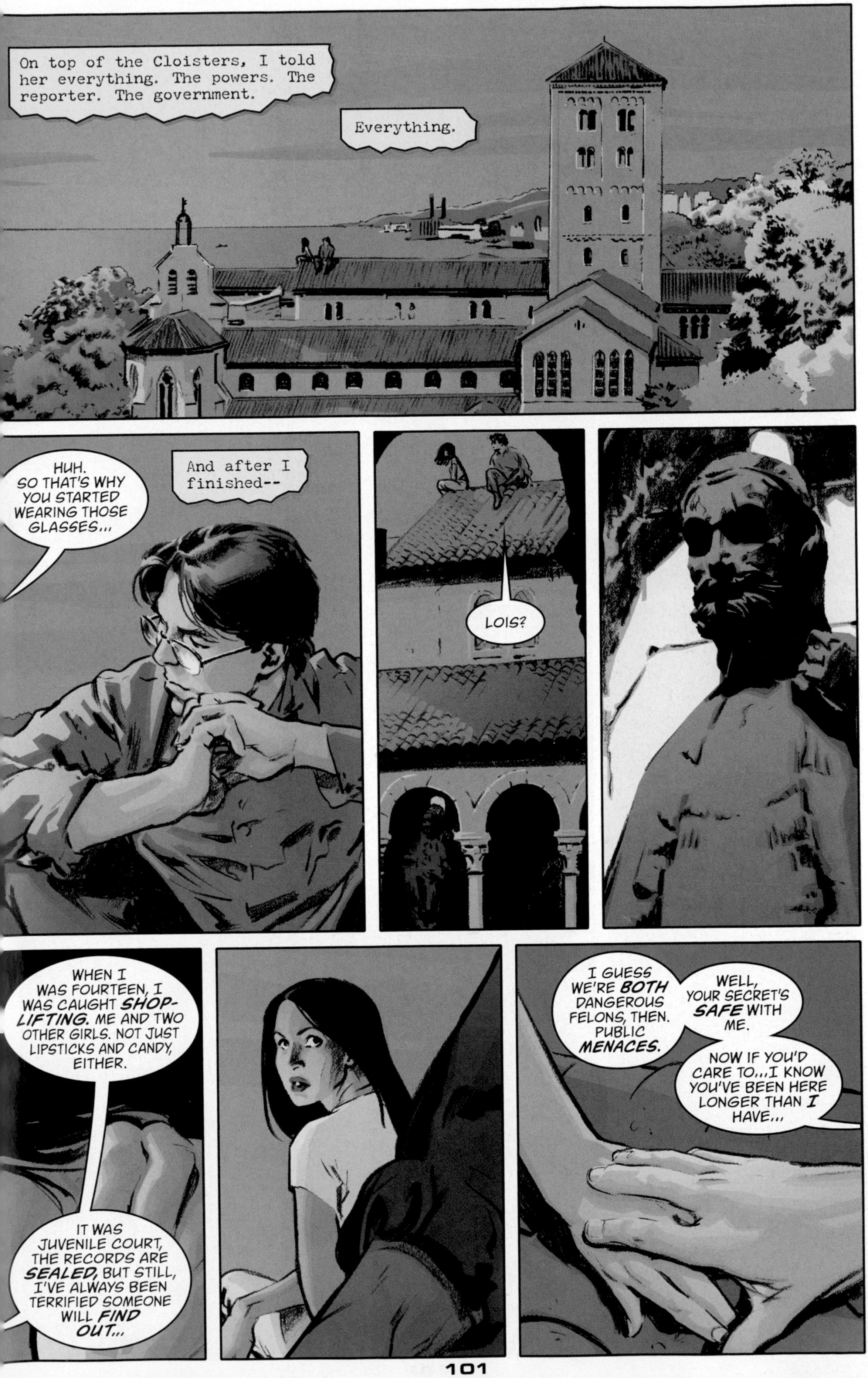
On top of the Cloisters, I told her everything. The powers. The reporter. The government.
Everything.
HUH. SO THAT'S WHY YOU STARTED WEARING THOSE GLASSES...
And after I finished--
LOIS?
WHEN I WAS FOURTEEN, I WAS CAUGHT SHOP-LIFTING. ME AND TWO OTHER GIRLS. NOT JUST LIPSTICKS AND CANDY, EITHER.
IT WAS JUVENILE COURT, THE RECORDS ARE SEALED, BUT STILL, I'VE ALWAYS BEEN TERRIFIED SOMEONE WILL FIND OUT...
I GUESS WE'RE BOTH DANGEROUS FELONS, THEN. PUBLIC MENACES.
WELL, YOUR SECRET'S SAFE WITH ME.
NOW IF YOU'D CARE TO...I KNOW YOU'VE BEEN HERE LONGER THAN I HAVE...

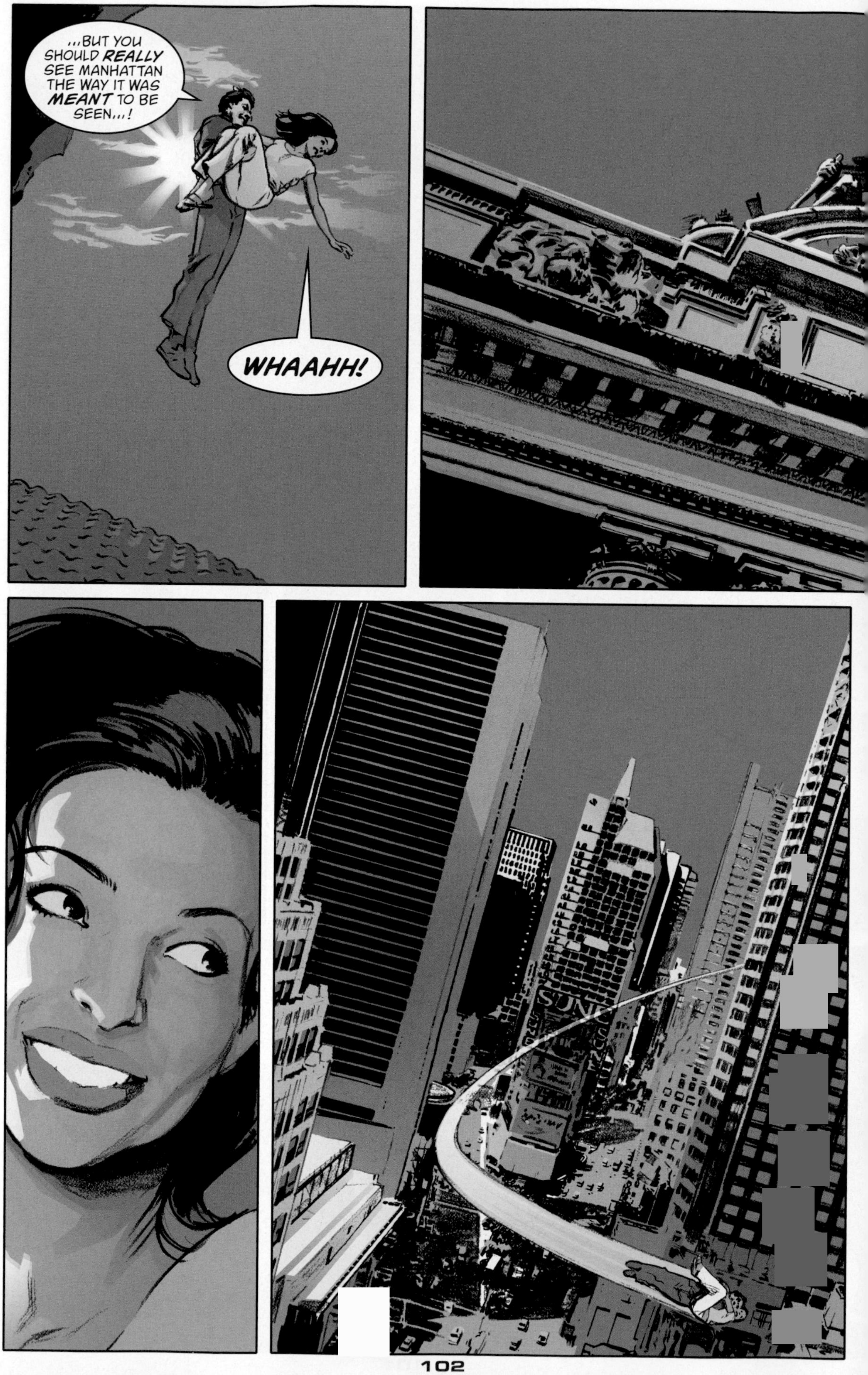
...BUT YOU SHOULD REALLY SEE MANHATTAN THE WAY IT WAS MEANT TO BE SEEN...!
WHAAHH!

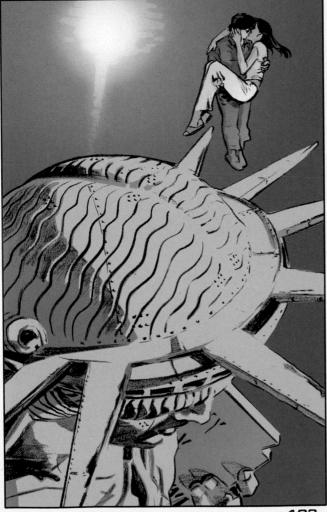

SO, WHAT'S NEXT? YOUR FORTRESS OF SOLITUDE?

WELL...I *DO* KNOW THIS GREAT *CRAB SHACK* ON THE OUTER BANKS IN NORTH CAROLINA. FOUND IT WHEN I WAS IN COLLEGE.

WE...WE COULDN'T. *COULD* WE?

FOR *YOU*, LOIS...

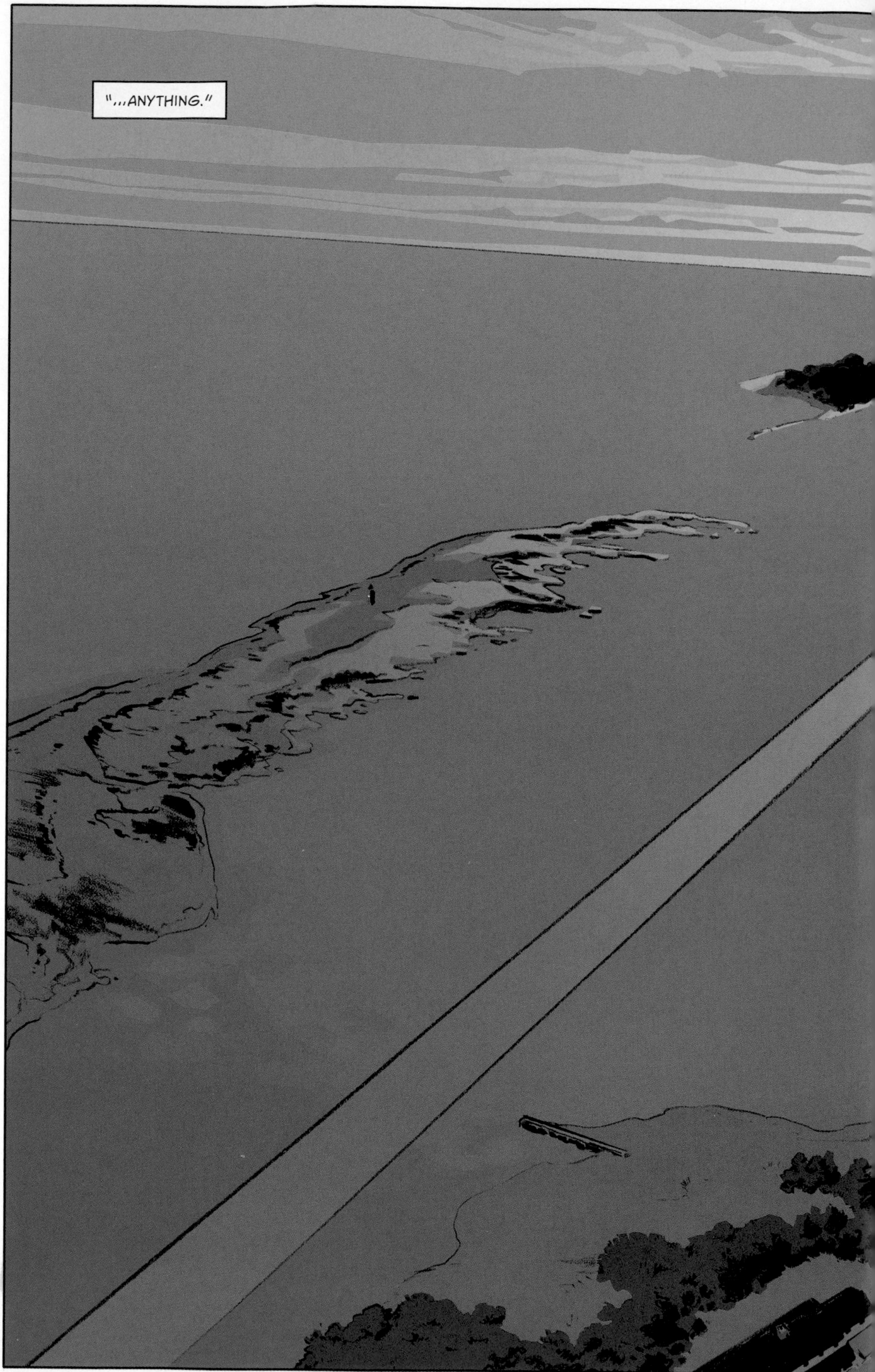
"...ANYTHING."

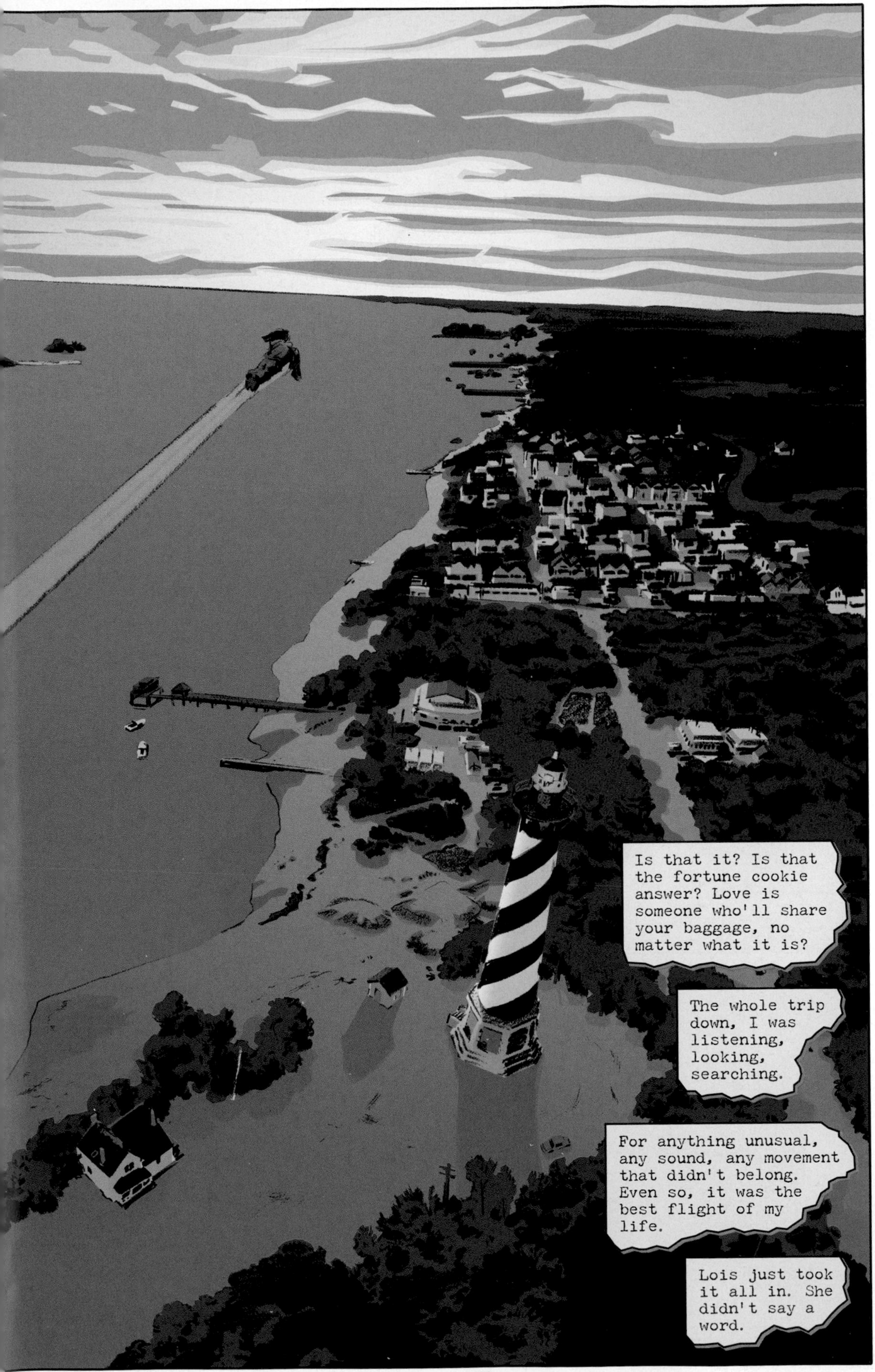
Is that it? Is that the fortune cookie answer? Love is someone who'll share your baggage, no matter what it is?
The whole trip down, I was listening, looking, searching.
For anything unusual, any sound, any movement that didn't belong. Even so, it was the best flight of my life.
Lois just took it all in. She didn't say a word.

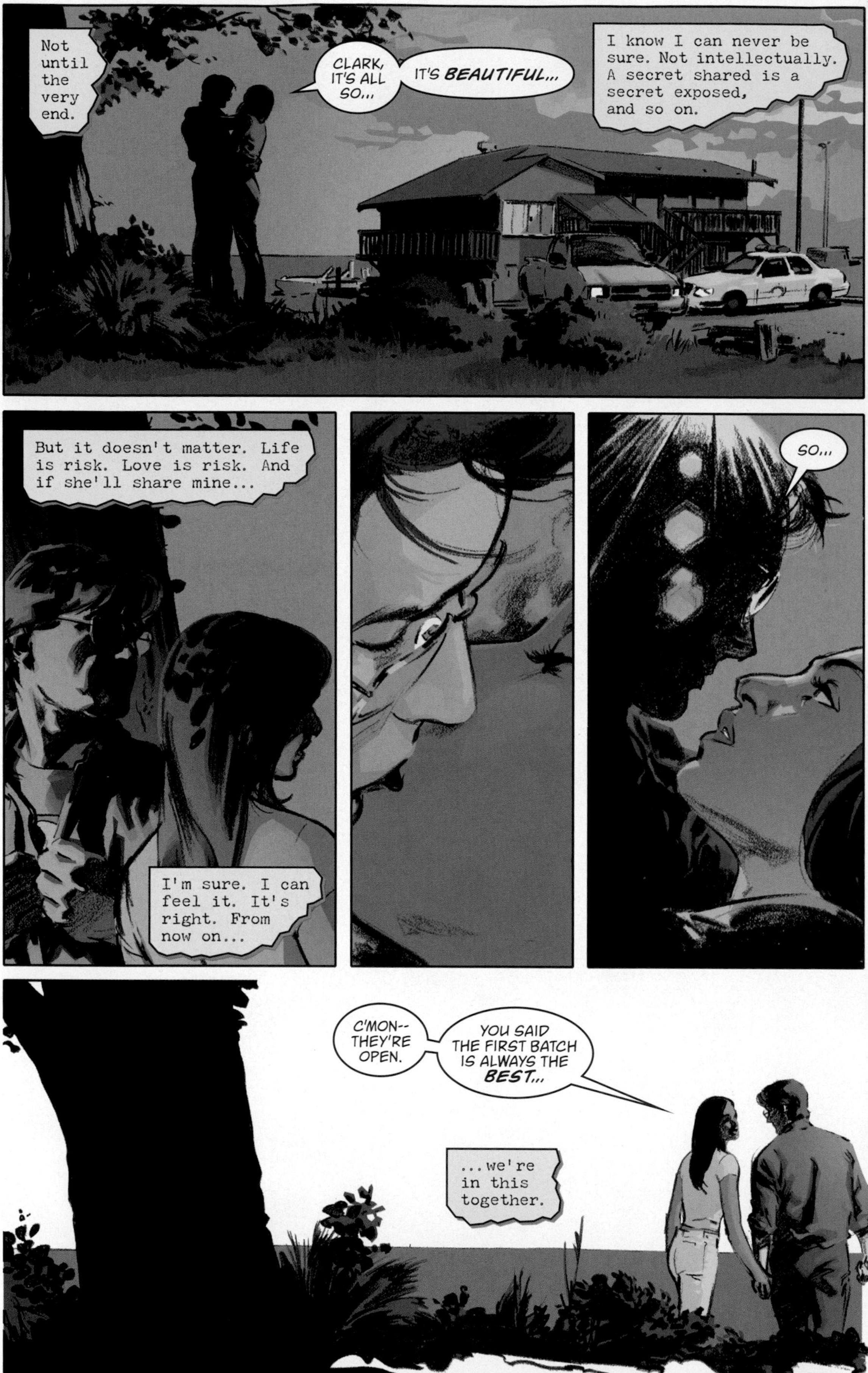

Not until the very end.
CLARK, IT'S ALL SO...
IT'S BEAUTIFUL...
I know I can never be sure. Not intellectually. A secret shared is a secret exposed, and so on.
But it doesn't matter. Life is risk. Love is risk. And if she'll share mine...
I'm sure. I can feel it. It's right. From now on...
SO...
C'MON-- THEY'RE OPEN.
YOU SAID THE FIRST BATCH IS ALWAYS THE BEST...
...we're in this together.

# chapter three **fortress**

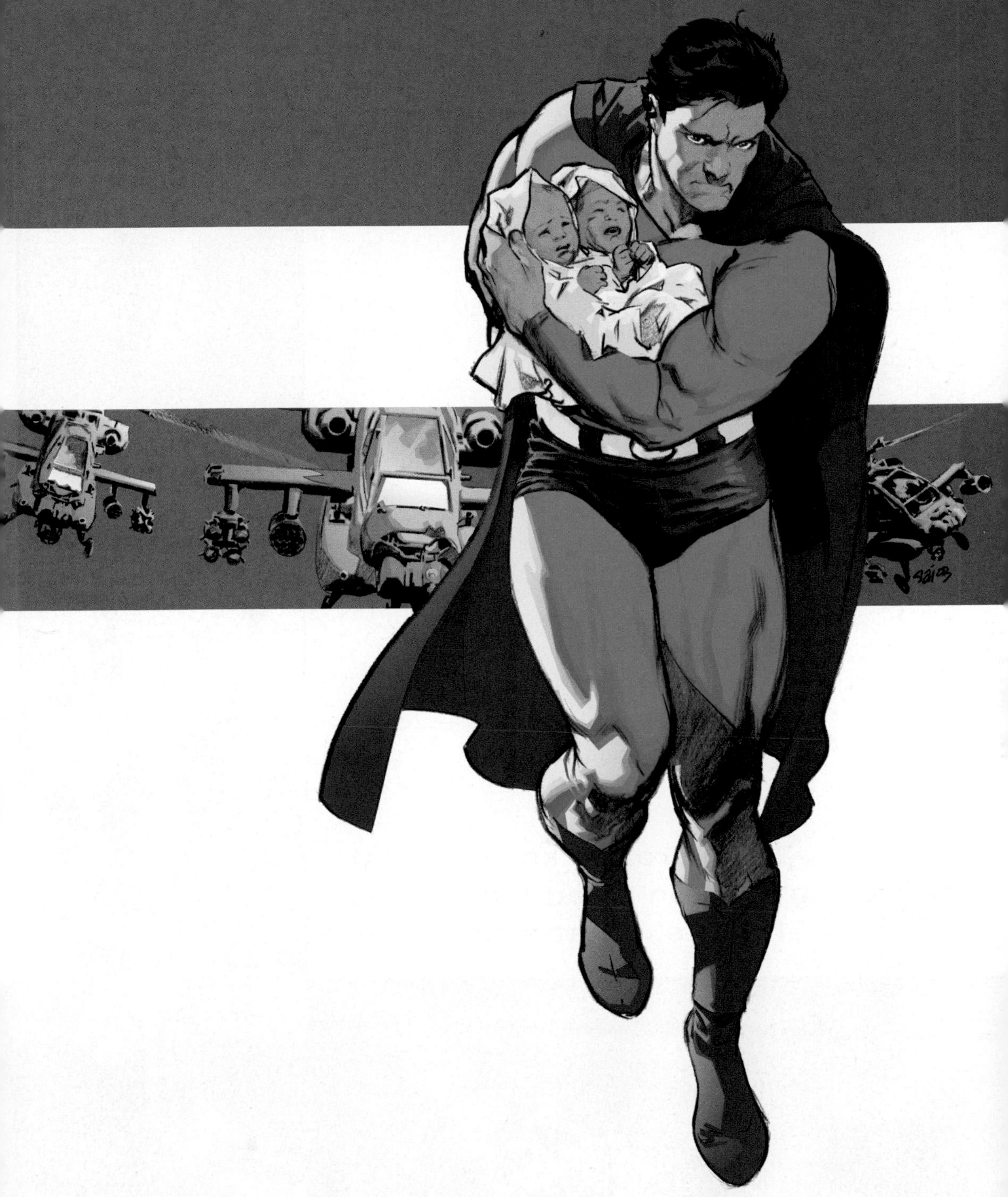

They already know I **exist**,
so as long as I don't lead them home,
I figure, **what's the harm**?

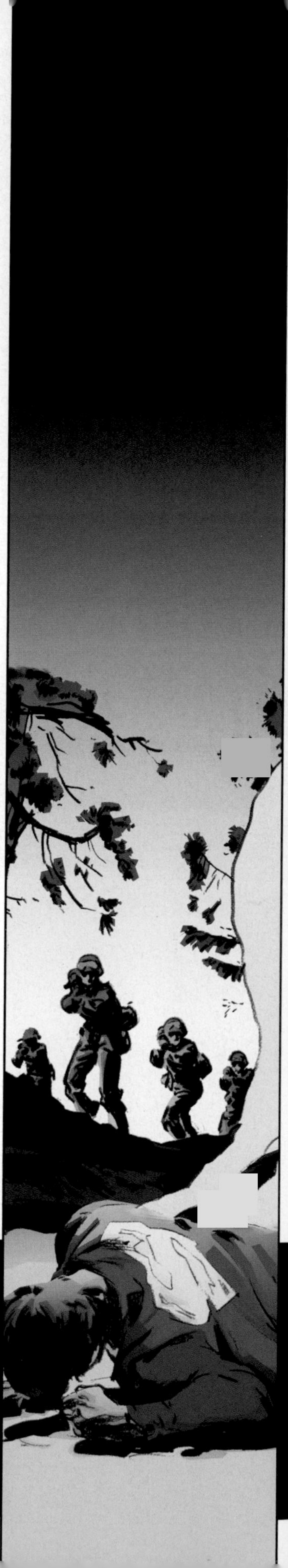

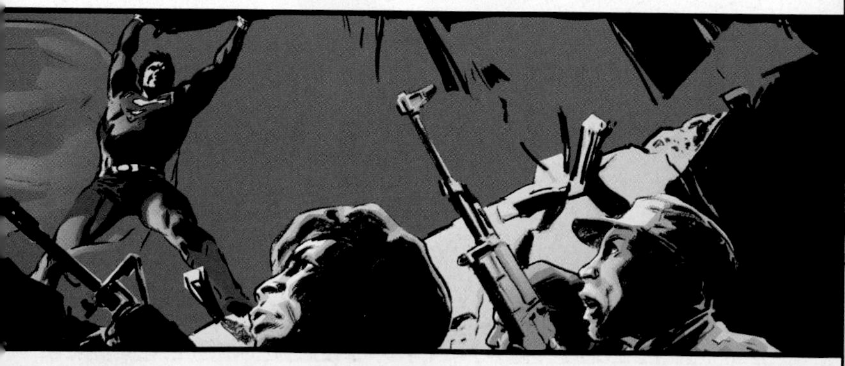

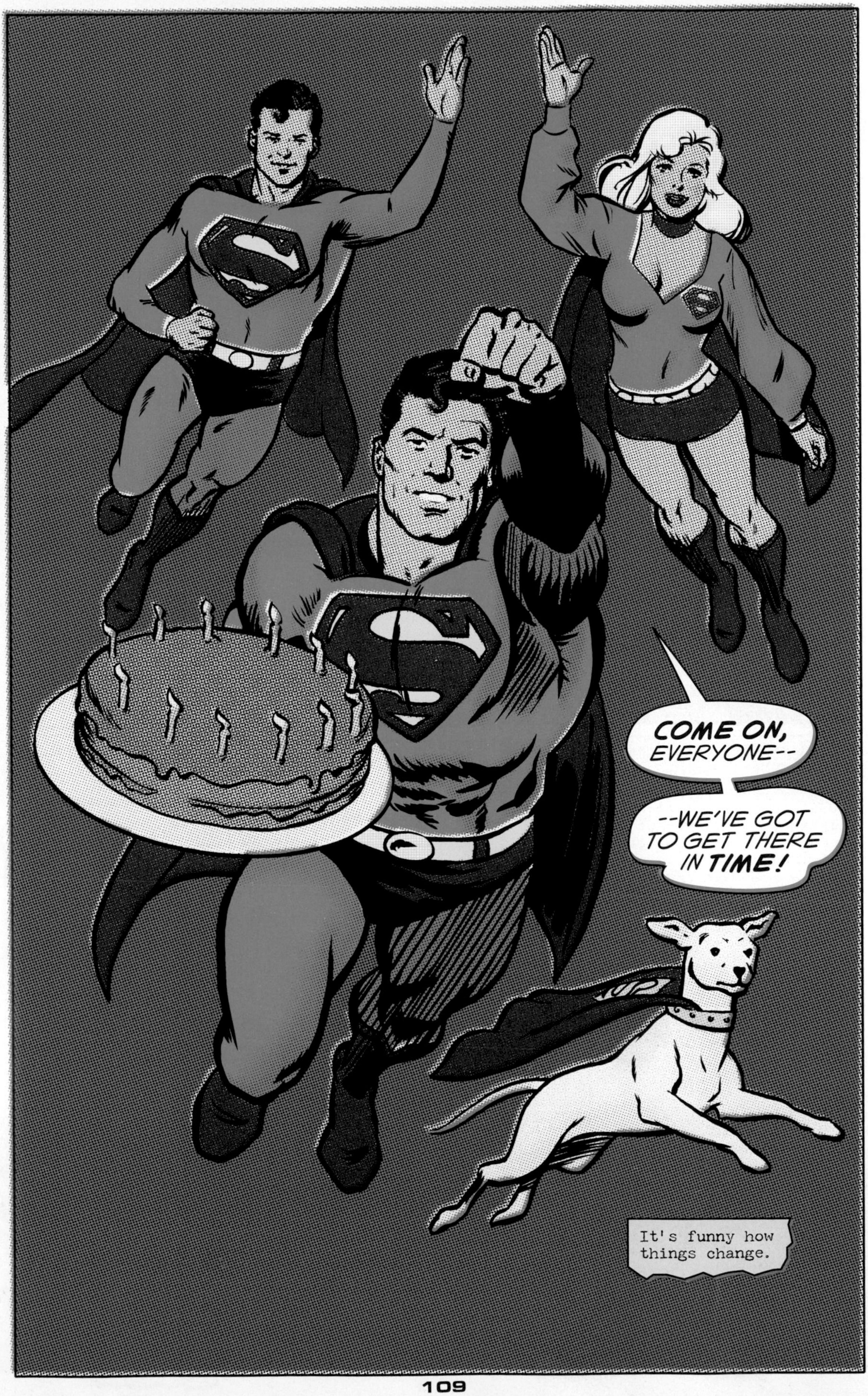
COME ON, EVERYONE--
--WE'VE GOT TO GET THERE IN TIME!
It's funny how things change.

A decade ago, it'd have annoyed me, but today, something as simple as a dopey card can touch my heart.

And it's nowhere near my birthday. She must have just seen it and thought of me.

Nice work in Ecuador! We'll see you soon. — Love, Lois

たんじょうびに おめでとう！

SUPERMAN FAMILY

It used to be such a pain, that whole "Ha ha yes, my name's Clark Kent, ha ha yes," like Superman" thing.

But it's different when it's not just you. When someone can make a face and roll their eyes for you, and you know they understand.

When they share your secret.

I find myself looking around a lot. Reassessing.

Lois is happy as an environmental designer--they've got her helping set up the new Toshiba building in Tokyo, and she's working in Dallas, London, Mexico City...

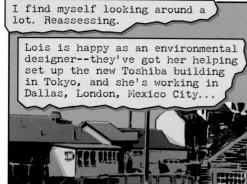

I miss her when she travels, but I'm glad she likes the work.

And me--

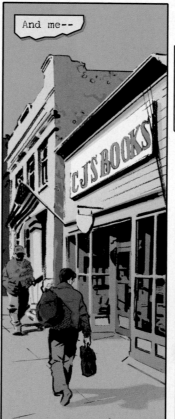

My last two books have made the BookSense 76 list.

To my surprise, <u>The View From Space</u>, which I thought was about cultural development, has become an intro-ductory textbook on systems analysis.

CLARK KENT

LOST FUTURES: Humanity's Changing Dreams

I'm speaking at an L.A. book festival next month.

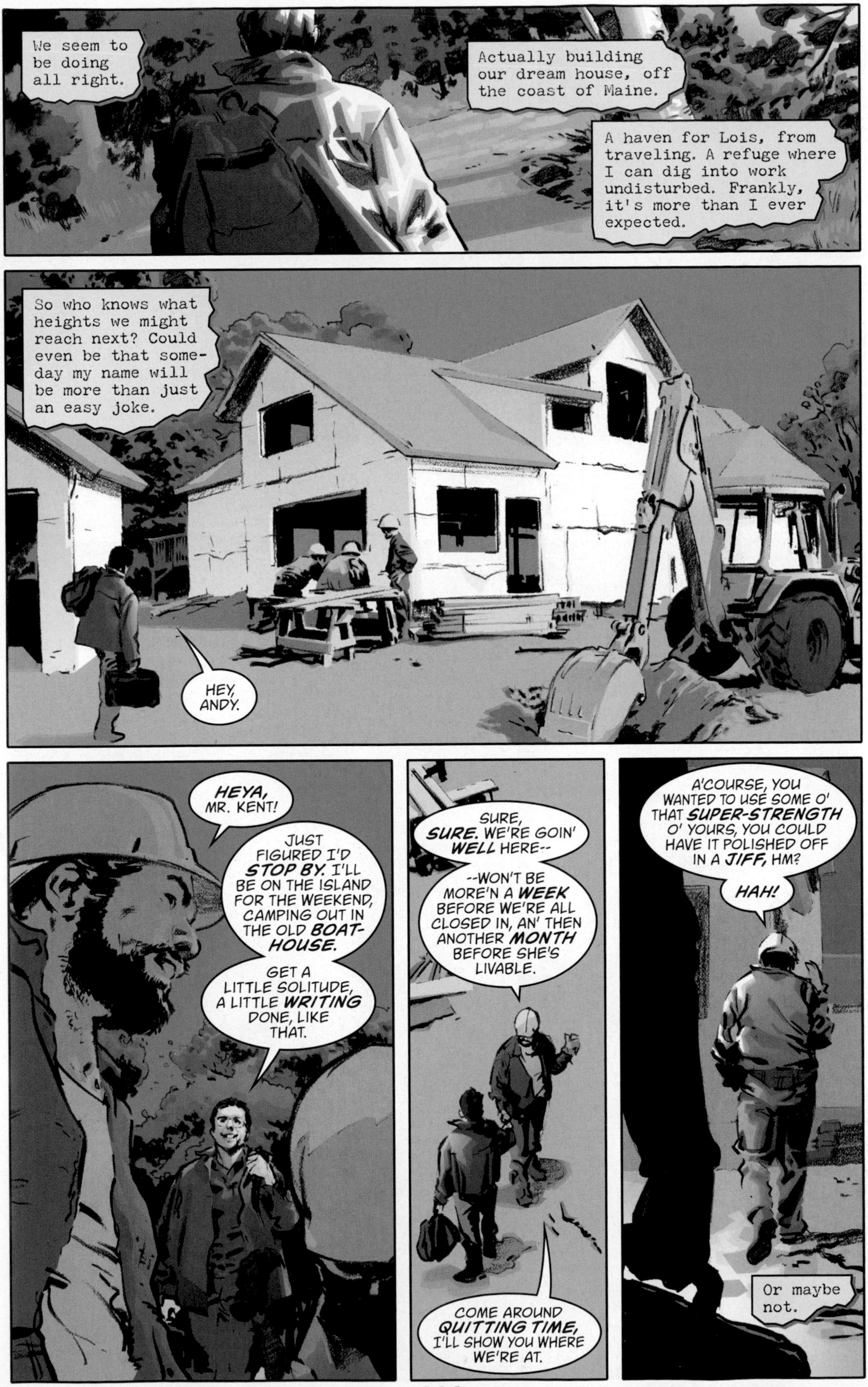
We seem to be doing all right.
Actually building our dream house, off the coast of Maine.
A haven for Lois, from traveling. A refuge where I can dig into work undisturbed. Frankly, it's more than I ever expected.
So who knows what heights we might reach next? Could even be that some-day my name will be more than just an easy joke.
HEY, ANDY.
HEYA, MR. KENT!
JUST FIGURED I'D STOP BY. I'LL BE ON THE ISLAND FOR THE WEEKEND, CAMPING OUT IN THE OLD BOAT-HOUSE.
GET A LITTLE SOLITUDE, A LITTLE WRITING DONE, LIKE THAT.
SURE, SURE. WE'RE GOIN' WELL HERE--
--WON'T BE MORE'N A WEEK BEFORE WE'RE ALL CLOSED IN, AN' THEN ANOTHER MONTH BEFORE SHE'S LIVABLE.
COME AROUND QUITTING TIME, I'LL SHOW YOU WHERE WE'RE AT.
A'COURSE, YOU WANTED TO USE SOME O' THAT SUPER-STRENGTH O' YOURS, YOU COULD HAVE IT POLISHED OFF IN A JIFF, HM?
HAH!
Or maybe not.

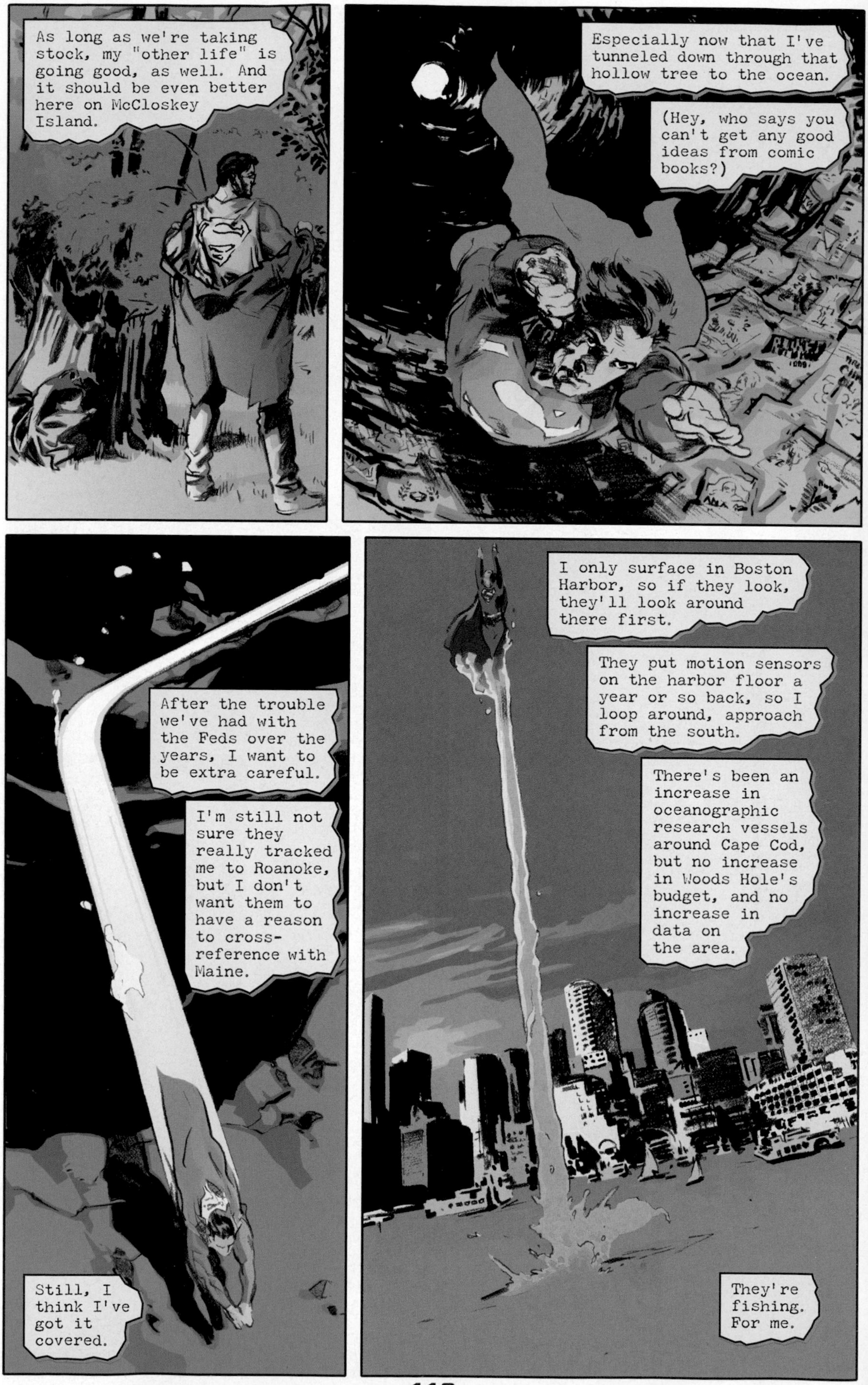
As long as we're taking stock, my "other life" is going good, as well. And it should be even better here on McCloskey Island.
Especially now that I've tunneled down through that hollow tree to the ocean.
(Hey, who says you can't get any good ideas from comic books?)
After the trouble we've had with the Feds over the years, I want to be extra careful.
I'm still not sure they really tracked me to Roanoke, but I don't want them to have a reason to cross-reference with Maine.
Still, I think I've got it covered.
I only surface in Boston Harbor, so if they look, they'll look around there first.
They put motion sensors on the harbor floor a year or so back, so I loop around, approach from the south.
There's been an increase in oceanographic research vessels around Cape Cod, but no increase in Woods Hole's budget, and no increase in data on the area.
They're fishing. For me.

Let them. As long as they're fishing in the wrong waters.

I've helped in seventy fires, over two hundred airplane or car crashes, two earthquakes and an avalanche since we moved.

Lately, though, I've been working on a thing in Africa.

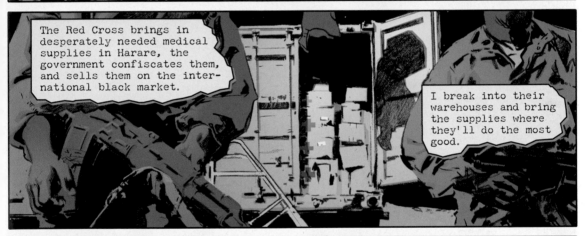

The Red Cross brings in desperately needed medical supplies in Harare, the government confiscates them, and sells them on the international black market.

I break into their warehouses and bring the supplies where they'll do the most good.

The government rails about thieves and vandals, but they know it's something more.

And whenever they send soldiers to reclaim the supplies, I use my heat vision to fuse all their ammo from orbit.

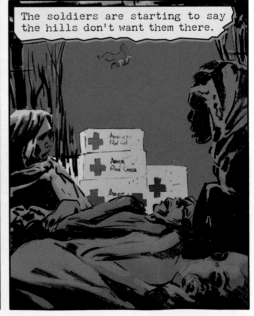

The soldiers are starting to say the hills don't want them there.

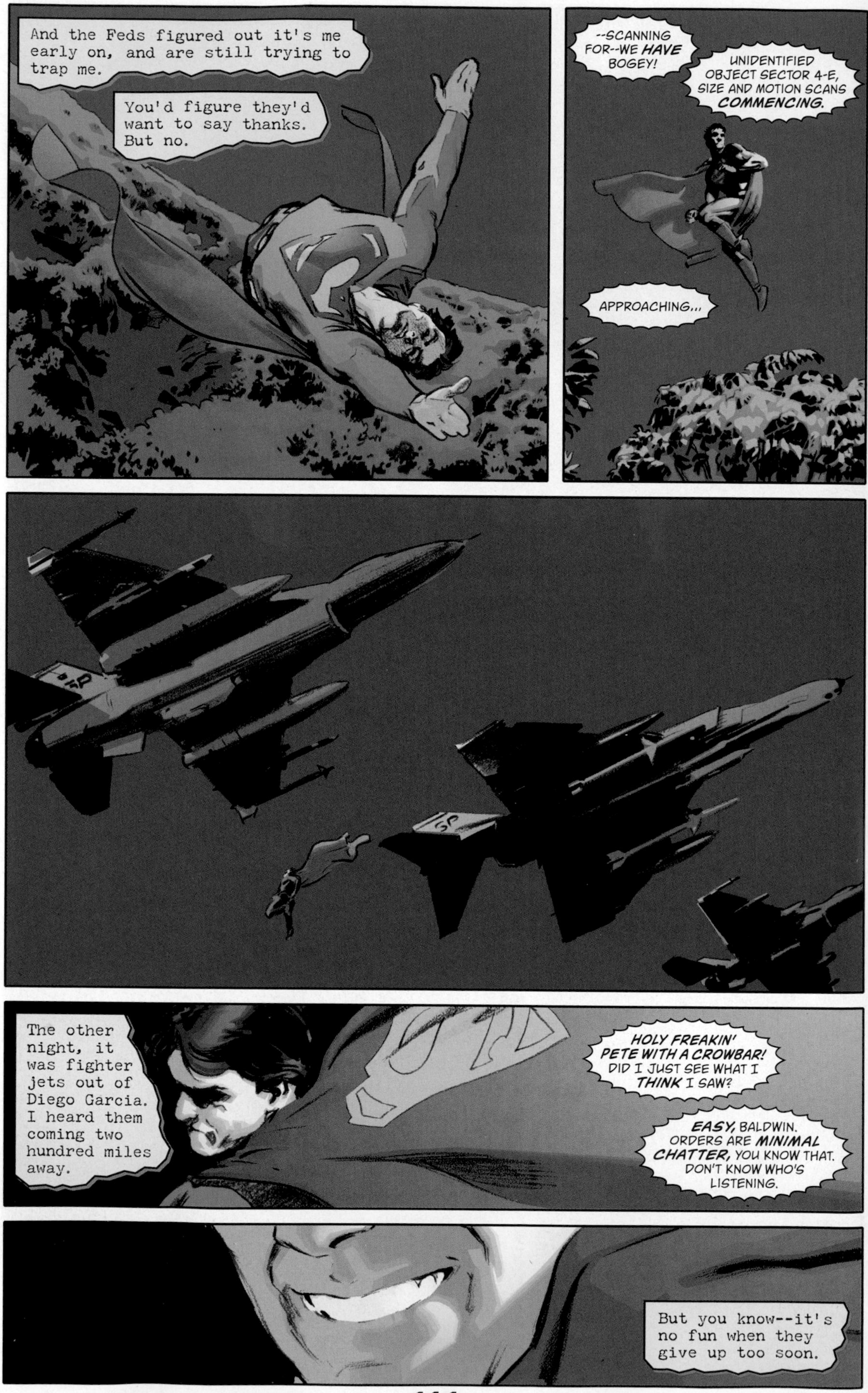
And the Feds figured out it's me early on, and are still trying to trap me.
You'd figure they'd want to say thanks. But no.
--SCANNING FOR--WE HAVE BOGEY!
UNIDENTIFIED OBJECT SECTOR 4-E, SIZE AND MOTION SCANS COMMENCING.
APPROACHING...
The other night, it was fighter jets out of Diego Garcia. I heard them coming two hundred miles away.
HOLY FREAKIN' PETE WITH A CROWBAR! DID I JUST SEE WHAT I THINK I SAW?
EASY, BALDWIN. ORDERS ARE MINIMAL CHATTER, YOU KNOW THAT. DON'T KNOW WHO'S LISTENING.
But you know--it's no fun when they give up too soon.

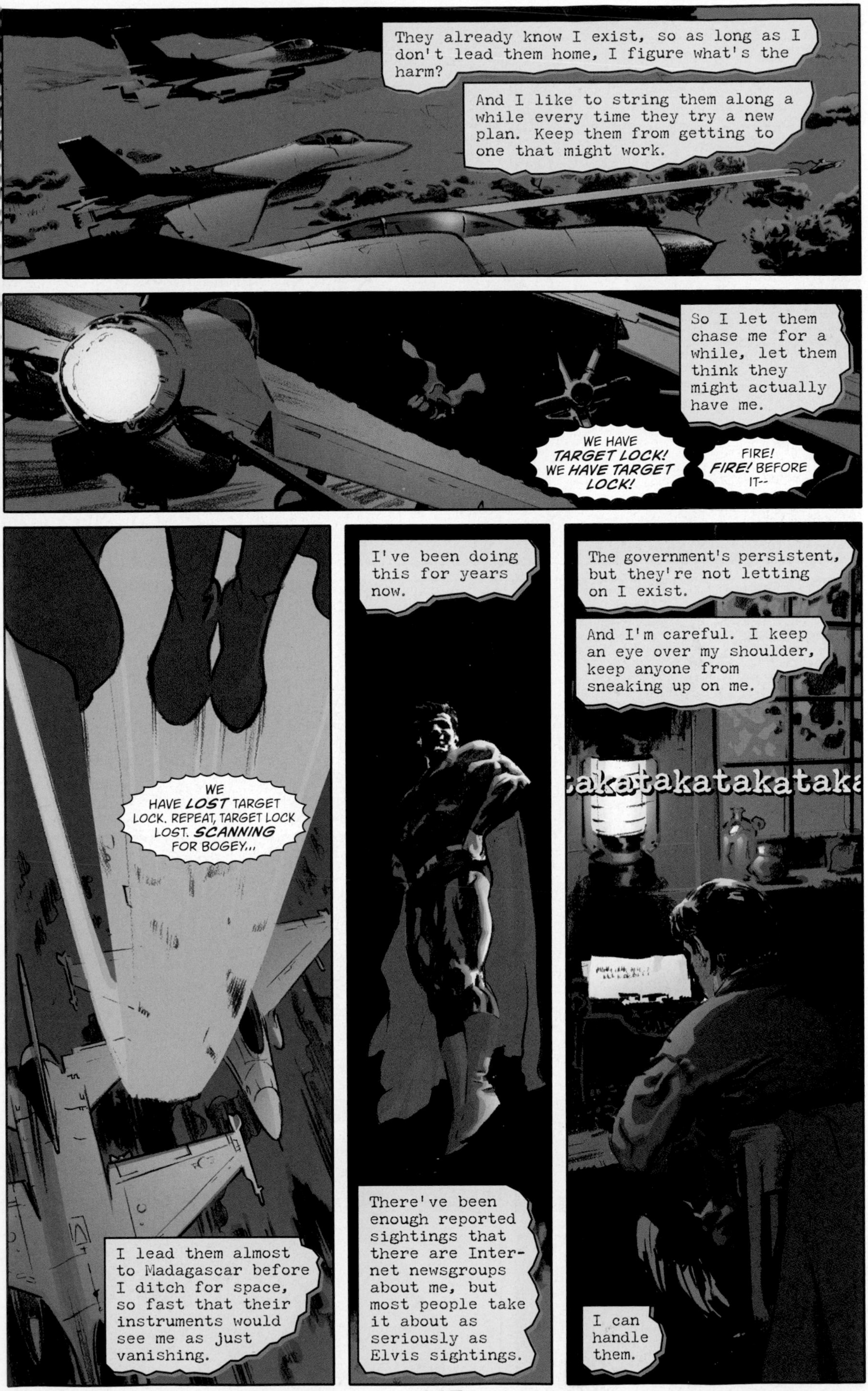
They already know I exist, so as long as I don't lead them home, I figure what's the harm?
And I like to string them along a while every time they try a new plan. Keep them from getting to one that might work.
So I let them chase me for a while, let them think they might actually have me.
WE HAVE TARGET LOCK! WE HAVE TARGET LOCK!
FIRE! FIRE! BEFORE IT--
WE HAVE LOST TARGET LOCK. REPEAT, TARGET LOCK LOST. SCANNING FOR BOGEY...
I lead them almost to Madagascar before I ditch for space, so fast that their instruments would see me as just vanishing.
I've been doing this for years now.
There've been enough reported sightings that there are Internet newsgroups about me, but most people take it about as seriously as Elvis sightings.
The government's persistent, but they're not letting on I exist.
And I'm careful. I keep an eye over my shoulder, keep anyone from sneaking up on me.
takatakatakataka
I can handle them.

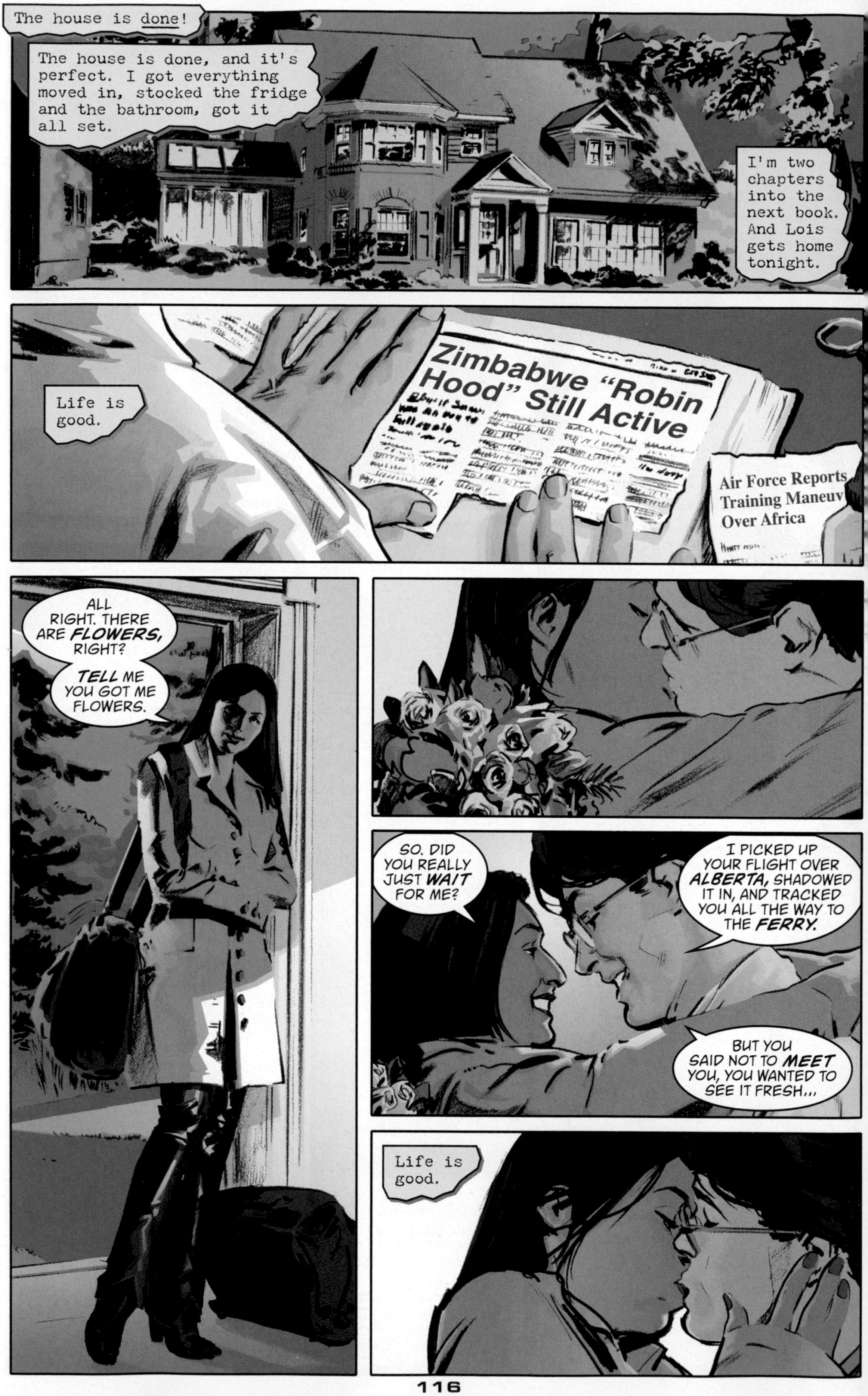
The house is done!
The house is done, and it's perfect. I got everything moved in, stocked the fridge and the bathroom, got it all set.
I'm two chapters into the next book. And Lois gets home tonight.
Life is good.
Zimbabwe "Robin Hood" Still Active
Air Force Reports Training Maneuv Over Africa
ALL RIGHT. THERE ARE FLOWERS, RIGHT?
TELL ME YOU GOT ME FLOWERS.
SO. DID YOU REALLY JUST WAIT FOR ME?
I PICKED UP YOUR FLIGHT OVER ALBERTA, SHADOWED IT IN, AND TRACKED YOU ALL THE WAY TO THE FERRY.
BUT YOU SAID NOT TO MEET YOU, YOU WANTED TO SEE IT FRESH...
Life is good.

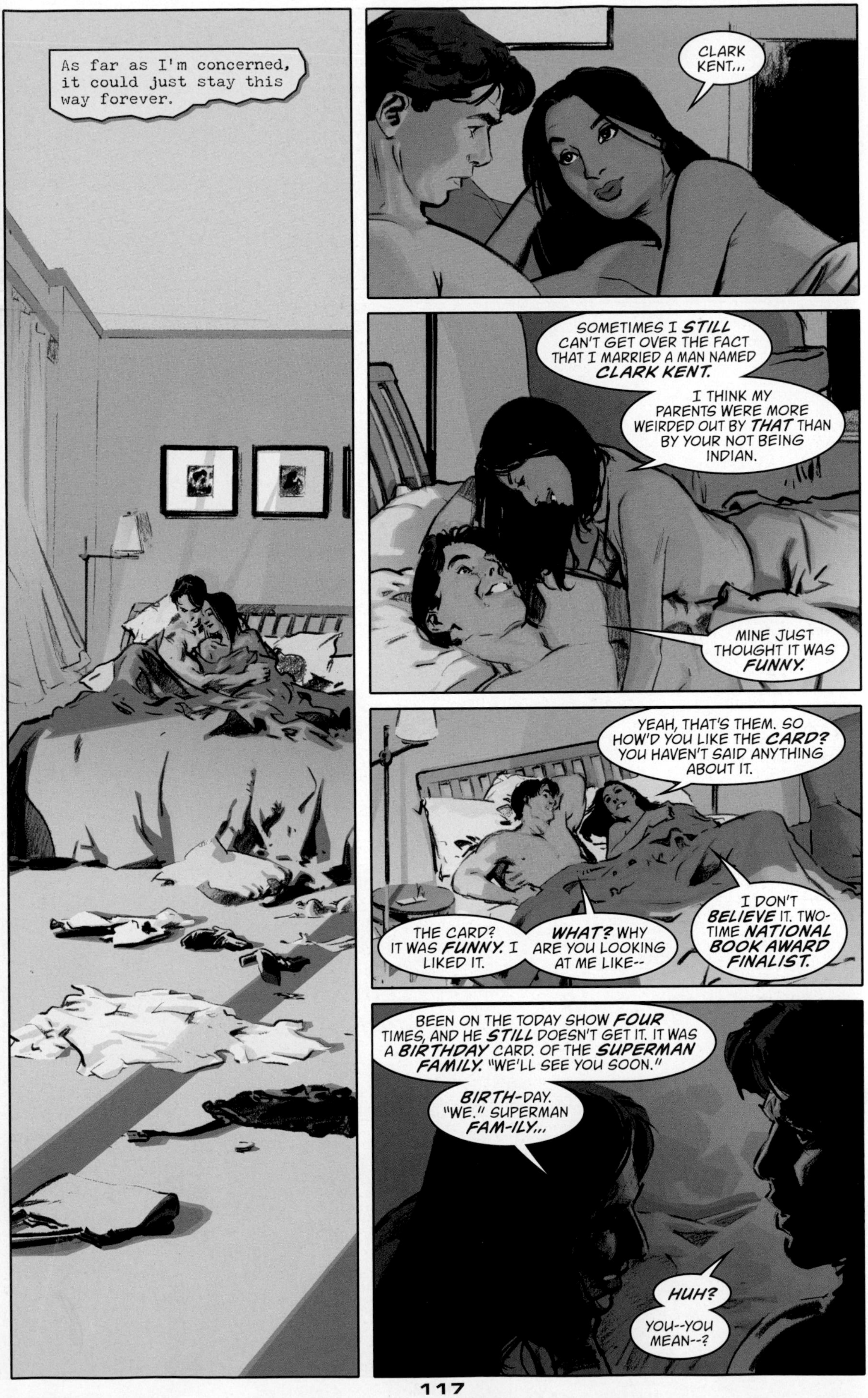
As far as I'm concerned, it could just stay this way forever.
CLARK KENT...
SOMETIMES I STILL CAN'T GET OVER THE FACT THAT I MARRIED A MAN NAMED CLARK KENT.
I THINK MY PARENTS WERE MORE WEIRDED OUT BY THAT THAN BY YOUR NOT BEING INDIAN.
MINE JUST THOUGHT IT WAS FUNNY.
YEAH, THAT'S THEM. SO HOW'D YOU LIKE THE CARD? YOU HAVEN'T SAID ANYTHING ABOUT IT.
THE CARD? IT WAS FUNNY. I LIKED IT.
WHAT? WHY ARE YOU LOOKING AT ME LIKE--
I DON'T BELIEVE IT. TWO-TIME NATIONAL BOOK AWARD FINALIST.
BEEN ON THE TODAY SHOW FOUR TIMES, AND HE STILL DOESN'T GET IT. IT WAS A BIRTHDAY CARD. OF THE SUPERMAN FAMILY. "WE'LL SEE YOU SOON."
BIRTH-DAY. "WE." SUPERMAN FAM-ILY...
HUH?
YOU--YOU MEAN--?

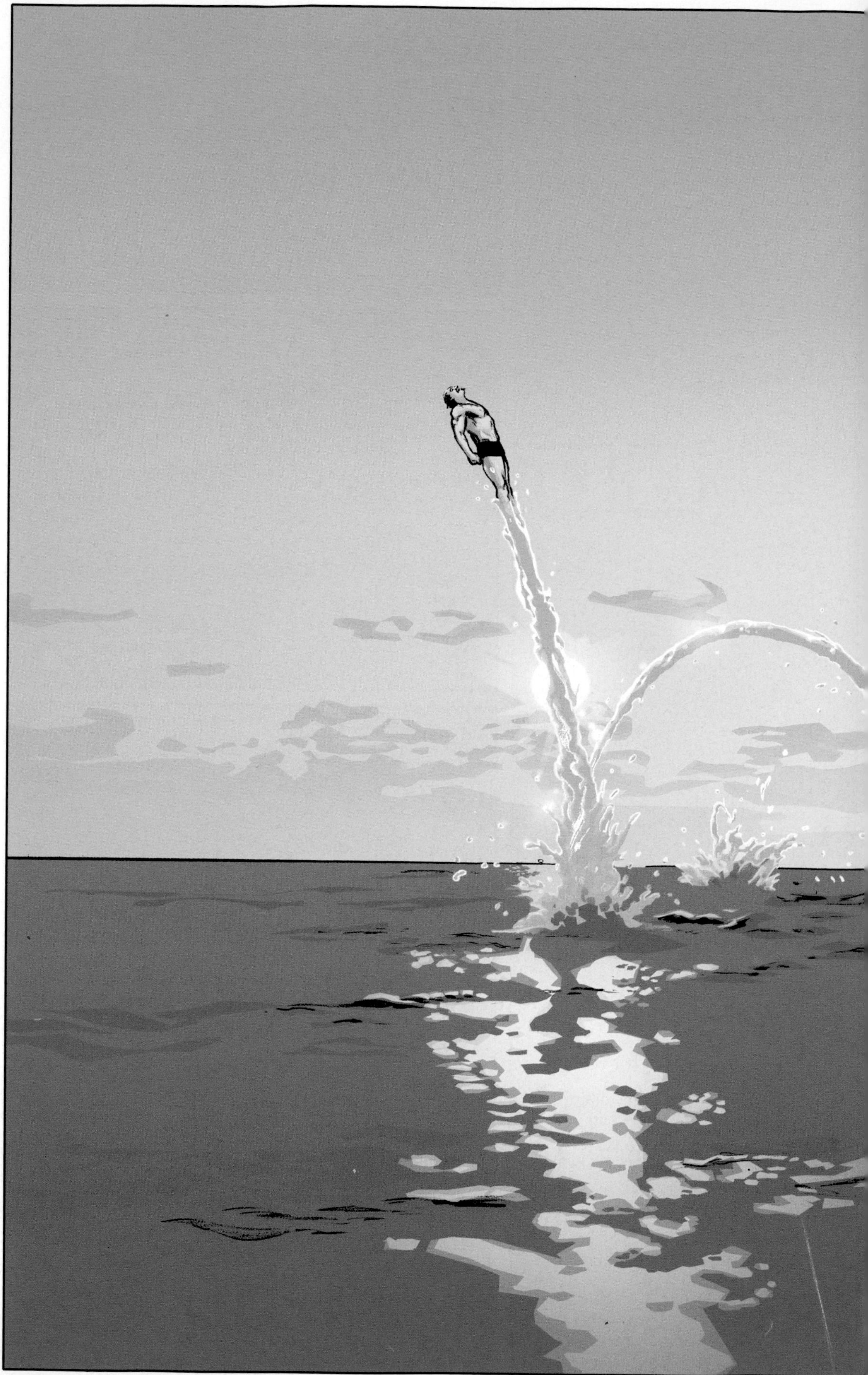

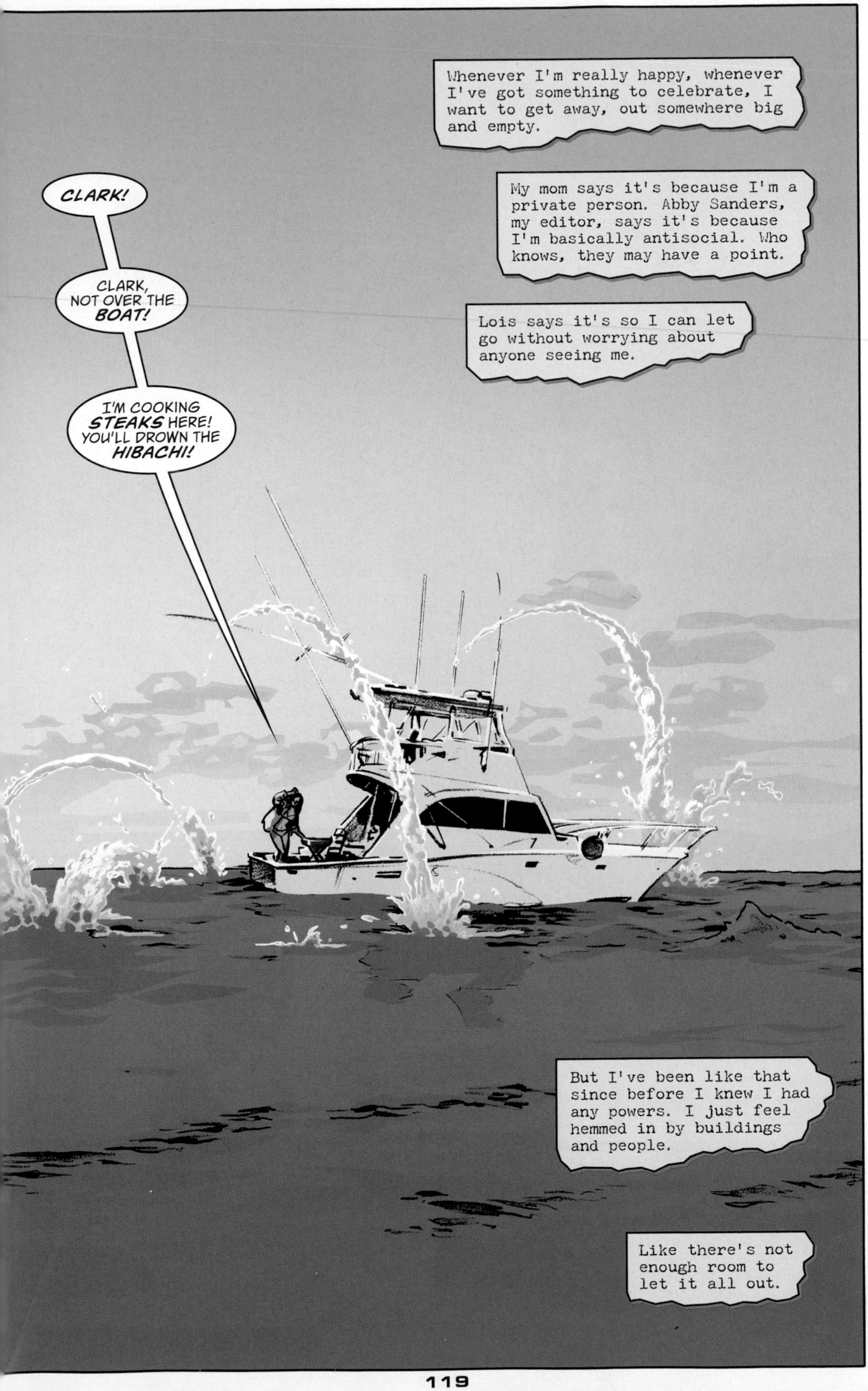
Whenever I'm really happy, whenever I've got something to celebrate, I want to get away, out somewhere big and empty.
My mom says it's because I'm a private person. Abby Sanders, my editor, says it's because I'm basically antisocial. Who knows, they may have a point.
Lois says it's so I can let go without worrying about anyone seeing me.
CLARK!
CLARK, NOT OVER THE BOAT!
I'M COOKING STEAKS HERE! YOU'LL DROWN THE HIBACHI!
But I've been like that since before I knew I had any powers. I just feel hemmed in by buildings and people.
Like there's not enough room to let it all out.

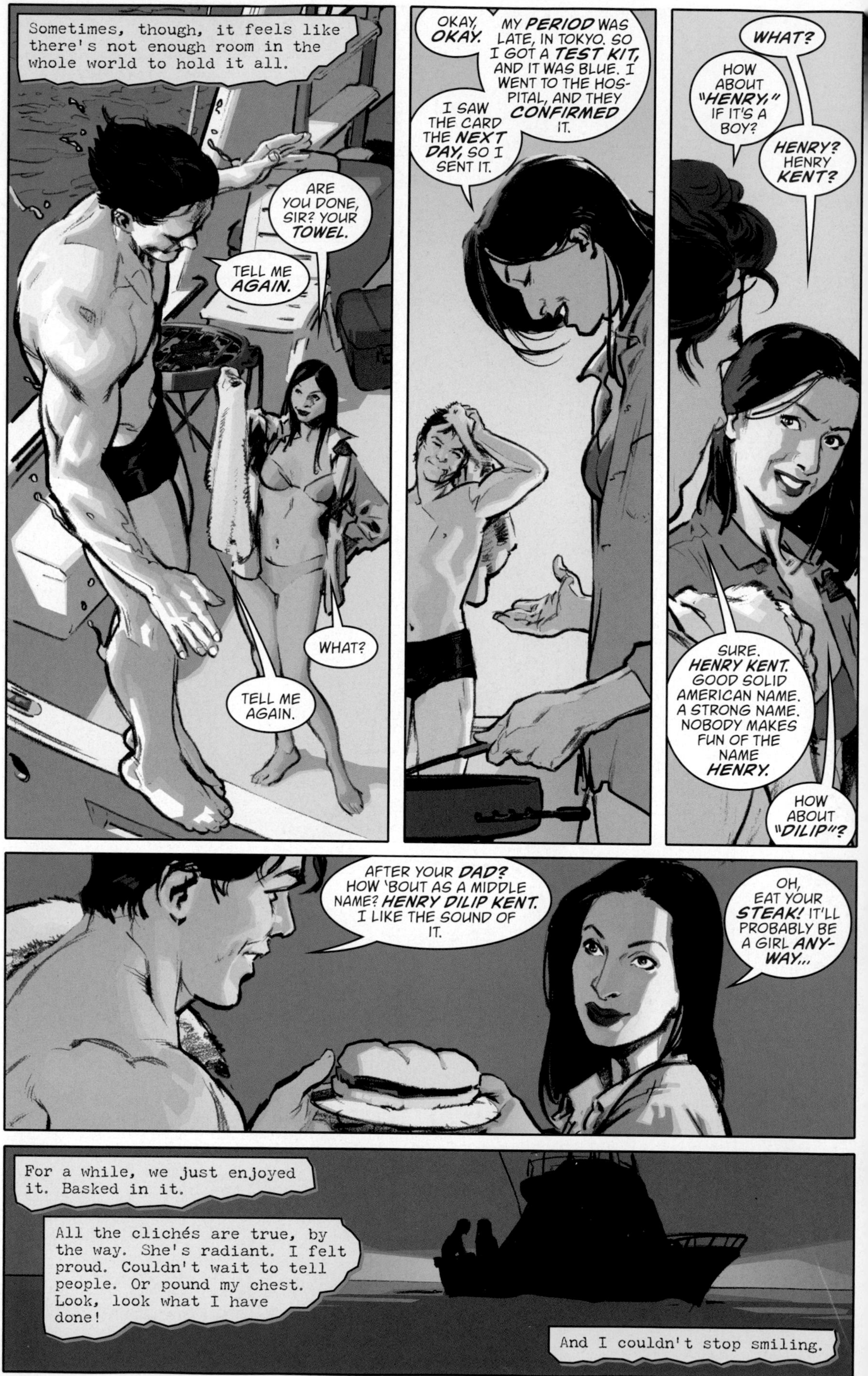
Sometimes, though, it feels like there's not enough room in the whole world to hold it all.
ARE YOU DONE, SIR? YOUR TOWEL.
TELL ME AGAIN.
WHAT?
TELL ME AGAIN.
OKAY, OKAY.
MY PERIOD WAS LATE, IN TOKYO. SO I GOT A TEST KIT, AND IT WAS BLUE. I WENT TO THE HOS-PITAL, AND THEY CONFIRMED IT.
I SAW THE CARD THE NEXT DAY, SO I SENT IT.
HOW ABOUT "HENRY," IF IT'S A BOY?
WHAT?
HENRY? HENRY KENT?
SURE. HENRY KENT. GOOD SOLID AMERICAN NAME. A STRONG NAME. NOBODY MAKES FUN OF THE NAME HENRY.
HOW ABOUT "DILIP"?
AFTER YOUR DAD? HOW 'BOUT AS A MIDDLE NAME? HENRY DILIP KENT. I LIKE THE SOUND OF IT.
OH, EAT YOUR STEAK! IT'LL PROBABLY BE A GIRL ANY-WAY...
For a while, we just enjoyed it. Basked in it.
All the clichés are true, by the way. She's radiant. I felt proud. Couldn't wait to tell people. Or pound my chest. Look, look what I have done!
And I couldn't stop smiling.

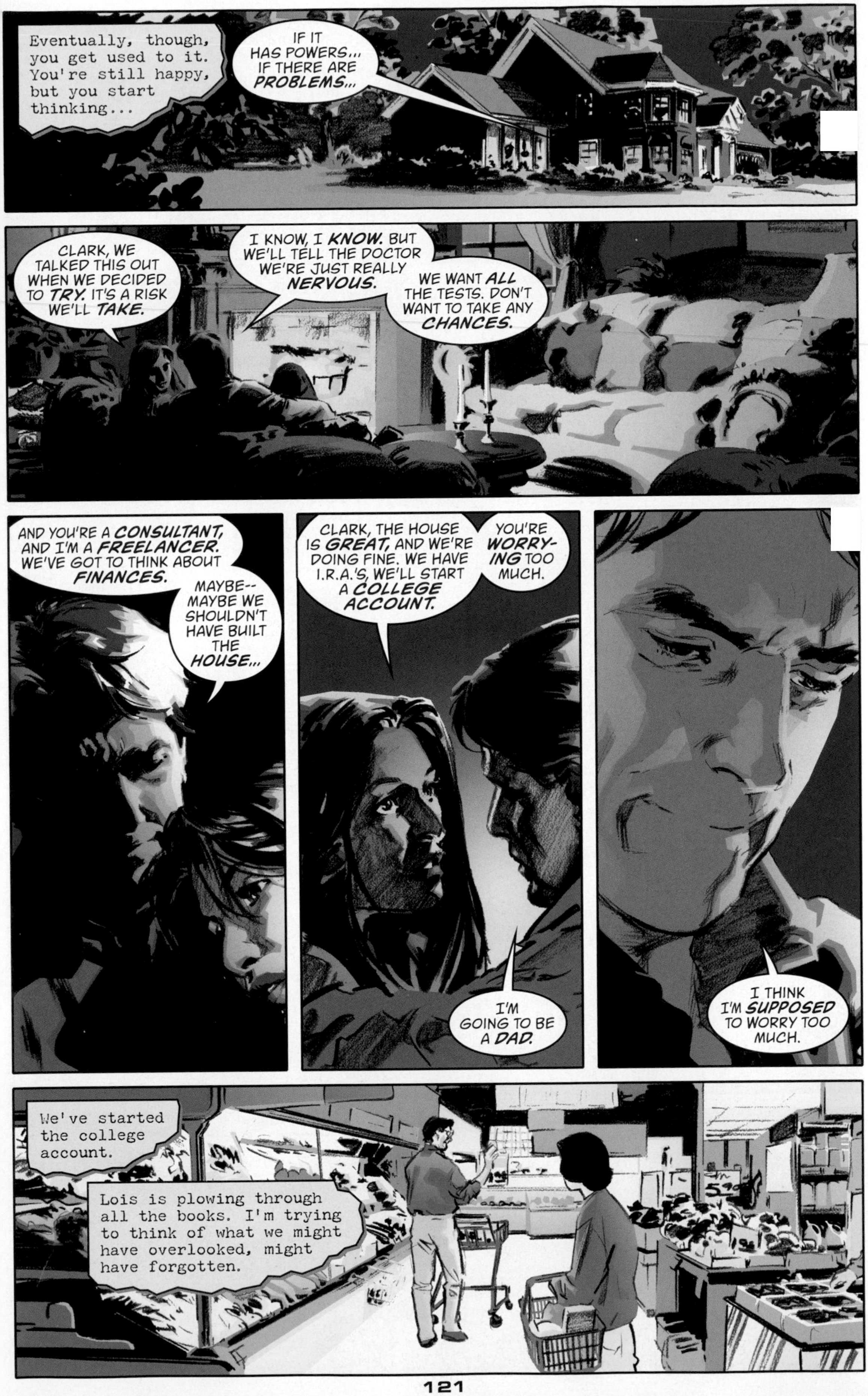
Eventually, though, you get used to it. You're still happy, but you start thinking...
IF IT HAS POWERS... IF THERE ARE PROBLEMS...
CLARK, WE TALKED THIS OUT WHEN WE DECIDED TO TRY. IT'S A RISK WE'LL TAKE.
I KNOW, I KNOW. BUT WE'LL TELL THE DOCTOR WE'RE JUST REALLY NERVOUS.
WE WANT ALL THE TESTS. DON'T WANT TO TAKE ANY CHANCES.
AND YOU'RE A CONSULTANT, AND I'M A FREELANCER. WE'VE GOT TO THINK ABOUT FINANCES.
MAYBE-- MAYBE WE SHOULDN'T HAVE BUILT THE HOUSE...
CLARK, THE HOUSE IS GREAT, AND WE'RE DOING FINE. WE HAVE I.R.A.'S, WE'LL START A COLLEGE ACCOUNT.
YOU'RE WORRYING TOO MUCH.
I'M GOING TO BE A DAD.
I THINK I'M SUPPOSED TO WORRY TOO MUCH.
We've started the college account.
Lois is plowing through all the books. I'm trying to think of what we might have overlooked, might have forgotten.

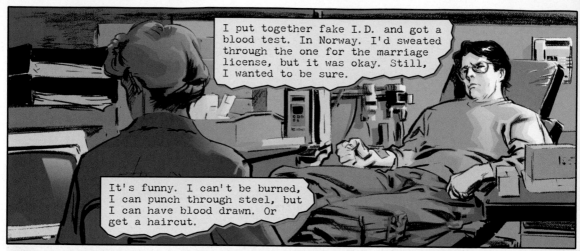

I put together fake I.D. and got a blood test. In Norway. I'd sweated through the one for the marriage license, but it was okay. Still, I wanted to be sure.

It's funny. I can't be burned, I can punch through steel, but I can have blood drawn. Or get a haircut.

I've started scouring the Internet again, UFO sites and more. Looking for any activity around when I was born.

Looking for some clue where I came from, how I got like this.

Not for me, I'm fine how I am. But for him or her. What if we need to know?

We did all the right things.

NOW, DOES EVERYONE HAVE A FOCUS OBJECT?

TWINS?

TWINS?!

LOOK, THERE THEY *ARE...*

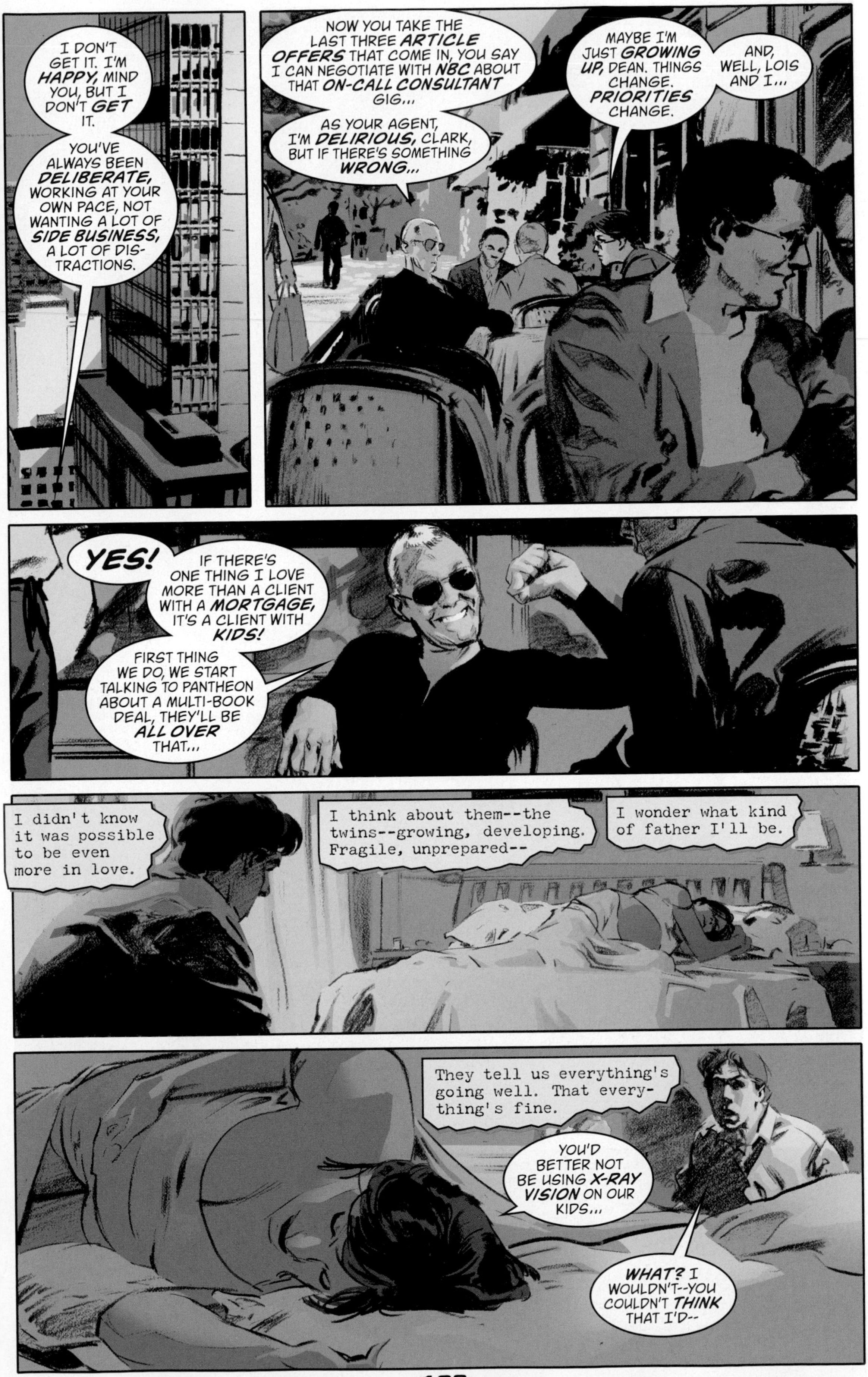

I DON'T GET IT. I'M HAPPY, MIND YOU, BUT I DON'T GET IT.
YOU'VE ALWAYS BEEN DELIBERATE, WORKING AT YOUR OWN PACE, NOT WANTING A LOT OF SIDE BUSINESS, A LOT OF DISTRACTIONS.
NOW YOU TAKE THE LAST THREE ARTICLE OFFERS THAT COME IN, YOU SAY I CAN NEGOTIATE WITH NBC ABOUT THAT ON-CALL CONSULTANT GIG...
AS YOUR AGENT, I'M DELIRIOUS, CLARK, BUT IF THERE'S SOMETHING WRONG...
MAYBE I'M JUST GROWING UP, DEAN. THINGS CHANGE. PRIORITIES CHANGE.
AND, WELL, LOIS AND I...
YES!
IF THERE'S ONE THING I LOVE MORE THAN A CLIENT WITH A MORTGAGE, IT'S A CLIENT WITH KIDS!
FIRST THING WE DO, WE START TALKING TO PANTHEON ABOUT A MULTI-BOOK DEAL, THEY'LL BE ALL OVER THAT...
I didn't know it was possible to be even more in love.
I think about them--the twins--growing, developing. Fragile, unprepared--
I wonder what kind of father I'll be.
They tell us everything's going well. That everything's fine.
YOU'D BETTER NOT BE USING X-RAY VISION ON OUR KIDS...
WHAT? I WOULDN'T--YOU COULDN'T THINK THAT I'D--

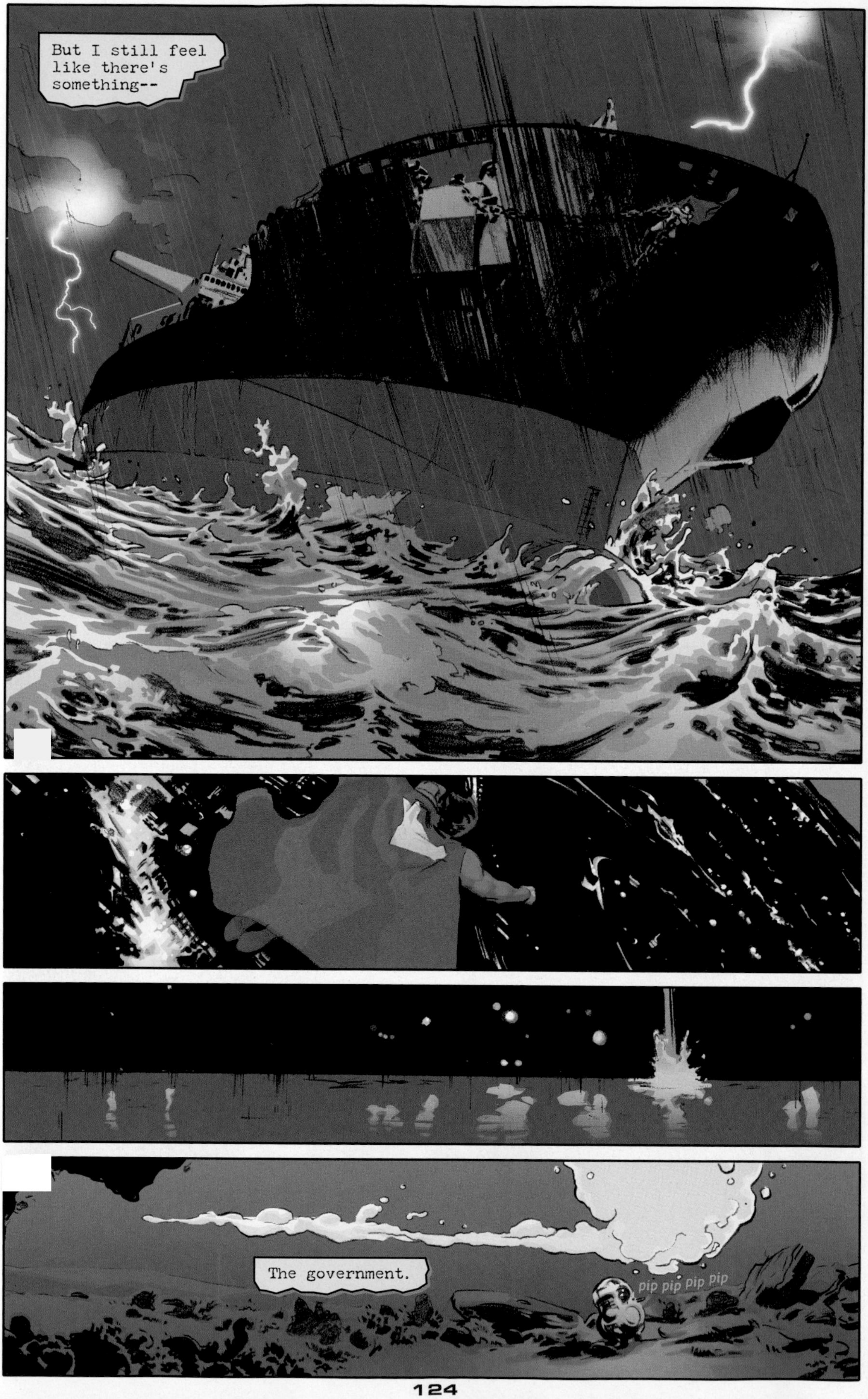
But I still feel like there's something--
The government.
pip pip pip pip

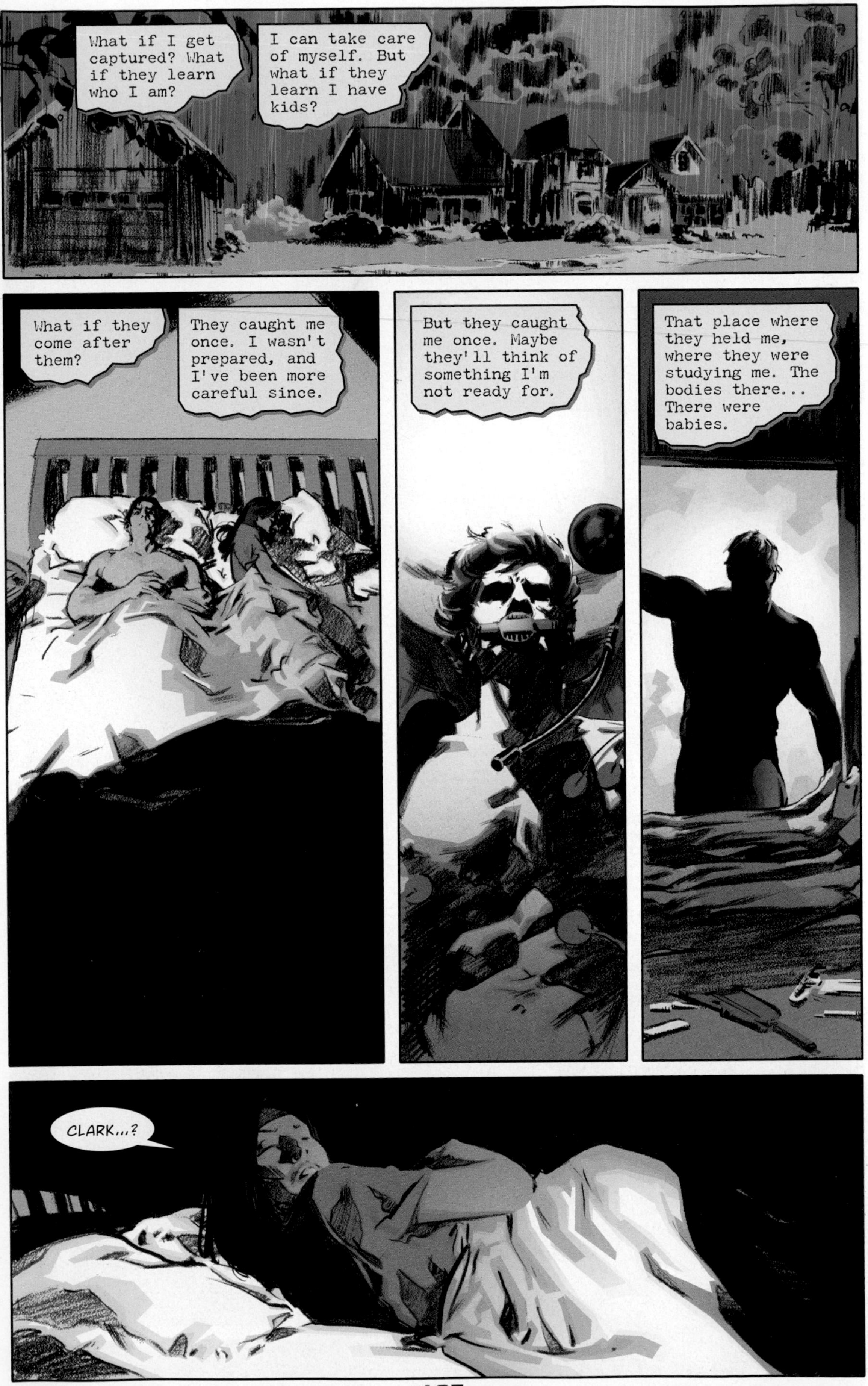
What if I get captured? What if they learn who I am?
I can take care of myself. But what if they learn I have kids?
What if they come after them?
They caught me once. I wasn't prepared, and I've been more careful since.
But they caught me once. Maybe they'll think of something I'm not ready for.
That place where they held me, where they were studying me. The bodies there... There were babies.
CLARK...?

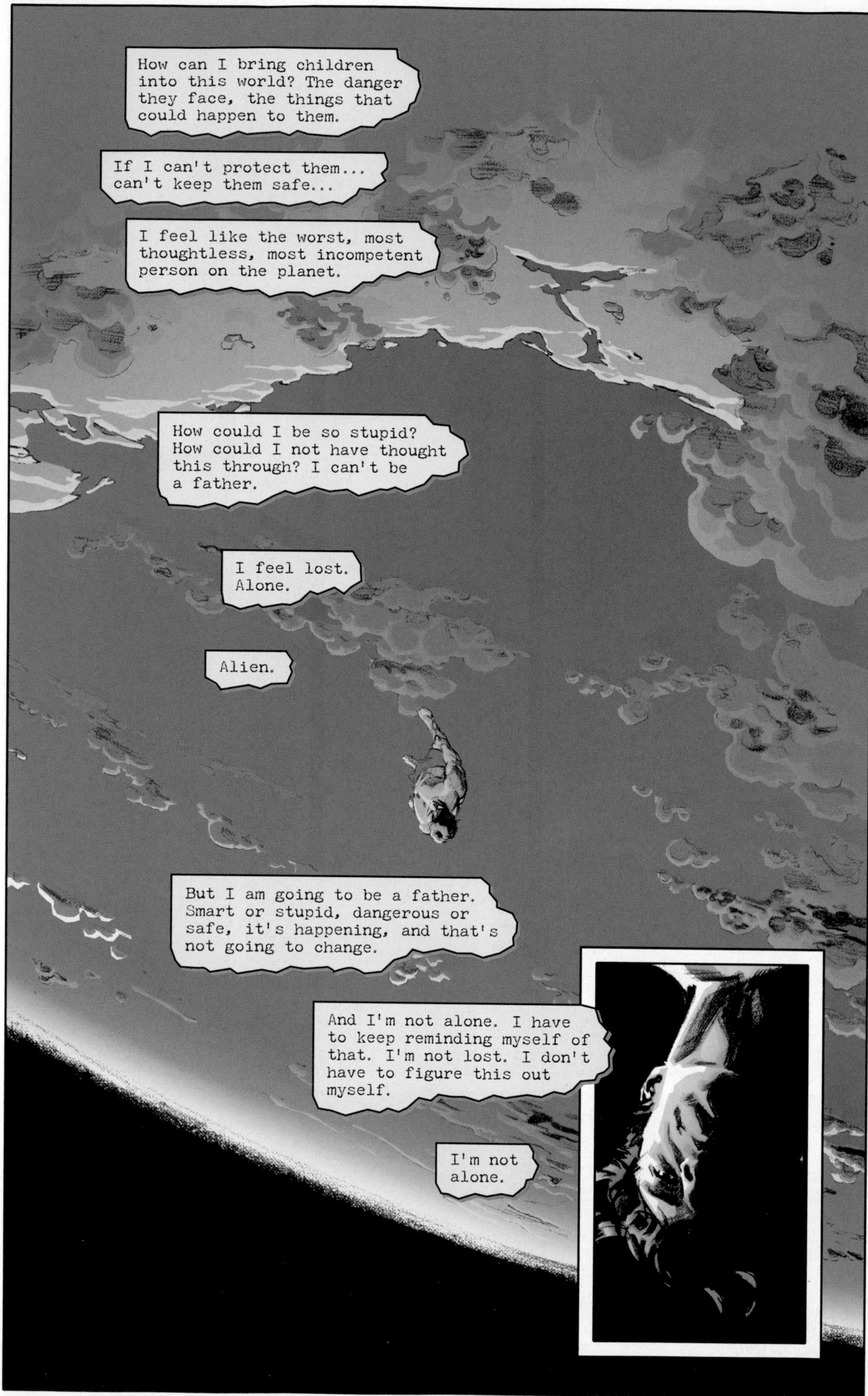
How can I bring children into this world? The danger they face, the things that could happen to them.
If I can't protect them... can't keep them safe...
I feel like the worst, most thoughtless, most incompetent person on the planet.
How could I be so stupid? How could I not have thought this through? I can't be a father.
I feel lost. Alone.
Alien.
But I am going to be a father. Smart or stupid, dangerous or safe, it's happening, and that's not going to change.
And I'm not alone. I have to keep reminding myself of that. I'm not lost. I don't have to figure this out myself.
I'm not alone.

I COULD **STOP.**

IF THEY DON'T HAVE ANY- ONE TO **LOOK FOR,** THERE'S NOTHING TO FIND.

NO, NO-- YOU CAN'T DO **THAT.**

BUT--

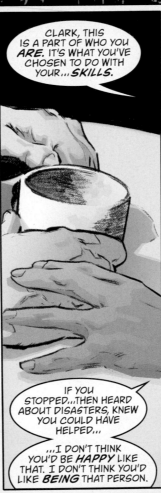

CLARK, THIS IS A PART OF WHO YOU **ARE.** IT'S WHAT YOU'VE CHOSEN TO DO WITH YOUR...**SKILLS.**

IF YOU STOPPED...THEN HEARD ABOUT DISASTERS, KNEW YOU COULD HAVE HELPED...

...I DON'T THINK YOU'D BE **HAPPY** LIKE THAT. I DON'T THINK YOU'D LIKE **BEING** THAT PERSON.

OKAY. I KNOW THAT **TOO,** I GUESS.

BUT...IT'S ONE THING TO RISK **MYSELF.** AND YOU...THEY WOULDN'T **CUT YOU UP,** WOULDN'T RUN TESTS ON YOU. I HOPE.

BUT OUR **CHILDREN**...

THIS CAN'T BE A **GAME** ANYMORE. EVEN IF I THINK I'LL KEEP WINNING, THE STAKES ARE **TOO HIGH.** I HAVE TO **DO** SOME- THING.

I HAVE TO GET THE GOVERNMENT **OFF MY BACK.**

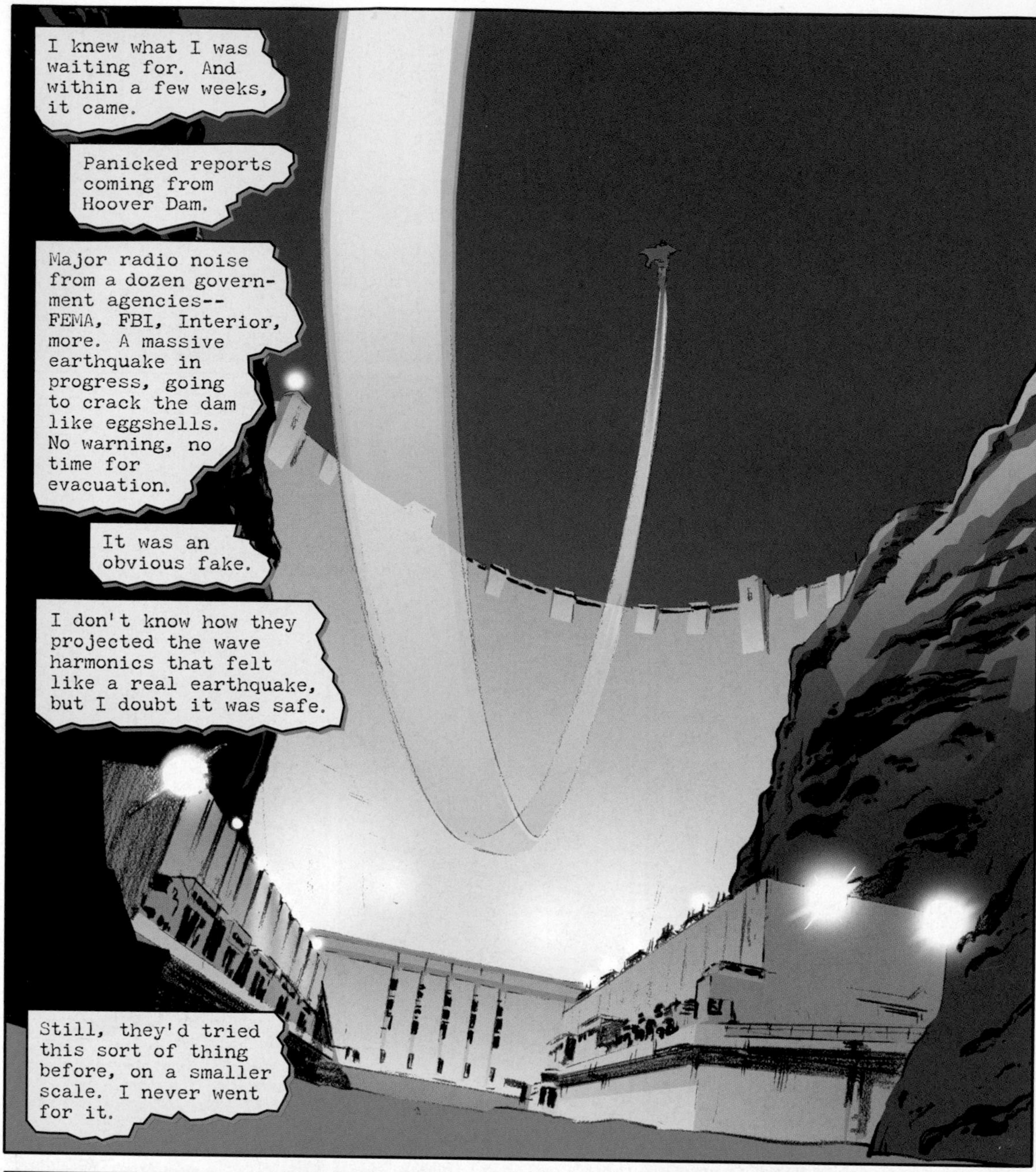
I knew what I was waiting for. And within a few weeks, it came.
Panicked reports coming from Hoover Dam.
Major radio noise from a dozen government agencies--FEMA, FBI, Interior, more. A massive earthquake in progress, going to crack the dam like eggshells. No warning, no time for evacuation.
It was an obvious fake.
I don't know how they projected the wave harmonics that felt like a real earthquake, but I doubt it was safe.
Still, they'd tried this sort of thing before, on a smaller scale. I never went for it.

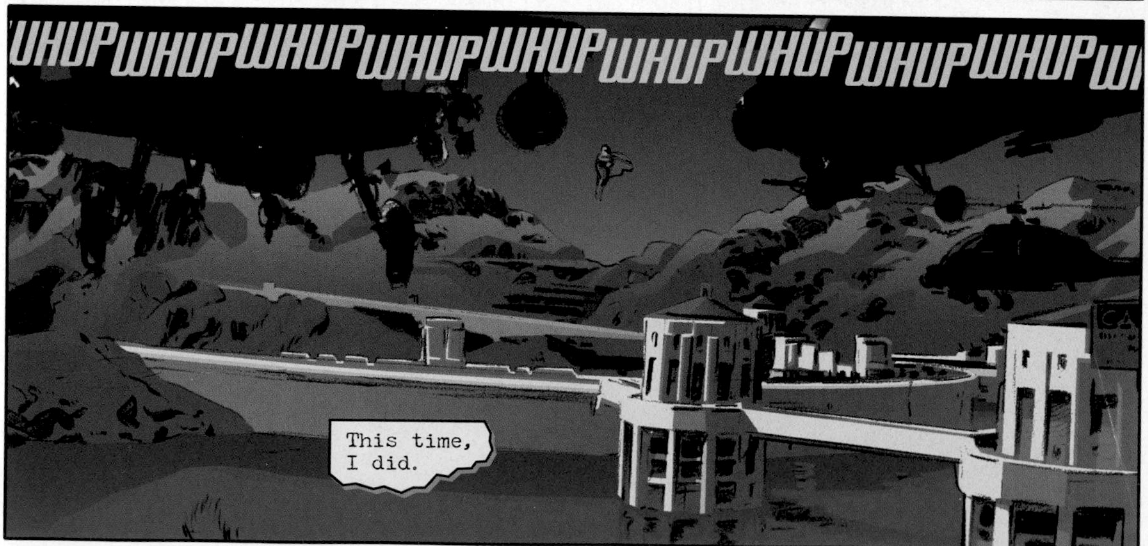
WHUPWHUPWHUPWHUPWHUPWHUPWHUPWHUPWHUP
This time, I did.

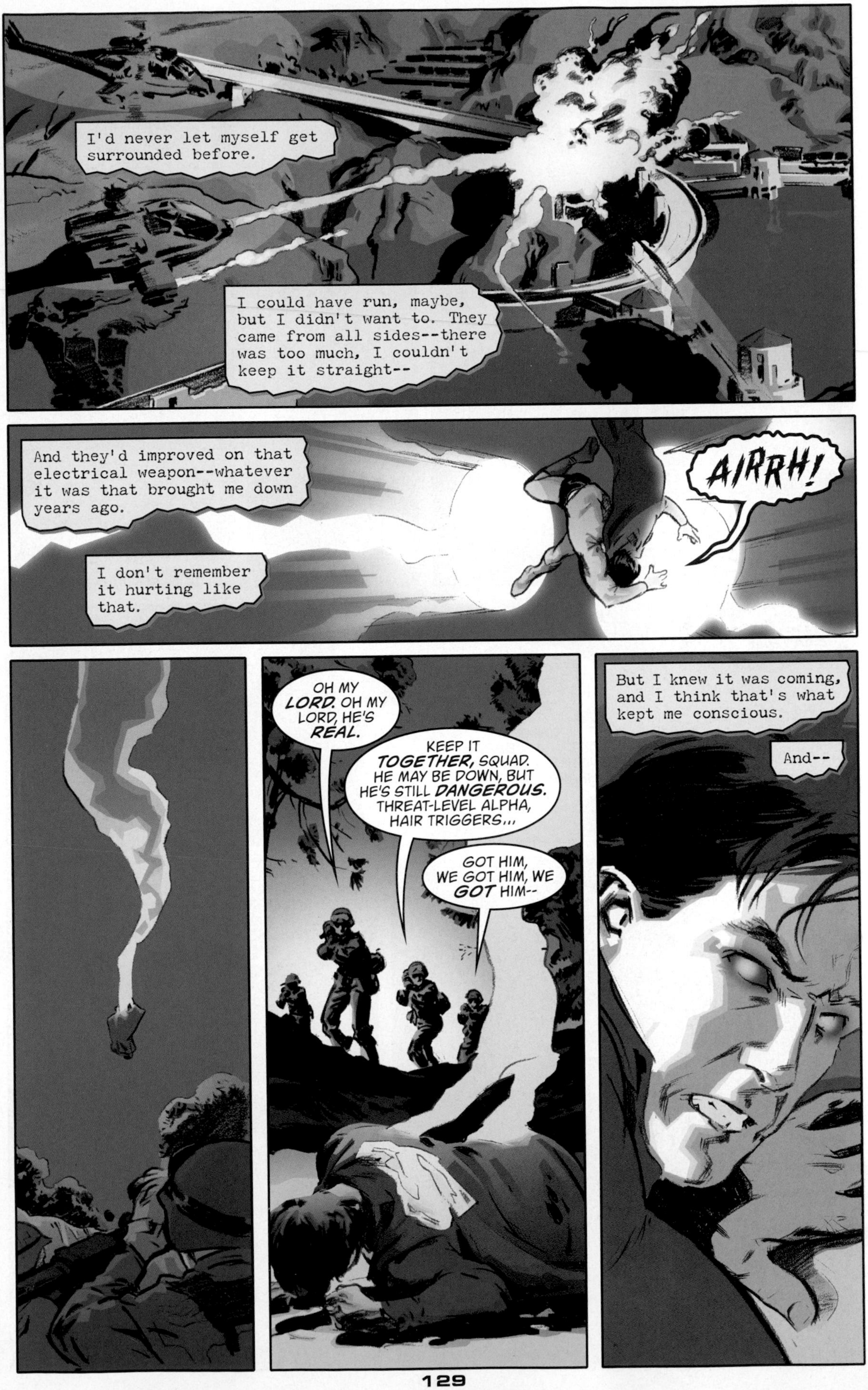

I'd never let myself get surrounded before.
I could have run, maybe, but I didn't want to. They came from all sides--there was too much, I couldn't keep it straight--
And they'd improved on that electrical weapon--whatever it was that brought me down years ago.
I don't remember it hurting like that.
AIRRH!
OH MY LORD. OH MY LORD, HE'S REAL.
KEEP IT TOGETHER, SQUAD. HE MAY BE DOWN, BUT HE'S STILL DANGEROUS. THREAT-LEVEL ALPHA, HAIR TRIGGERS...
GOT HIM, WE GOT HIM, WE GOT HIM--
But I knew it was coming, and I think that's what kept me conscious.
And--

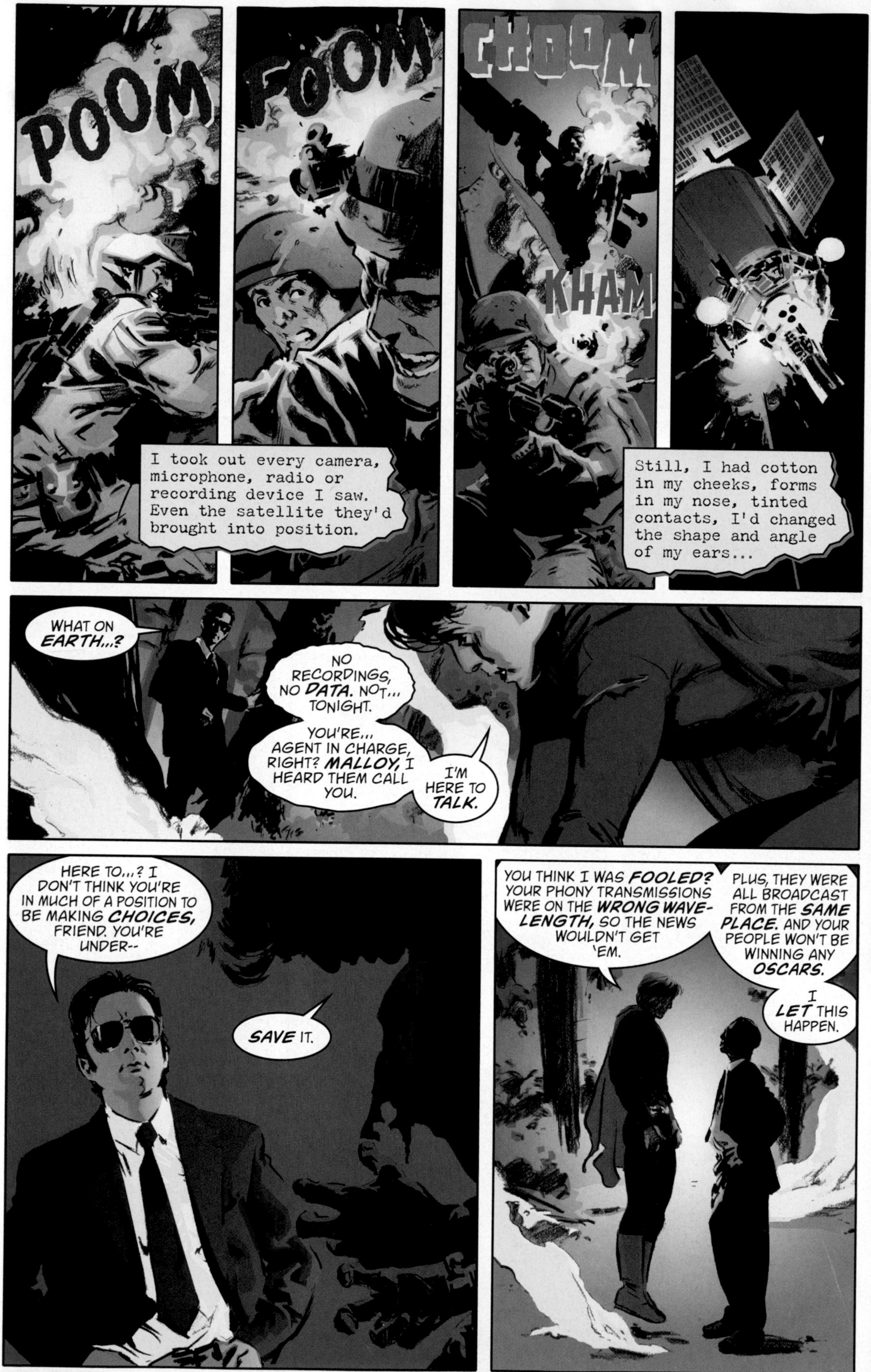
POOM
FOOM
CHOOM
KHAM
I took out every camera, microphone, radio or recording device I saw. Even the satellite they'd brought into position.
Still, I had cotton in my cheeks, forms in my nose, tinted contacts, I'd changed the shape and angle of my ears...
WHAT ON EARTH...?
NO RECORDINGS, NO DATA. NOT... TONIGHT.
YOU'RE... AGENT IN CHARGE, RIGHT? MALLOY, I HEARD THEM CALL YOU.
I'M HERE TO TALK.
HERE TO...? I DON'T THINK YOU'RE IN MUCH OF A POSITION TO BE MAKING CHOICES, FRIEND. YOU'RE UNDER--
SAVE IT.
YOU THINK I WAS FOOLED? YOUR PHONY TRANSMISSIONS WERE ON THE WRONG WAVE-LENGTH, SO THE NEWS WOULDN'T GET 'EM.
PLUS, THEY WERE ALL BROADCAST FROM THE SAME PLACE. AND YOUR PEOPLE WON'T BE WINNING ANY OSCARS.
I LET THIS HAPPEN.

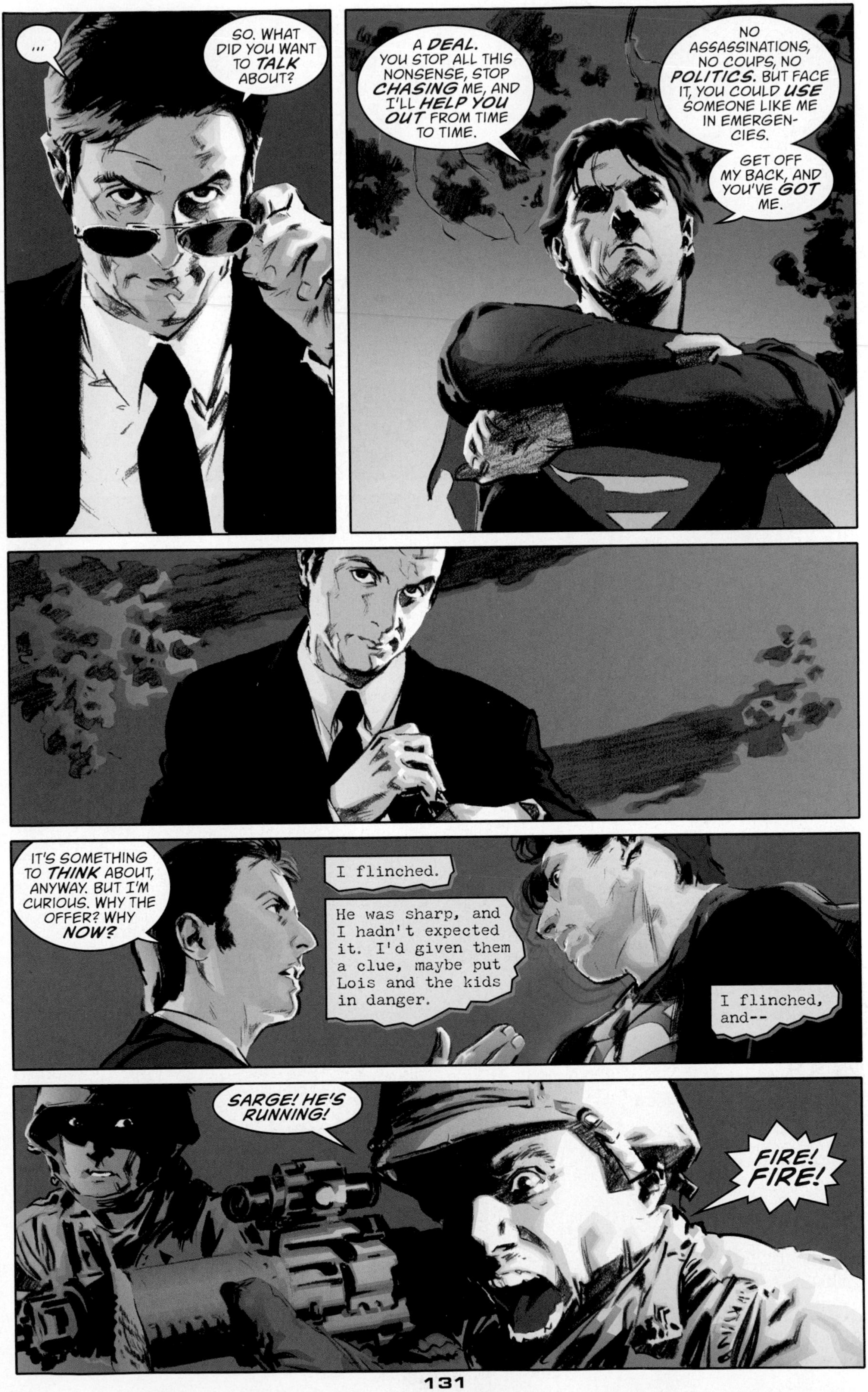
...
SO. WHAT DID YOU WANT TO TALK ABOUT?
A DEAL. YOU STOP ALL THIS NONSENSE, STOP CHASING ME, AND I'LL HELP YOU OUT FROM TIME TO TIME.
NO ASSASSINATIONS, NO COUPS, NO POLITICS. BUT FACE IT, YOU COULD USE SOMEONE LIKE ME IN EMERGEN-CIES.
GET OFF MY BACK, AND YOU'VE GOT ME.
IT'S SOMETHING TO THINK ABOUT, ANYWAY. BUT I'M CURIOUS. WHY THE OFFER? WHY NOW?
I flinched.
He was sharp, and I hadn't expected it. I'd given them a clue, maybe put Lois and the kids in danger.
I flinched, and--
SARGE! HE'S RUNNING!
FIRE! FIRE!

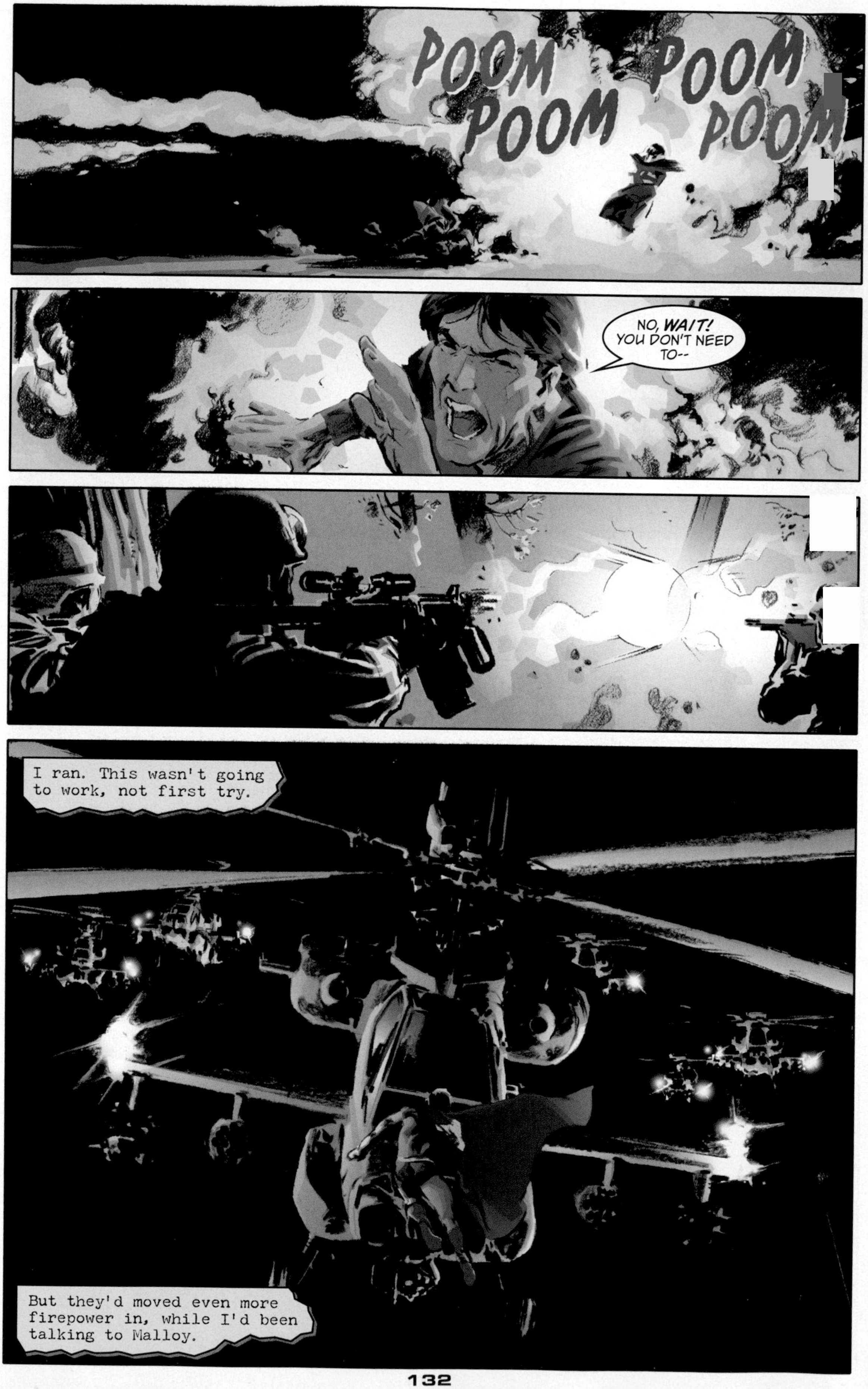
POOM POOM
POOM POOM
NO, WAIT! YOU DON'T NEED TO--
I ran. This wasn't going to work, not first try.
But they'd moved even more firepower in, while I'd been talking to Malloy.

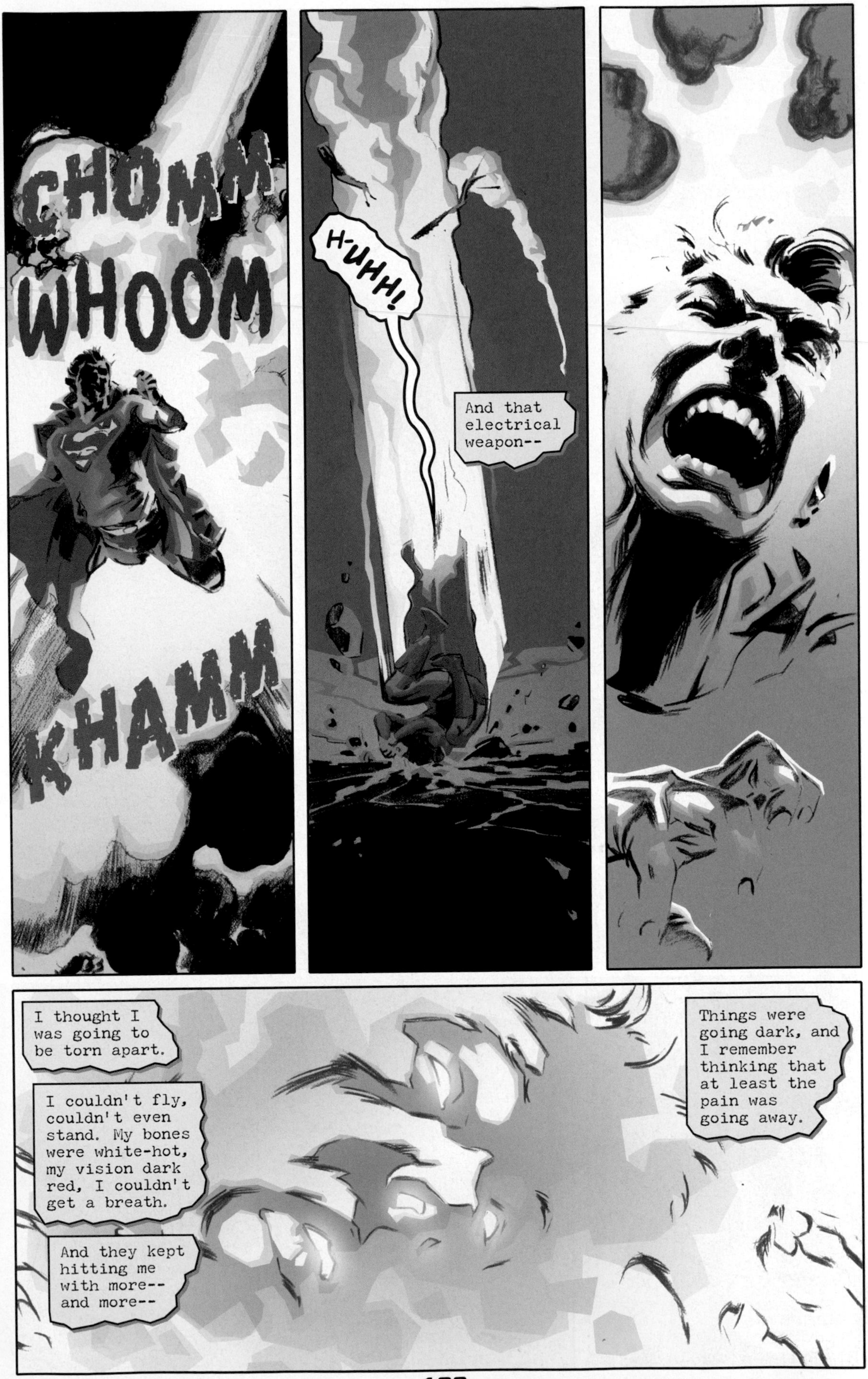
CHOMM
WHOOM
KHAMM
H-UHH!
And that electrical weapon--
I thought I was going to be torn apart.
I couldn't fly, couldn't even stand. My bones were white-hot, my vision dark red, I couldn't get a breath.
And they kept hitting me with more-- and more--
Things were going dark, and I remember thinking that at least the pain was going away.

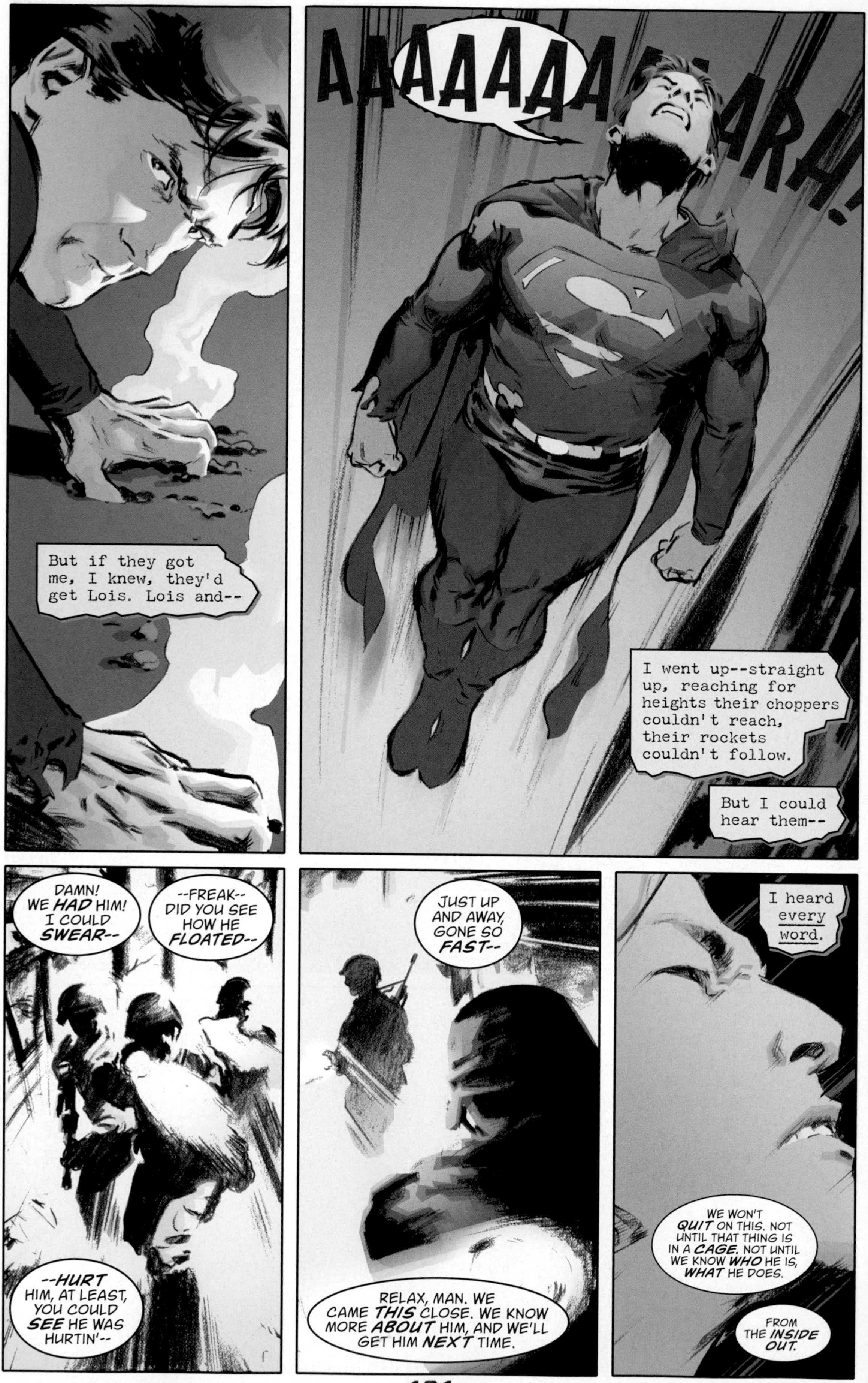

But if they got me, I knew, they'd get Lois. Lois and--
AAAAAAAAARRH!
I went up--straight up, reaching for heights their choppers couldn't reach, their rockets couldn't follow.
But I could hear them--
DAMN! WE HAD HIM! I COULD SWEAR--
--FREAK-- DID YOU SEE HOW HE FLOATED--
--HURT HIM, AT LEAST, YOU COULD SEE HE WAS HURTIN'--
JUST UP AND AWAY, GONE SO FAST--
RELAX, MAN. WE CAME THIS CLOSE. WE KNOW MORE ABOUT HIM, AND WE'LL GET HIM NEXT TIME.
I heard every word.
WE WON'T QUIT ON THIS. NOT UNTIL THAT THING IS IN A CAGE. NOT UNTIL WE KNOW WHO HE IS, WHAT HE DOES.
FROM THE INSIDE OUT.

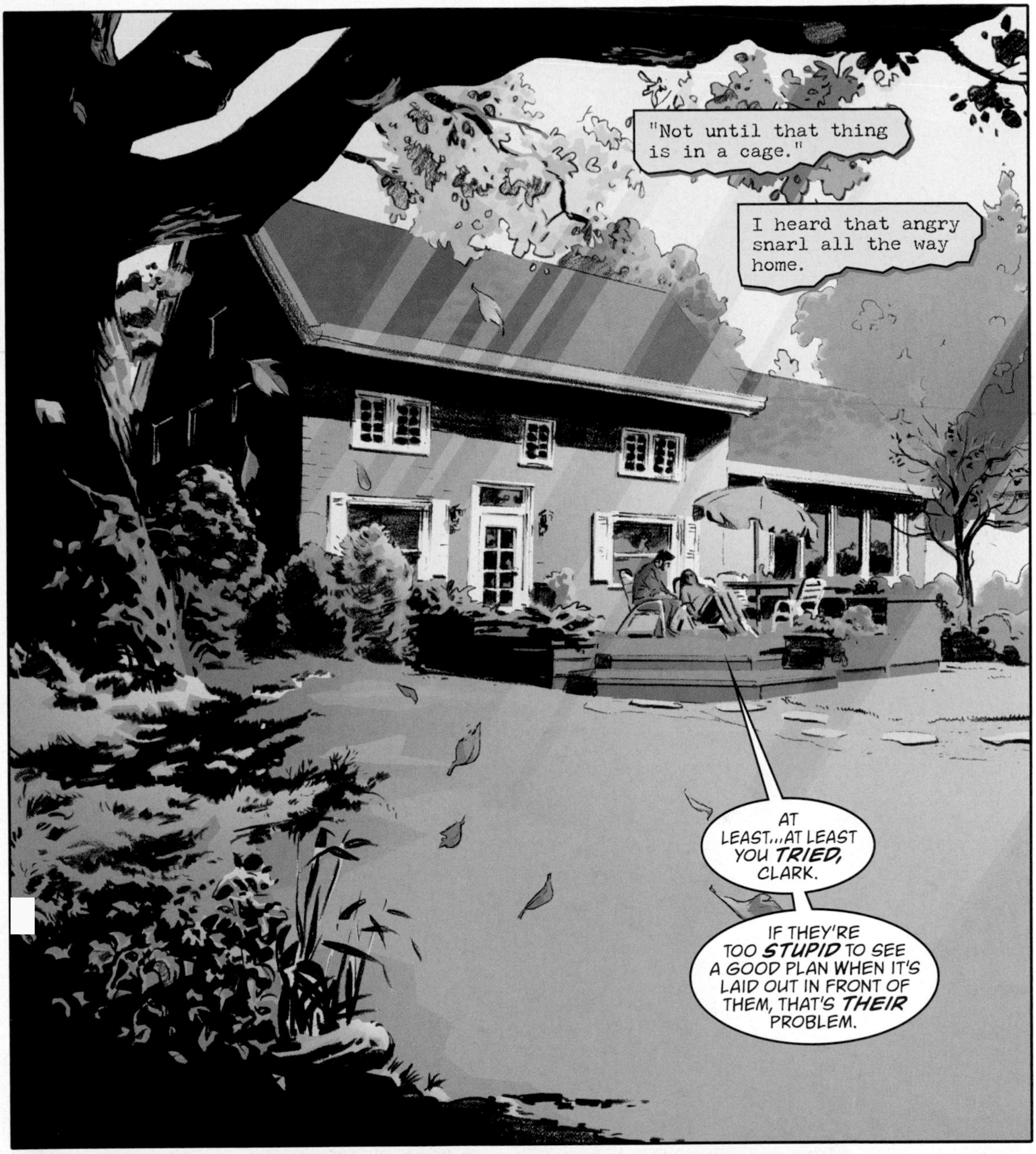
"Not until that thing is in a cage."
I heard that angry snarl all the way home.
AT LEAST...AT LEAST YOU TRIED, CLARK.
IF THEY'RE TOO STUPID TO SEE A GOOD PLAN WHEN IT'S LAID OUT IN FRONT OF THEM, THAT'S THEIR PROBLEM.

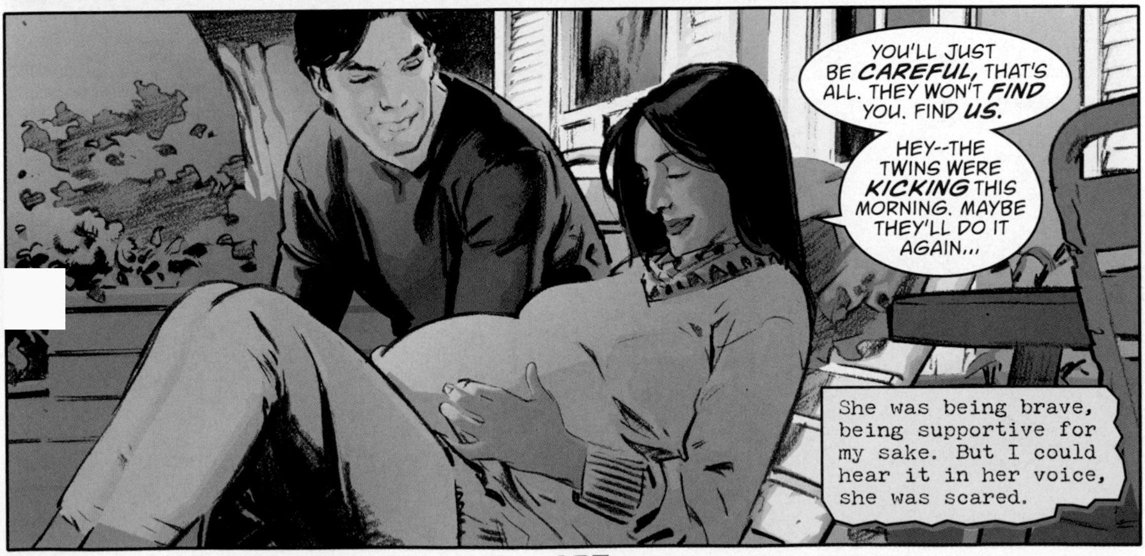
YOU'LL JUST BE CAREFUL, THAT'S ALL. THEY WON'T FIND YOU. FIND US.
HEY--THE TWINS WERE KICKING THIS MORNING. MAYBE THEY'LL DO IT AGAIN...
She was being brave, being supportive for my sake. But I could hear it in her voice, she was scared.

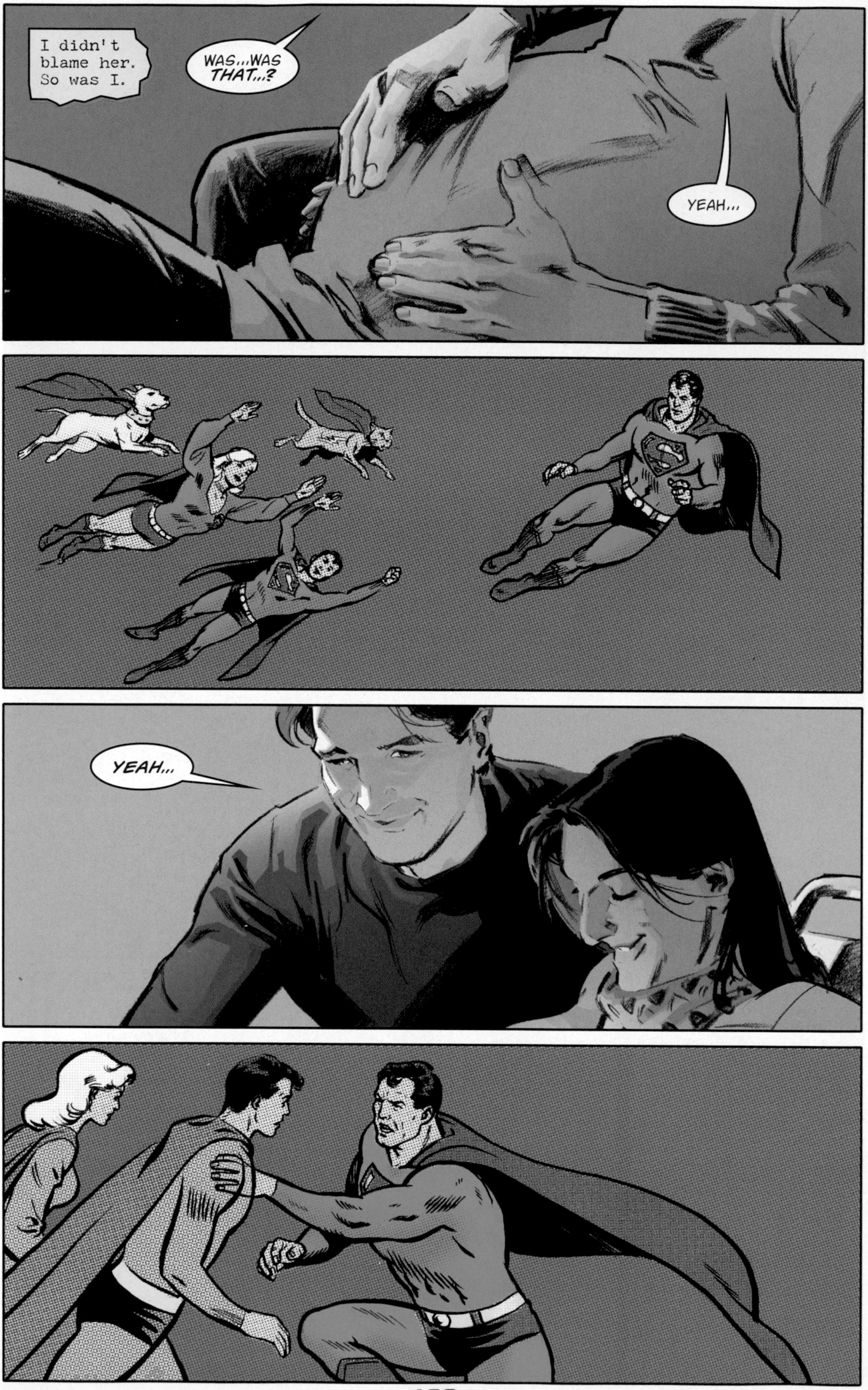
I didn't blame her. So was I.
WAS...WAS THAT...?
YEAH...
YEAH...

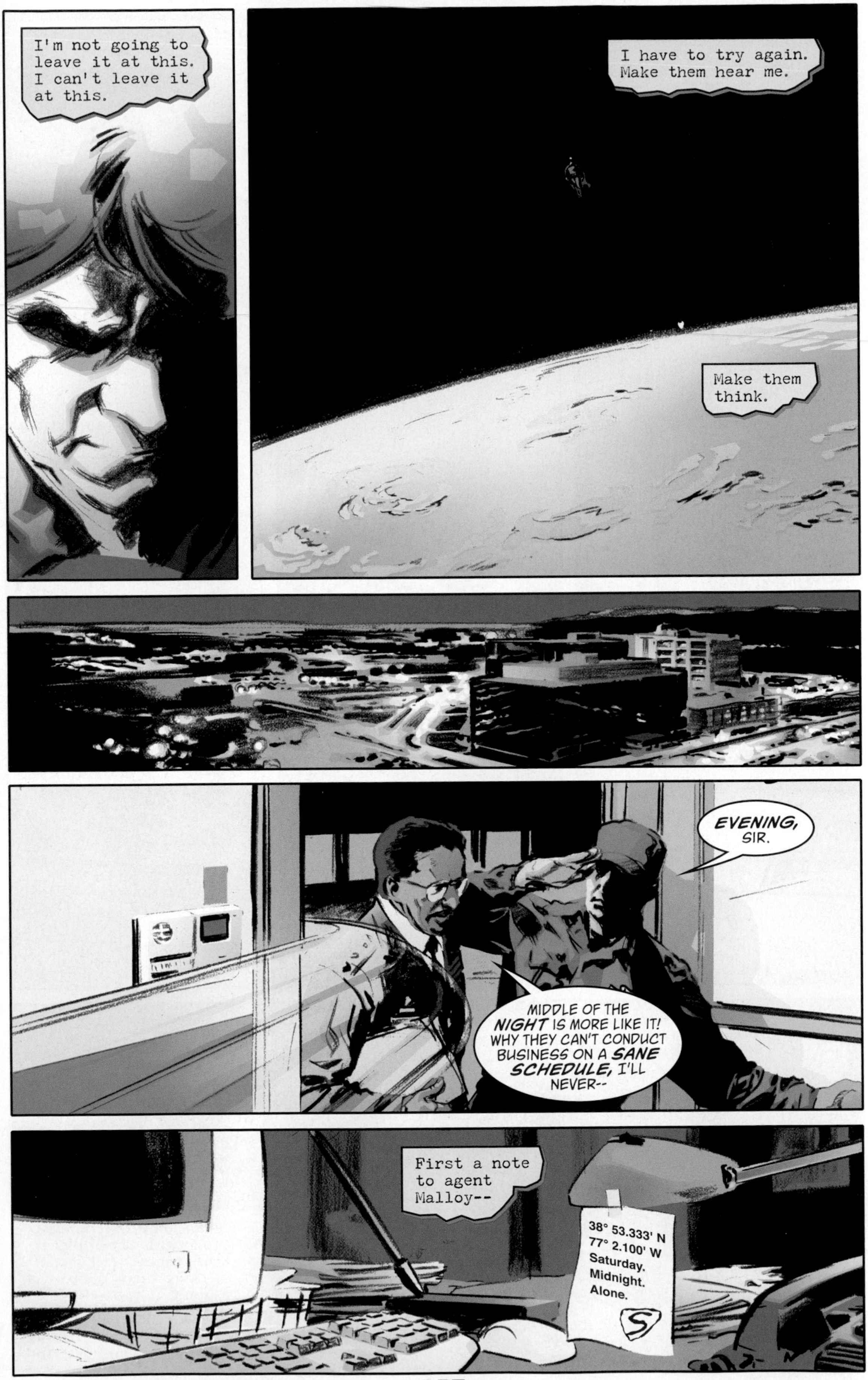
I'm not going to leave it at this. I can't leave it at this.
I have to try again. Make them hear me.
Make them think.
EVENING, SIR.
MIDDLE OF THE NIGHT IS MORE LIKE IT! WHY THEY CAN'T CONDUCT BUSINESS ON A SANE SCHEDULE, I'LL NEVER--
First a note to agent Malloy--
38° 53.333' N
77° 2.100' W
Saturday.
Midnight.
Alone.

I figure the CIA director's office should be pretty secure. Not a place they want strangers wandering into unannounced.

So that's where I'll start, on Monday.

HELEN?

HELEN, WHAT *IS* THIS?

SIR?

Tuesday, it's the Navy's turn.

I don't know how they'll react to finding the nuclear missiles from a carrier in the Pacific swapped with the missiles on a carrier in the Atlantic--

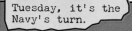
A-OOGA A-OOGA

--but I imagine it'll cause a stir.

SIR, I DON'T KNOW... DON'T KNOW HOW...

GET ME *CINCPAC.* NOW.

I'd swap guns for butter, if I thought they'd get the reference. But that might have been over-statement.

And it'd alter our defense capabilities, and I didn't want to do that.

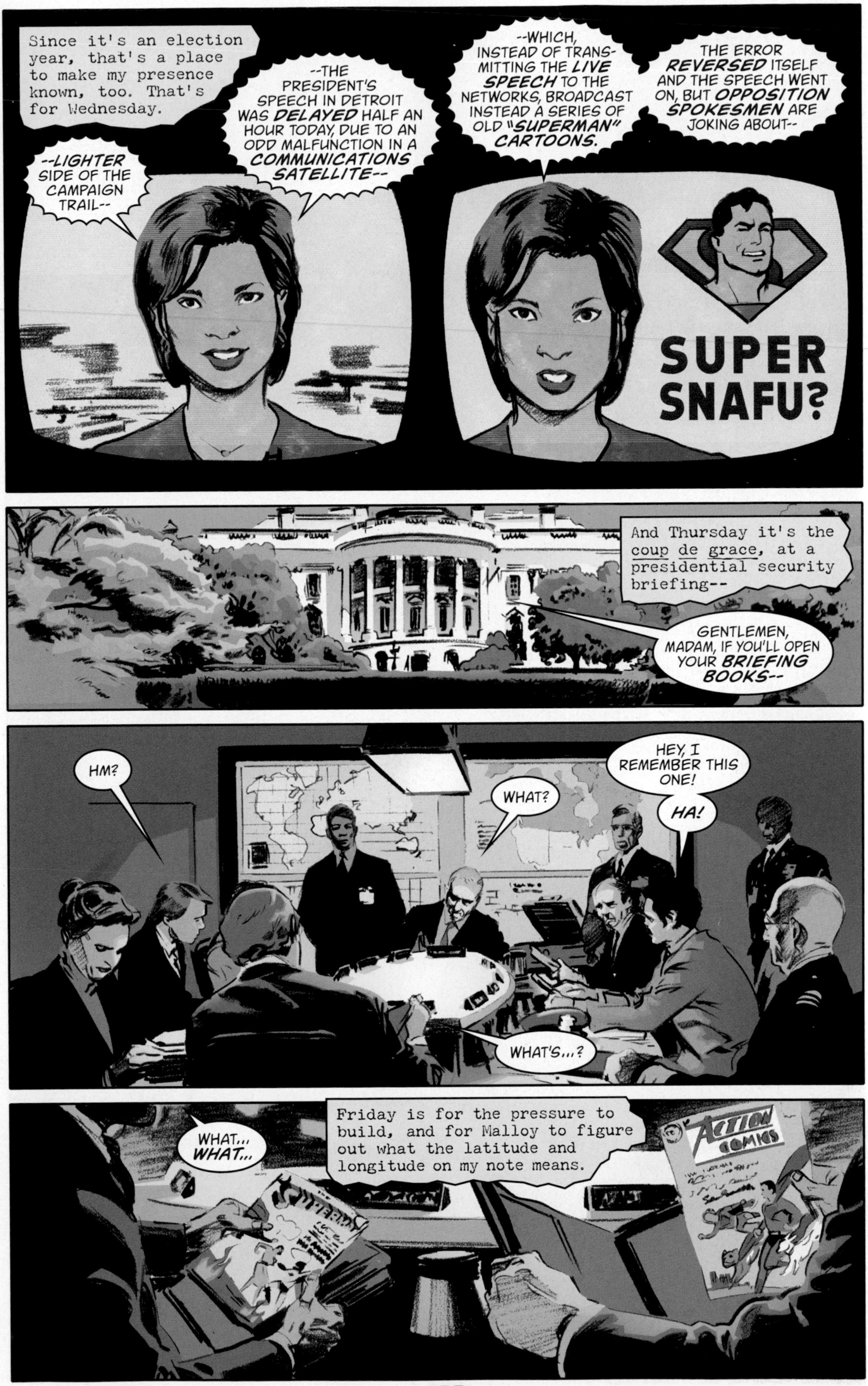
Since it's an election year, that's a place to make my presence known, too. That's for Wednesday.
--LIGHTER SIDE OF THE CAMPAIGN TRAIL--
--THE PRESIDENT'S SPEECH IN DETROIT WAS DELAYED HALF AN HOUR TODAY, DUE TO AN ODD MALFUNCTION IN A COMMUNICATIONS SATELLITE--
--WHICH, INSTEAD OF TRANS-MITTING THE LIVE SPEECH TO THE NETWORKS, BROADCAST INSTEAD A SERIES OF OLD "SUPERMAN" CARTOONS.
THE ERROR REVERSED ITSELF AND THE SPEECH WENT ON, BUT OPPOSITION SPOKESMEN ARE JOKING ABOUT--
SUPER SNAFU?
And Thursday it's the coup de grace, at a presidential security briefing--
GENTLEMEN, MADAM, IF YOU'LL OPEN YOUR BRIEFING BOOKS--
HM?
WHAT?
HEY, I REMEMBER THIS ONE!
HA!
WHAT'S...?
WHAT... WHAT...
Friday is for the pressure to build, and for Malloy to figure out what the latitude and longitude on my note means.
ACTION COMICS

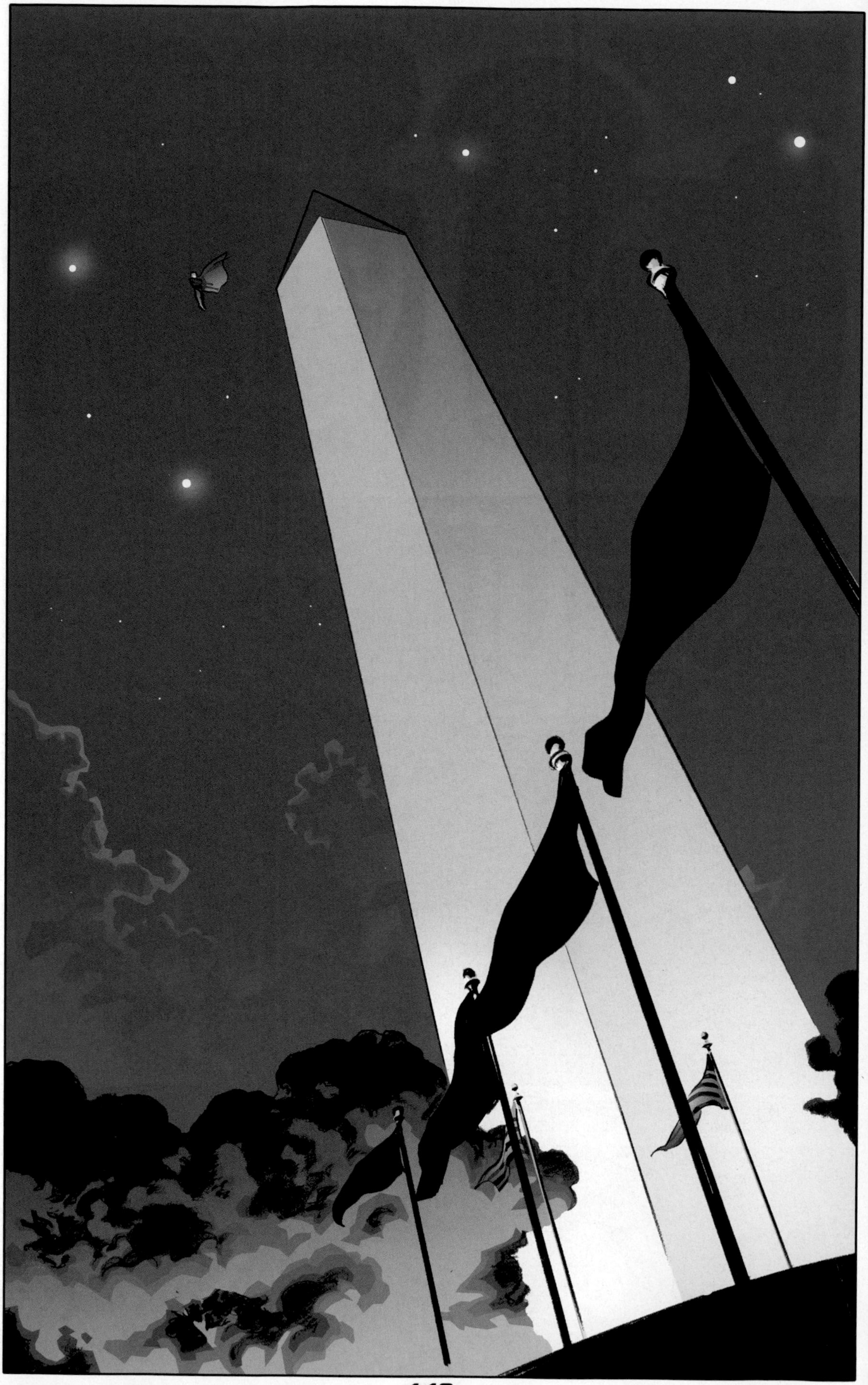

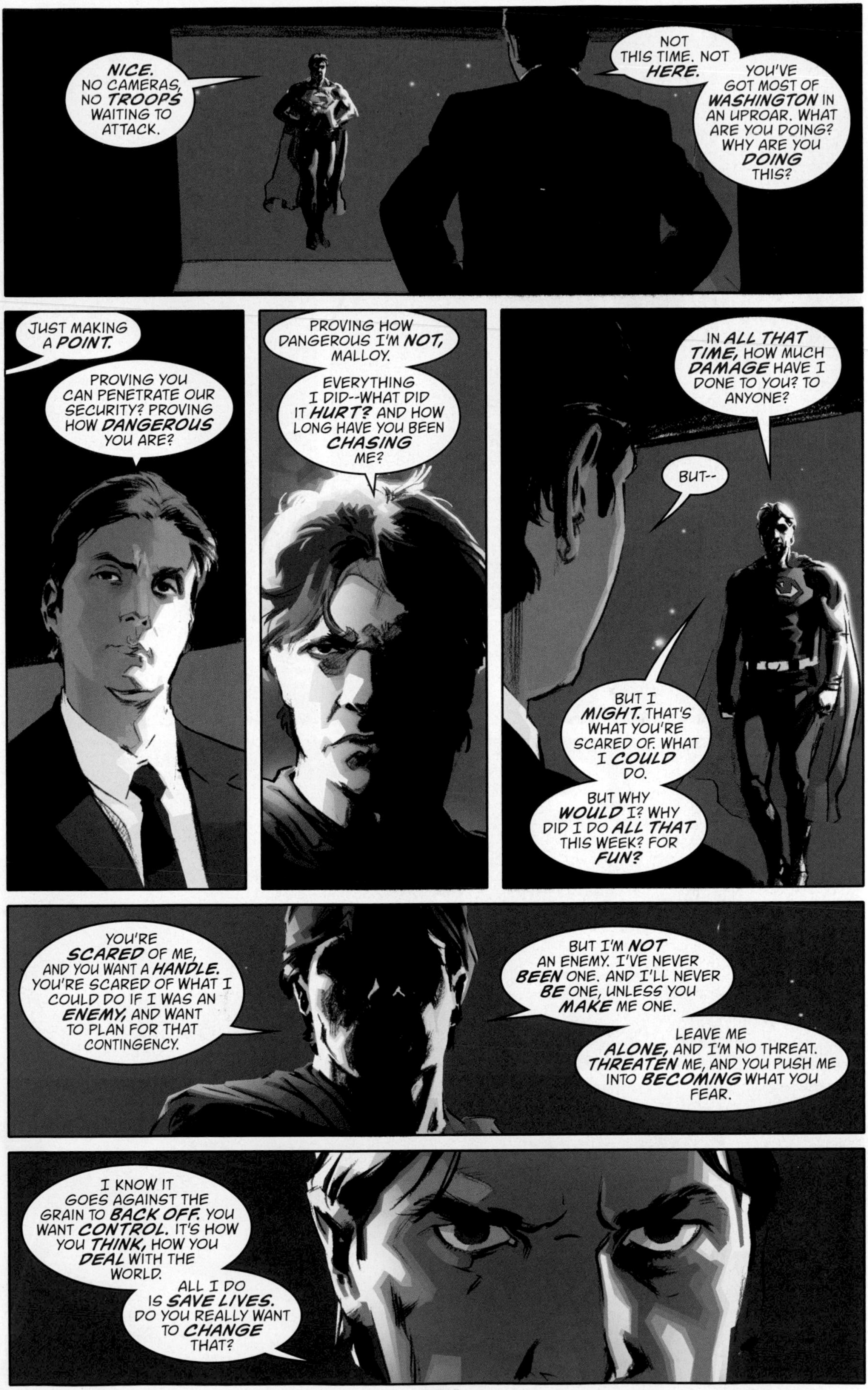
NICE. NO CAMERAS, NO TROOPS WAITING TO ATTACK.
NOT THIS TIME. NOT HERE.
YOU'VE GOT MOST OF WASHINGTON IN AN UPROAR. WHAT ARE YOU DOING? WHY ARE YOU DOING THIS?
JUST MAKING A POINT.
PROVING YOU CAN PENETRATE OUR SECURITY? PROVING HOW DANGEROUS YOU ARE?
PROVING HOW DANGEROUS I'M NOT, MALLOY.
EVERYTHING I DID--WHAT DID IT HURT? AND HOW LONG HAVE YOU BEEN CHASING ME?
IN ALL THAT TIME, HOW MUCH DAMAGE HAVE I DONE TO YOU? TO ANYONE?
BUT--
BUT I MIGHT. THAT'S WHAT YOU'RE SCARED OF. WHAT I COULD DO.
BUT WHY WOULD I? WHY DID I DO ALL THAT THIS WEEK? FOR FUN?
YOU'RE SCARED OF ME, AND YOU WANT A HANDLE. YOU'RE SCARED OF WHAT I COULD DO IF I WAS AN ENEMY, AND WANT TO PLAN FOR THAT CONTINGENCY.
BUT I'M NOT AN ENEMY. I'VE NEVER BEEN ONE. AND I'LL NEVER BE ONE, UNLESS YOU MAKE ME ONE.
LEAVE ME ALONE, AND I'M NO THREAT. THREATEN ME, AND YOU PUSH ME INTO BECOMING WHAT YOU FEAR.
I KNOW IT GOES AGAINST THE GRAIN TO BACK OFF. YOU WANT CONTROL. IT'S HOW YOU THINK, HOW YOU DEAL WITH THE WORLD.
ALL I DO IS SAVE LIVES. DO YOU REALLY WANT TO CHANGE THAT?

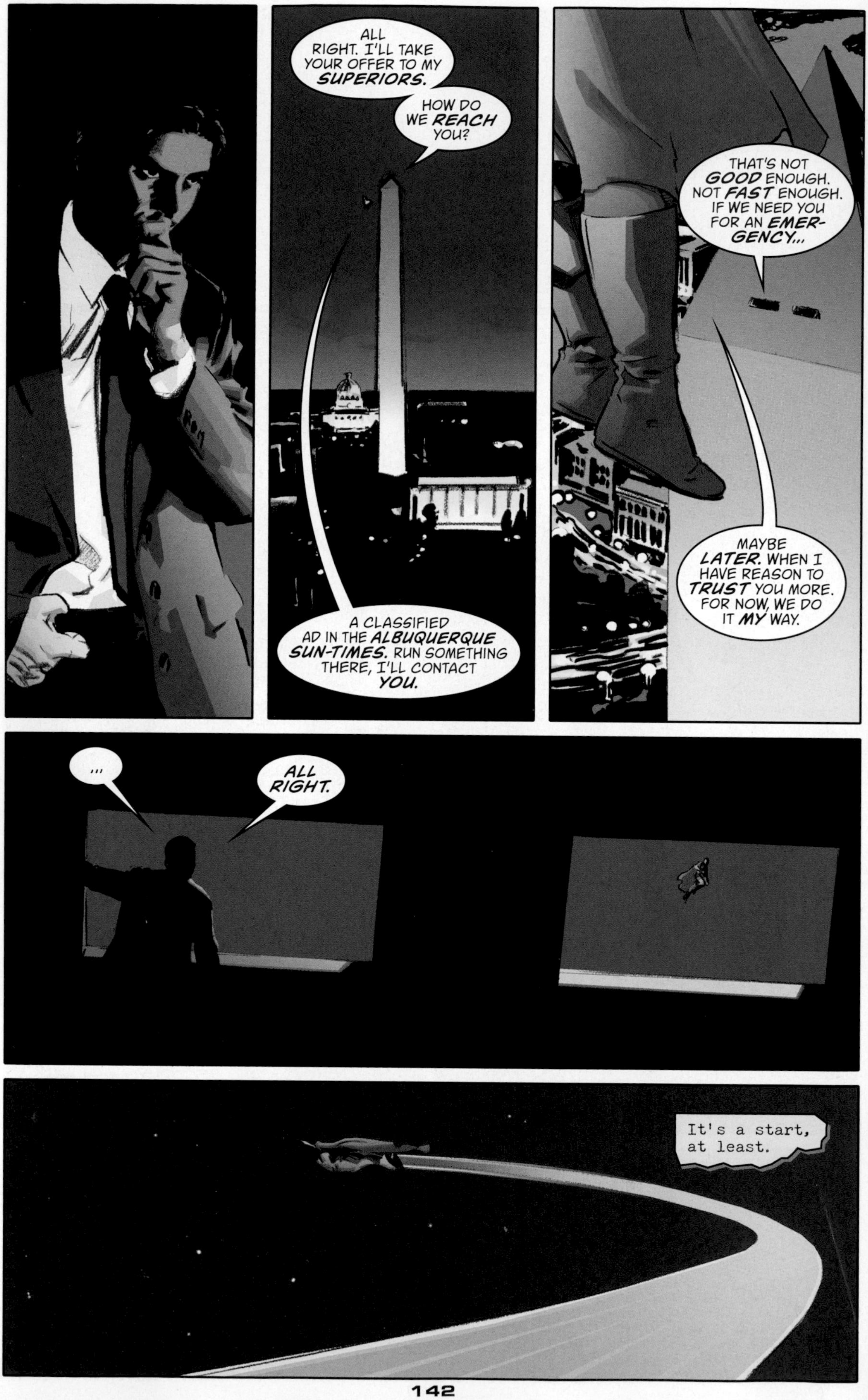
ALL RIGHT. I'LL TAKE YOUR OFFER TO MY SUPERIORS.
HOW DO WE REACH YOU?
A CLASSIFIED AD IN THE ALBUQUERQUE SUN-TIMES. RUN SOMETHING THERE, I'LL CONTACT YOU.
THAT'S NOT GOOD ENOUGH. NOT FAST ENOUGH. IF WE NEED YOU FOR AN EMERGENCY...
MAYBE LATER. WHEN I HAVE REASON TO TRUST YOU MORE. FOR NOW, WE DO IT MY WAY.
...
ALL RIGHT.
It's a start, at least.

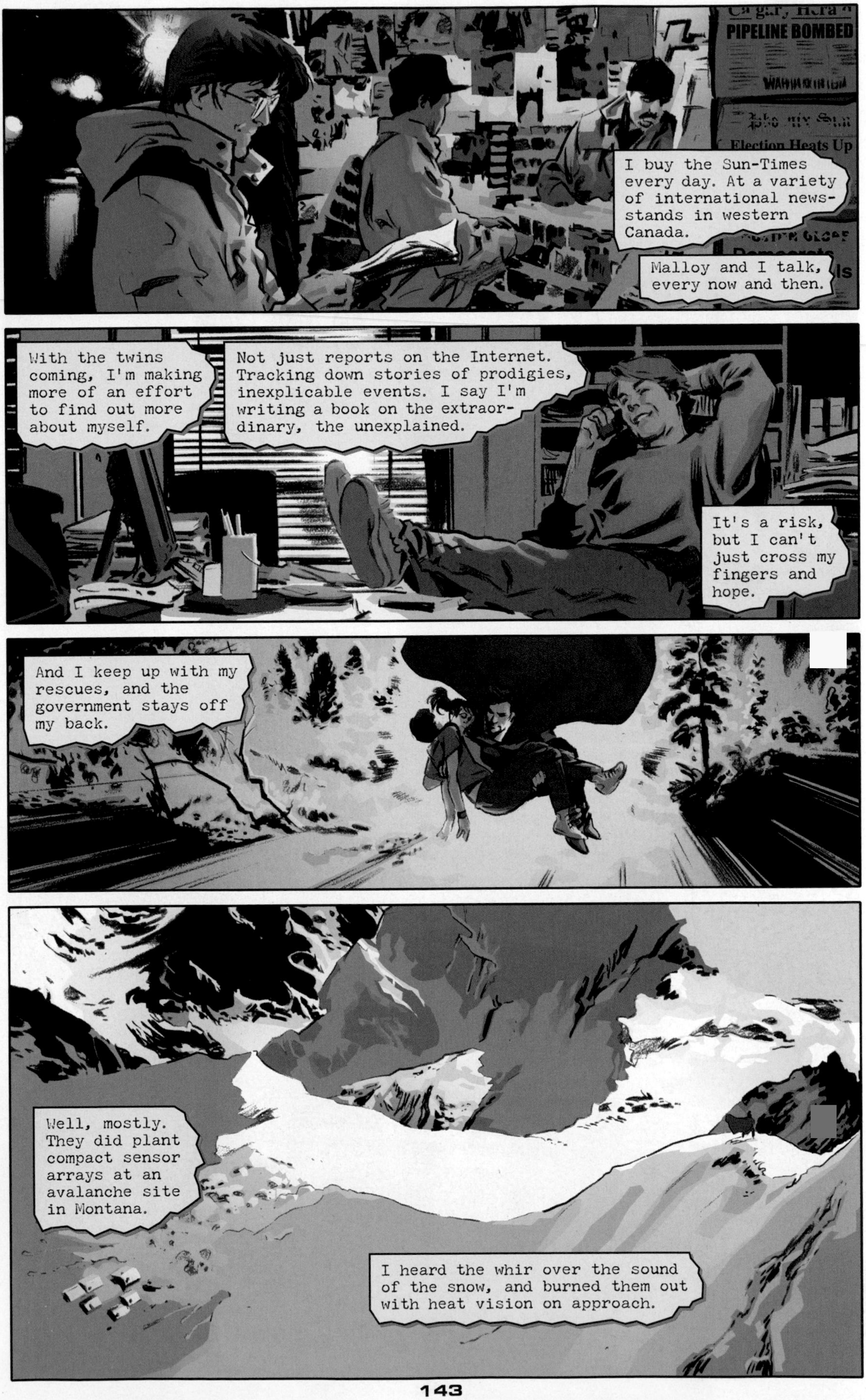
PIPELINE BOMBED
Election Heats Up
I buy the Sun-Times every day. At a variety of international news-stands in western Canada.
Malloy and I talk, every now and then.
With the twins coming, I'm making more of an effort to find out more about myself.
Not just reports on the Internet. Tracking down stories of prodigies, inexplicable events. I say I'm writing a book on the extraordinary, the unexplained.
It's a risk, but I can't just cross my fingers and hope.
And I keep up with my rescues, and the government stays off my back.
Well, mostly. They did plant compact sensor arrays at an avalanche site in Montana.
I heard the whir over the sound of the snow, and burned them out with heat vision on approach.

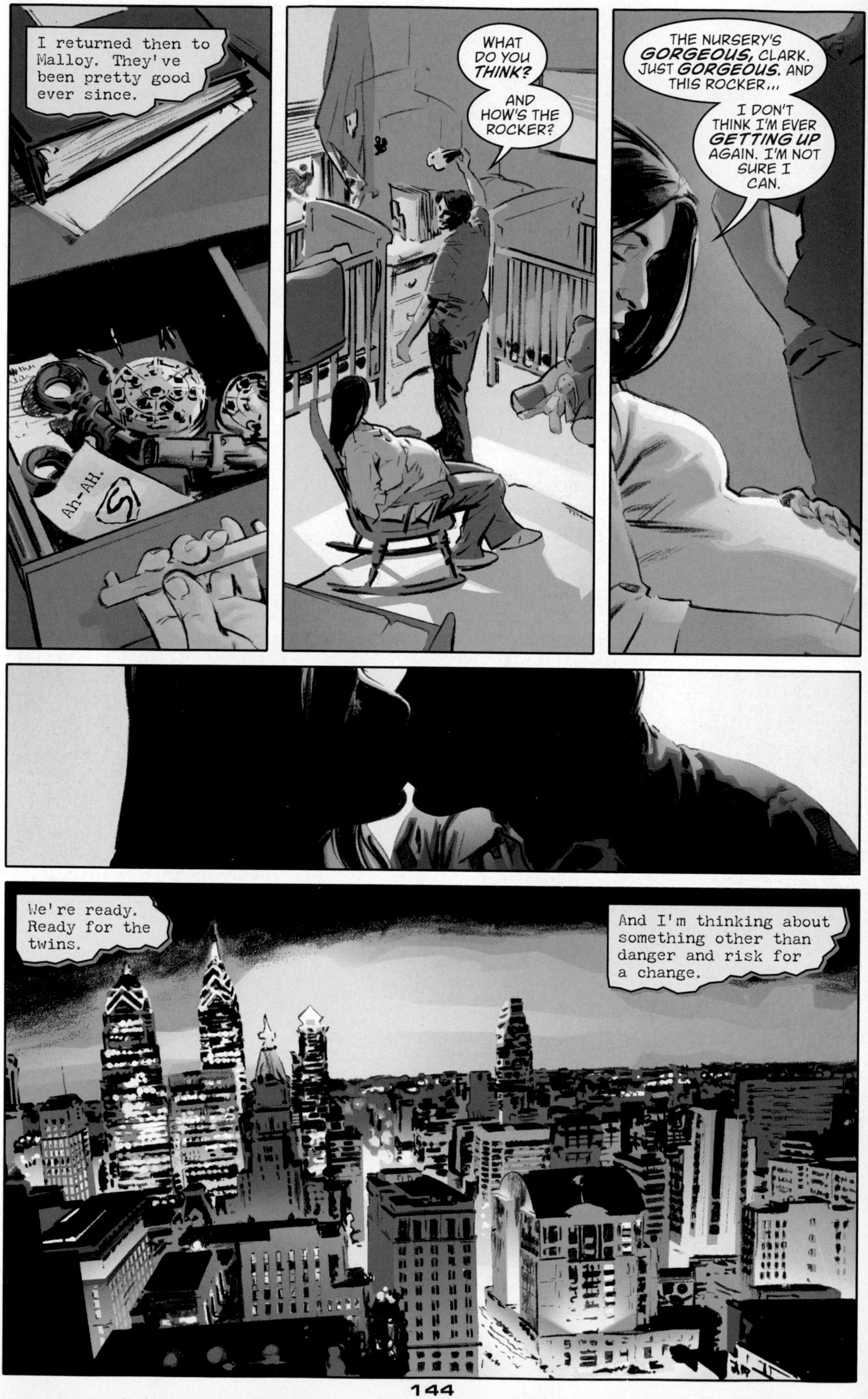
I returned then to Malloy. They've been pretty good ever since.
Ah-AH.
WHAT DO YOU THINK?
AND HOW'S THE ROCKER?
THE NURSERY'S GORGEOUS, CLARK. JUST GORGEOUS. AND THIS ROCKER...
I DON'T THINK I'M EVER GETTING UP AGAIN. I'M NOT SURE I CAN.
We're ready. Ready for the twins.
And I'm thinking about something other than danger and risk for a change.

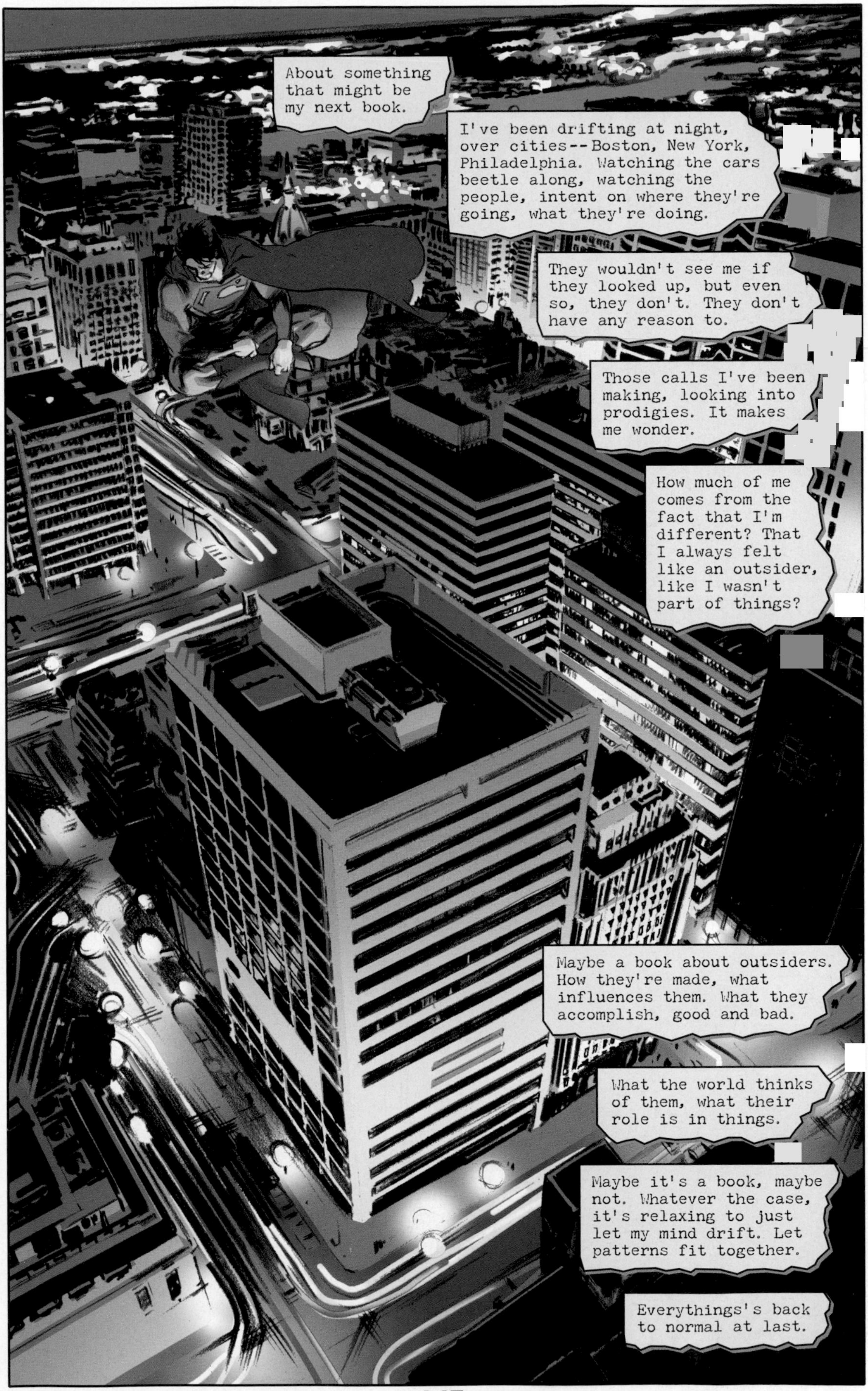
About something that might be my next book.
I've been drifting at night, over cities--Boston, New York, Philadelphia. Watching the cars beetle along, watching the people, intent on where they're going, what they're doing.
They wouldn't see me if they looked up, but even so, they don't. They don't have any reason to.
Those calls I've been making, looking into prodigies. It makes me wonder.
How much of me comes from the fact that I'm different? That I always felt like an outsider, like I wasn't part of things?
Maybe a book about outsiders. How they're made, what influences them. What they accomplish, good and bad.
What the world thinks of them, what their role is in things.
Maybe it's a book, maybe not. Whatever the case, it's relaxing to just let my mind drift. Let patterns fit together.
Everythings's back to normal at last.

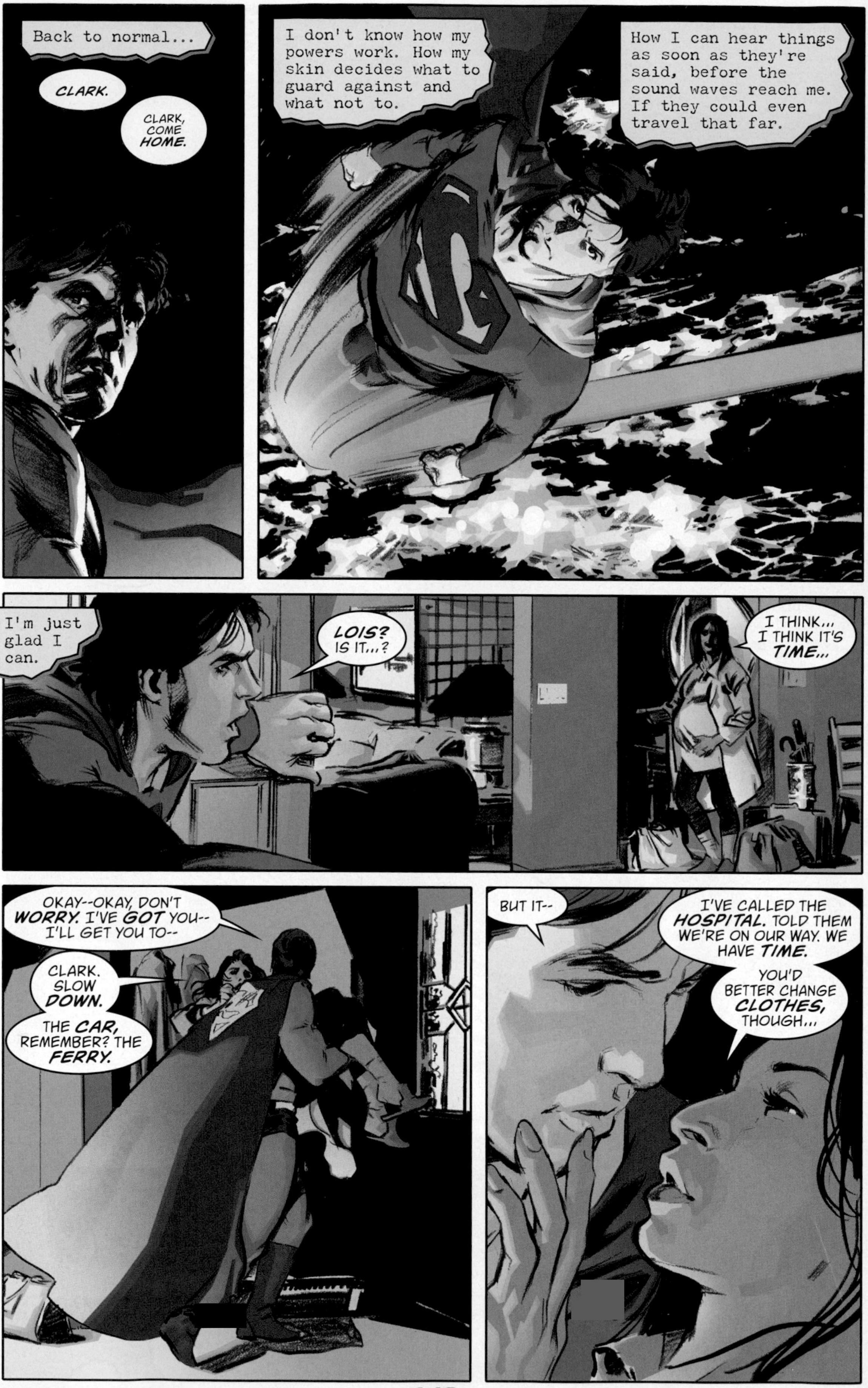
Back to normal...
CLARK.
CLARK, COME HOME.
I don't know how my powers work. How my skin decides what to guard against and what not to.
How I can hear things as soon as they're said, before the sound waves reach me. If they could even travel that far.
I'm just glad I can.
LOIS? IS IT...?
I THINK... I THINK IT'S TIME...
OKAY--OKAY, DON'T WORRY. I'VE GOT YOU-- I'LL GET YOU TO--
CLARK. SLOW DOWN.
THE CAR, REMEMBER? THE FERRY.
BUT IT--
I'VE CALLED THE HOSPITAL. TOLD THEM WE'RE ON OUR WAY. WE HAVE TIME.
YOU'D BETTER CHANGE CLOTHES, THOUGH...

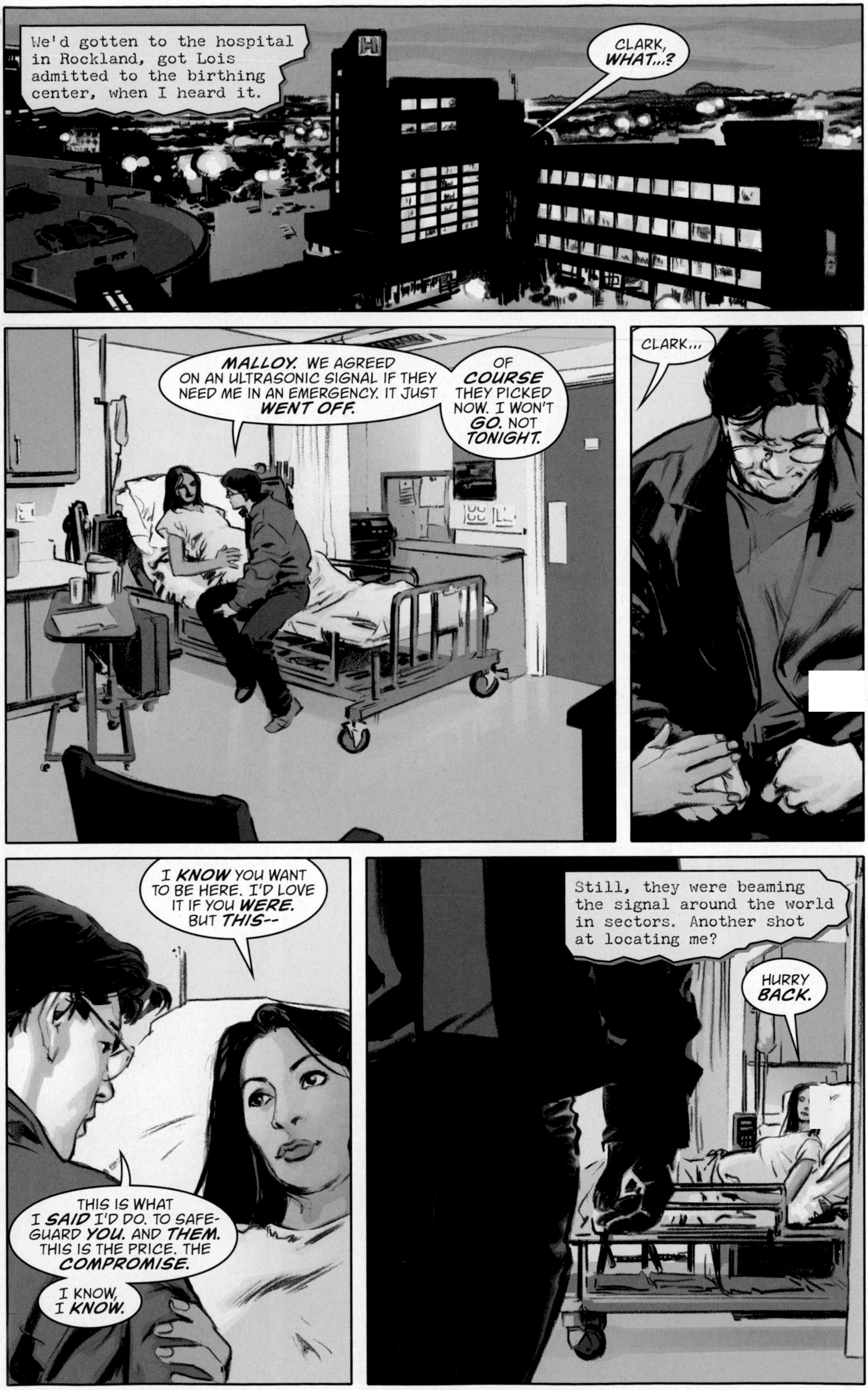
We'd gotten to the hospital in Rockland, got Lois admitted to the birthing center, when I heard it.
CLARK, WHAT...?
MALLOY. WE AGREED ON AN ULTRASONIC SIGNAL IF THEY NEED ME IN AN EMERGENCY. IT JUST WENT OFF.
OF COURSE THEY PICKED NOW. I WON'T GO. NOT TONIGHT.
CLARK...
I KNOW YOU WANT TO BE HERE. I'D LOVE IT IF YOU WERE. BUT THIS--
THIS IS WHAT I SAID I'D DO. TO SAFE-GUARD YOU. AND THEM. THIS IS THE PRICE. THE COMPROMISE.
I KNOW, I KNOW.
Still, they were beaming the signal around the world in sectors. Another shot at locating me?
HURRY BACK.

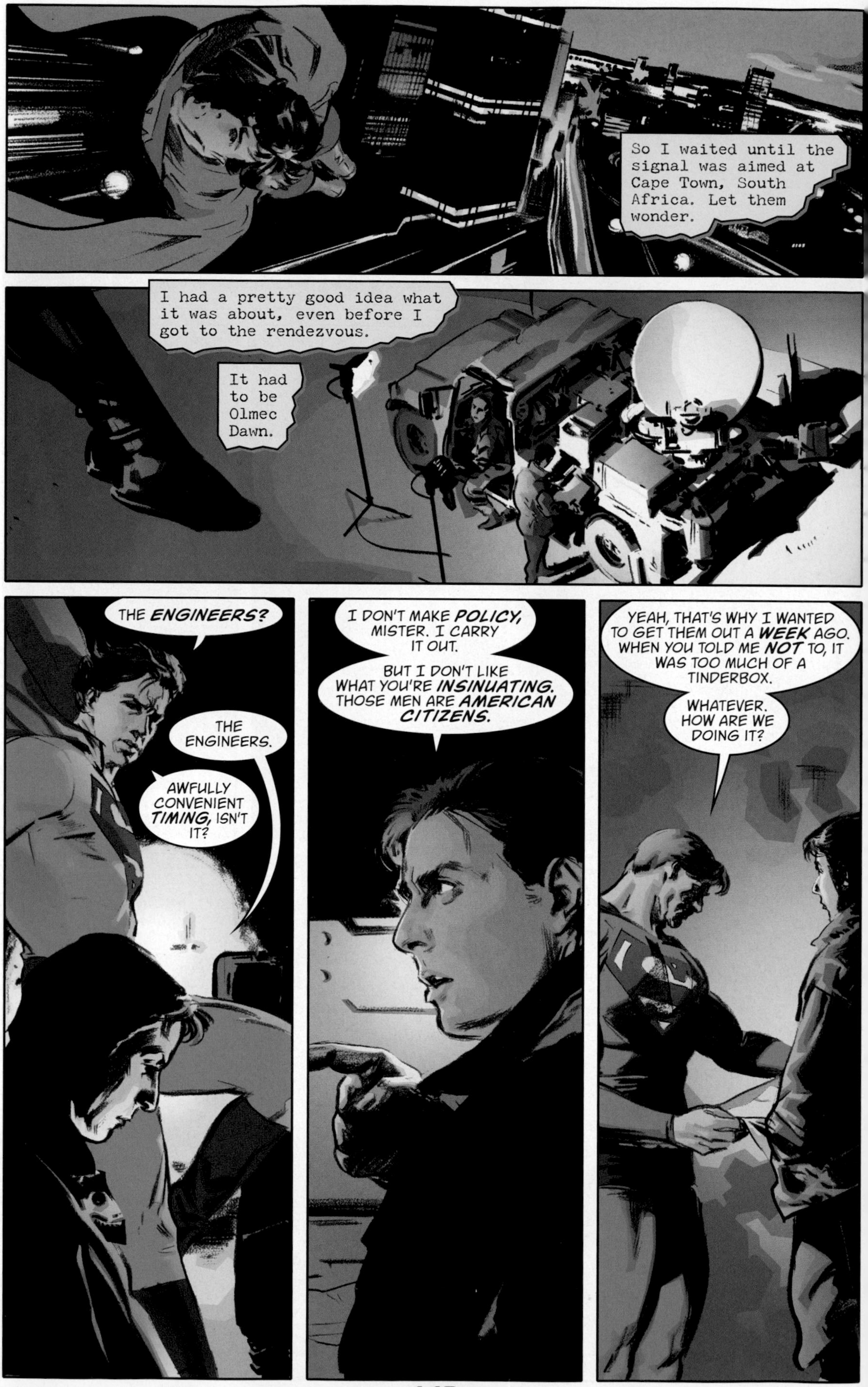

So I waited until the signal was aimed at Cape Town, South Africa. Let them wonder.
I had a pretty good idea what it was about, even before I got to the rendezvous.
It had to be Olmec Dawn.
THE ENGINEERS?
THE ENGINEERS.
AWFULLY CONVENIENT TIMING, ISN'T IT?
I DON'T MAKE POLICY, MISTER. I CARRY IT OUT.
BUT I DON'T LIKE WHAT YOU'RE INSINUATING. THOSE MEN ARE AMERICAN CITIZENS.
YEAH, THAT'S WHY I WANTED TO GET THEM OUT A WEEK AGO. WHEN YOU TOLD ME NOT TO, IT WAS TOO MUCH OF A TINDERBOX.
WHATEVER. HOW ARE WE DOING IT?

As I headed south, I listened for Lois.

Even if I couldn't be there, I wanted to know what was going on.

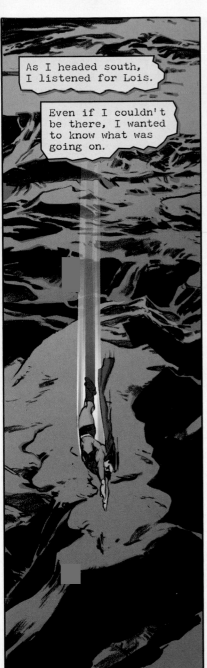

YOUR **HUSBAND**...?

HE HAD TO **GO**. BUSINESS.

I'LL BE **OKAY**.

**MEN**. ISN'T IT ALWAYS THE **WAY**?

*HMPH.*

Olmec Dawn was said to be a multinational paramilitary group, made up of rogue factions in various South American armies, cocaine warlords, more.

They wanted to unite the continent under military rule. Theirs, of course.

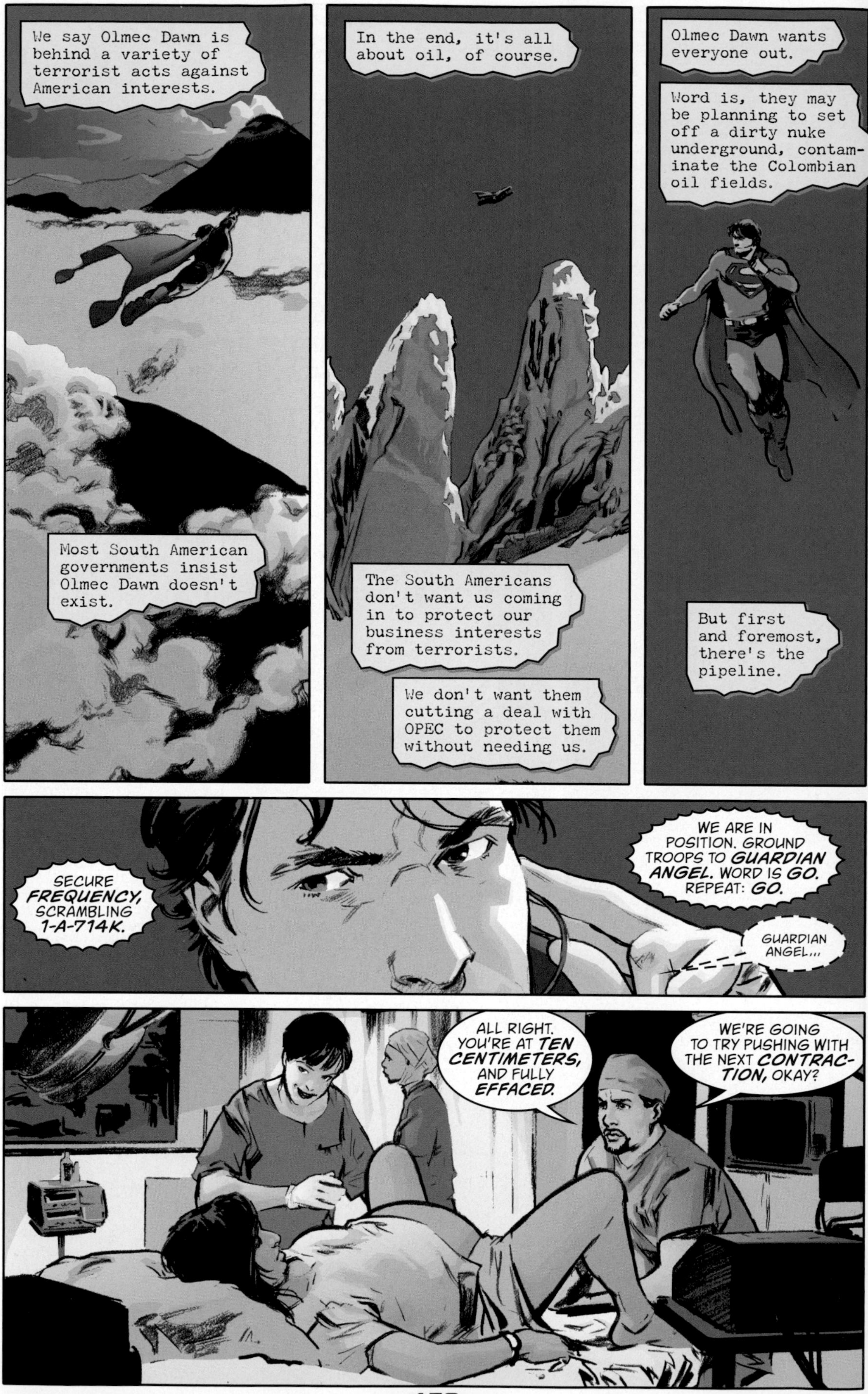

We say Olmec Dawn is behind a variety of terrorist acts against American interests.
Most South American governments insist Olmec Dawn doesn't exist.
In the end, it's all about oil, of course.
The South Americans don't want us coming in to protect our business interests from terrorists.
We don't want them cutting a deal with OPEC to protect them without needing us.
Olmec Dawn wants everyone out.
Word is, they may be planning to set off a dirty nuke underground, contaminate the Colombian oil fields.
But first and foremost, there's the pipeline.
SECURE FREQUENCY, SCRAMBLING 1-A-714K.
WE ARE IN POSITION. GROUND TROOPS TO GUARDIAN ANGEL. WORD IS GO. REPEAT: GO.
GUARDIAN ANGEL...
ALL RIGHT. YOU'RE AT TEN CENTIMETERS, AND FULLY EFFACED.
WE'RE GOING TO TRY PUSHING WITH THE NEXT CONTRACTION, OKAY?

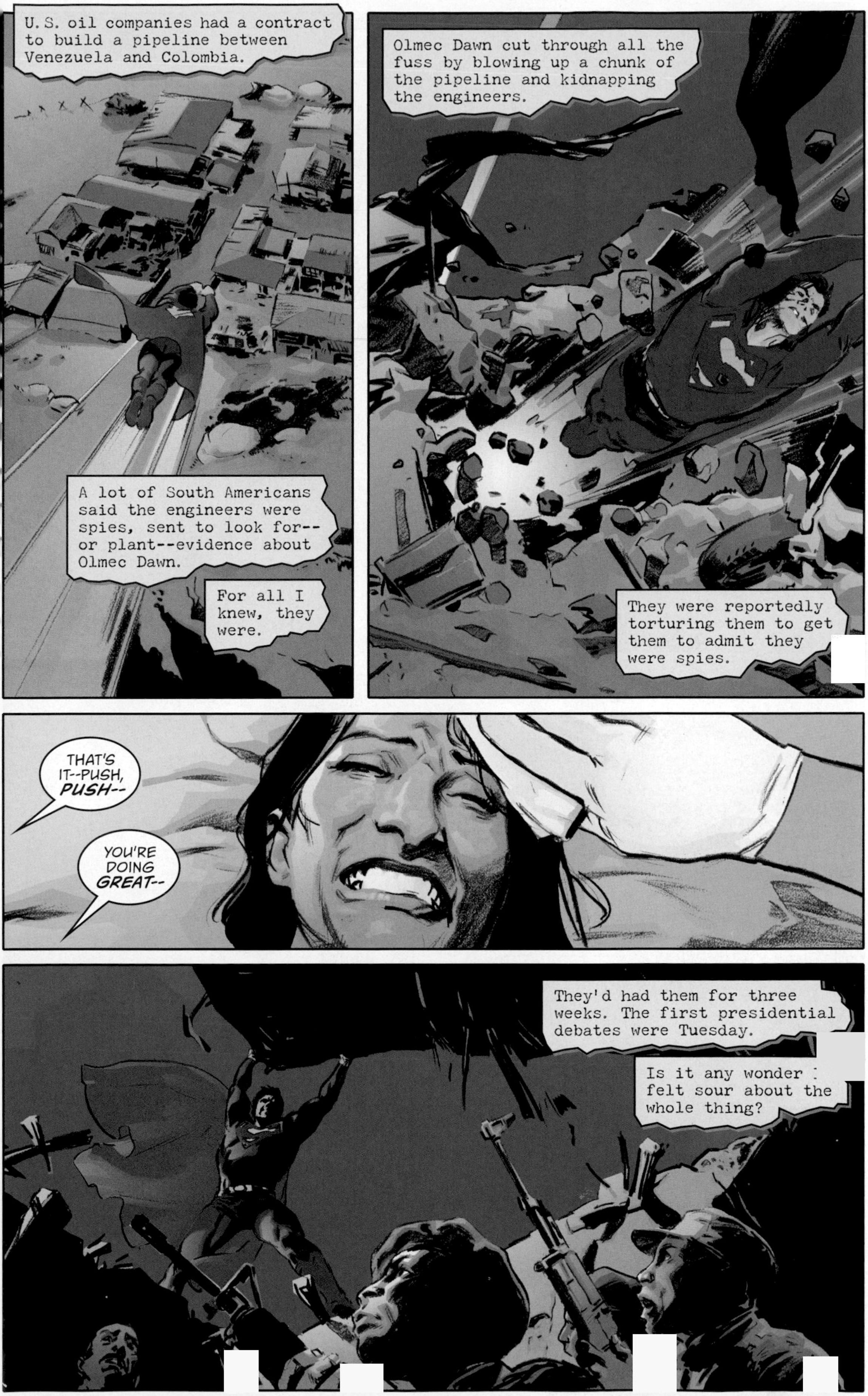
U.S. oil companies had a contract to build a pipeline between Venezuela and Colombia.
Olmec Dawn cut through all the fuss by blowing up a chunk of the pipeline and kidnapping the engineers.
A lot of South Americans said the engineers were spies, sent to look for--or plant--evidence about Olmec Dawn.
For all I knew, they were.
They were reportedly torturing them to get them to admit they were spies.
THAT'S IT--PUSH, *PUSH--*
YOU'RE DOING *GREAT--*
They'd had them for three weeks. The first presidential debates were Tuesday.
Is it any wonder
felt sour about the whole thing?

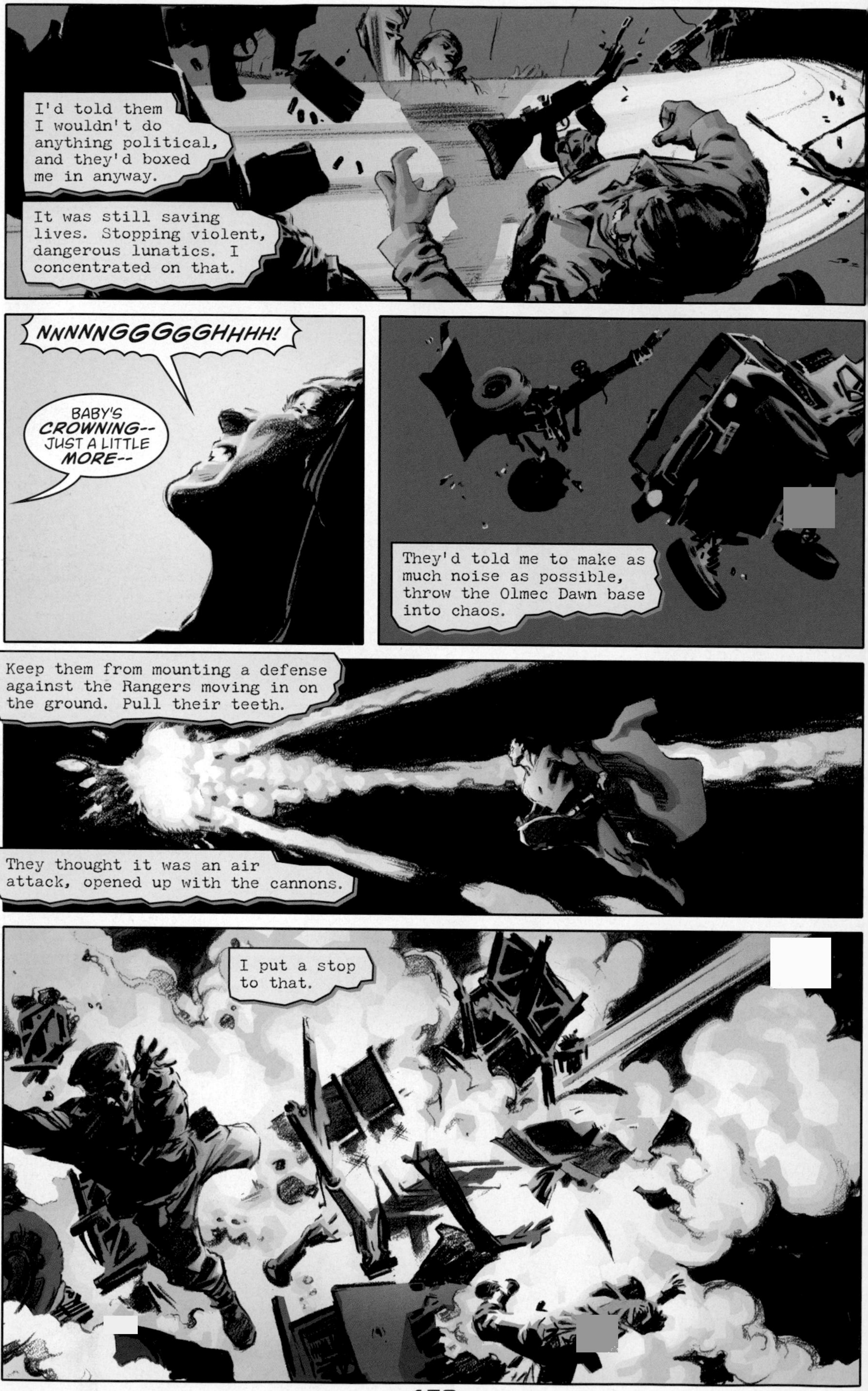
I'd told them I wouldn't do anything political, and they'd boxed me in anyway.
It was still saving lives. Stopping violent, dangerous lunatics. I concentrated on that.
NNNNNGGGGGHHHHH!
BABY'S CROWNING-- JUST A LITTLE MORE--
They'd told me to make as much noise as possible, throw the Olmec Dawn base into chaos.
Keep them from mounting a defense against the Rangers moving in on the ground. Pull their teeth.
They thought it was an air attack, opened up with the cannons.
I put a stop to that.

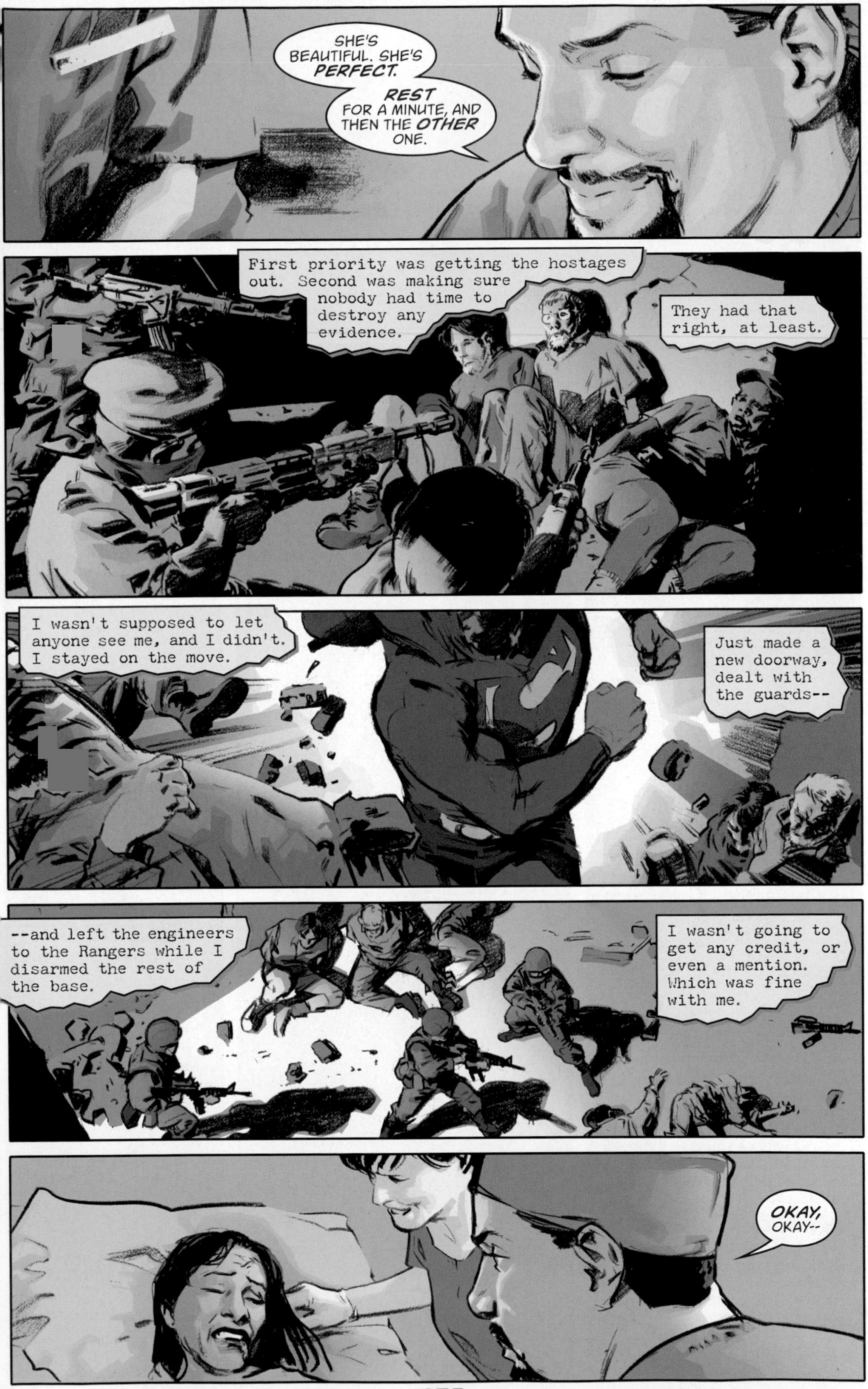
SHE'S BEAUTIFUL. SHE'S PERFECT.
REST FOR A MINUTE, AND THEN THE OTHER ONE.
First priority was getting the hostages out. Second was making sure nobody had time to destroy any evidence.
They had that right, at least.
I wasn't supposed to let anyone see me, and I didn't. I stayed on the move.
Just made a new doorway, dealt with the guards--
--and left the engineers to the Rangers while I disarmed the rest of the base.
I wasn't going to get any credit, or even a mention. Which was fine with me.
OKAY, OKAY--

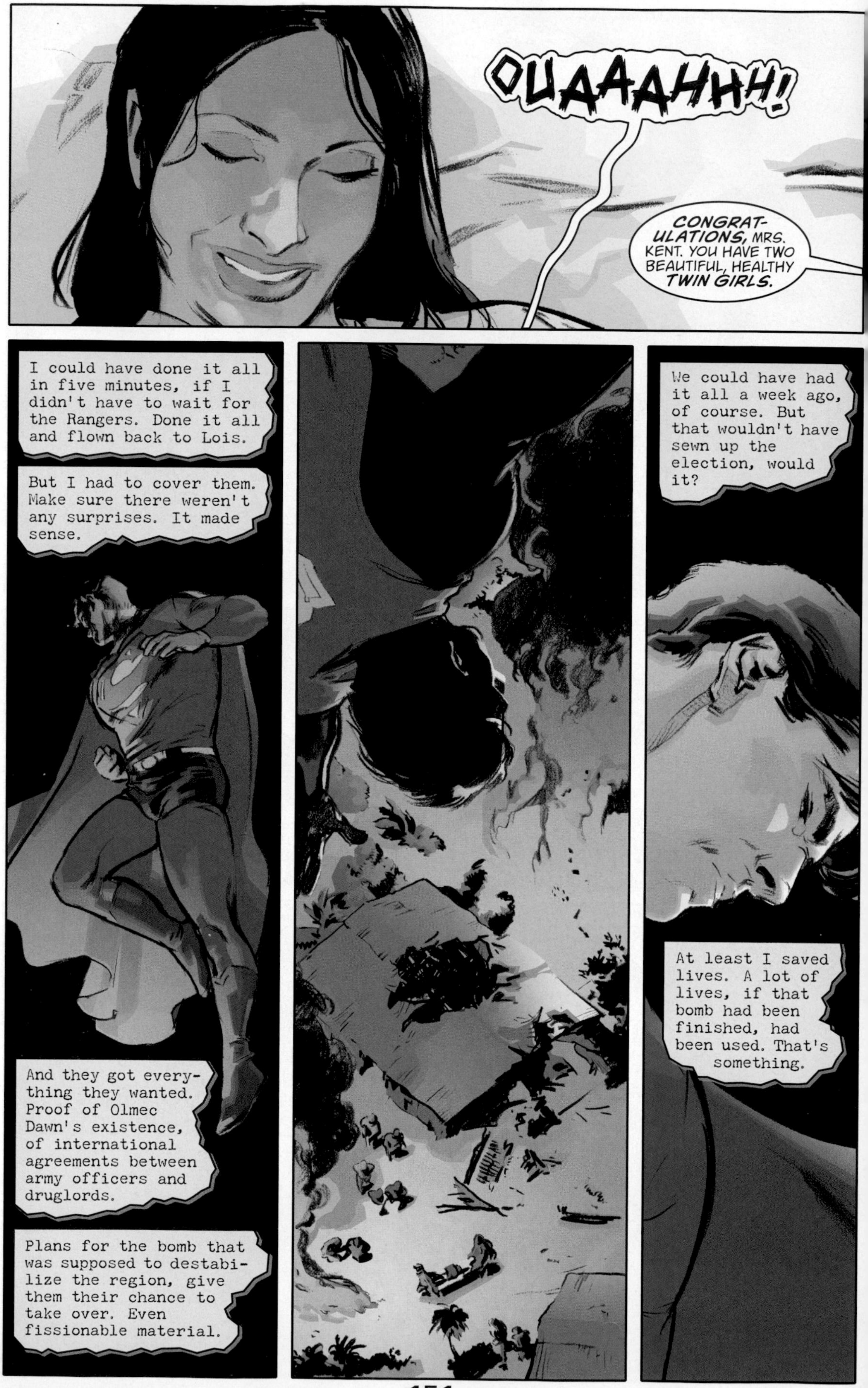
OUAAAHHH!
CONGRAT-ULATIONS, MRS. KENT. YOU HAVE TWO BEAUTIFUL, HEALTHY TWIN GIRLS.
I could have done it all in five minutes, if I didn't have to wait for the Rangers. Done it all and flown back to Lois.
But I had to cover them. Make sure there weren't any surprises. It made sense.
And they got every-thing they wanted. Proof of Olmec Dawn's existence, of international agreements between army officers and druglords.
Plans for the bomb that was supposed to destabi-lize the region, give them their chance to take over. Even fissionable material.
We could have had it all a week ago, of course. But that wouldn't have sewn up the election, would it?
At least I saved lives. A lot of lives, if that bomb had been finished, had been used. That's something.

I wish I could have been there, Lois. I know you understand. I know you approved.

But I wish I could have been there.

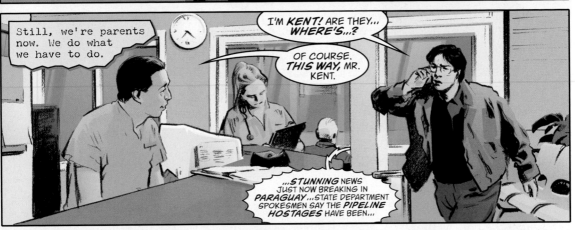

Still, we're parents now. We do what we have to do.

I'M *KENT!* ARE THEY... *WHERE'S...?*

OF COURSE. *THIS WAY,* MR. KENT.

...*STUNNING* NEWS JUST NOW BREAKING IN *PARAGUAY*...STATE DEPARTMENT SPOKESMEN SAY THE *PIPELINE HOSTAGES* HAVE BEEN...

Whatever we have to do.

THEY'RE... *THEY'RE...*

HI, CLARK. THIS IS YOUR *DADDY,* GIRLS.

WANT TO *HOLD* THEM?

HI. I HEARD YOU BEING *BORN.* YOU *TOO.* I HEARD IT *ALL.*

AND I WANT TO MAKE YOU *TWO* PROMISES. FIRST, WE WON'T NAME YOU *LANA* OR *LORI* OR *KARA* OR ANYTHING REMOTELY LIKE IT.

AND SECOND, YOUR MOM AND I WILL *PROTECT* YOU. KEEP YOU *SAFE.*

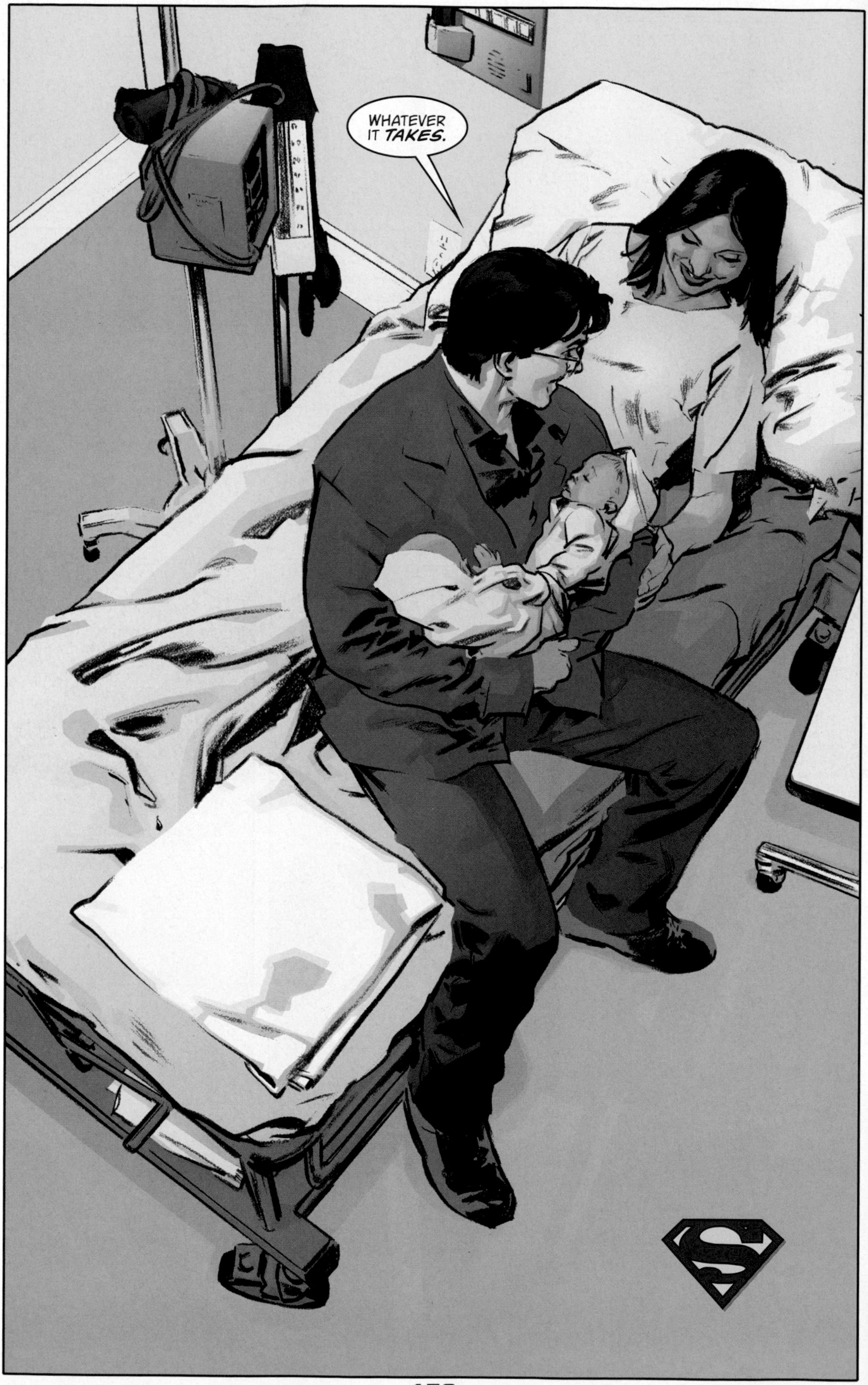
WHATEVER IT TAKES.

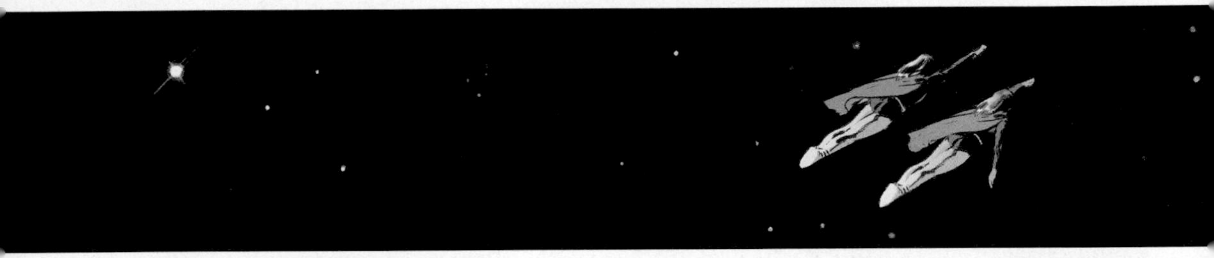
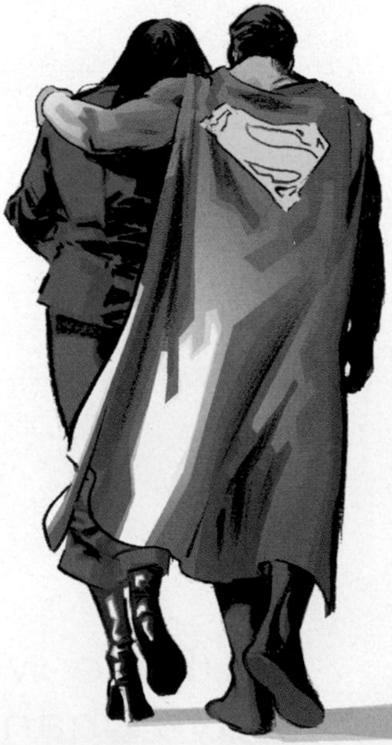

the world is **changing.**

but the world
always changes.

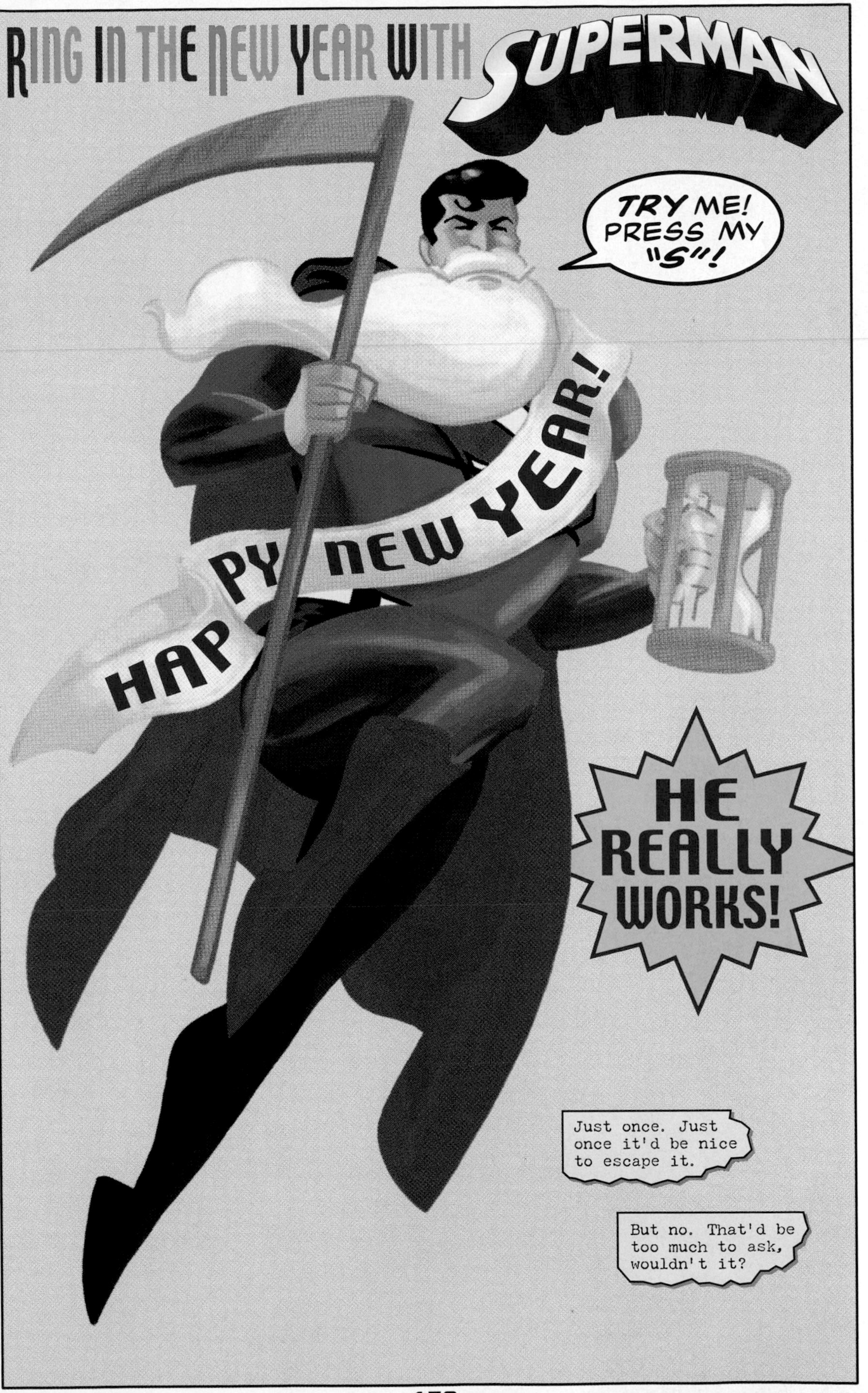
RING IN THE NEW YEAR WITH SUPERMAN
TRY ME! PRESS MY "S"!
HAPPY NEW YEAR!
HE REALLY WORKS!
Just once. Just once it'd be nice to escape it.
But no. That'd be too much to ask, wouldn't it?

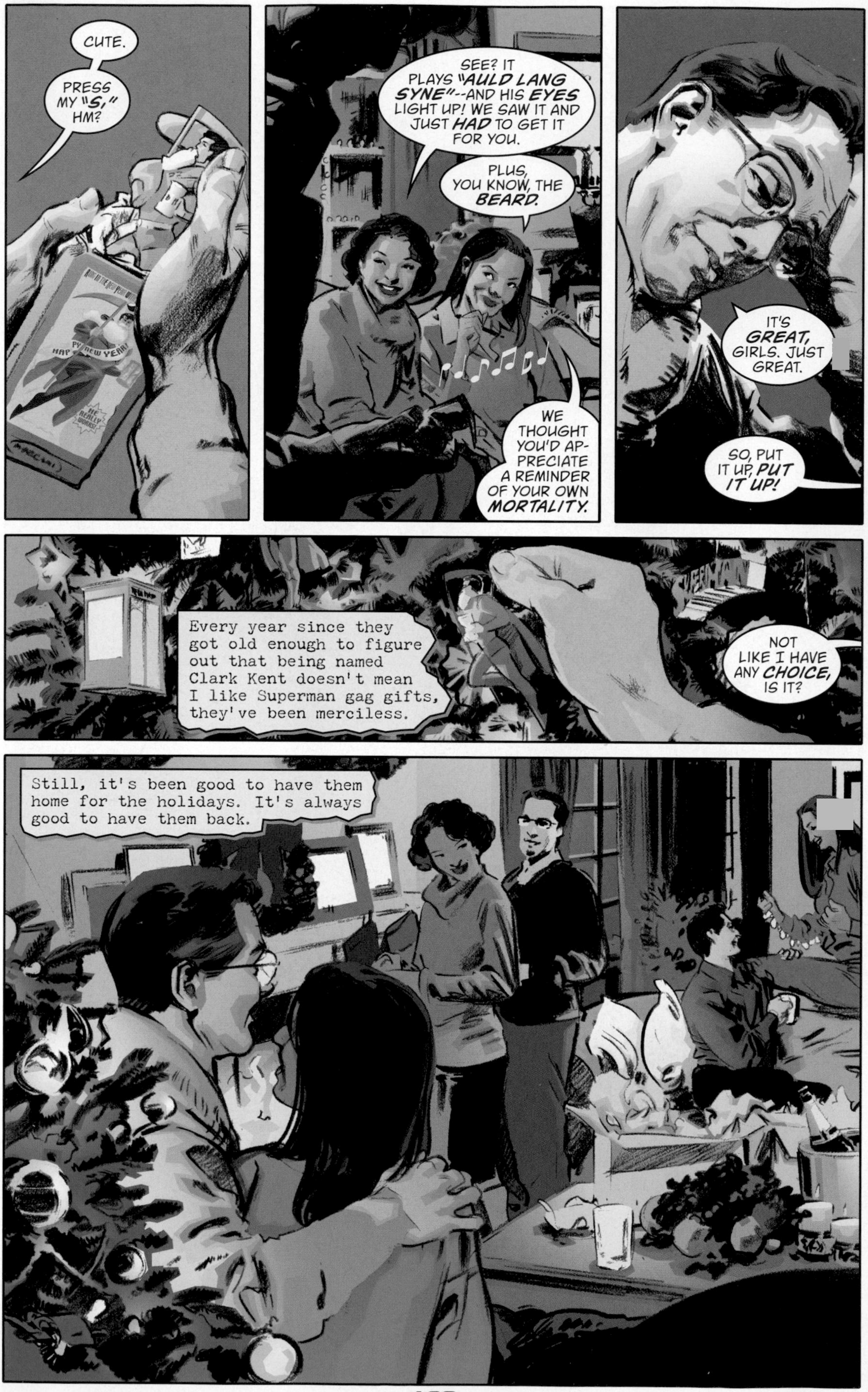
CUTE.
PRESS MY "S," HM?
SEE? IT PLAYS "AULD LANG SYNE"--AND HIS EYES LIGHT UP! WE SAW IT AND JUST HAD TO GET IT FOR YOU.
PLUS, YOU KNOW, THE BEARD.
WE THOUGHT YOU'D AP-PRECIATE A REMINDER OF YOUR OWN MORTALITY.
IT'S GREAT, GIRLS. JUST GREAT.
SO, PUT IT UP, PUT IT UP!
Every year since they got old enough to figure out that being named Clark Kent doesn't mean I like Superman gag gifts, they've been merciless.
NOT LIKE I HAVE ANY CHOICE, IS IT?
Still, it's been good to have them home for the holidays. It's always good to have them back.

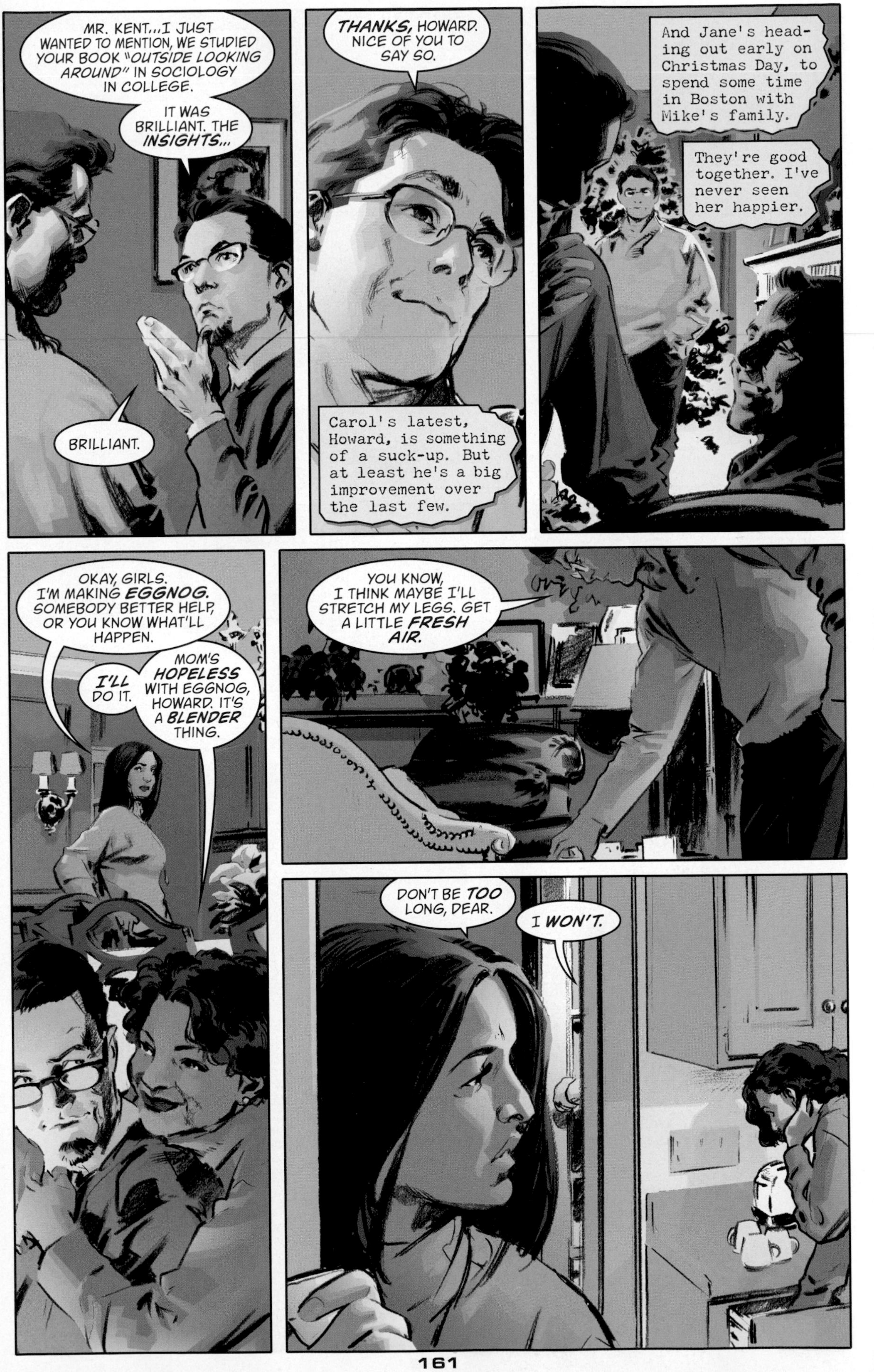
MR. KENT...I JUST WANTED TO MENTION, WE STUDIED YOUR BOOK "OUTSIDE LOOKING AROUND" IN SOCIOLOGY IN COLLEGE.
IT WAS BRILLIANT. THE INSIGHTS...
BRILLIANT.
THANKS, HOWARD. NICE OF YOU TO SAY SO.
Carol's latest, Howard, is something of a suck-up. But at least he's a big improvement over the last few.
And Jane's heading out early on Christmas Day, to spend some time in Boston with Mike's family.
They're good together. I've never seen her happier.
OKAY, GIRLS. I'M MAKING EGGNOG. SOMEBODY BETTER HELP, OR YOU KNOW WHAT'LL HAPPEN.
I'LL DO IT.
MOM'S HOPELESS WITH EGGNOG, HOWARD. IT'S A BLENDER THING.
YOU KNOW, I THINK MAYBE I'LL STRETCH MY LEGS. GET A LITTLE FRESH AIR.
DON'T BE TOO LONG, DEAR.
I WON'T.

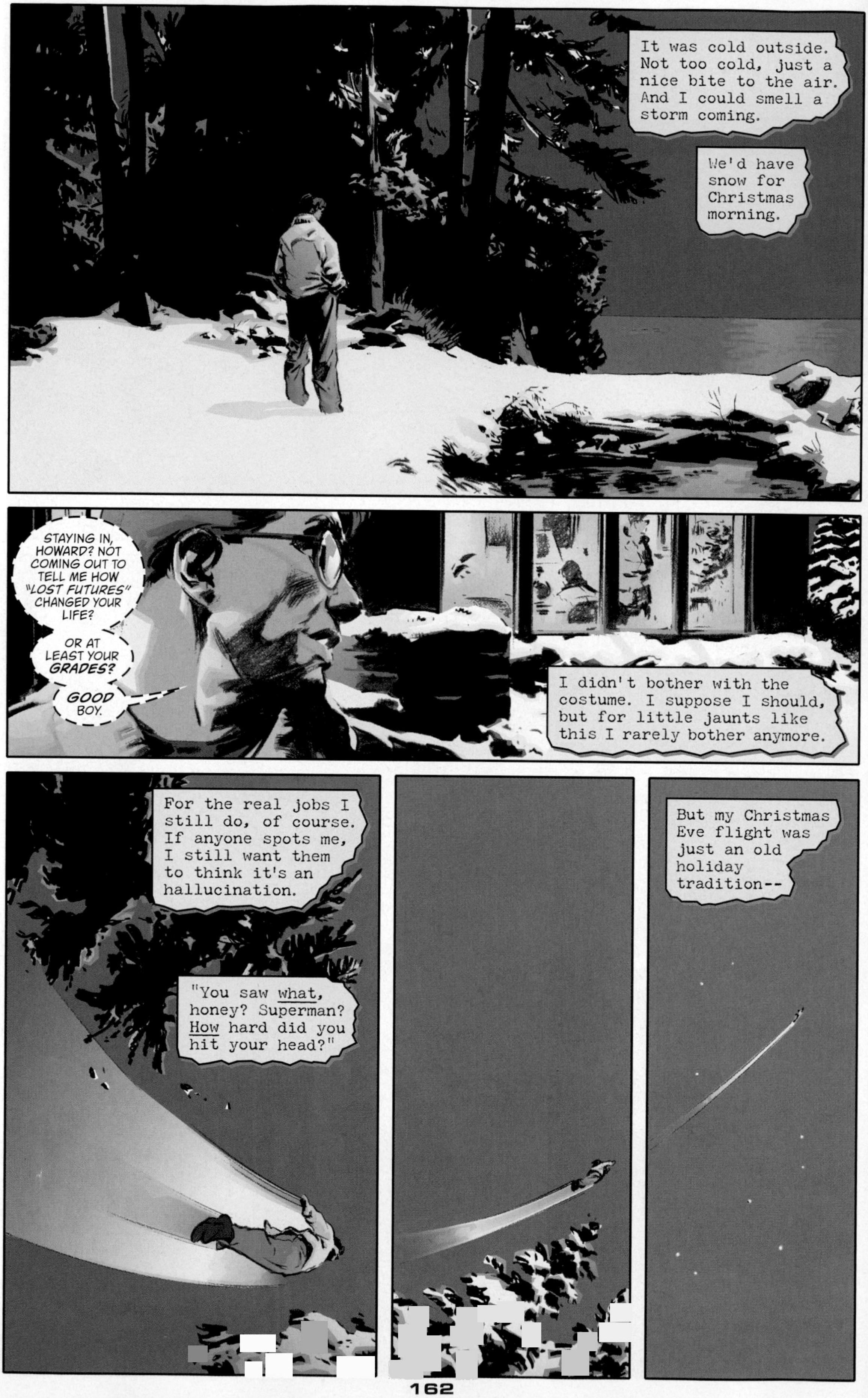

It was cold outside. Not too cold, just a nice bite to the air. And I could smell a storm coming.
We'd have snow for Christmas morning.
STAYING IN, HOWARD? NOT COMING OUT TO TELL ME HOW "LOST FUTURES" CHANGED YOUR LIFE?
OR AT LEAST YOUR GRADES?
GOOD BOY.
I didn't bother with the costume. I suppose I should, but for little jaunts like this I rarely bother anymore.
For the real jobs I still do, of course. If anyone spots me, I still want them to think it's an hallucination.
"You saw what, honey? Superman? How hard did you hit your head?"
But my Christmas Eve flight was just an old holiday tradition--

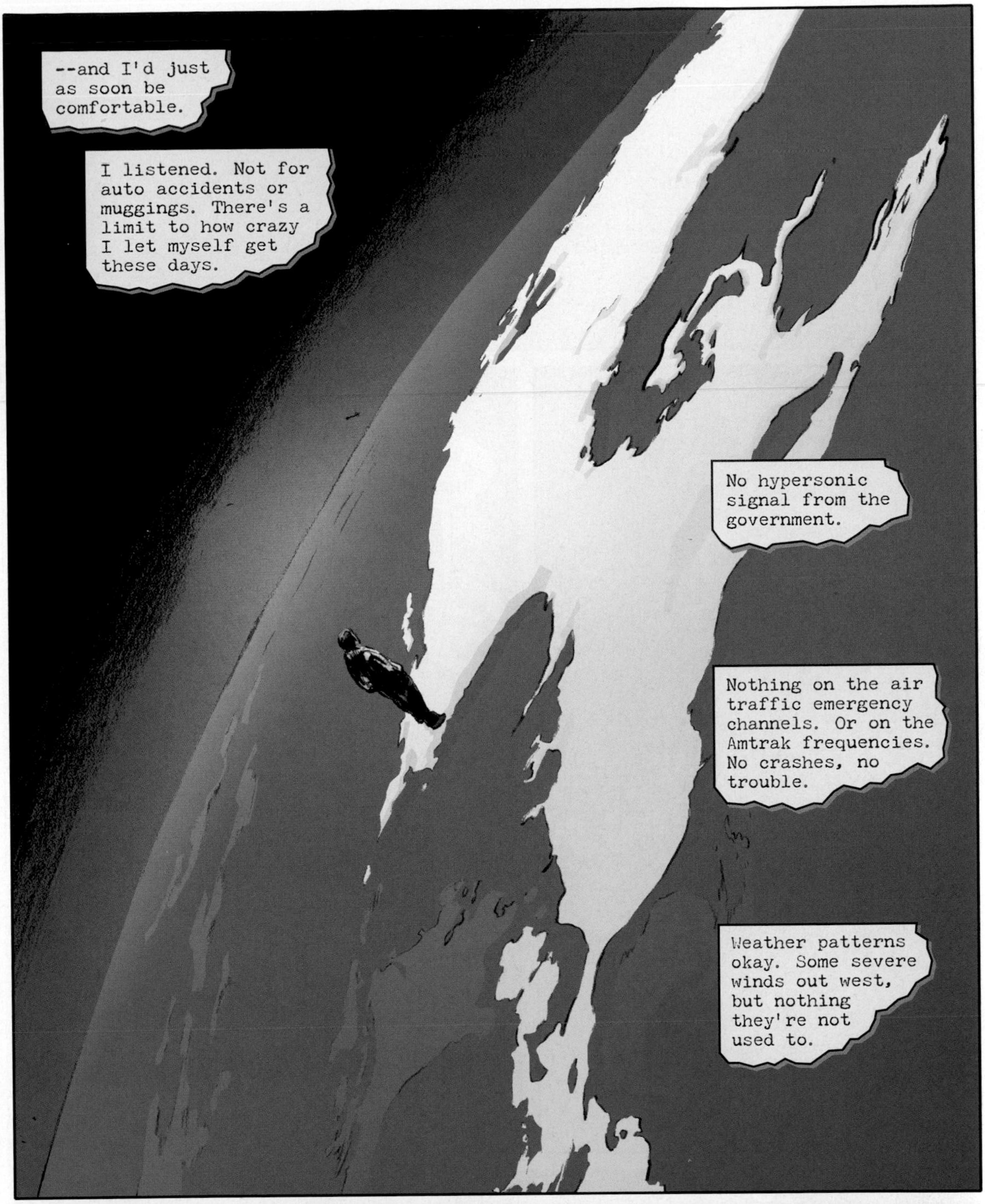
--and I'd just as soon be comfortable.
I listened. Not for auto accidents or muggings. There's a limit to how crazy I let myself get these days.
No hypersonic signal from the government.
Nothing on the air traffic emergency channels. Or on the Amtrak frequencies. No crashes, no trouble.
Weather patterns okay. Some severe winds out west, but nothing they're not used to.

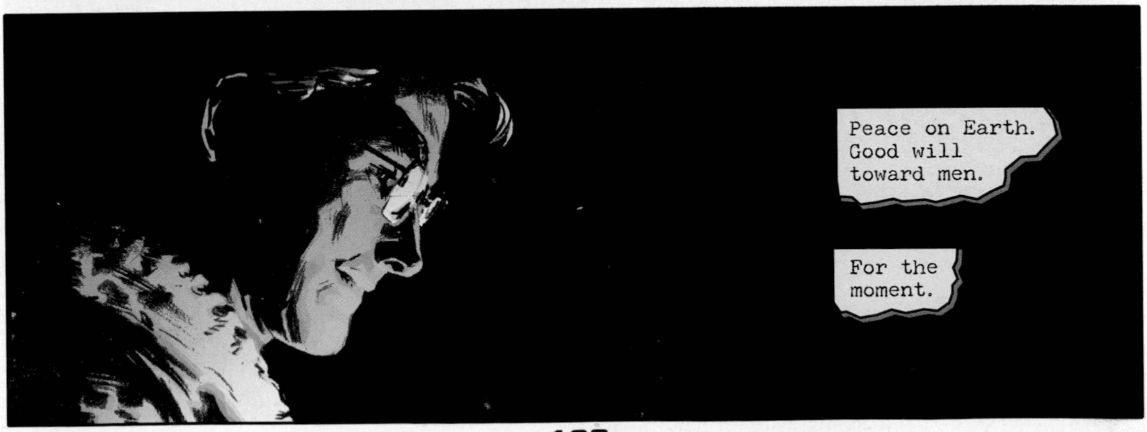
Peace on Earth. Good will toward men.
For the moment.

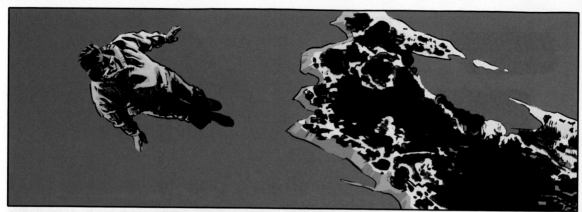

Lois was waiting, by the old hollow tree I used to use. One of her traditions.

I BROUGHT YOU SOME *EGGNOG.* JANE PRONOUNCED IT ALMOST *DRINK-ABLE.*

HOW *IS* IT? OUT THERE.

THANKS.

QUIET.

*GOOD.* YOU'RE NOT GETTING ANY *YOUNGER,* YOU KNOW.

NO. *NO,* I GUESS I'M *NOT.*

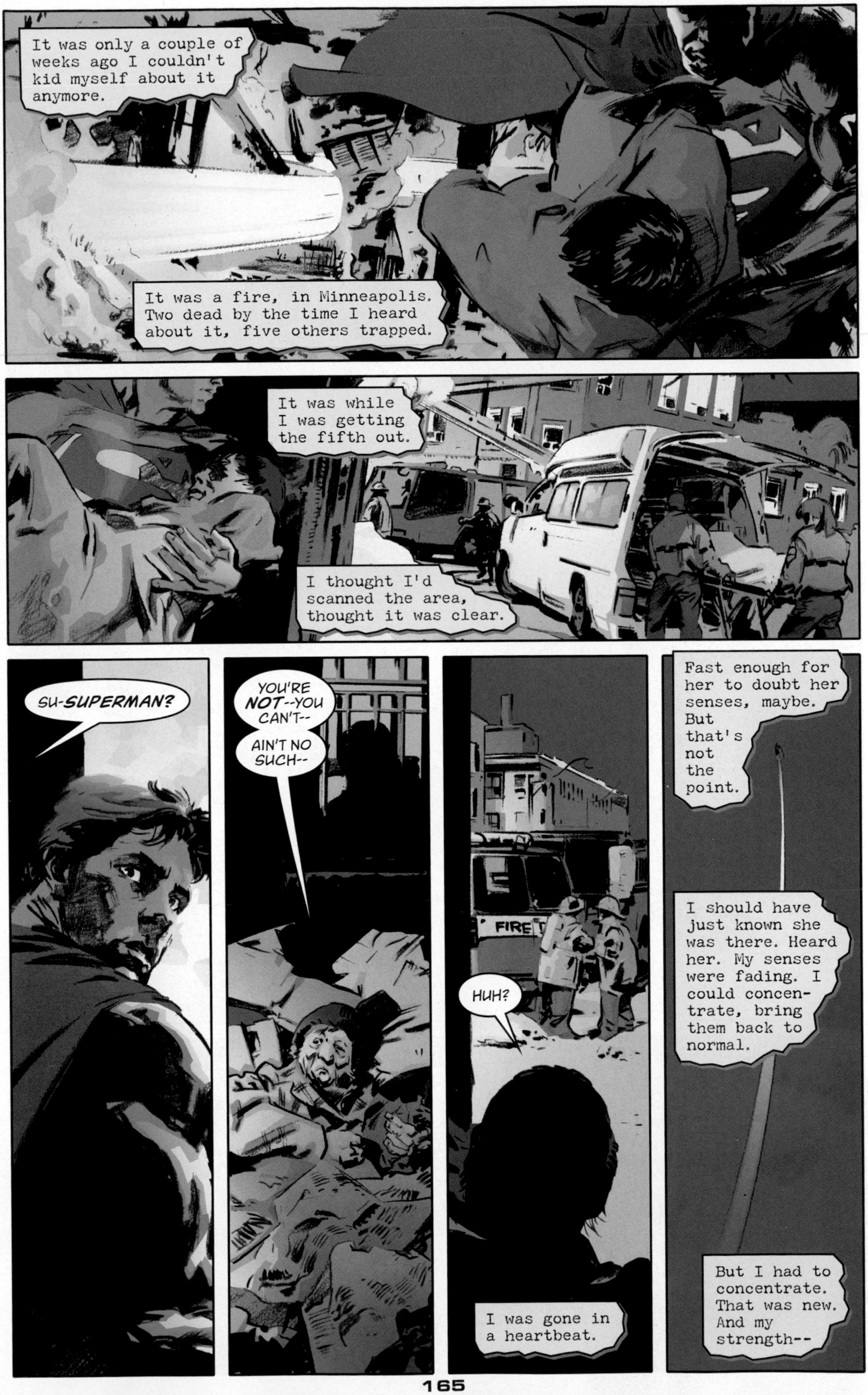
It was only a couple of weeks ago I couldn't kid myself about it anymore.
It was a fire, in Minneapolis. Two dead by the time I heard about it, five others trapped.
It was while I was getting the fifth out.
I thought I'd scanned the area, thought it was clear.
SU-SUPERMAN?
YOU'RE NOT--YOU CAN'T--
AIN'T NO SUCH--
HUH?
I was gone in a heartbeat.
Fast enough for her to doubt her senses, maybe. But that's not the point.
I should have just known she was there. Heard her. My senses were fading. I could concentrate, bring them back to normal.
But I had to concentrate. That was new. And my strength--

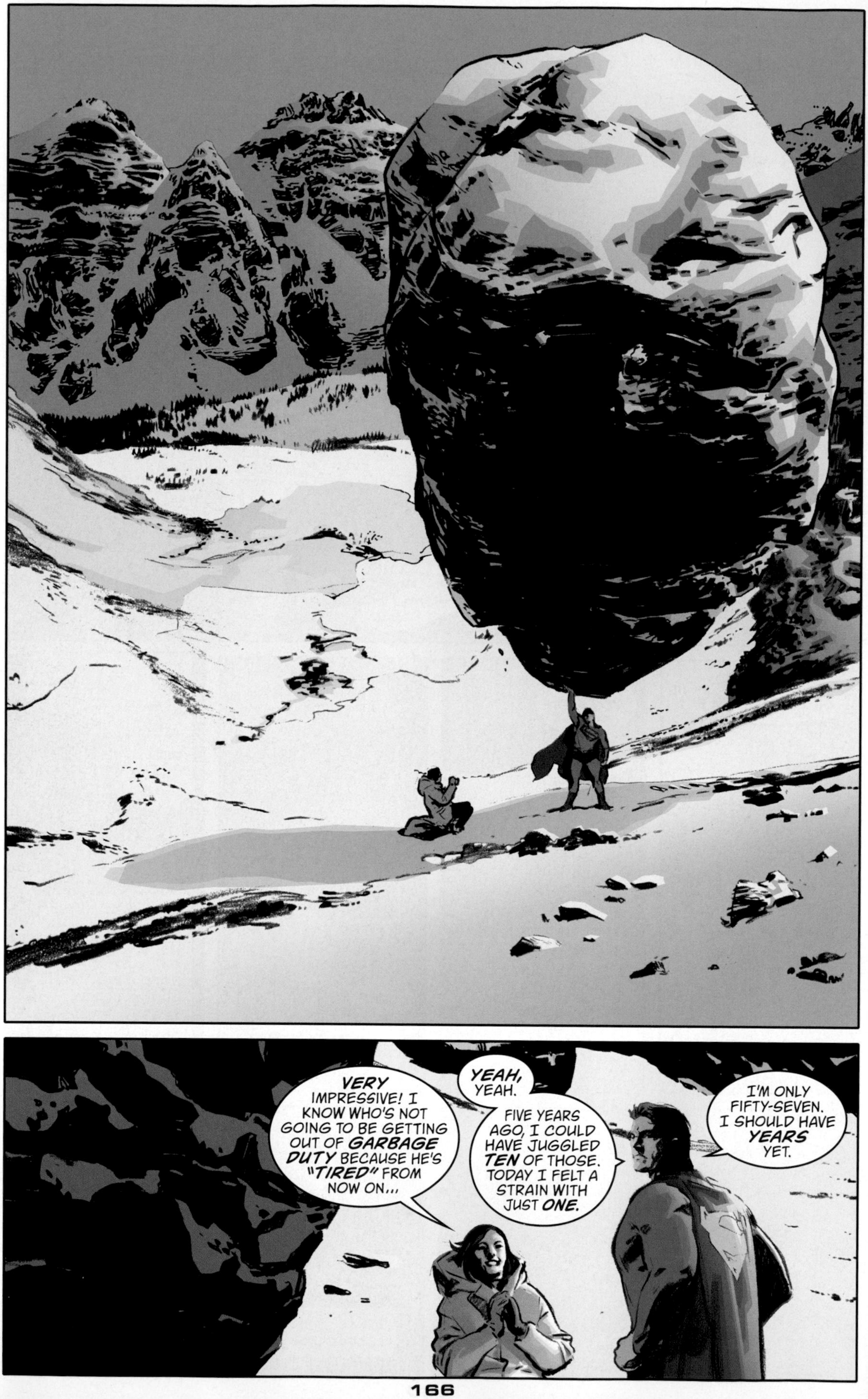
VERY IMPRESSIVE! I KNOW WHO'S NOT GOING TO BE GETTING OUT OF GARBAGE DUTY BECAUSE HE'S "TIRED" FROM NOW ON...
YEAH, YEAH.
FIVE YEARS AGO, I COULD HAVE JUGGLED TEN OF THOSE. TODAY I FELT A STRAIN WITH JUST ONE.
I'M ONLY FIFTY-SEVEN. I SHOULD HAVE YEARS YET.

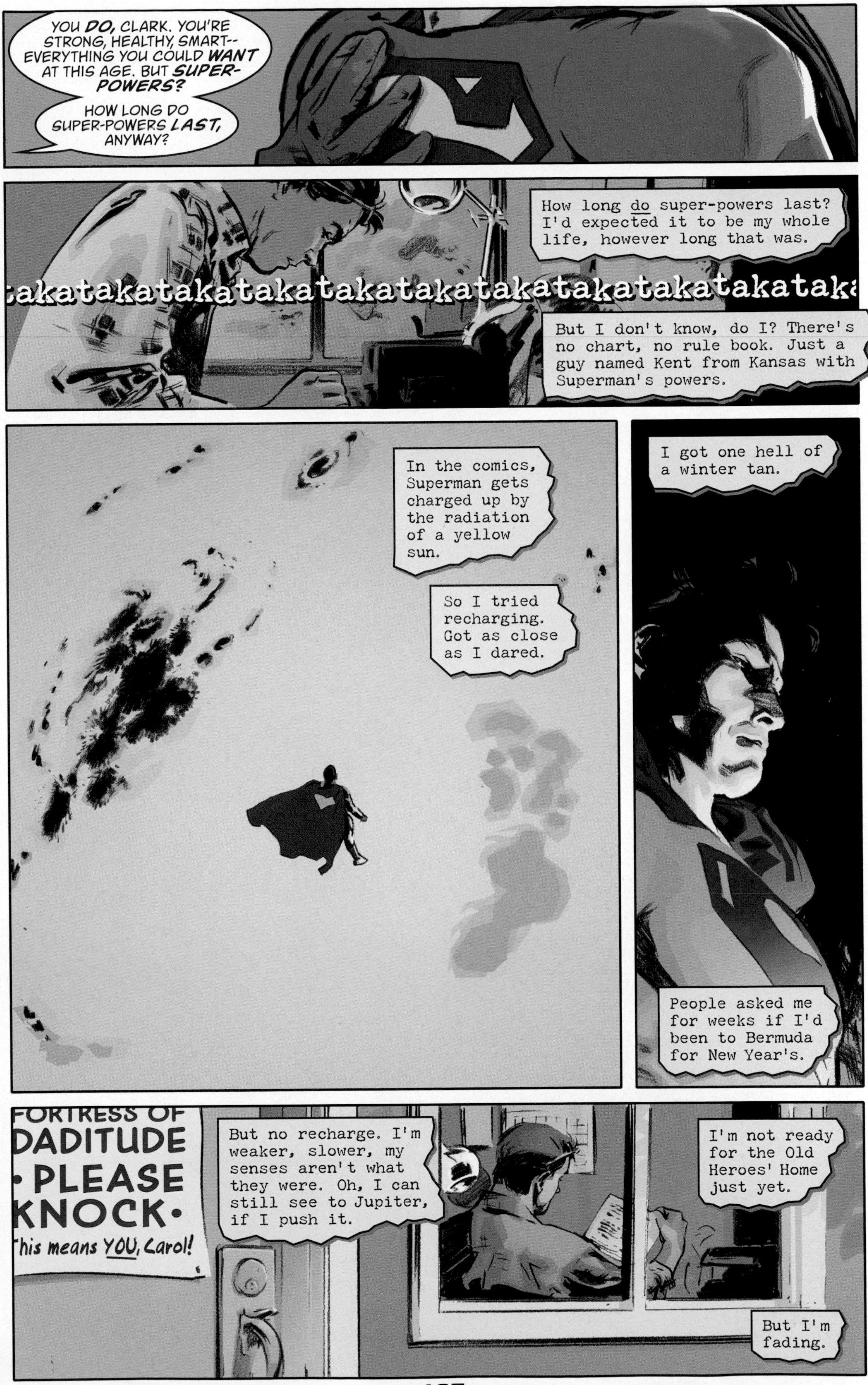
YOU DO, CLARK. YOU'RE STRONG, HEALTHY, SMART-- EVERYTHING YOU COULD WANT AT THIS AGE. BUT SUPER-POWERS?
HOW LONG DO SUPER-POWERS LAST, ANYWAY?
How long do super-powers last? I'd expected it to be my whole life, however long that was.
takatakatakatakatakatakatakatakataka
But I don't know, do I? There's no chart, no rule book. Just a guy named Kent from Kansas with Superman's powers.
In the comics, Superman gets charged up by the radiation of a yellow sun.
So I tried recharging. Got as close as I dared.
I got one hell of a winter tan.
People asked me for weeks if I'd been to Bermuda for New Year's.
FORTRESS OF DADITUDE • PLEASE KNOCK • This means YOU, Carol!
But no recharge. I'm weaker, slower, my senses aren't what they were. Oh, I can still see to Jupiter, if I push it.
I'm not ready for the Old Heroes' Home just yet.
But I'm fading.

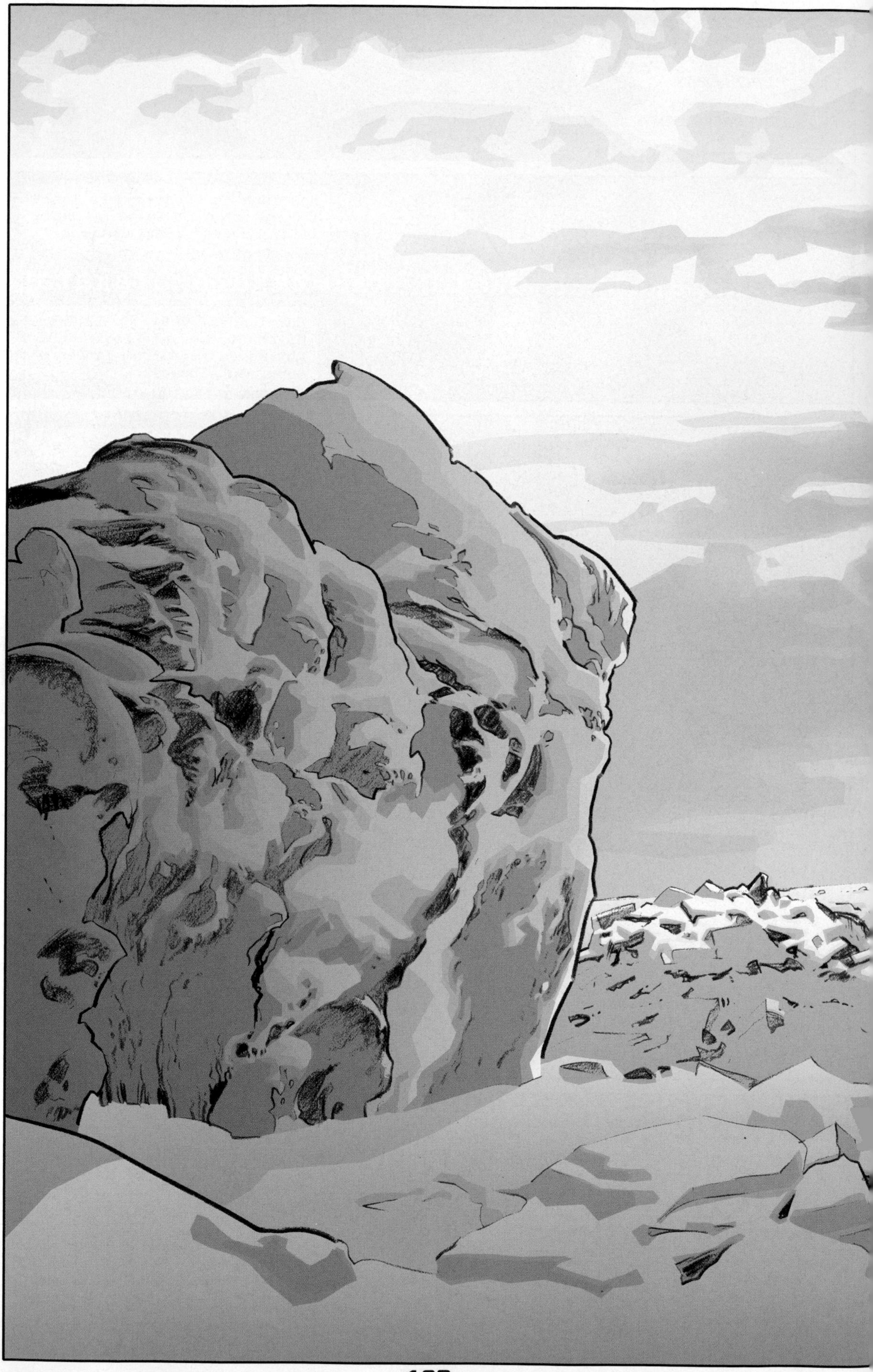

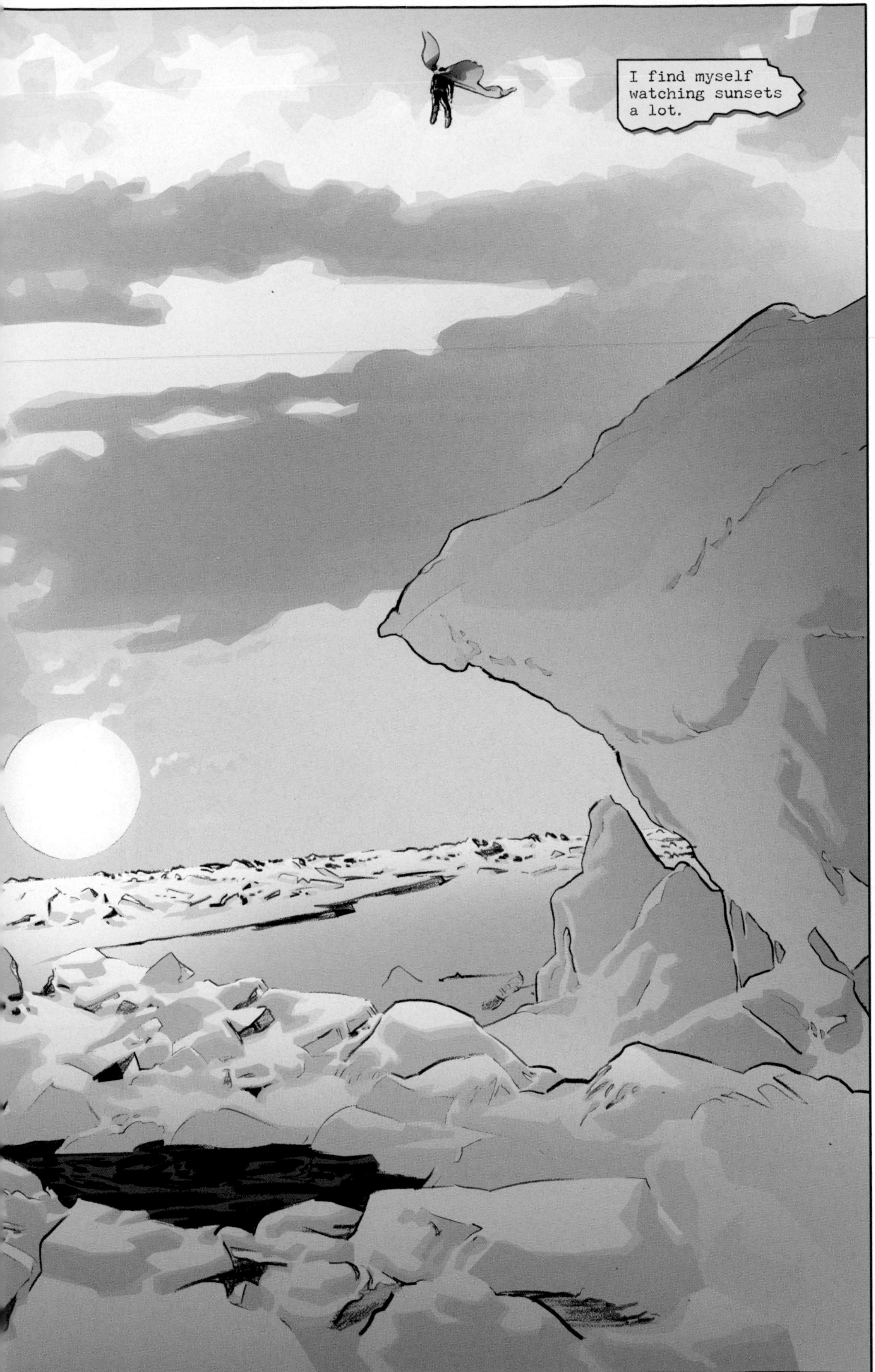
I find myself watching sunsets a lot.

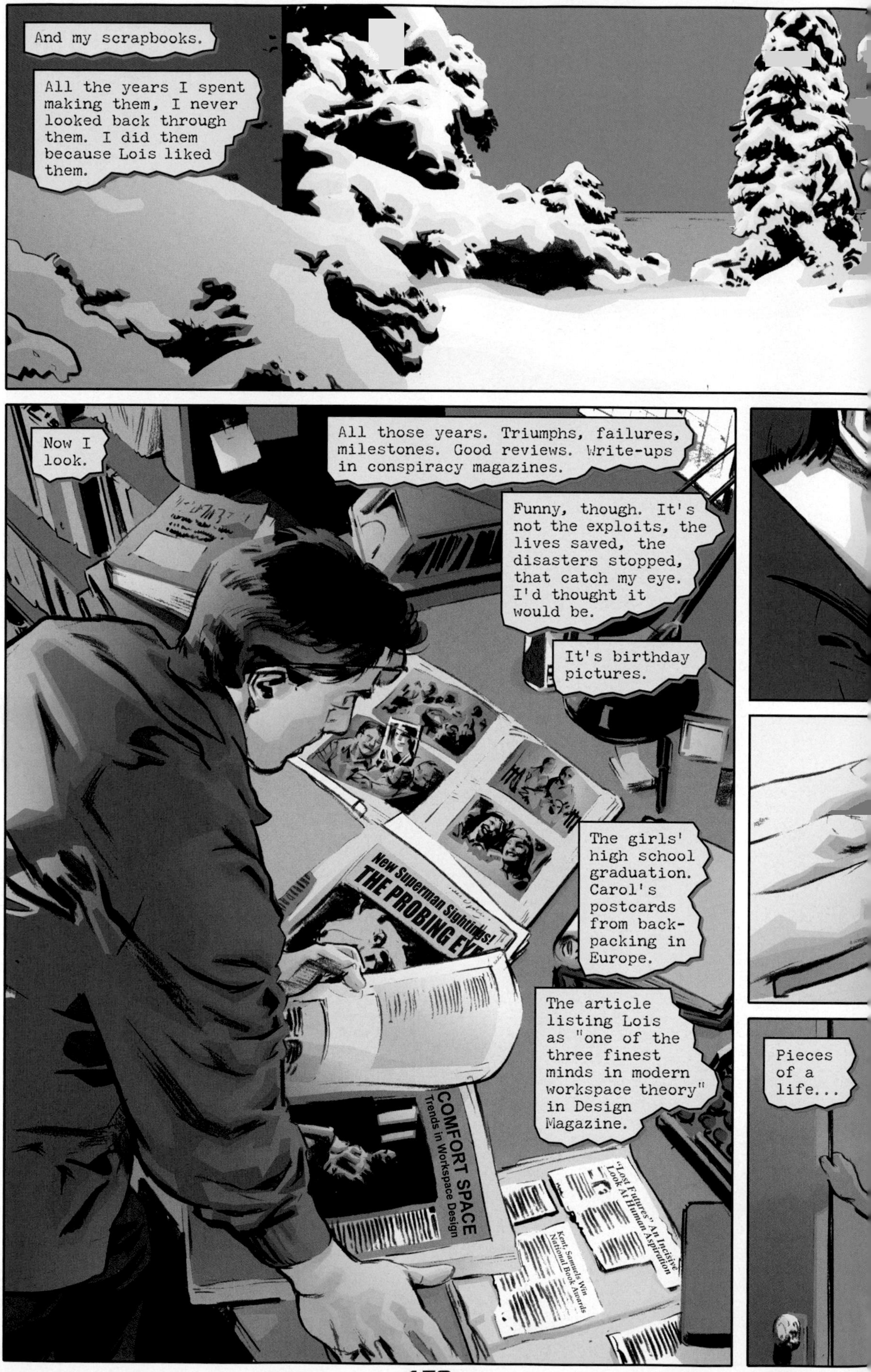
And my scrapbooks.
All the years I spent making them, I never looked back through them. I did them because Lois liked them.
Now I look.
All those years. Triumphs, failures, milestones. Good reviews. Write-ups in conspiracy magazines.
Funny, though. It's not the exploits, the lives saved, the disasters stopped, that catch my eye. I'd thought it would be.
It's birthday pictures.
New Superman Sightings!
THE PROBING
The girls' high school graduation. Carol's postcards from back-packing in Europe.
The article listing Lois as "one of the three finest minds in modern workspace theory" in Design Magazine.
COMFORT SPACE
Trends in Workspace Design
"Lost Futures" An Incisive Look At Human Aspiration
Kent, Samuels Win National Book Awards
Pieces of a life...

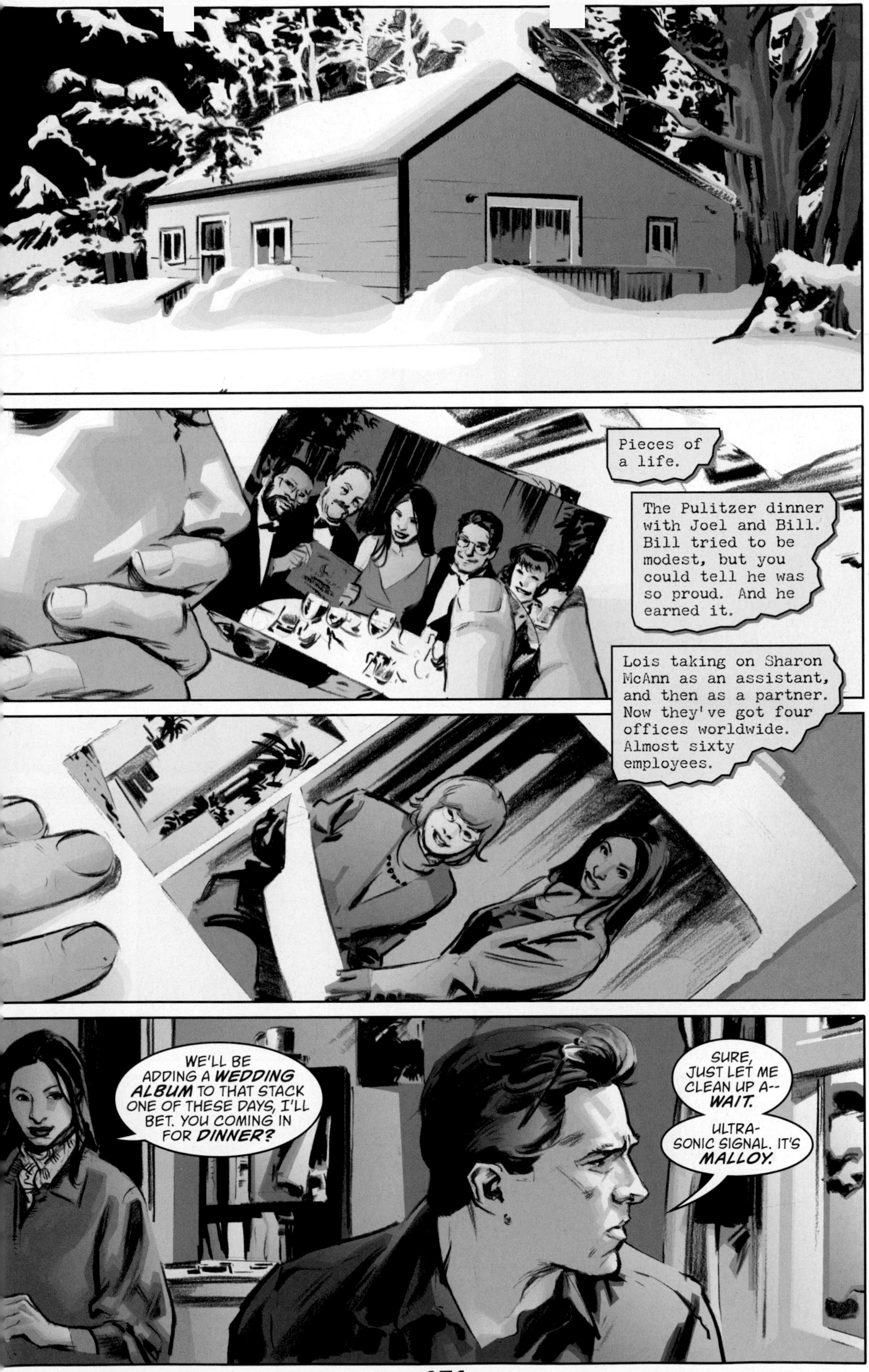

Pieces of a life.
The Pulitzer dinner with Joel and Bill. Bill tried to be modest, but you could tell he was so proud. And he earned it.
Lois taking on Sharon McAnn as an assistant, and then as a partner. Now they've got four offices worldwide. Almost sixty employees.
WE'LL BE ADDING A WEDDING ALBUM TO THAT STACK ONE OF THESE DAYS, I'LL BET. YOU COMING IN FOR DINNER?
SURE, JUST LET ME CLEAN UP A-- WAIT.
ULTRA-SONIC SIGNAL. IT'S MALLOY.

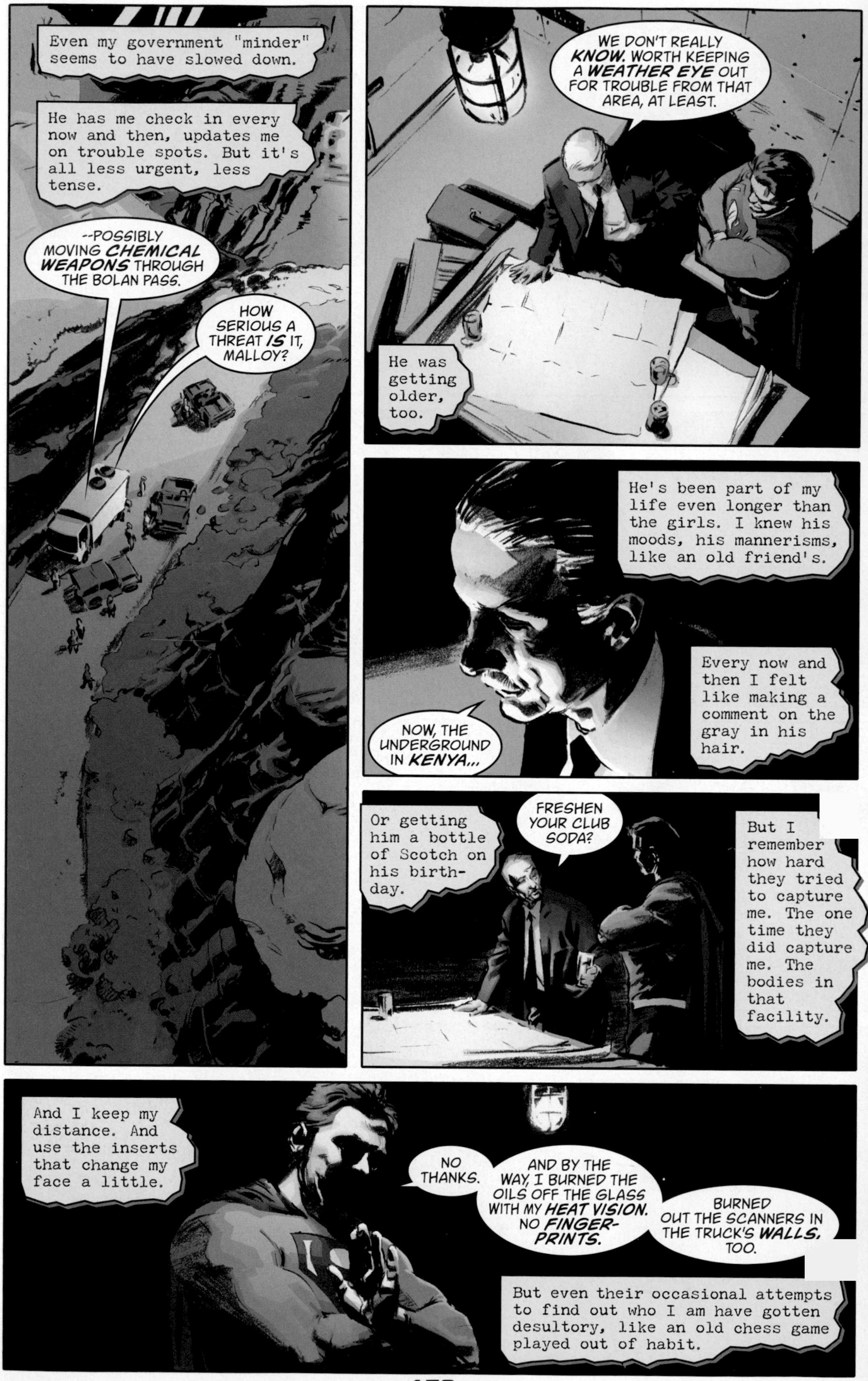
Even my government "minder" seems to have slowed down.
He has me check in every now and then, updates me on trouble spots. But it's all less urgent, less tense.
--POSSIBLY MOVING CHEMICAL WEAPONS THROUGH THE BOLAN PASS.
HOW SERIOUS A THREAT IS IT, MALLOY?
WE DON'T REALLY KNOW. WORTH KEEPING A WEATHER EYE OUT FOR TROUBLE FROM THAT AREA, AT LEAST.
He was getting older, too.
He's been part of my life even longer than the girls. I knew his moods, his mannerisms, like an old friend's.
NOW, THE UNDERGROUND IN KENYA...
Every now and then I felt like making a comment on the gray in his hair.
Or getting him a bottle of Scotch on his birth-day.
FRESHEN YOUR CLUB SODA?
But I remember how hard they tried to capture me. The one time they did capture me. The bodies in that facility.
And I keep my distance. And use the inserts that change my face a little.
NO THANKS.
AND BY THE WAY, I BURNED THE OILS OFF THE GLASS WITH MY HEAT VISION. NO FINGER-PRINTS.
BURNED OUT THE SCANNERS IN THE TRUCK'S WALLS, TOO.
But even their occasional attempts to find out who I am have gotten desultory, like an old chess game played out of habit.

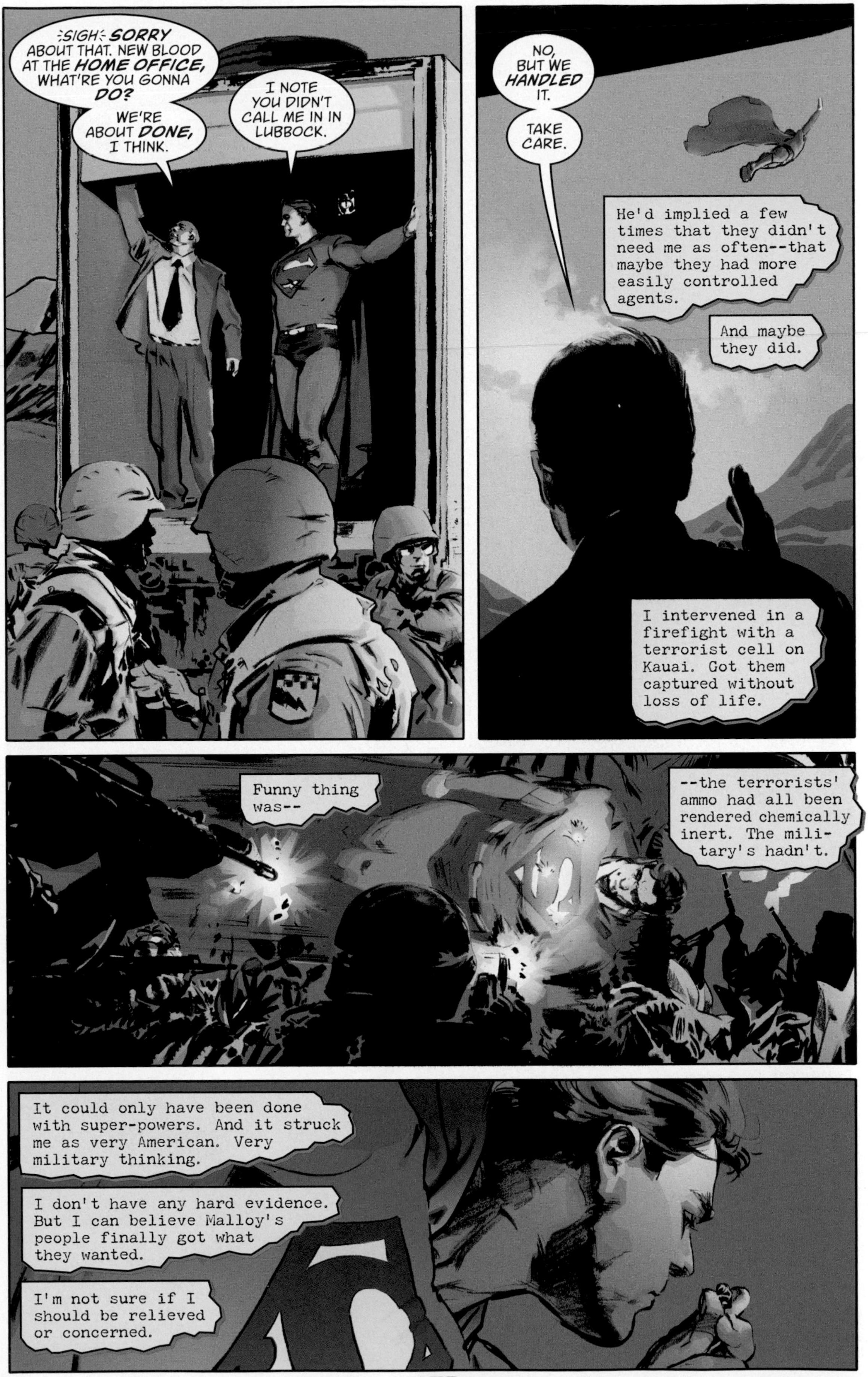

:SIGH: SORRY ABOUT THAT. NEW BLOOD AT THE HOME OFFICE, WHAT'RE YOU GONNA DO?
WE'RE ABOUT DONE, I THINK.
I NOTE YOU DIDN'T CALL ME IN IN LUBBOCK.
NO, BUT WE HANDLED IT.
TAKE CARE.
He'd implied a few times that they didn't need me as often--that maybe they had more easily controlled agents.
And maybe they did.
I intervened in a firefight with a terrorist cell on Kauai. Got them captured without loss of life.
Funny thing was--
--the terrorists' ammo had all been rendered chemically inert. The mili-tary's hadn't.
It could only have been done with super-powers. And it struck me as very American. Very military thinking.
I don't have any hard evidence. But I can believe Malloy's people finally got what they wanted.
I'm not sure if I should be relieved or concerned.

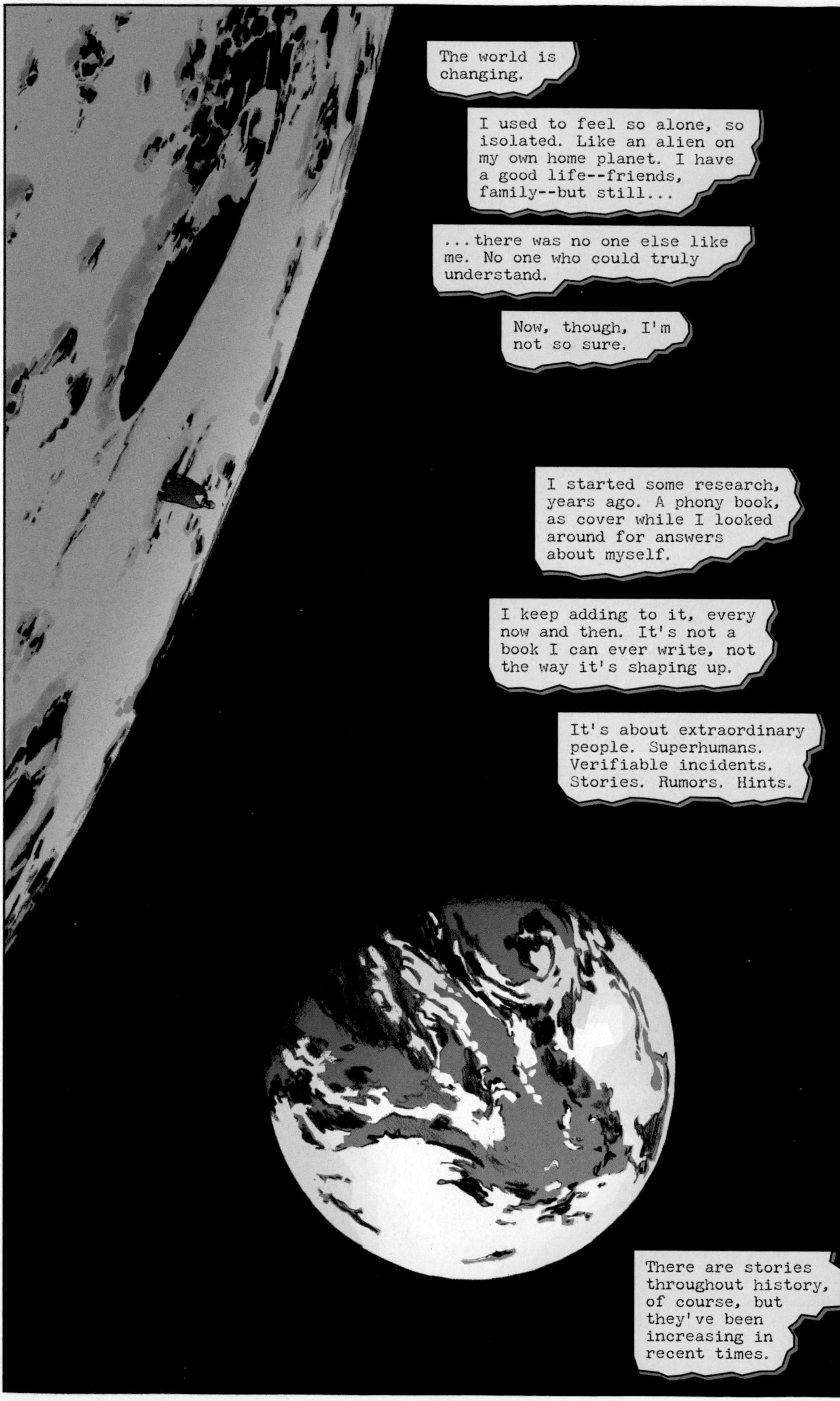
The world is changing.
I used to feel so alone, so isolated. Like an alien on my own home planet. I have a good life--friends, family--but still...
...there was no one else like me. No one who could truly understand.
Now, though, I'm not so sure.
I started some research, years ago. A phony book, as cover while I looked around for answers about myself.
I keep adding to it, every now and then. It's not a book I can ever write, not the way it's shaping up.
It's about extraordinary people. Superhumans. Verifiable incidents. Stories. Rumors. Hints.
There are stories throughout history, of course, but they've been increasing in recent times.

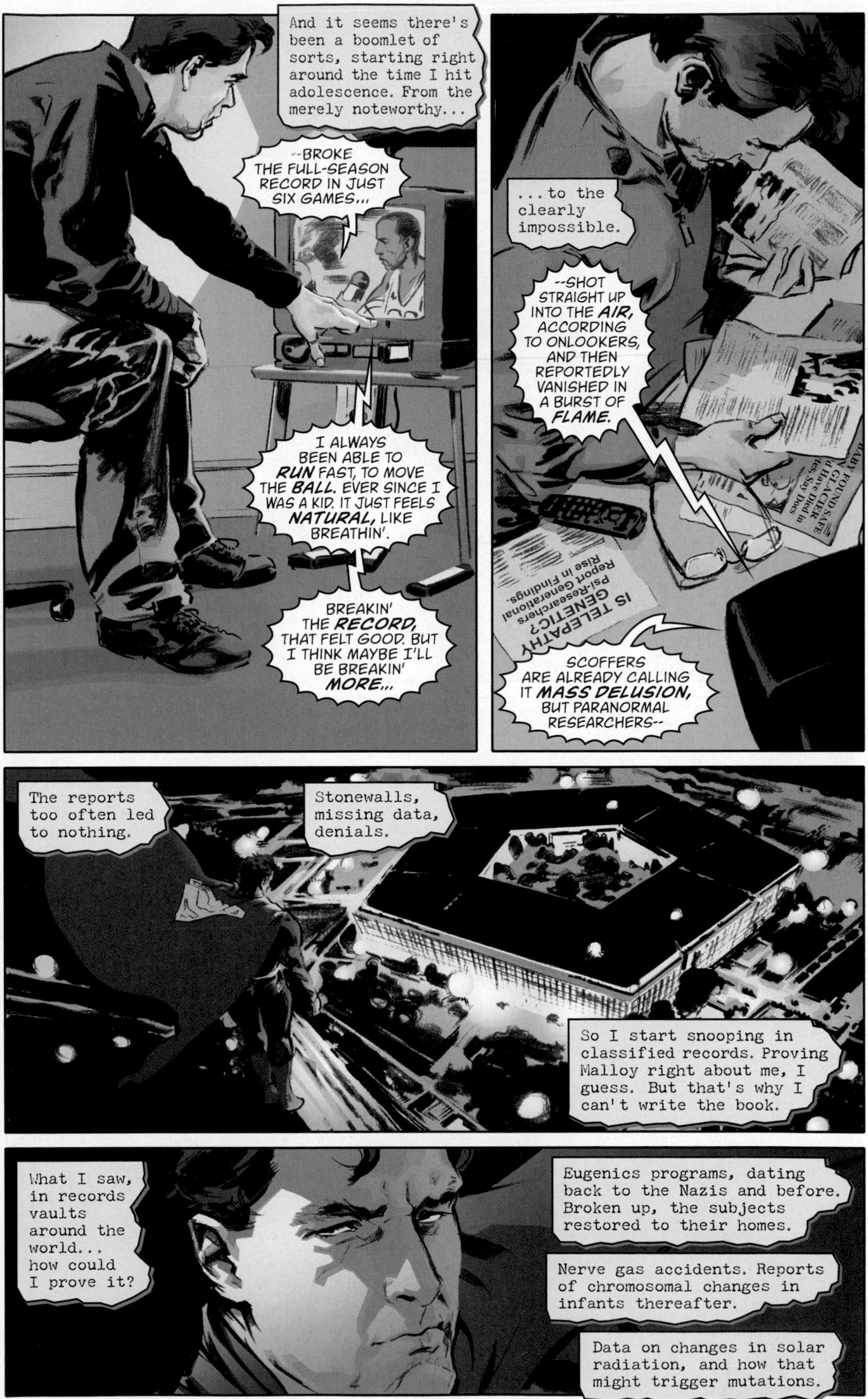
And it seems there's been a boomlet of sorts, starting right around the time I hit adolescence. From the merely noteworthy...
--BROKE THE FULL-SEASON RECORD IN JUST SIX GAMES...
I ALWAYS BEEN ABLE TO RUN FAST, TO MOVE THE BALL. EVER SINCE I WAS A KID. IT JUST FEELS NATURAL, LIKE BREATHIN'.
BREAKIN' THE RECORD, THAT FELT GOOD. BUT I THINK MAYBE I'LL BE BREAKIN' MORE...
...to the clearly impossible.
--SHOT STRAIGHT UP INTO THE AIR, ACCORDING TO ONLOOKERS, AND THEN REPORTEDLY VANISHED IN A BURST OF FLAME.
IS TELEPATHY GENETIC? Psi-Researchers Report Generational Rise in Findings.
SCOFFERS ARE ALREADY CALLING IT MASS DELUSION, BUT PARANORMAL RESEARCHERS--
The reports too often led to nothing.
Stonewalls, missing data, denials.
So I start snooping in classified records. Proving Malloy right about me, I guess. But that's why I can't write the book.
What I saw, in records vaults around the world... how could I prove it?
Eugenics programs, dating back to the Nazis and before. Broken up, the subjects restored to their homes.
Nerve gas accidents. Reports of chromosomal changes in infants thereafter.
Data on changes in solar radiation, and how that might trigger mutations.

More.

HERE IT IS. I COPIED IT AS WELL AS I COULD. *METEOR STRIKES* AROUND THE WORLD IN 1988. SEVERAL IN *KANSAS.*

UNKNOWN *CHEMICAL COMPOUNDS* AND *RADIATION* RELEASED INTO THE WATER TABLE. TESTS. COVER-UPS. I WAS *13.*

OH, CLARK. IS THAT...?

IS THAT WHAT HAPPENED TO *ME?*

IT *CHANGED* ME SOMEHOW? AND I GAVE *MYSELF* POWERS, SHAPED THEM *SUBCONSCIOUSLY?* IT WOULD EXPLAIN A LOT. BUT I DON'T *KNOW.*

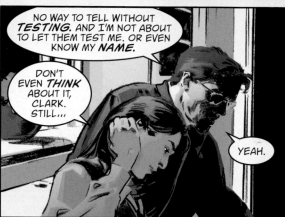

NO WAY TO TELL WITHOUT *TESTING.* AND I'M NOT ABOUT TO LET THEM TEST ME. OR EVEN KNOW MY *NAME.*

DON'T EVEN *THINK* ABOUT IT, CLARK. STILL...

YEAH.

It'd be nice to know. I don't really care on my own account. I've accepted who I am, and it doesn't matter to me how I got that way.

Still, it'd be nice to know for the girls' sake.

The girls. We worried so much, after they were born.

Not whether they'd have my powers, but whether we'd know how to deal with it if they did.

Whether they'd be discovered, and we wouldn't be able to protect them.

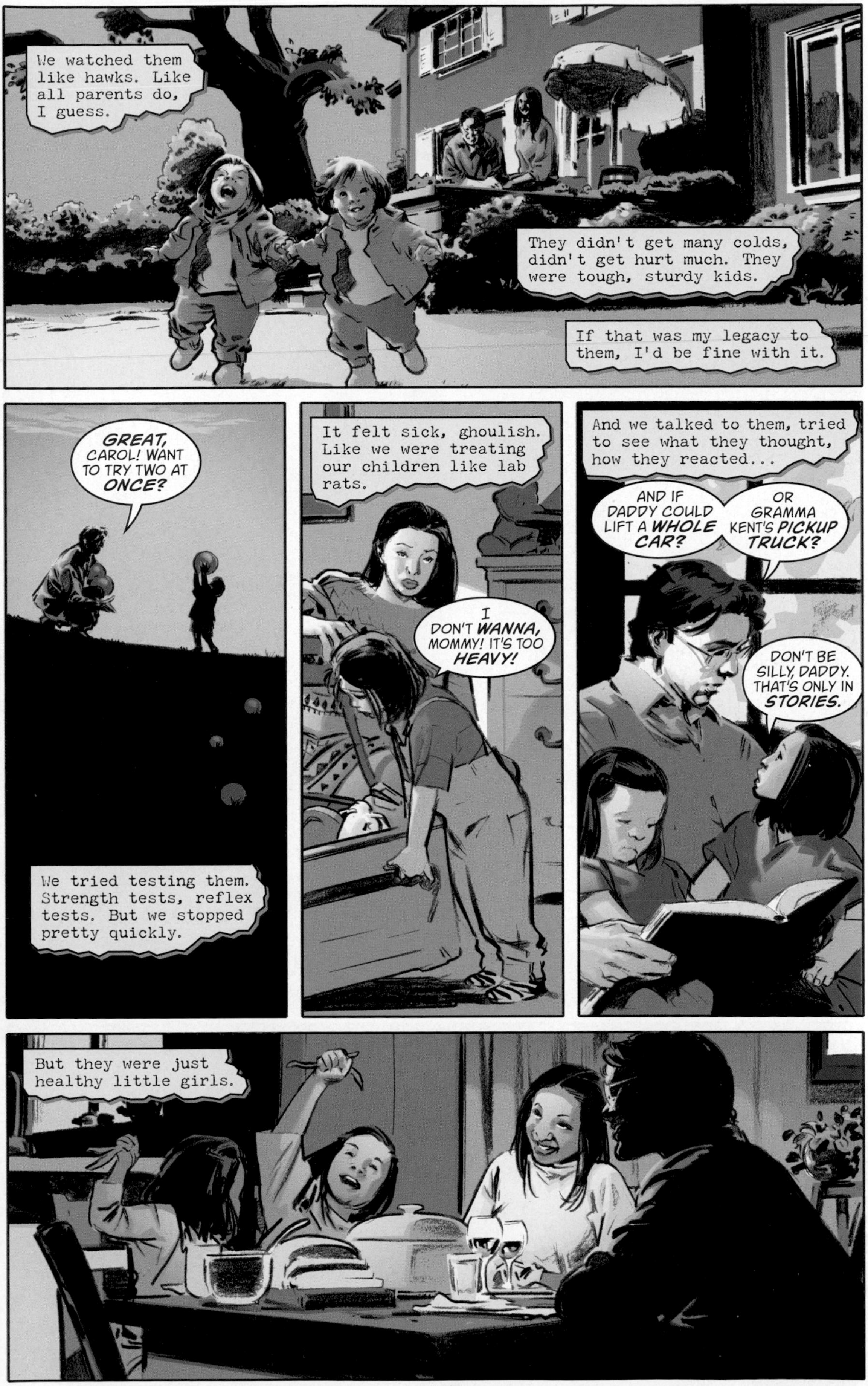
We watched them like hawks. Like all parents do, I guess.
They didn't get many colds, didn't get hurt much. They were tough, sturdy kids.
If that was my legacy to them, I'd be fine with it.
GREAT, CAROL! WANT TO TRY TWO AT ONCE?
We tried testing them. Strength tests, reflex tests. But we stopped pretty quickly.
It felt sick, ghoulish. Like we were treating our children like lab rats.
I DON'T WANNA, MOMMY! IT'S TOO HEAVY!
And we talked to them, tried to see what they thought, how they reacted...
AND IF DADDY COULD LIFT A WHOLE CAR?
OR GRAMMA KENT'S PICKUP TRUCK?
DON'T BE SILLY, DADDY. THAT'S ONLY IN STORIES.
But they were just healthy little girls.

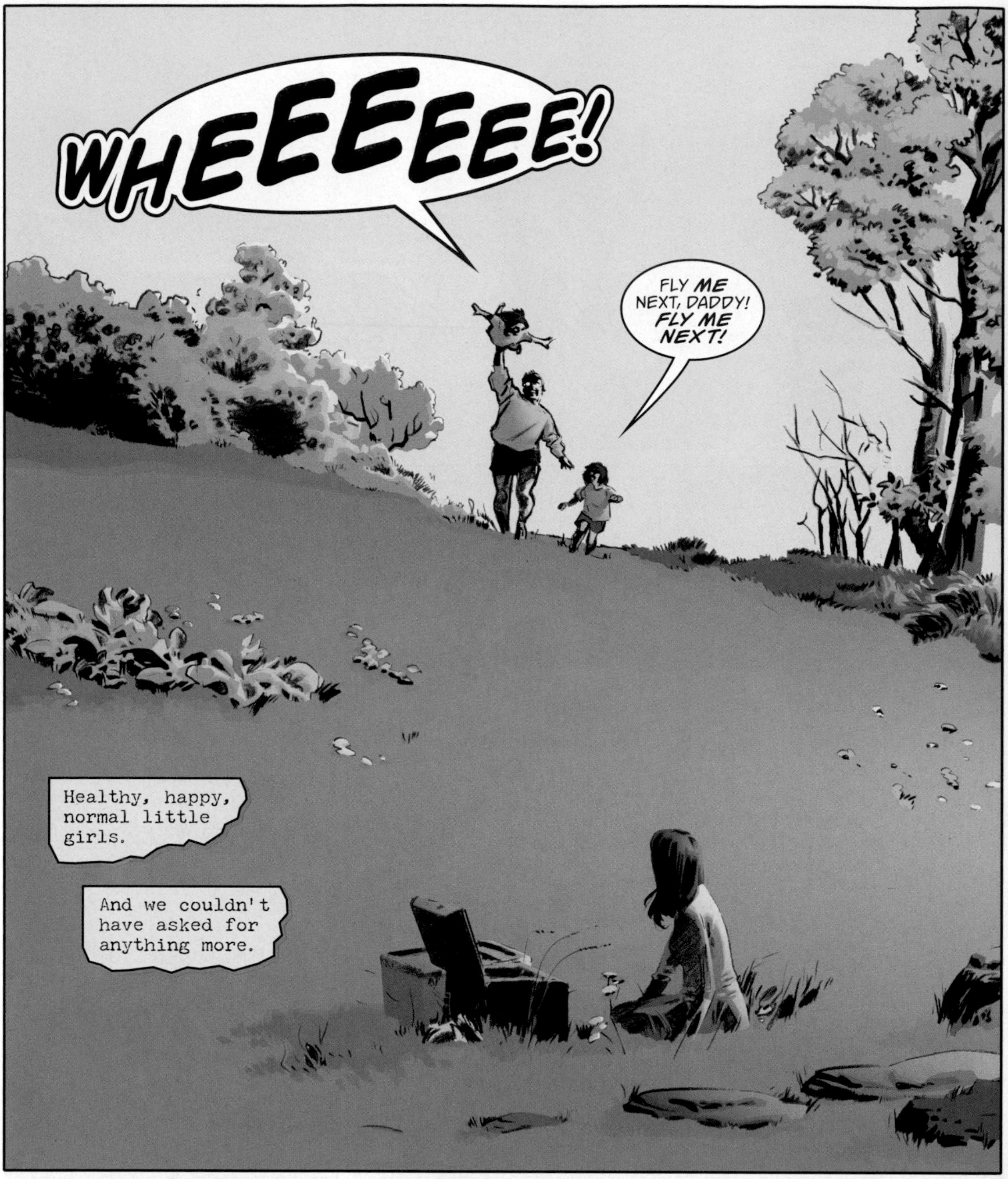
WHEEEEEEE!
FLY ME NEXT, DADDY! FLY ME NEXT!
Healthy, happy, normal little girls.
And we couldn't have asked for anything more.

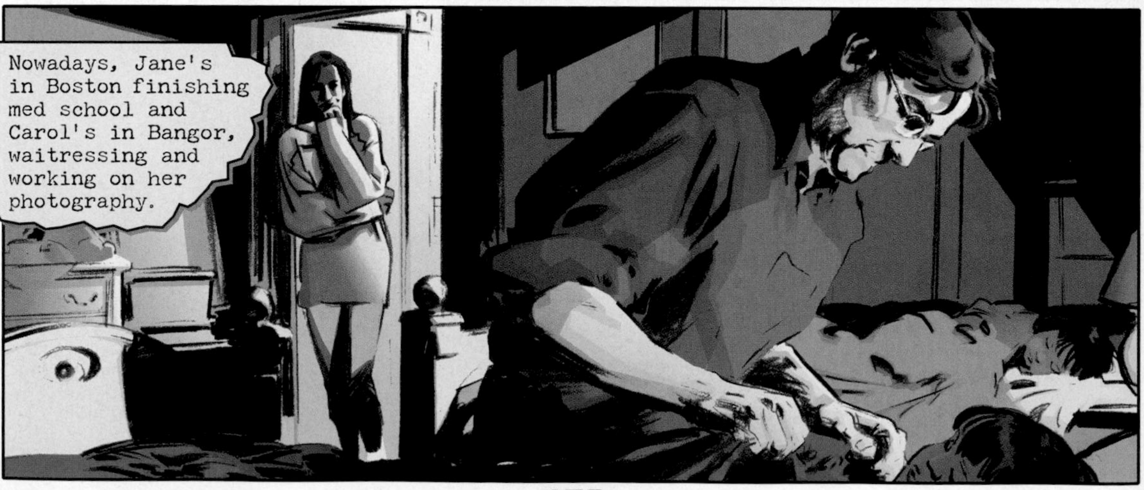
Nowadays, Jane's in Boston finishing med school and Carol's in Bangor, waitressing and working on her photography.

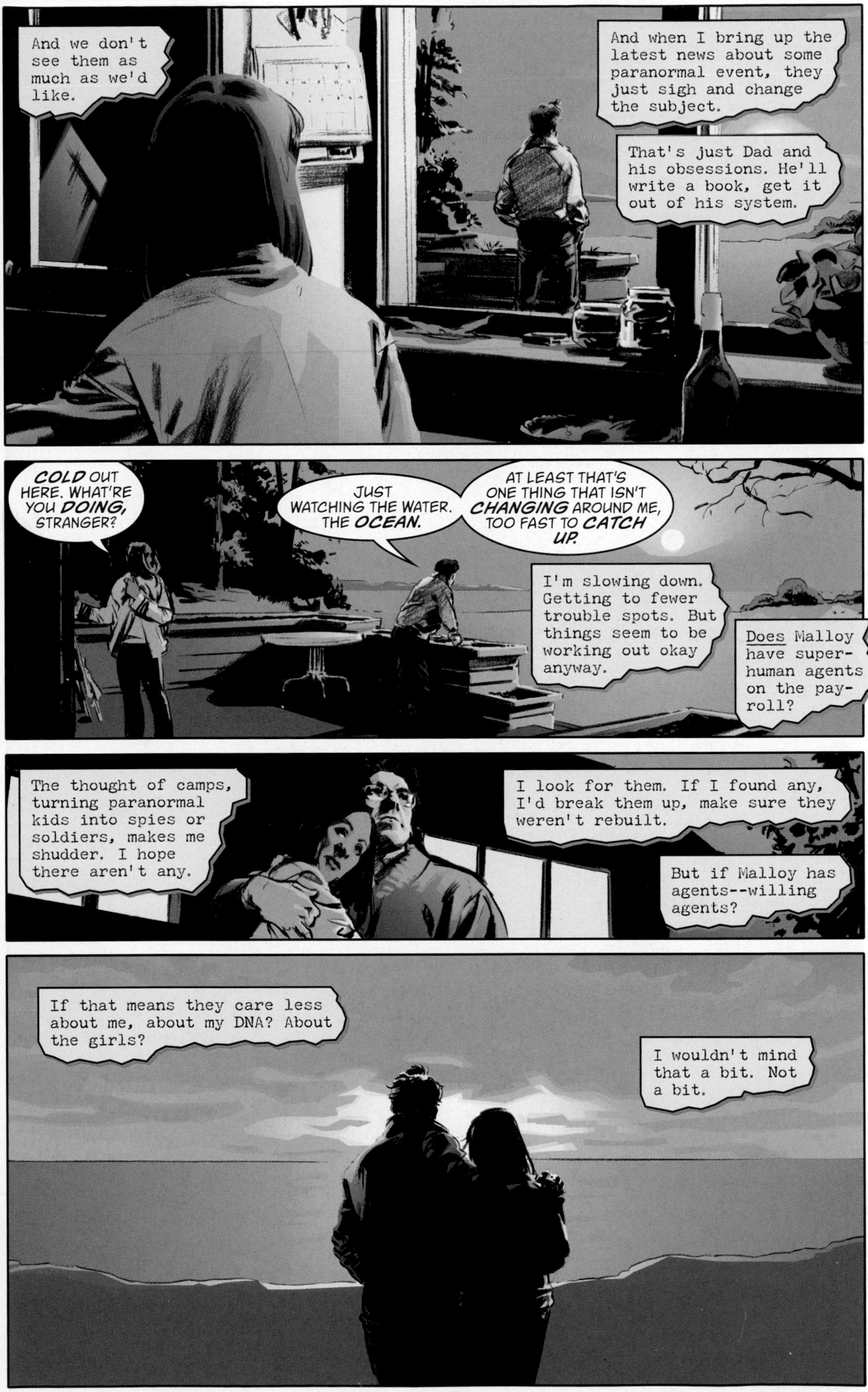
And we don't see them as much as we'd like.
And when I bring up the latest news about some paranormal event, they just sigh and change the subject.
That's just Dad and his obsessions. He'll write a book, get it out of his system.
COLD OUT HERE. WHAT'RE YOU DOING, STRANGER?
JUST WATCHING THE WATER. THE OCEAN.
AT LEAST THAT'S ONE THING THAT ISN'T CHANGING AROUND ME, TOO FAST TO CATCH UP.
I'm slowing down. Getting to fewer trouble spots. But things seem to be working out okay anyway.
Does Malloy have super-human agents on the pay-roll?
The thought of camps, turning paranormal kids into spies or soldiers, makes me shudder. I hope there aren't any.
I look for them. If I found any, I'd break them up, make sure they weren't rebuilt.
But if Malloy has agents--willing agents?
If that means they care less about me, about my DNA? About the girls?
I wouldn't mind that a bit. Not a bit.

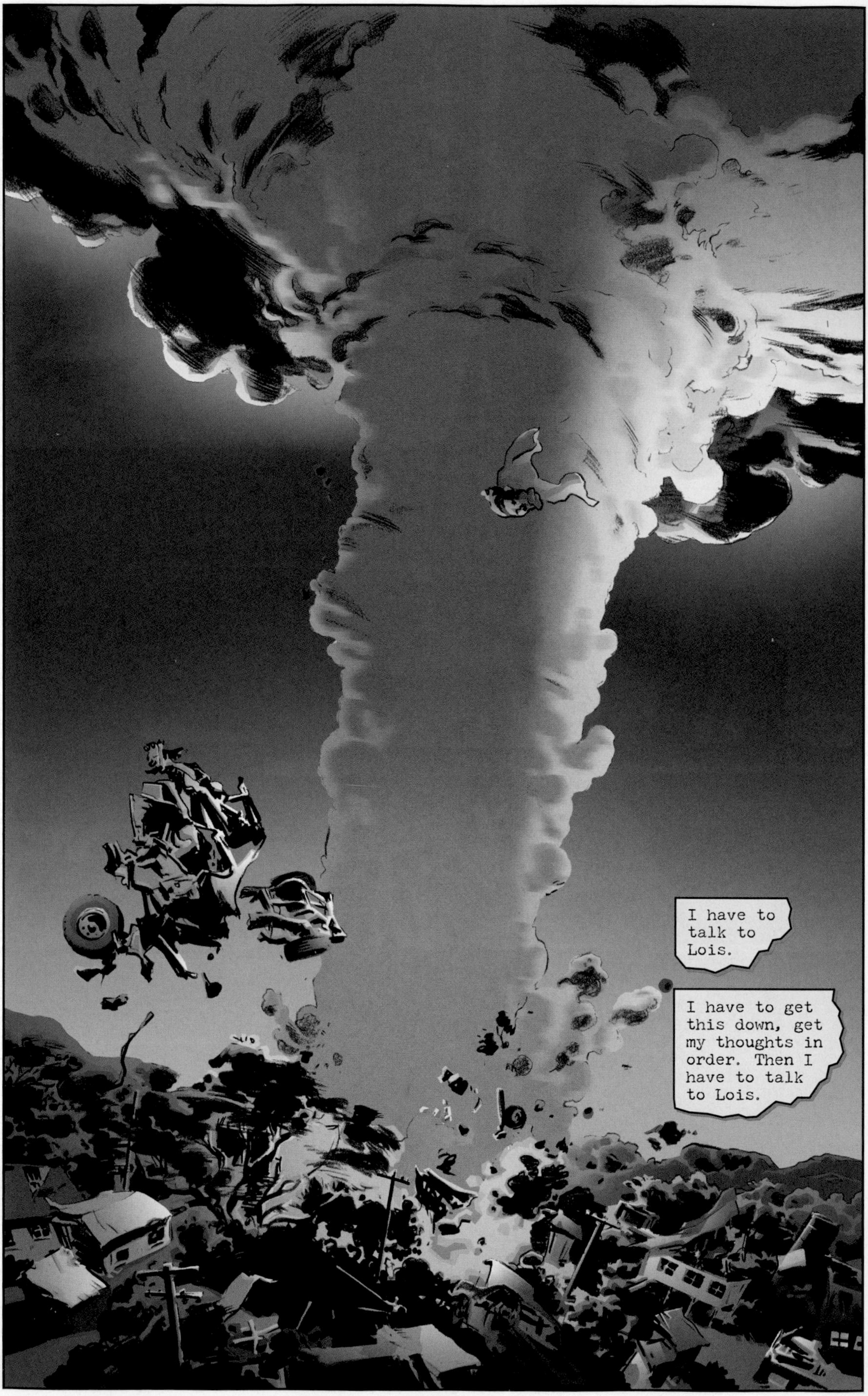
I have to talk to Lois.
I have to get this down, get my thoughts in order. Then I have to talk to Lois.

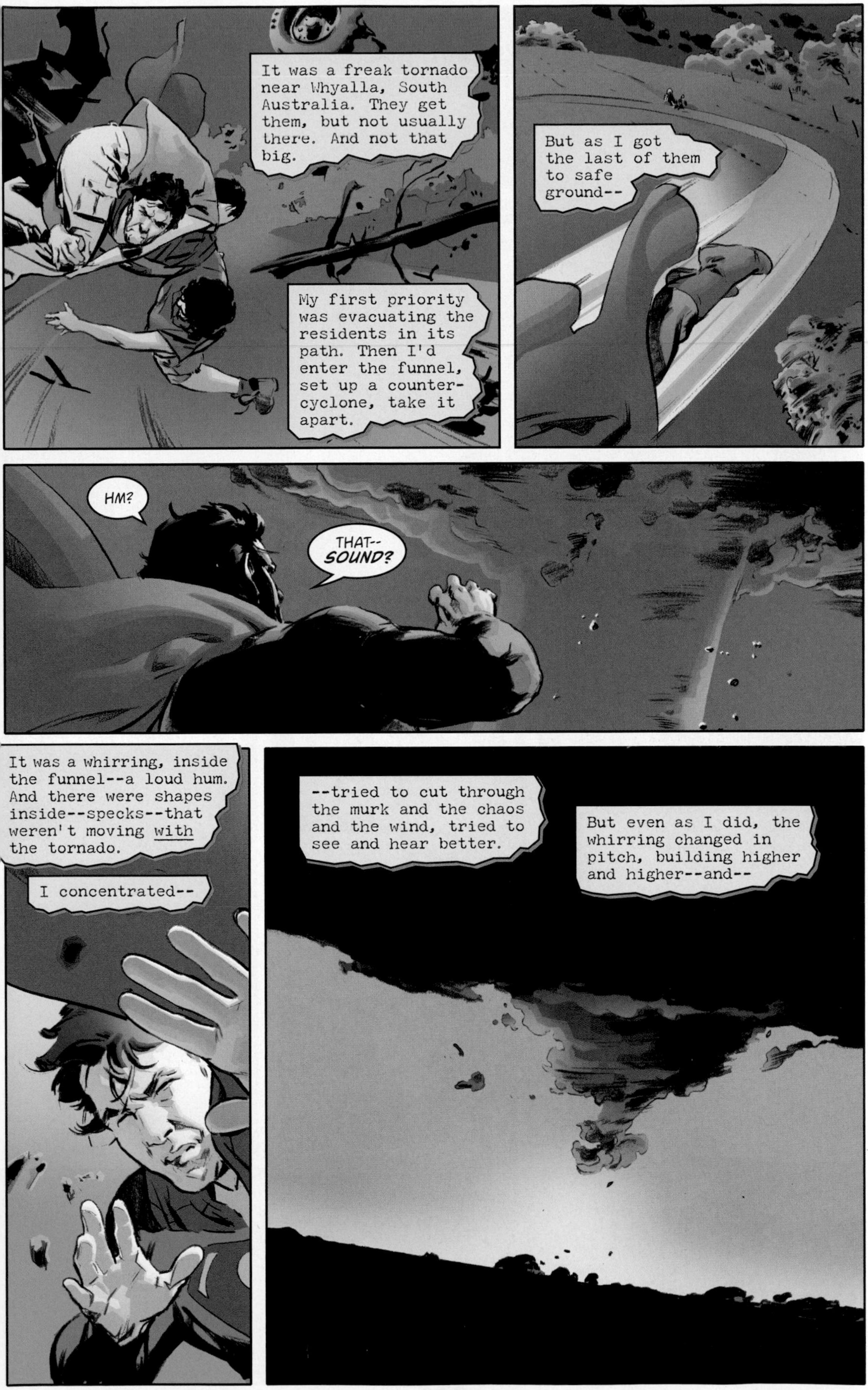
It was a freak tornado near Whyalla, South Australia. They get them, but not usually there. And not that big.
My first priority was evacuating the residents in its path. Then I'd enter the funnel, set up a counter-cyclone, take it apart.
But as I got the last of them to safe ground--
HM?
THAT-- SOUND?
It was a whirring, inside the funnel--a loud hum. And there were shapes inside--specks--that weren't moving with the tornado.
I concentrated--
--tried to cut through the murk and the chaos and the wind, tried to see and hear better.
But even as I did, the whirring changed in pitch, building higher and higher--and--

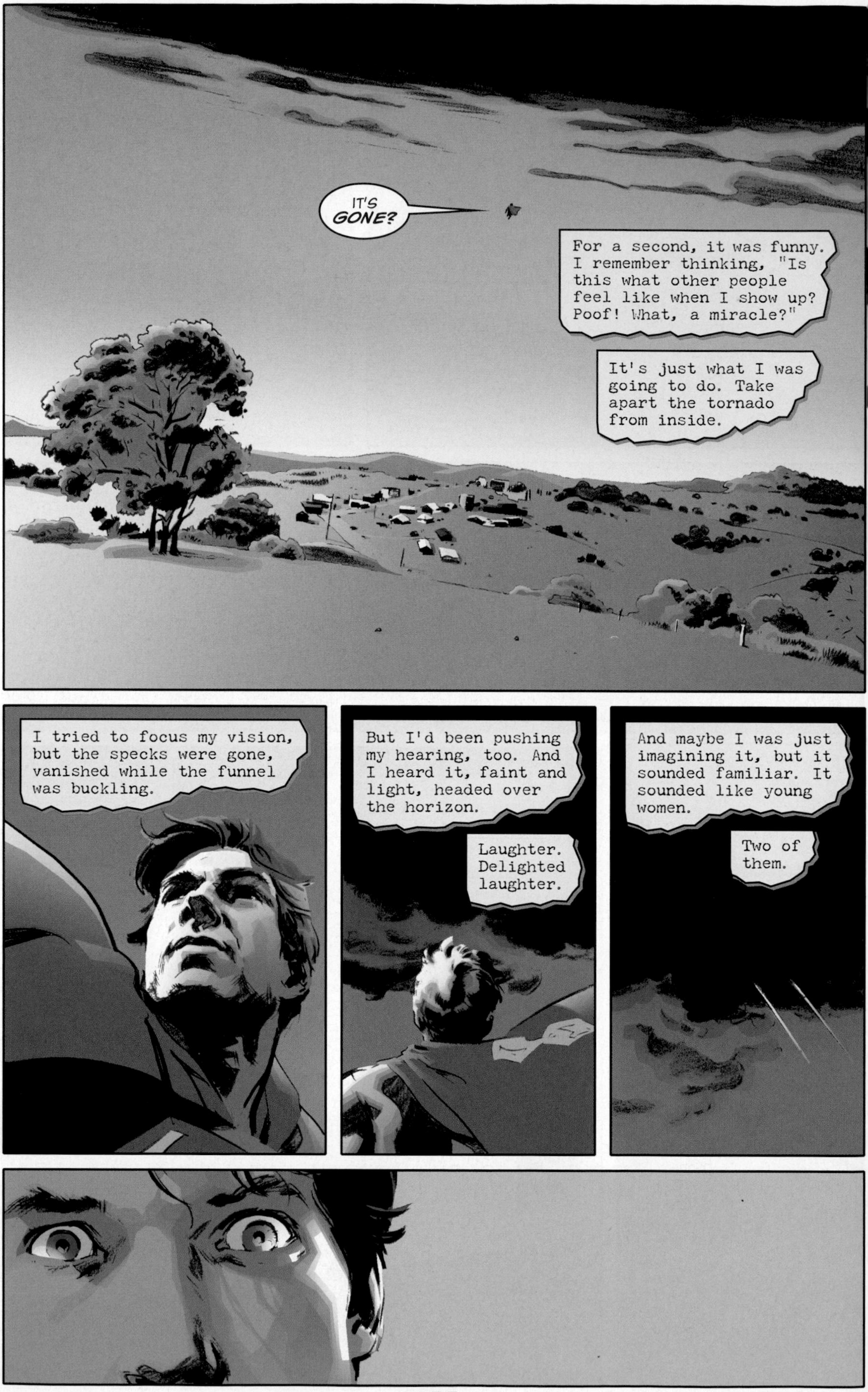
IT'S GONE?
For a second, it was funny. I remember thinking, "Is this what other people feel like when I show up? Poof! What, a miracle?"
It's just what I was going to do. Take apart the tornado from inside.
I tried to focus my vision, but the specks were gone, vanished while the funnel was buckling.
But I'd been pushing my hearing, too. And I heard it, faint and light, headed over the horizon.
Laughter. Delighted laughter.
And maybe I was just imagining it, but it sounded familiar. It sounded like young women.
Two of them.

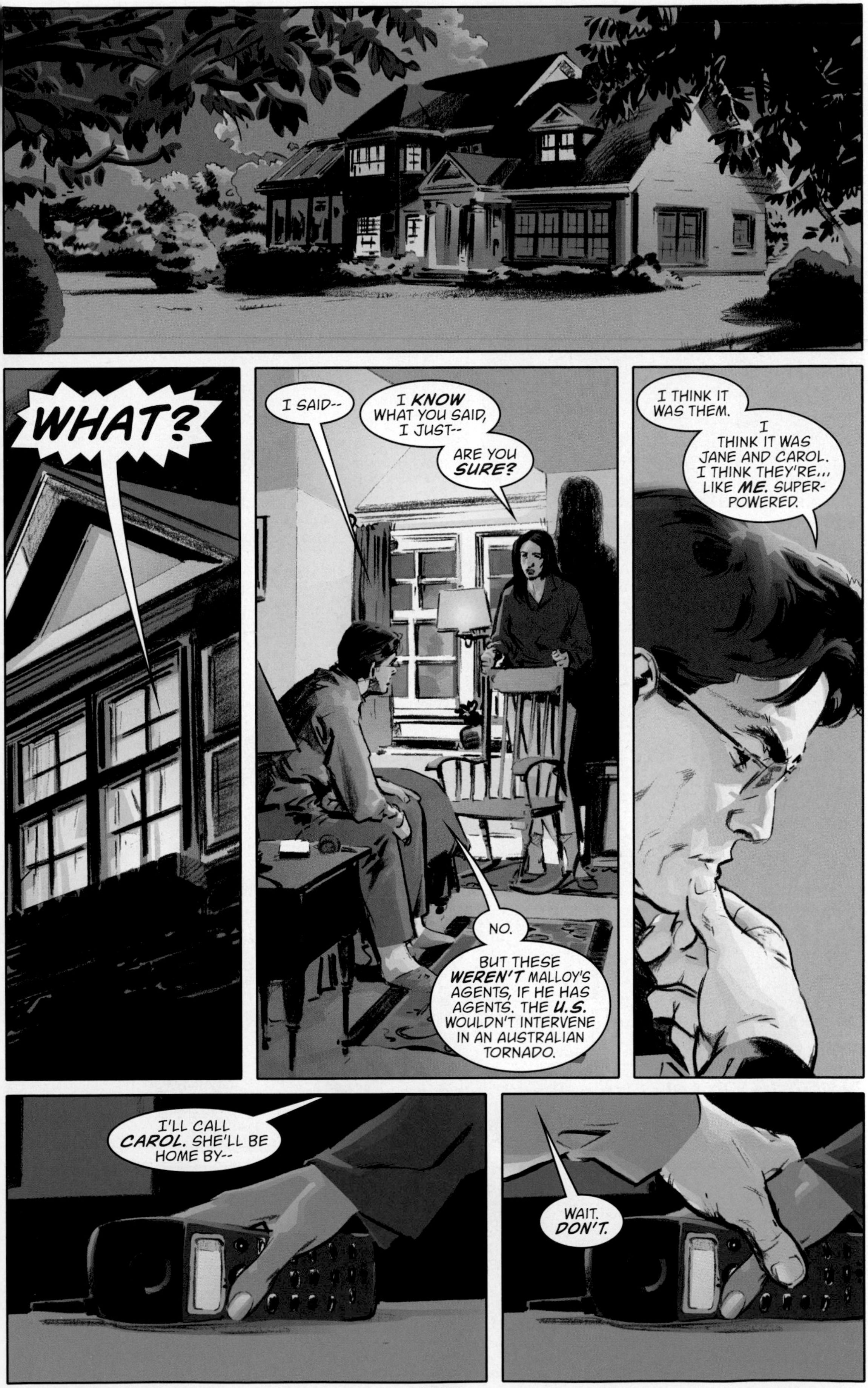
WHAT?
I SAID--
I KNOW WHAT YOU SAID, I JUST--
ARE YOU SURE?
NO.
BUT THESE WEREN'T MALLOY'S AGENTS, IF HE HAS AGENTS. THE U.S. WOULDN'T INTERVENE IN AN AUSTRALIAN TORNADO.
I THINK IT WAS THEM.
I THINK IT WAS JANE AND CAROL. I THINK THEY'RE... LIKE ME. SUPER-POWERED.
I'LL CALL CAROL. SHE'LL BE HOME BY--
WAIT. DON'T.

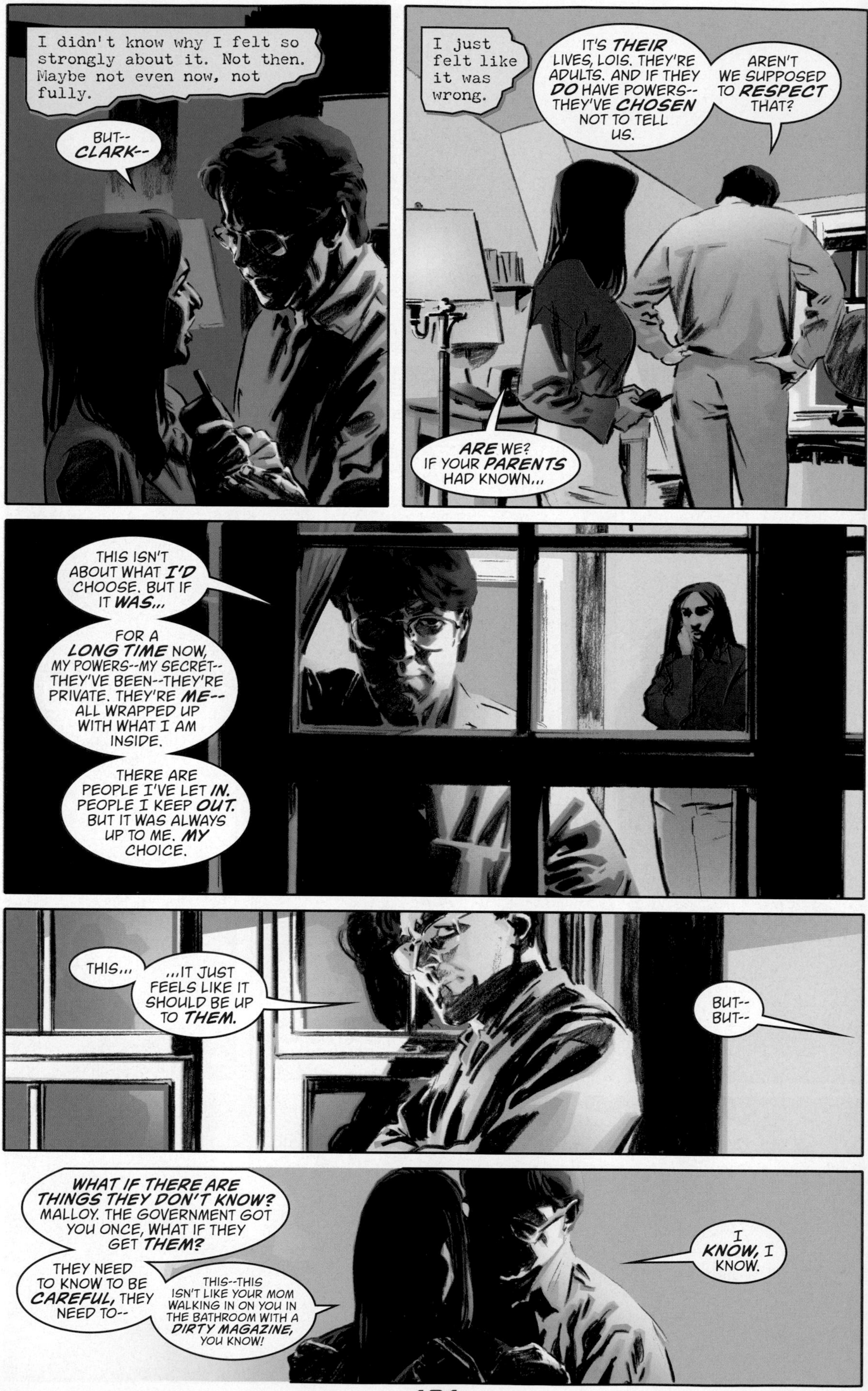
I didn't know why I felt so strongly about it. Not then. Maybe not even now, not fully.
BUT-- CLARK--
I just felt like it was wrong.
IT'S THEIR LIVES, LOIS. THEY'RE ADULTS. AND IF THEY DO HAVE POWERS-- THEY'VE CHOSEN NOT TO TELL US.
AREN'T WE SUPPOSED TO RESPECT THAT?
ARE WE? IF YOUR PARENTS HAD KNOWN...
THIS ISN'T ABOUT WHAT I'D CHOOSE. BUT IF IT WAS...
FOR A LONG TIME NOW, MY POWERS--MY SECRET-- THEY'VE BEEN--THEY'RE PRIVATE. THEY'RE ME-- ALL WRAPPED UP WITH WHAT I AM INSIDE.
THERE ARE PEOPLE I'VE LET IN. PEOPLE I KEEP OUT. BUT IT WAS ALWAYS UP TO ME. MY CHOICE.
THIS...
...IT JUST FEELS LIKE IT SHOULD BE UP TO THEM.
BUT-- BUT--
WHAT IF THERE ARE THINGS THEY DON'T KNOW? MALLOY. THE GOVERNMENT GOT YOU ONCE, WHAT IF THEY GET THEM?
THEY NEED TO KNOW TO BE CAREFUL, THEY NEED TO--
THIS--THIS ISN'T LIKE YOUR MOM WALKING IN ON YOU IN THE BATHROOM WITH A DIRTY MAGAZINE, YOU KNOW!
I KNOW, I KNOW.

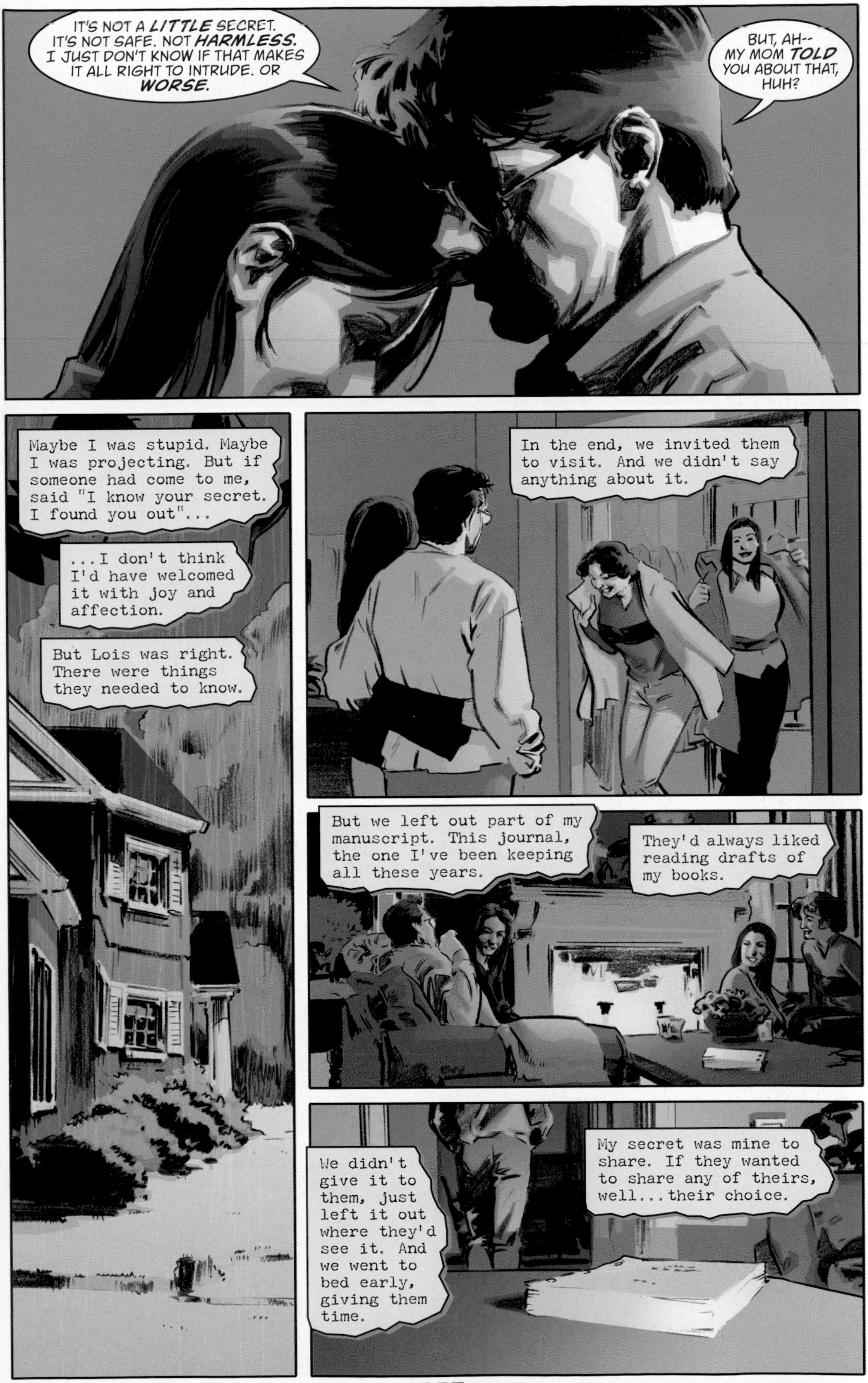
IT'S NOT A LITTLE SECRET. IT'S NOT SAFE. NOT HARMLESS. I JUST DON'T KNOW IF THAT MAKES IT ALL RIGHT TO INTRUDE. OR WORSE.
BUT, AH-- MY MOM TOLD YOU ABOUT THAT, HUH?
Maybe I was stupid. Maybe I was projecting. But if someone had come to me, said "I know your secret. I found you out"...
...I don't think I'd have welcomed it with joy and affection.
But Lois was right. There were things they needed to know.
In the end, we invited them to visit. And we didn't say anything about it.
But we left out part of my manuscript. This journal, the one I've been keeping all these years.
They'd always liked reading drafts of my books.
We didn't give it to them, just left it out where they'd see it. And we went to bed early, giving them time.
My secret was mine to share. If they wanted to share any of theirs, well...their choice.

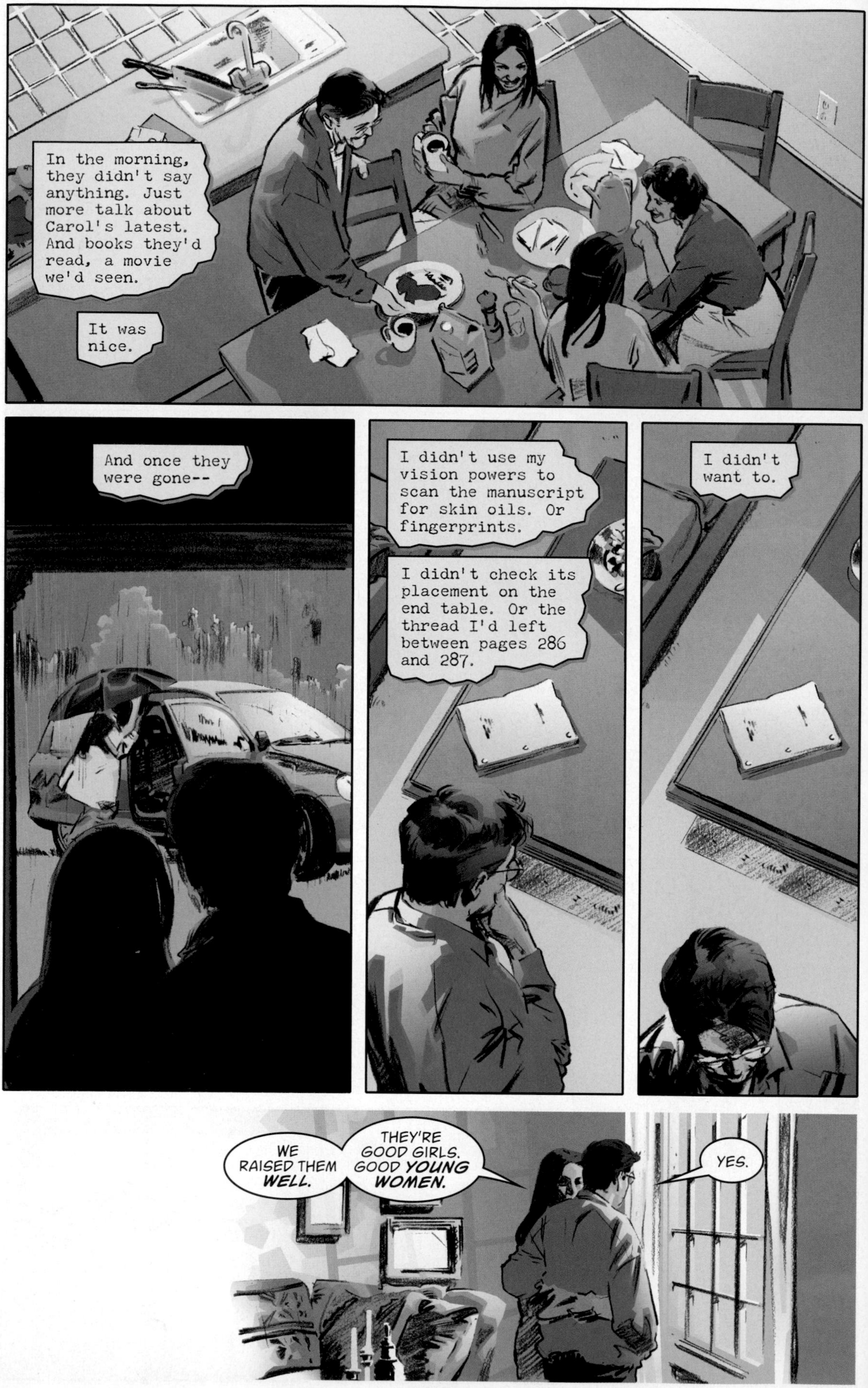
In the morning, they didn't say anything. Just more talk about Carol's latest. And books they'd read, a movie we'd seen.
It was nice.
And once they were gone--
I didn't use my vision powers to scan the manuscript for skin oils. Or fingerprints.
I didn't check its placement on the end table. Or the thread I'd left between pages 286 and 287.
I didn't want to.
WE RAISED THEM WELL.
THEY'RE GOOD GIRLS. GOOD YOUNG WOMEN.
YES.

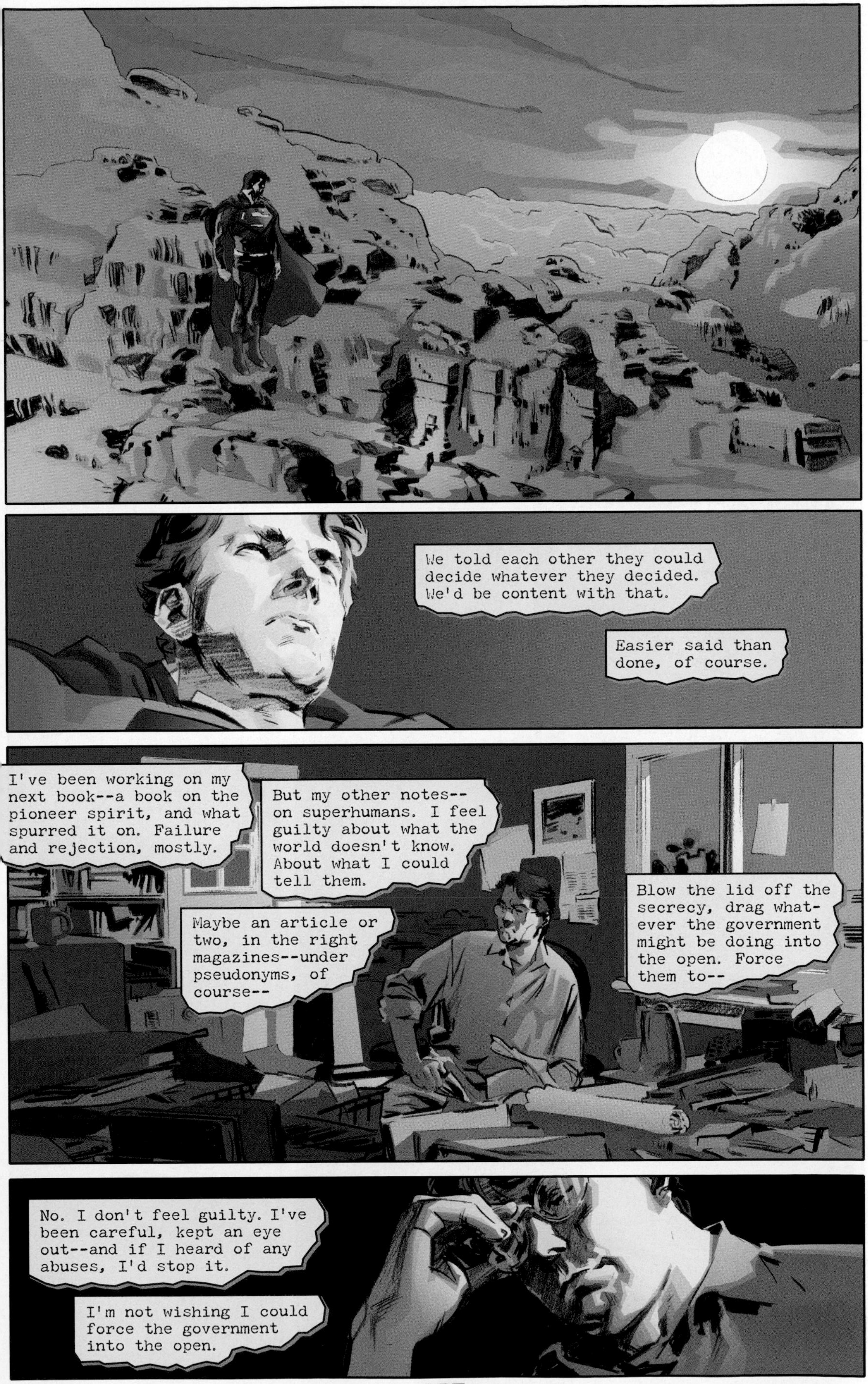

We told each other they could decide whatever they decided. We'd be content with that.
Easier said than done, of course.
I've been working on my next book--a book on the pioneer spirit, and what spurred it on. Failure and rejection, mostly.
But my other notes--on superhumans. I feel guilty about what the world doesn't know. About what I could tell them.
Maybe an article or two, in the right magazines--under pseudonyms, of course--
Blow the lid off the secrecy, drag whatever the government might be doing into the open. Force them to--
No. I don't feel guilty. I've been careful, kept an eye out--and if I heard of any abuses, I'd stop it.
I'm not wishing I could force the government into the open.

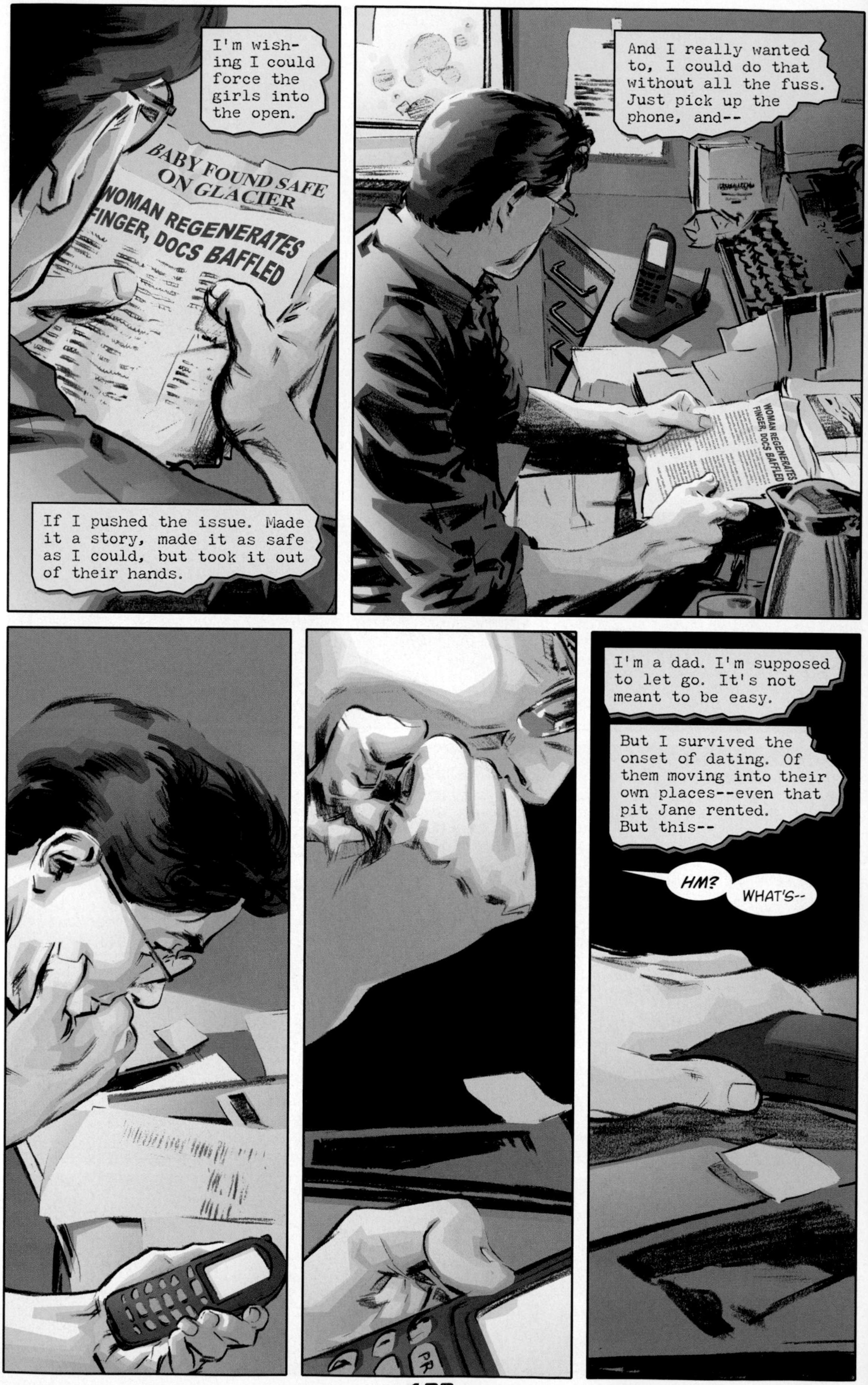

I'm wishing I could force the girls into the open.
BABY FOUND SAFE ON GLACIER
WOMAN REGENERATES FINGER, DOCS BAFFLED
If I pushed the issue. Made it a story, made it as safe as I could, but took it out of their hands.
And I really wanted to, I could do that without all the fuss. Just pick up the phone, and--
WOMAN REGENERATES FINGER, DOCS BAFFLED
I'm a dad. I'm supposed to let go. It's not meant to be easy.
But I survived the onset of dating. Of them moving into their own places--even that pit Jane rented. But this--
HM?
WHAT'S--

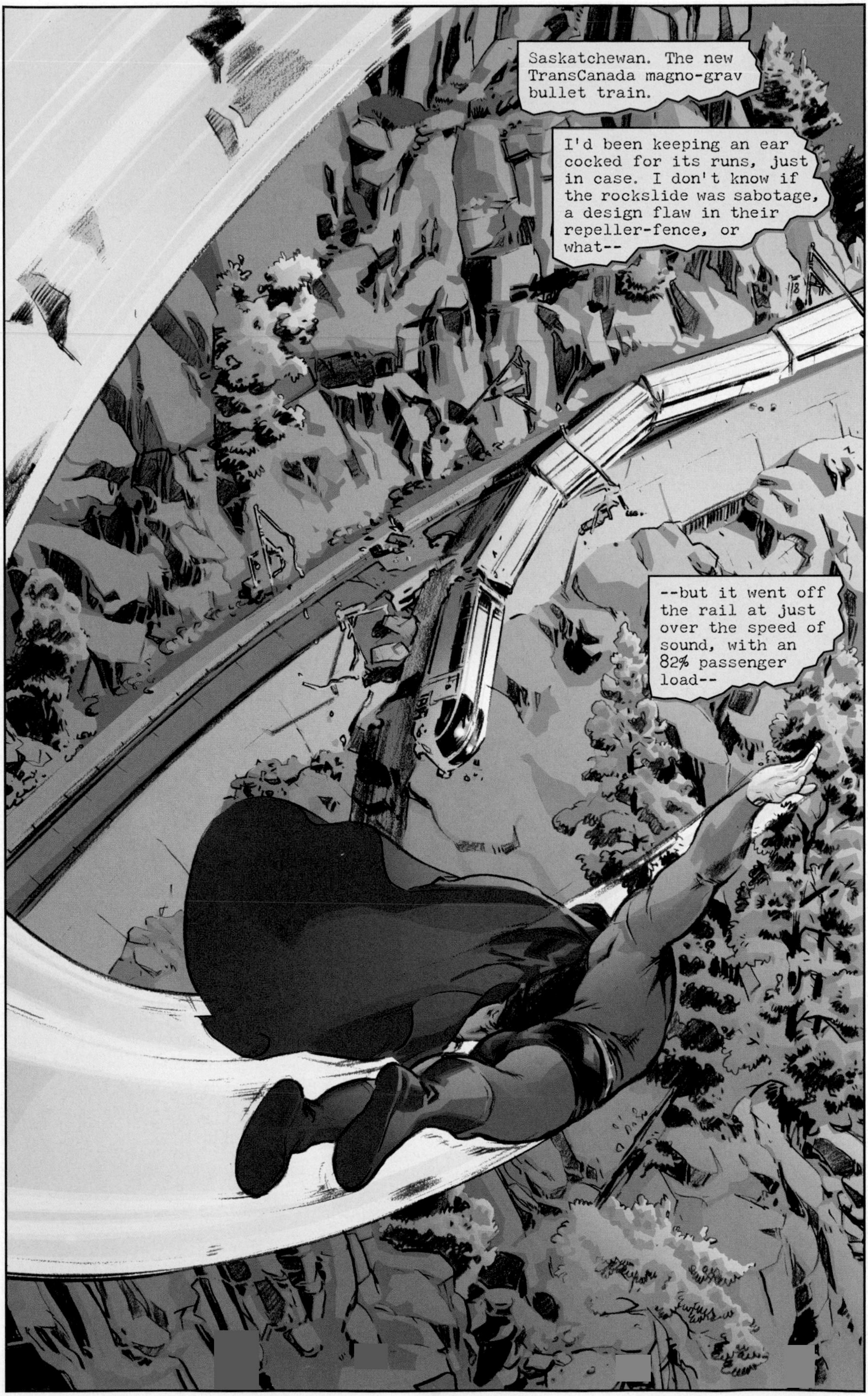
Saskatchewan. The new TransCanada magno-grav bullet train.
I'd been keeping an ear cocked for its runs, just in case. I don't know if the rockslide was sabotage, a design flaw in their repeller-fence, or what--
--but it went off the rail at just over the speed of sound, with an 82% passenger load--

Catching it was no trouble, of course.

But keeping it from whiplashing, keeping the cars in an arc, so I could decelerate them all together--

--well, imagine backing a car with a heavy trailer out of your driveway--

--but it's 142 trailers in a row, you're backing at 600 mph, and you've got to do it all in one shot.

Ten years ago, it'd have been no problem.

Heck, two years ago. Today...

I'm sure I could have done it. It was just a little trickier, and I'd end up sore. But--

WH--?

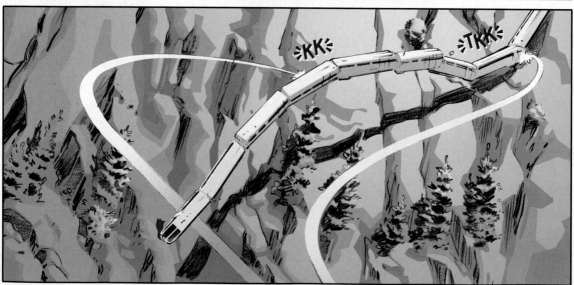

*KK*

*TKK*

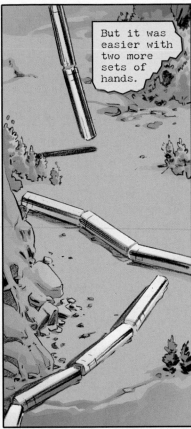

But it was easier with two more sets of hands.

WELL.

MAN. YOU HAVE **GOT** TO SHOW ME HOW YOU DO THAT.

BALANCING **THAT** MANY CARS--AT THAT **SPEED**--

CAROL, IS THAT **REALLY** THE FIRST THING YOU WANT TO TALK ABOUT?

IT WAS **AUSTRALIA**-- RIGHT, DAD? YOU FIGURED IT OUT IN AUSTRALIA.

I THOUGHT MAYBE.

BUT LOOK, I WANT TO HEAR **EVERY- THING**. BUT YOUR MOM'S GOING TO WANT TO HEAR IT **TOO**.

COME ON--

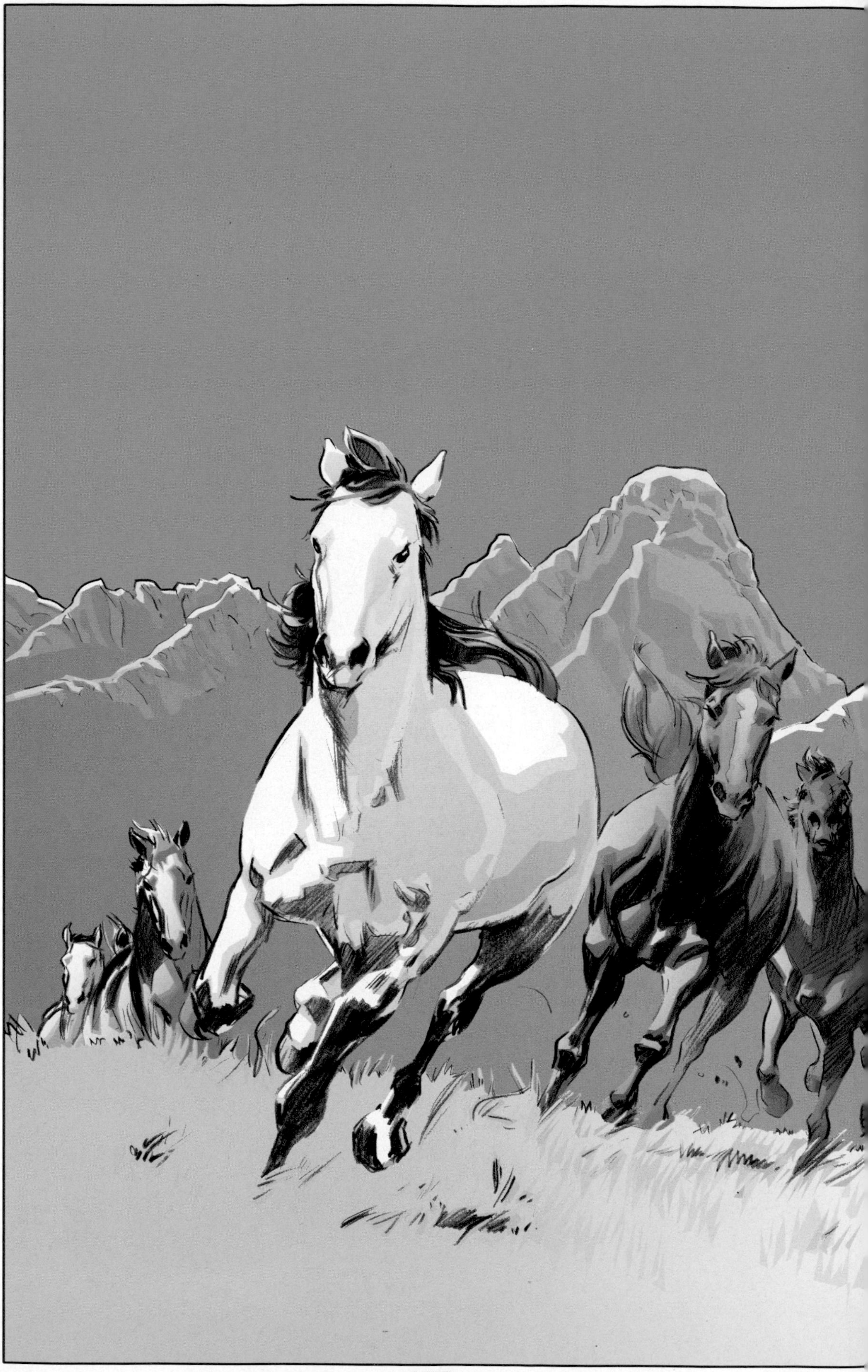

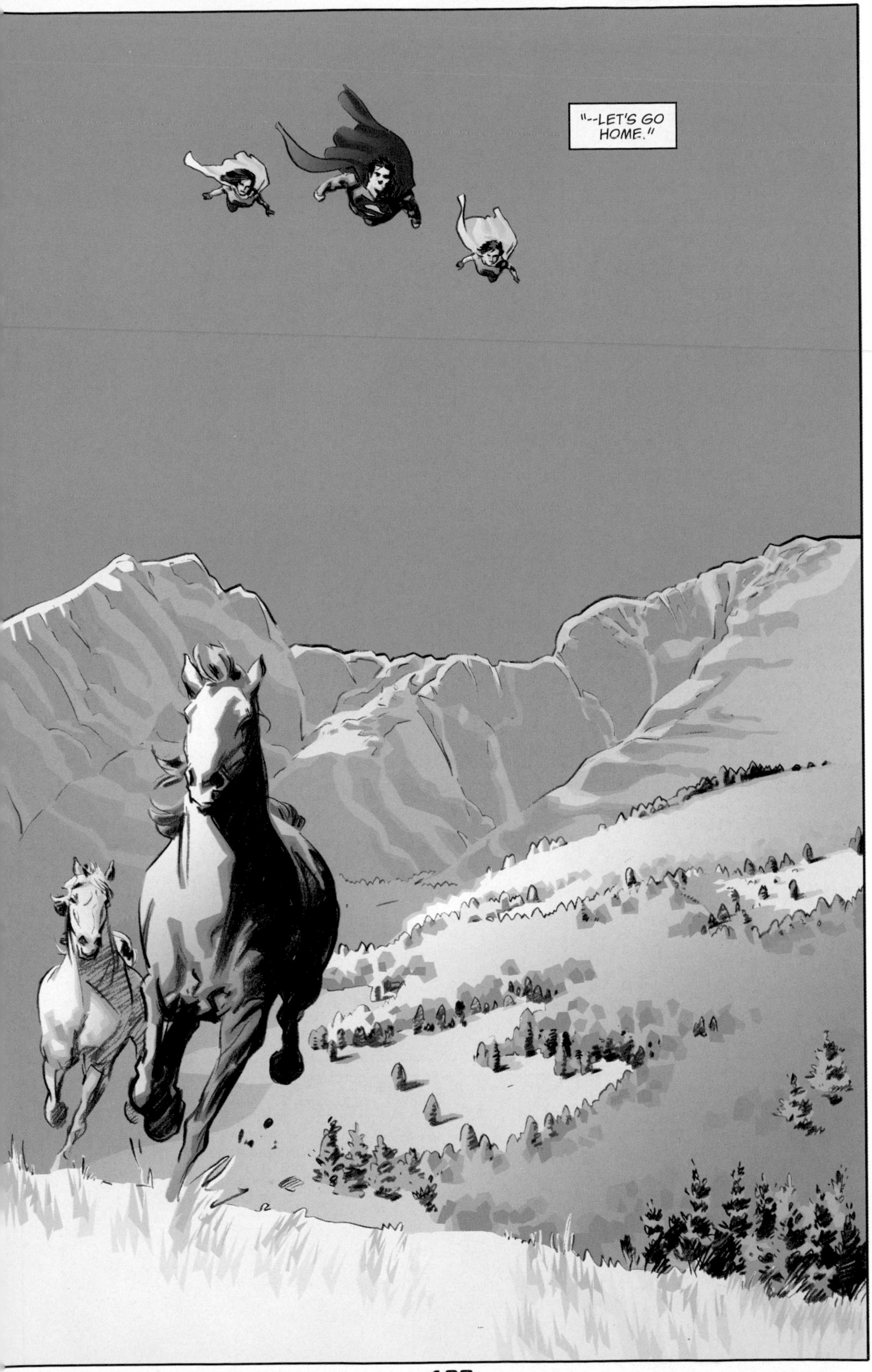
"--LET'S GO HOME."

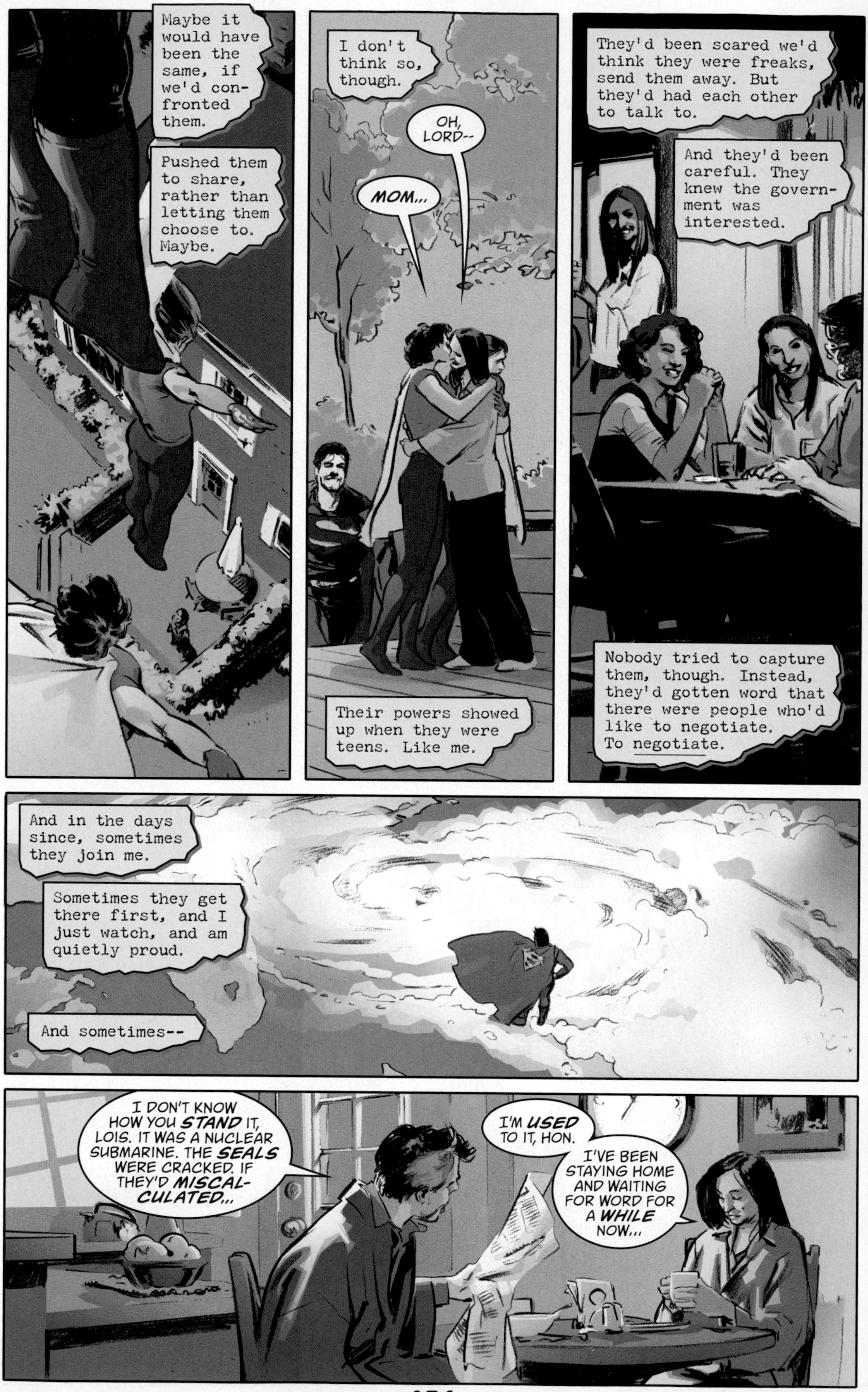
Maybe it would have been the same, if we'd confronted them.
Pushed them to share, rather than letting them choose to. Maybe.
I don't think so, though.
OH, LORD--
MOM...
Their powers showed up when they were teens. Like me.
They'd been scared we'd think they were freaks, send them away. But they'd had each other to talk to.
And they'd been careful. They knew the government was interested.
Nobody tried to capture them, though. Instead, they'd gotten word that there were people who'd like to negotiate. To negotiate.
And in the days since, sometimes they join me.
Sometimes they get there first, and I just watch, and am quietly proud.
And sometimes--
I DON'T KNOW HOW YOU STAND IT, LOIS. IT WAS A NUCLEAR SUBMARINE. THE SEALS WERE CRACKED. IF THEY'D MISCALCULATED...
I'M USED TO IT, HON.
I'VE BEEN STAYING HOME AND WAITING FOR WORD FOR A WHILE NOW...

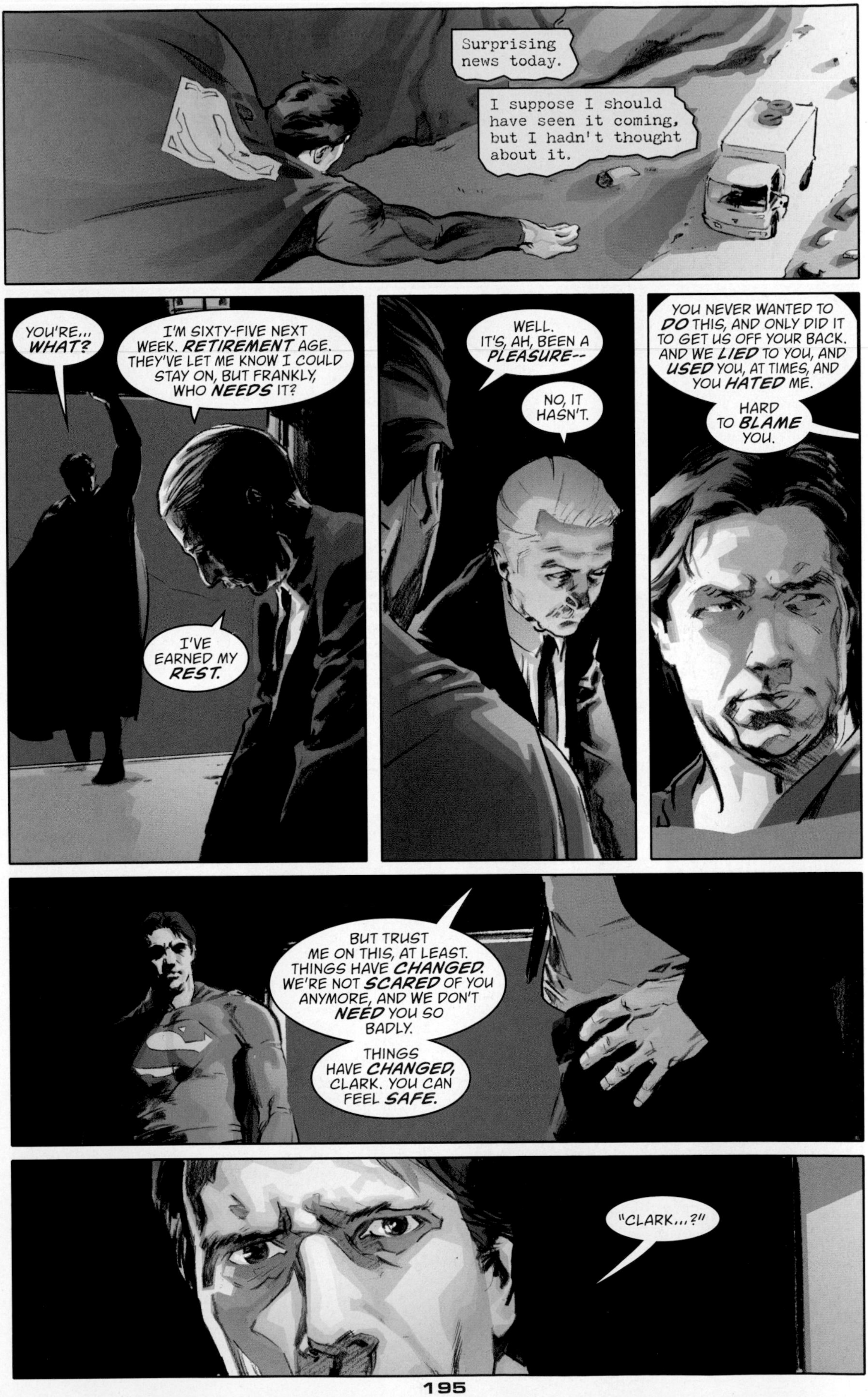
Surprising news today.
I suppose I should have seen it coming, but I hadn't thought about it.
YOU'RE... WHAT?
I'M SIXTY-FIVE NEXT WEEK. RETIREMENT AGE. THEY'VE LET ME KNOW I COULD STAY ON, BUT FRANKLY, WHO NEEDS IT?
I'VE EARNED MY REST.
WELL. IT'S, AH, BEEN A PLEASURE--
NO, IT HASN'T.
YOU NEVER WANTED TO DO THIS, AND ONLY DID IT TO GET US OFF YOUR BACK. AND WE LIED TO YOU, AND USED YOU, AT TIMES, AND YOU HATED ME.
HARD TO BLAME YOU.
BUT TRUST ME ON THIS, AT LEAST. THINGS HAVE CHANGED. WE'RE NOT SCARED OF YOU ANYMORE, AND WE DON'T NEED YOU SO BADLY.
THINGS HAVE CHANGED, CLARK. YOU CAN FEEL SAFE.
"CLARK...?"

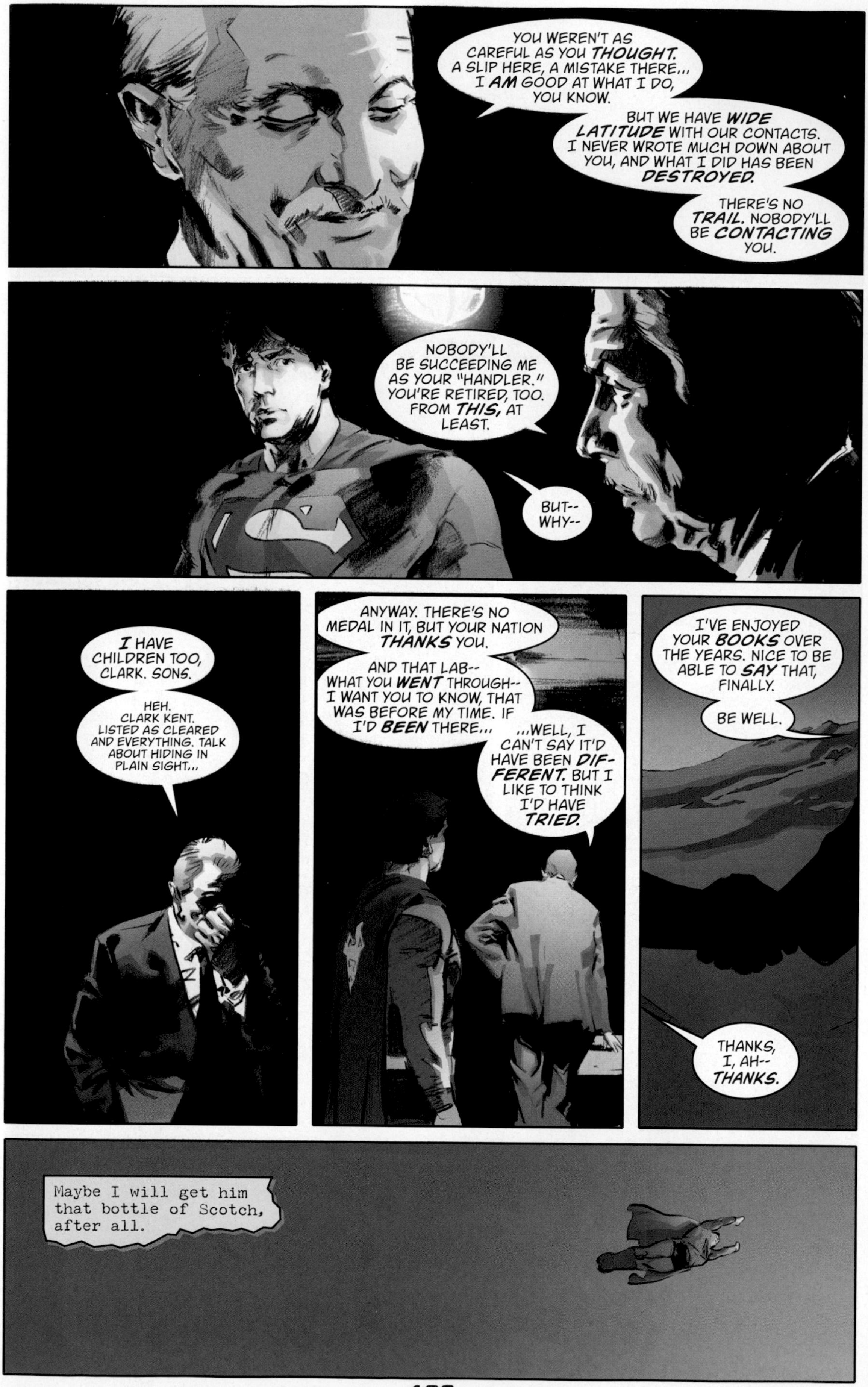
YOU WEREN'T AS CAREFUL AS YOU THOUGHT. A SLIP HERE, A MISTAKE THERE... I AM GOOD AT WHAT I DO, YOU KNOW.
BUT WE HAVE WIDE LATITUDE WITH OUR CONTACTS. I NEVER WROTE MUCH DOWN ABOUT YOU, AND WHAT I DID HAS BEEN DESTROYED.
THERE'S NO TRAIL. NOBODY'LL BE CONTACTING YOU.
NOBODY'LL BE SUCCEEDING ME AS YOUR "HANDLER." YOU'RE RETIRED, TOO. FROM THIS, AT LEAST.
BUT-- WHY--
I HAVE CHILDREN TOO, CLARK. SONS.
HEH. CLARK KENT. LISTED AS CLEARED AND EVERYTHING. TALK ABOUT HIDING IN PLAIN SIGHT...
ANYWAY. THERE'S NO MEDAL IN IT, BUT YOUR NATION THANKS YOU.
AND THAT LAB-- WHAT YOU WENT THROUGH-- I WANT YOU TO KNOW, THAT WAS BEFORE MY TIME. IF I'D BEEN THERE...
...WELL, I CAN'T SAY IT'D HAVE BEEN DIF-FERENT. BUT I LIKE TO THINK I'D HAVE TRIED.
I'VE ENJOYED YOUR BOOKS OVER THE YEARS. NICE TO BE ABLE TO SAY THAT, FINALLY.
BE WELL.
THANKS, I, AH-- THANKS.
Maybe I will get him that bottle of Scotch, after all.

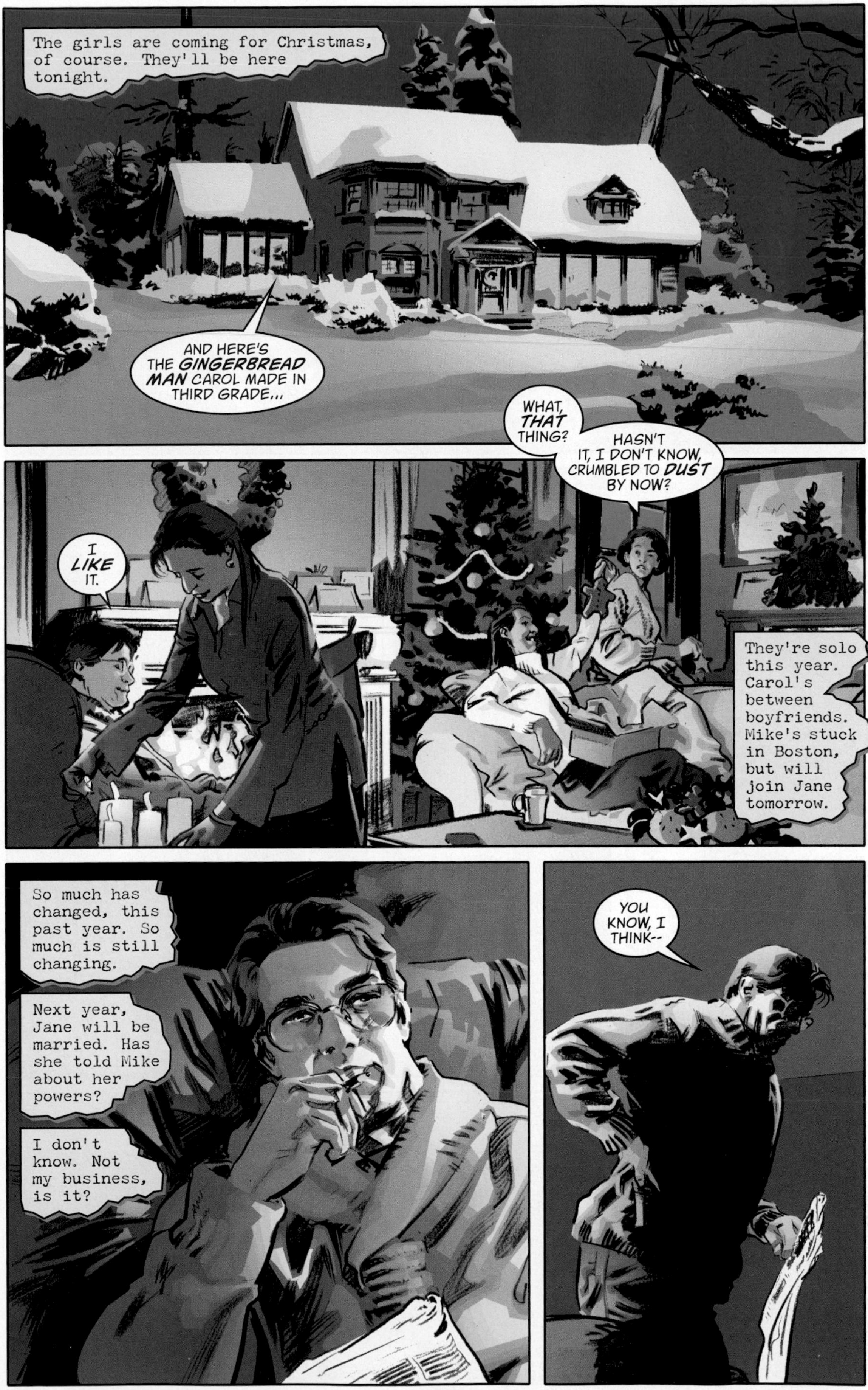
The girls are coming for Christmas, of course. They'll be here tonight.
AND HERE'S THE GINGERBREAD MAN CAROL MADE IN THIRD GRADE...
WHAT, THAT THING?
HASN'T IT, I DON'T KNOW, CRUMBLED TO DUST BY NOW?
I LIKE IT.
They're solo this year. Carol's between boyfriends. Mike's stuck in Boston, but will join Jane tomorrow.
So much has changed, this past year. So much is still changing.
Next year, Jane will be married. Has she told Mike about her powers?
I don't know. Not my business, is it?
YOU KNOW, I THINK--

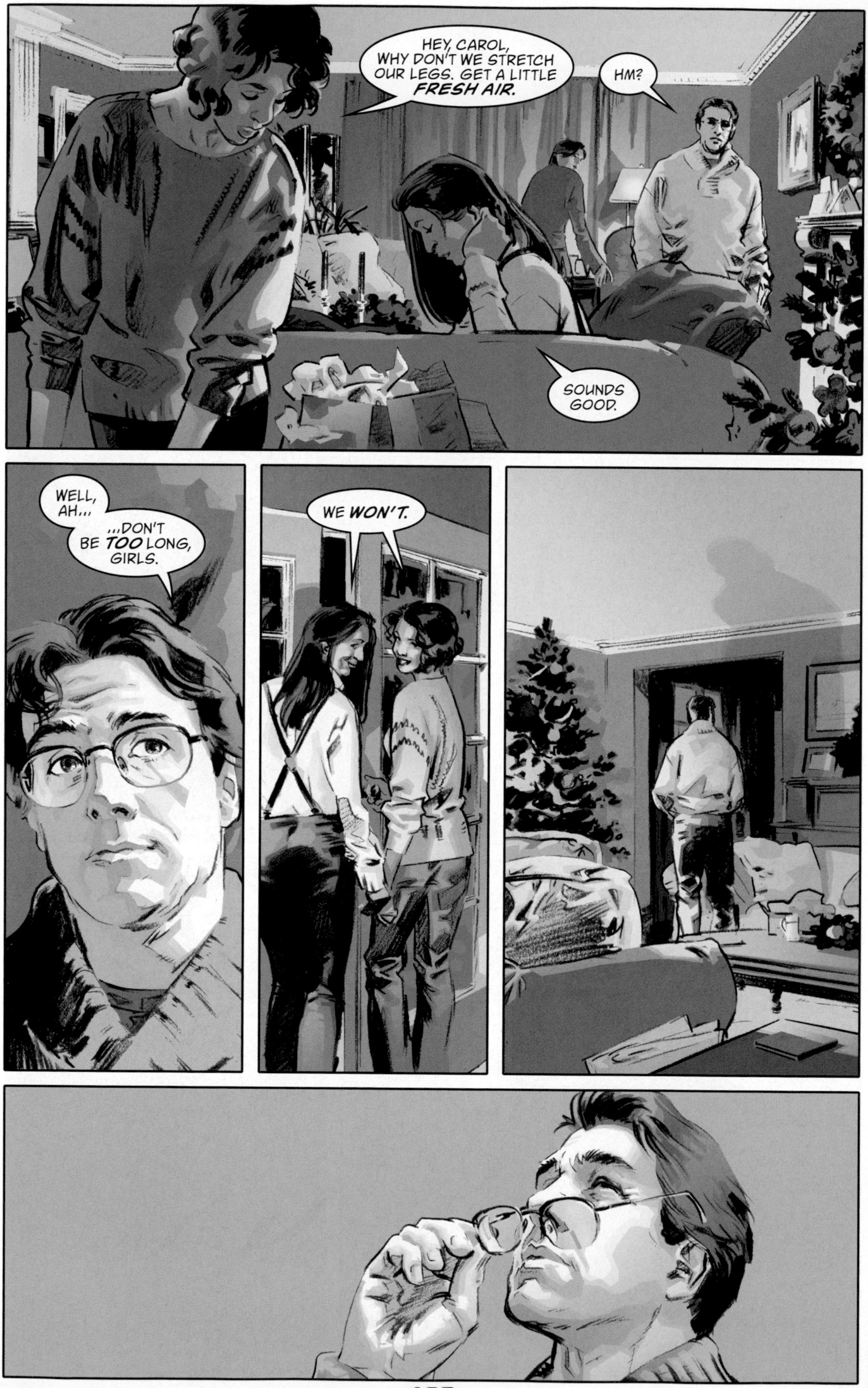
HEY, CAROL, WHY DON'T WE STRETCH OUR LEGS. GET A LITTLE FRESH AIR.
HM?
SOUNDS GOOD.
WELL, AH...
...DON'T BE TOO LONG, GIRLS.
WE WON'T.

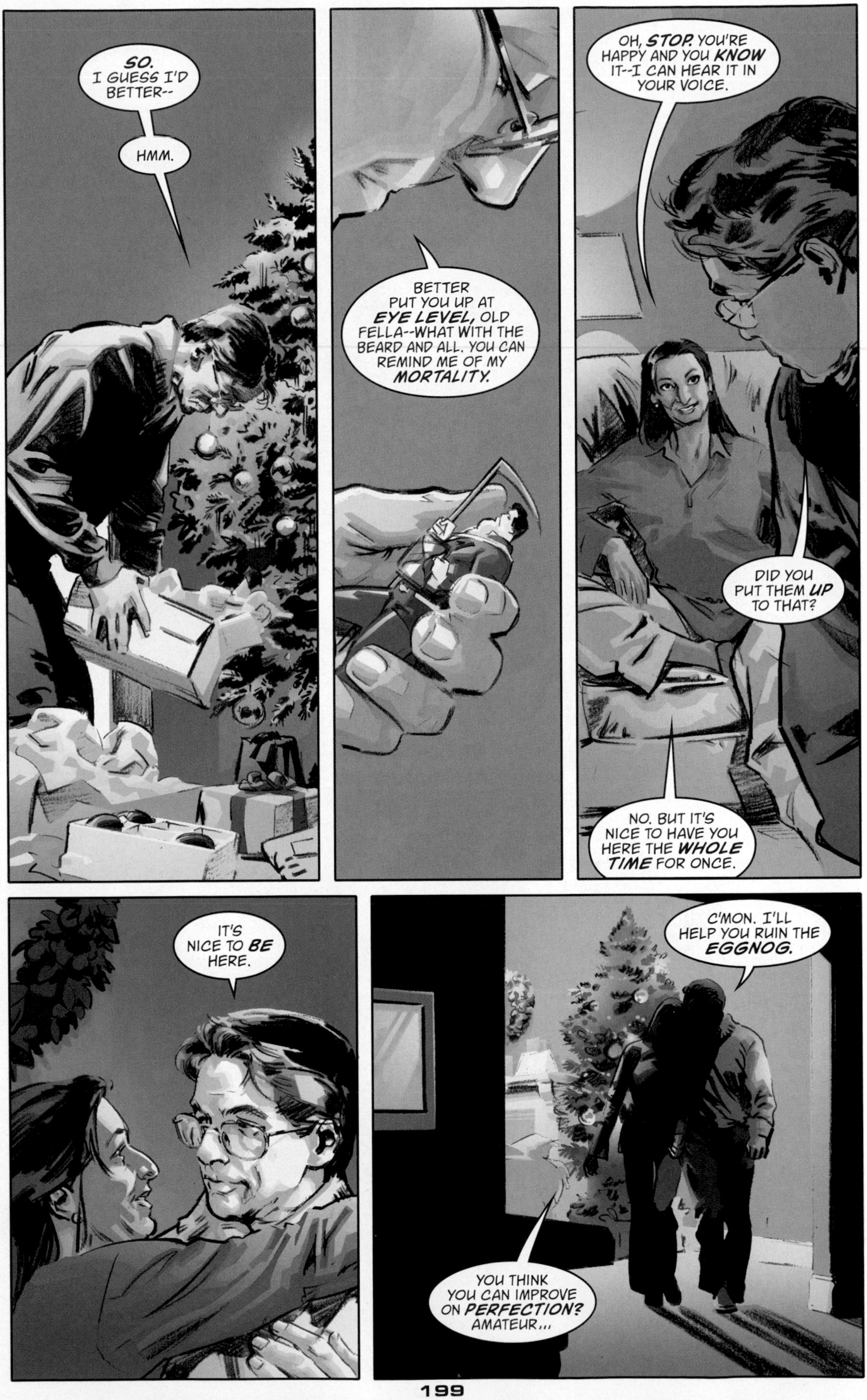
SO. I GUESS I'D BETTER--
HMM.
BETTER PUT YOU UP AT EYE LEVEL, OLD FELLA--WHAT WITH THE BEARD AND ALL. YOU CAN REMIND ME OF MY MORTALITY.
OH, STOP. YOU'RE HAPPY AND YOU KNOW IT--I CAN HEAR IT IN YOUR VOICE.
DID YOU PUT THEM UP TO THAT?
NO. BUT IT'S NICE TO HAVE YOU HERE THE WHOLE TIME FOR ONCE.
IT'S NICE TO BE HERE.
C'MON. I'LL HELP YOU RUIN THE EGGNOG.
YOU THINK YOU CAN IMPROVE ON PERFECTION? AMATEUR...

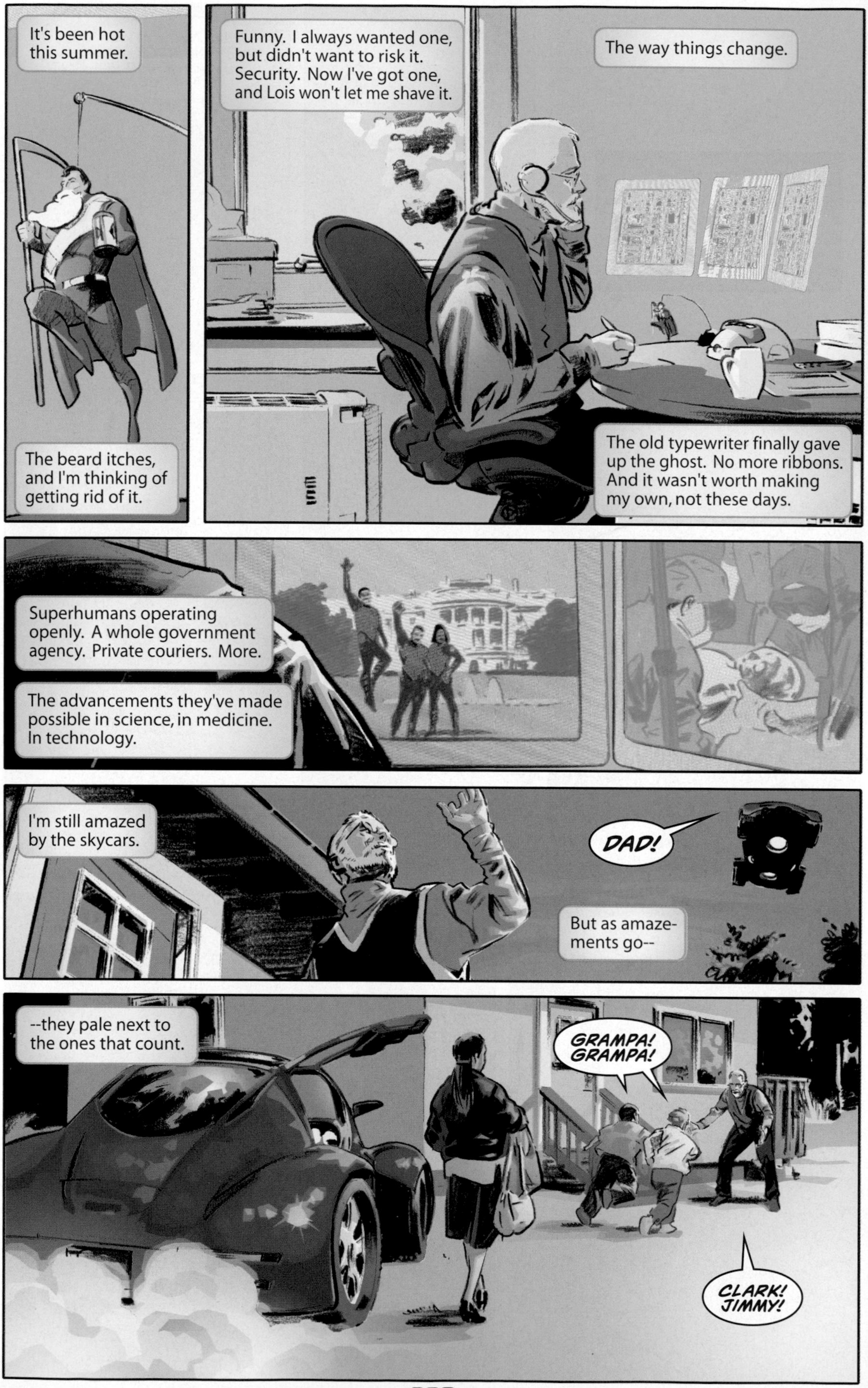
It's been hot this summer.
The beard itches, and I'm thinking of getting rid of it.
Funny. I always wanted one, but didn't want to risk it. Security. Now I've got one, and Lois won't let me shave it.
The way things change.
The old typewriter finally gave up the ghost. No more ribbons. And it wasn't worth making my own, not these days.
Superhumans operating openly. A whole government agency. Private couriers. More.
The advancements they've made possible in science, in medicine. In technology.
I'm still amazed by the skycars.
DAD!
But as amaze-ments go--
--they pale next to the ones that count.
GRAMPA! GRAMPA!
CLARK! JIMMY!

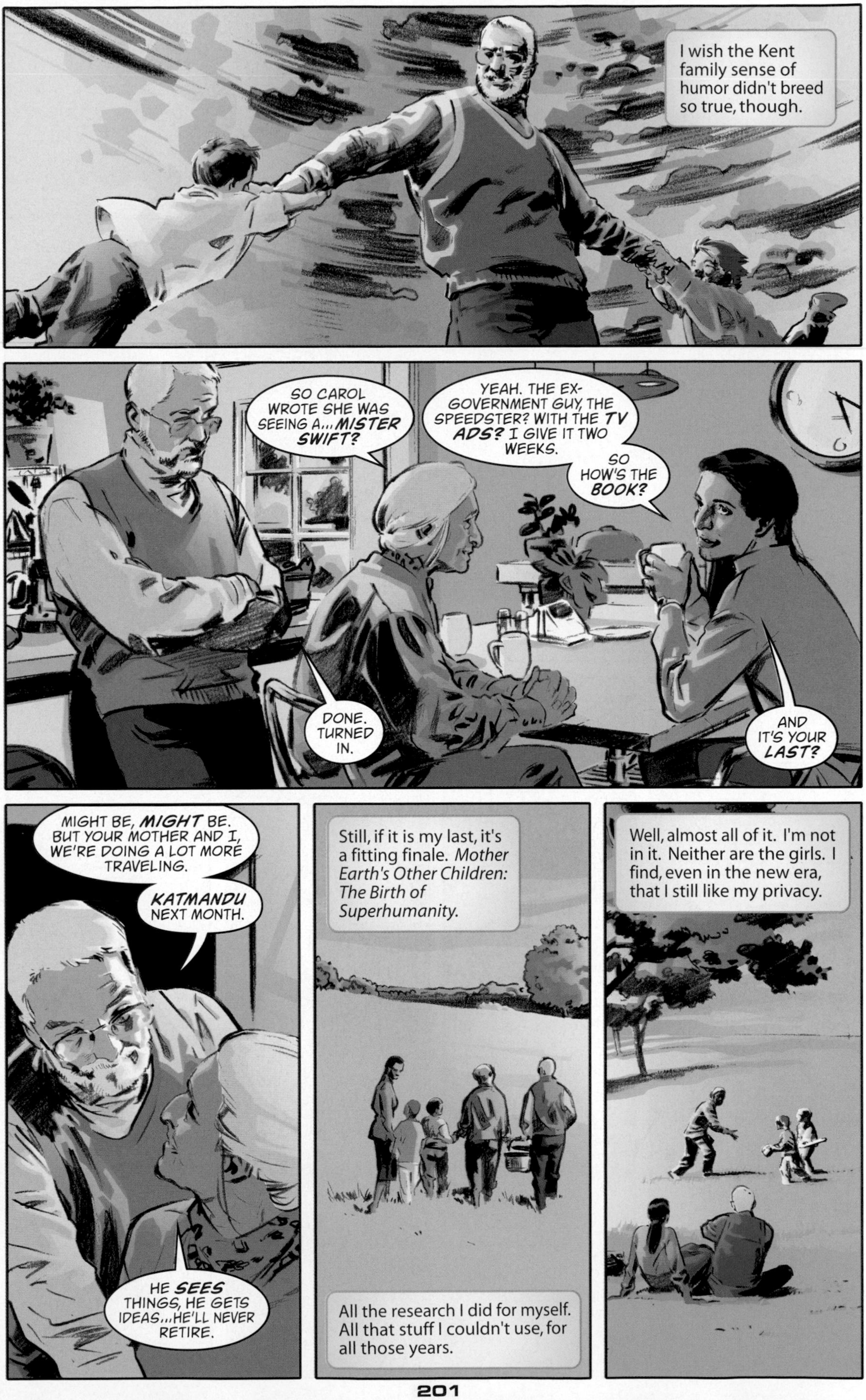
I wish the Kent family sense of humor didn't breed so true, though.
SO CAROL WROTE SHE WAS SEEING A... MISTER SWIFT?
YEAH. THE EX-GOVERNMENT GUY, THE SPEEDSTER? WITH THE TV ADS? I GIVE IT TWO WEEKS.
SO HOW'S THE BOOK?
DONE. TURNED IN.
AND IT'S YOUR LAST?
MIGHT BE, MIGHT BE. BUT YOUR MOTHER AND I, WE'RE DOING A LOT MORE TRAVELING.
KATMANDU NEXT MONTH.
HE SEES THINGS, HE GETS IDEAS... HE'LL NEVER RETIRE.
Still, if it is my last, it's a fitting finale. Mother Earth's Other Children: The Birth of Superhumanity.
All the research I did for myself. All that stuff I couldn't use, for all those years.
Well, almost all of it. I'm not in it. Neither are the girls. I find, even in the new era, that I still like my privacy.

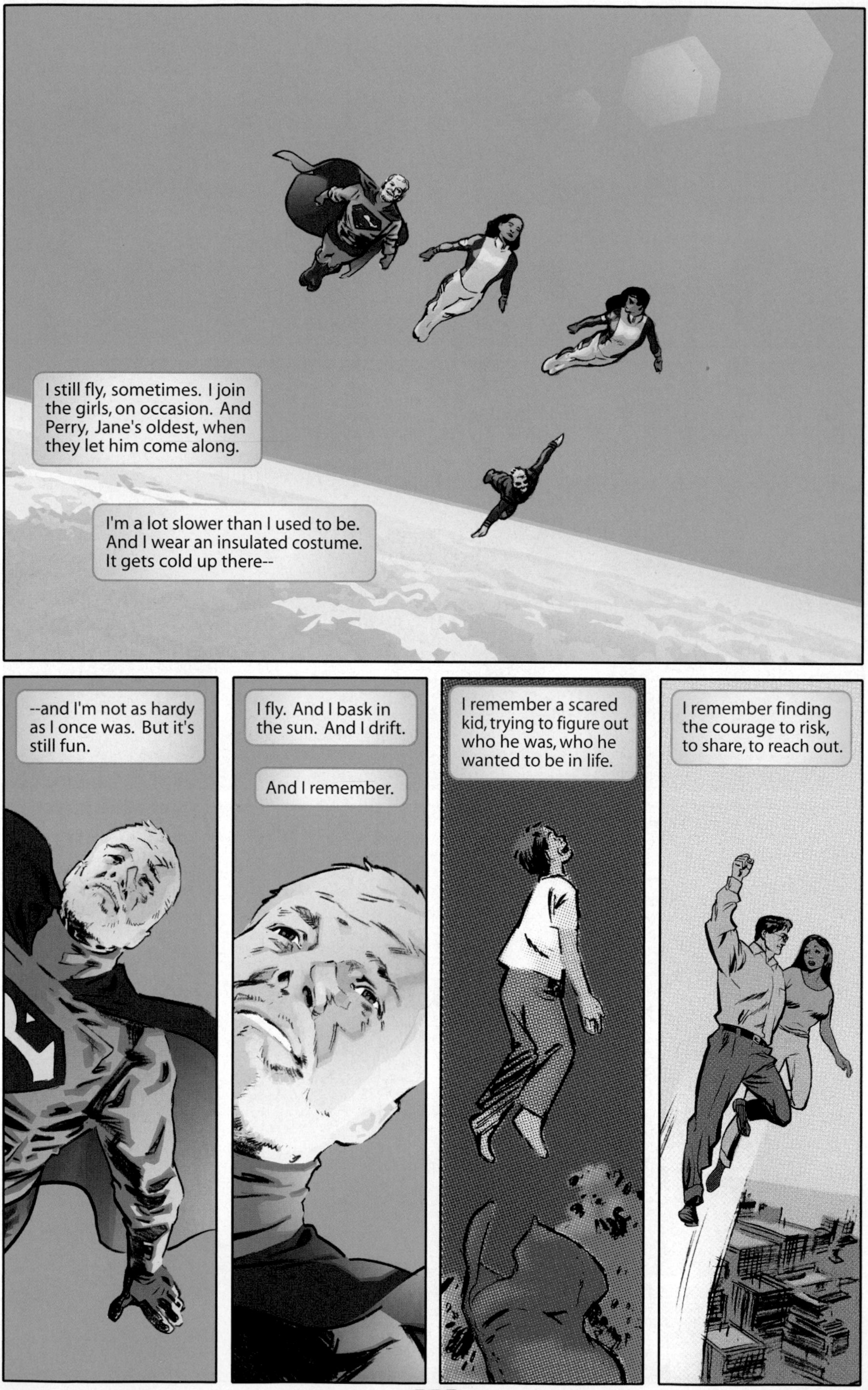
I still fly, sometimes. I join the girls, on occasion. And Perry, Jane's oldest, when they let him come along.
I'm a lot slower than I used to be. And I wear an insulated costume. It gets cold up there--
--and I'm not as hardy as I once was. But it's still fun.
I fly. And I bask in the sun. And I drift.
And I remember.
I remember a scared kid, trying to figure out who he was, who he wanted to be in life.
I remember finding the courage to risk, to share, to reach out.

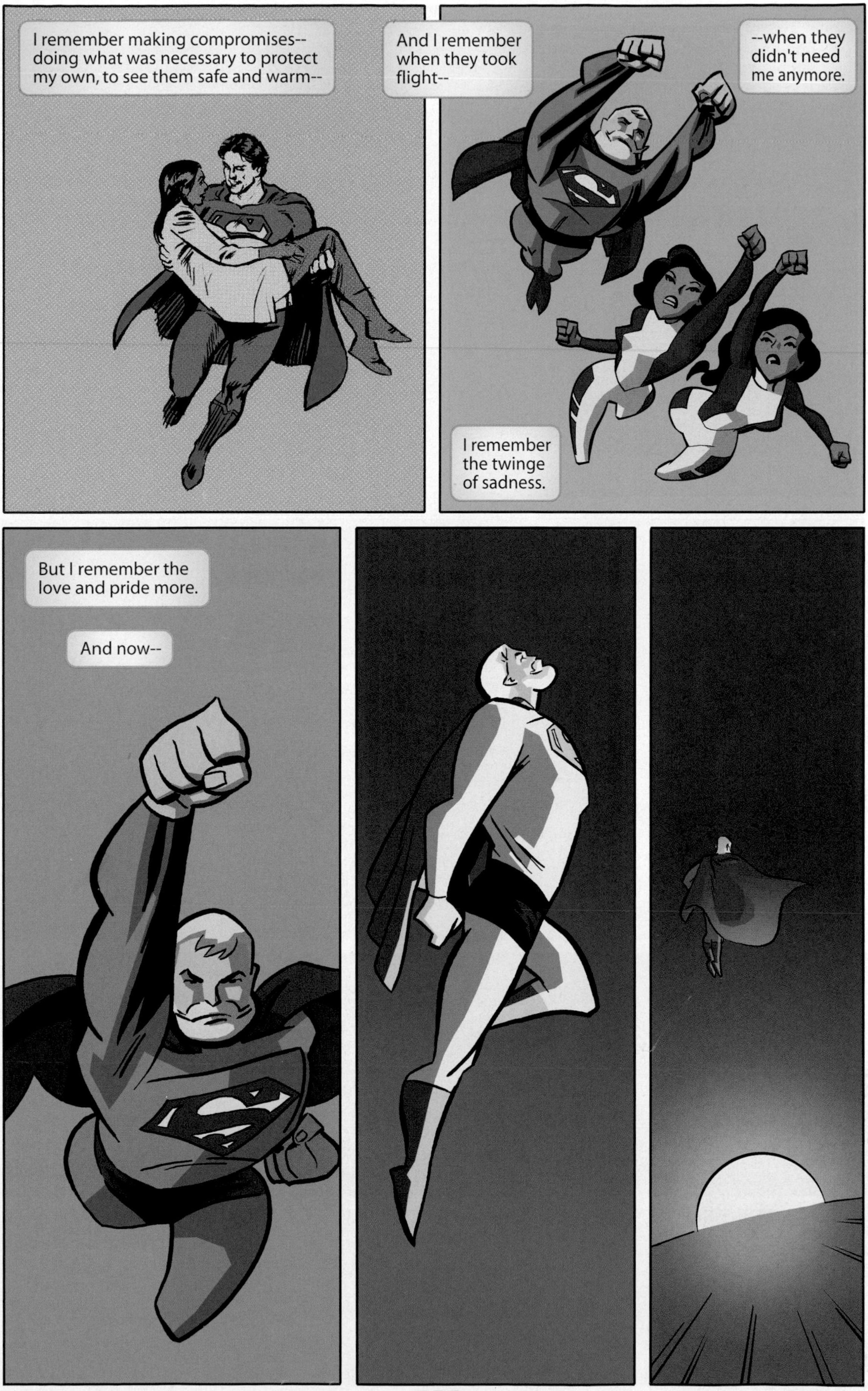
I remember making compromises--doing what was necessary to protect my own, to see them safe and warm--
And I remember when they took flight--
--when they didn't need me anymore.
I remember the twinge of sadness.
But I remember the love and pride more.
And now--

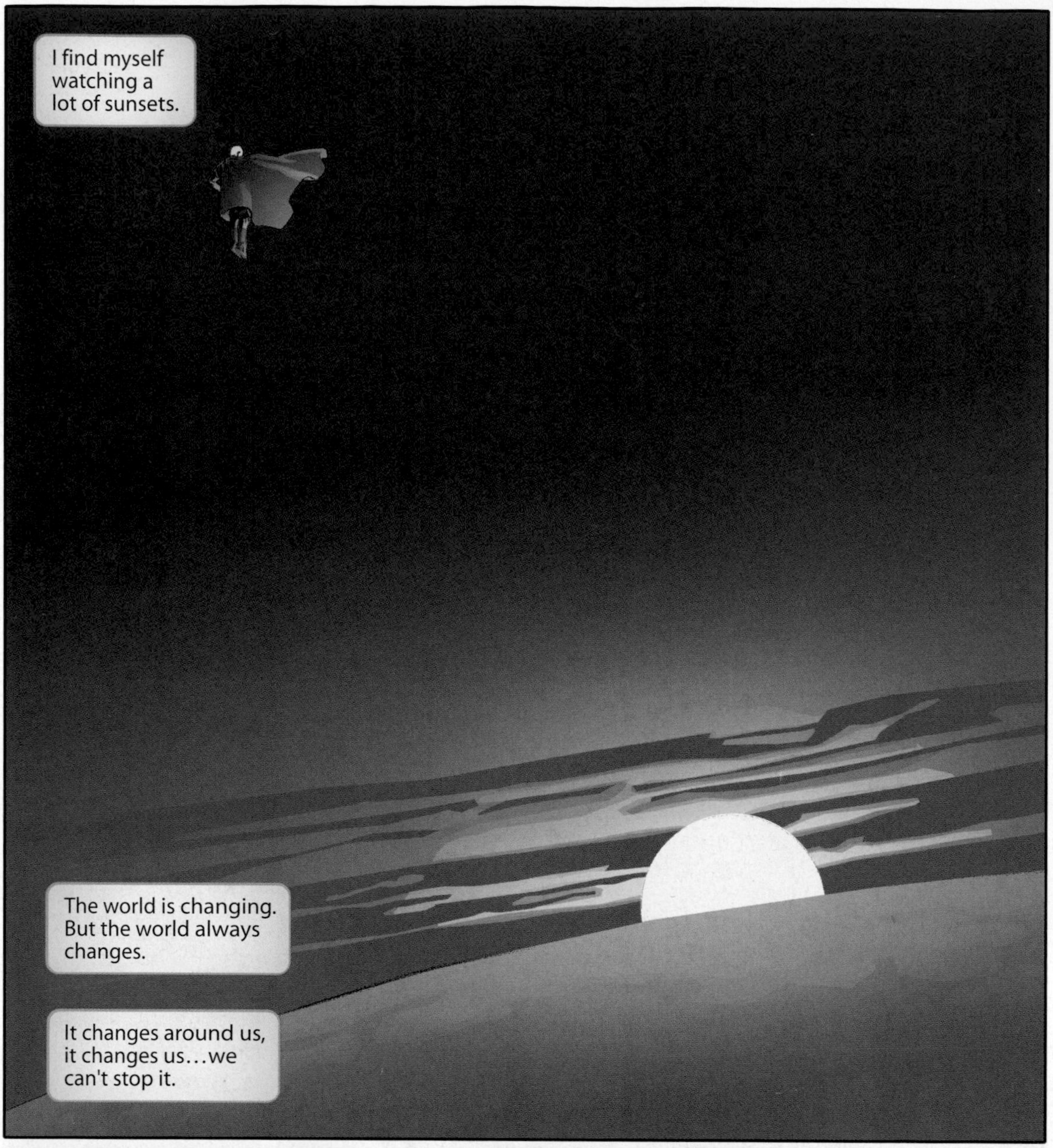
I find myself watching a lot of sunsets.
The world is changing. But the world always changes.
It changes around us, it changes us…we can't stop it.

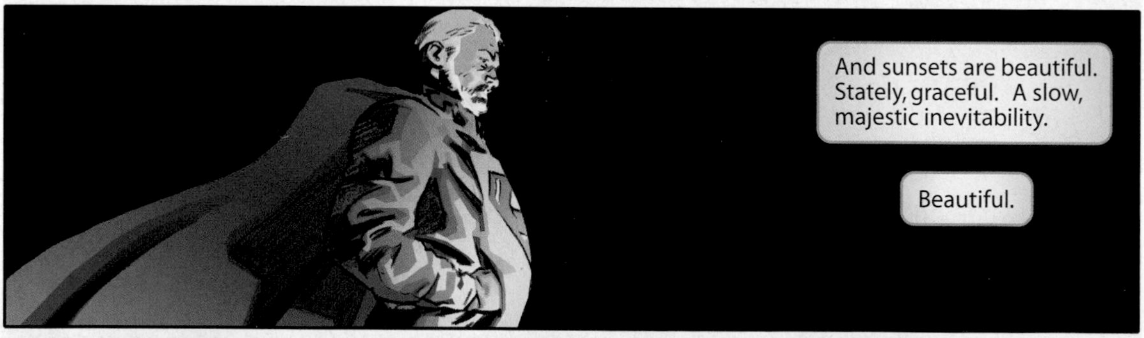
And sunsets are beautiful. Stately, graceful. A slow, majestic inevitability.
Beautiful.

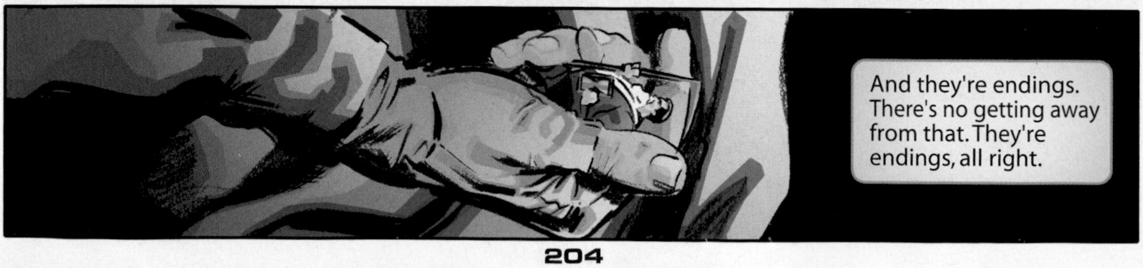
And they're endings. There's no getting away from that. They're endings, all right.

I've had a good life.

Different from most, but not all *that* different. Maybe I had a "secret identity," but then when you think about it, don't we all?

A part of ourselves very few people ever get to see.

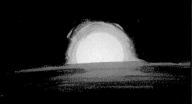

The part we think of as "me." The part that deals with the big stuff. Makes the real choices. The part everything else is a reflection of.

Mine was just a little… louder than most.

Katmandu. Belize. Lois has been talking about Antarctica next.

And Perry's graduation, and Carol's business troubles. She should really go out on her own. Her mom could tell her.

And that's the thing about sunsets. They're majestic, stately, lovely and inevitable.

And then, a little ways to the east…

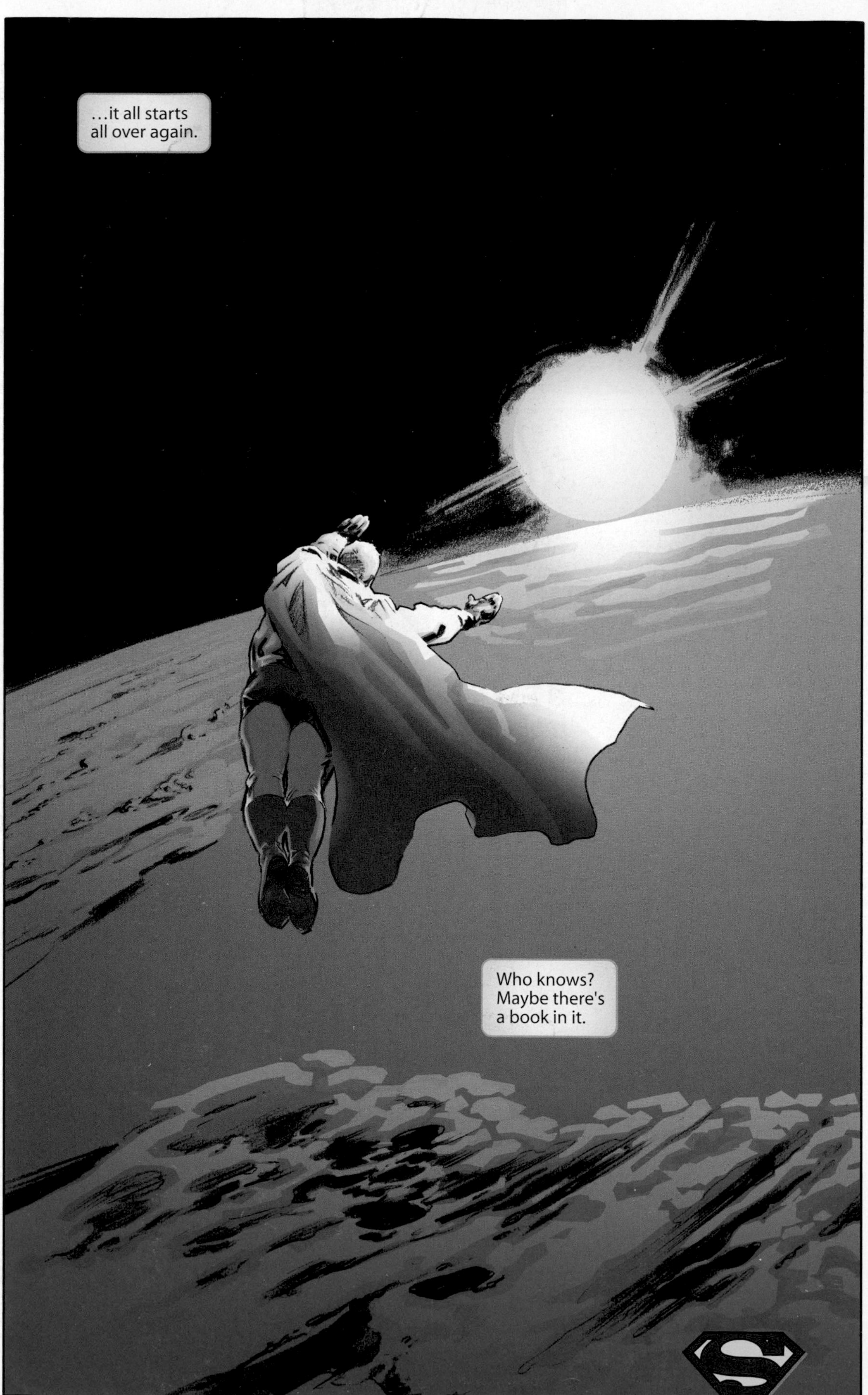
...it all starts all over again.
Who knows? Maybe there's a book in it.

# biographies

**KURT BUSIEK** was born in Boston, Massachusetts in 1960. He began writing comics professionally in 1982, selling stories to DC and Marvel Comics in the same month, both of which came out the same day. Since then, he's written series and characters ranging from Mickey Mouse to Vampirella, including Superman, Spider-Man, Iron Man, the Avengers and more. He is best known for the *Marvels* miniseries and for his co-creation, ASTRO CITY, both of which have garnered numerous industry awards, as well as runs on *Untold Tales of Spider-Man, Thunderbolts* (another co-creation) and a long run on Marvel's *Avengers* series with his JLA/AVENGERS partner George Pérez. In late 2004, Kurt became the regular writer on JLA. He lives in the Pacific Northwest with his wife, Ann, and his two daughters. He started writing and drawing his own JLA/AVENGERS clash in 1977.

**STUART IMMONEN** has, since 1986, pursued a career in the entertainment arts. His first endeavor in comics, after attending Toronto's York University, was the self-published series *Playground*, with partner Kathryn Kuder, and was followed up with a one-shot edition from Caliber Press. Together, they co-edited three issues of the humor anthology *Headcheese*. In 1993, following several jobs at RipOff Press, Innovation and Revolutionary Comics, Stuart found work at DC and Marvel, which quickly led to long stints on a variety of high-profile and critically successful series, including SUPERMAN, *X-Men, Fantastic Four, The Incredible Hulk, Ultimate Fantastic Four,* and the LEGION OF SUPER-HEROES. In addition to providing art chores for these series, Stuart also wrote and drew the INFERNO mini-series, and DC's first original Superman hardcover graphic novel, SUPERMAN: END OF THE CENTURY.

**TODD KLEIN** has been lettering comics since 1977. A highlight of his career is his work with Neil Gaiman on nearly all the original issues of THE SANDMAN, as well as BLACK ORCHID, DEATH and THE BOOKS OF MAGIC. Additionally, Todd has written stories featuring the Green Lantern Corps and THE OMEGA MEN. Currently, he is teamed with Alan Moore on all the AMERICA'S BEST COMICS titles in addition to FABLES. Todd has won numerous Eisner and Harvey Awards for his work.

DC COMICS™

*"It's fresh air. I like this all-too-human Superman, and I think a lot of you will, too."*
*—SCRIPPS HOWARD NEWS SERVICE*

START AT THE BEGINNING!

# SUPERMAN: ACTION COMICS VOLUME 1: SUPERMAN AND THE MEN OF STEEL

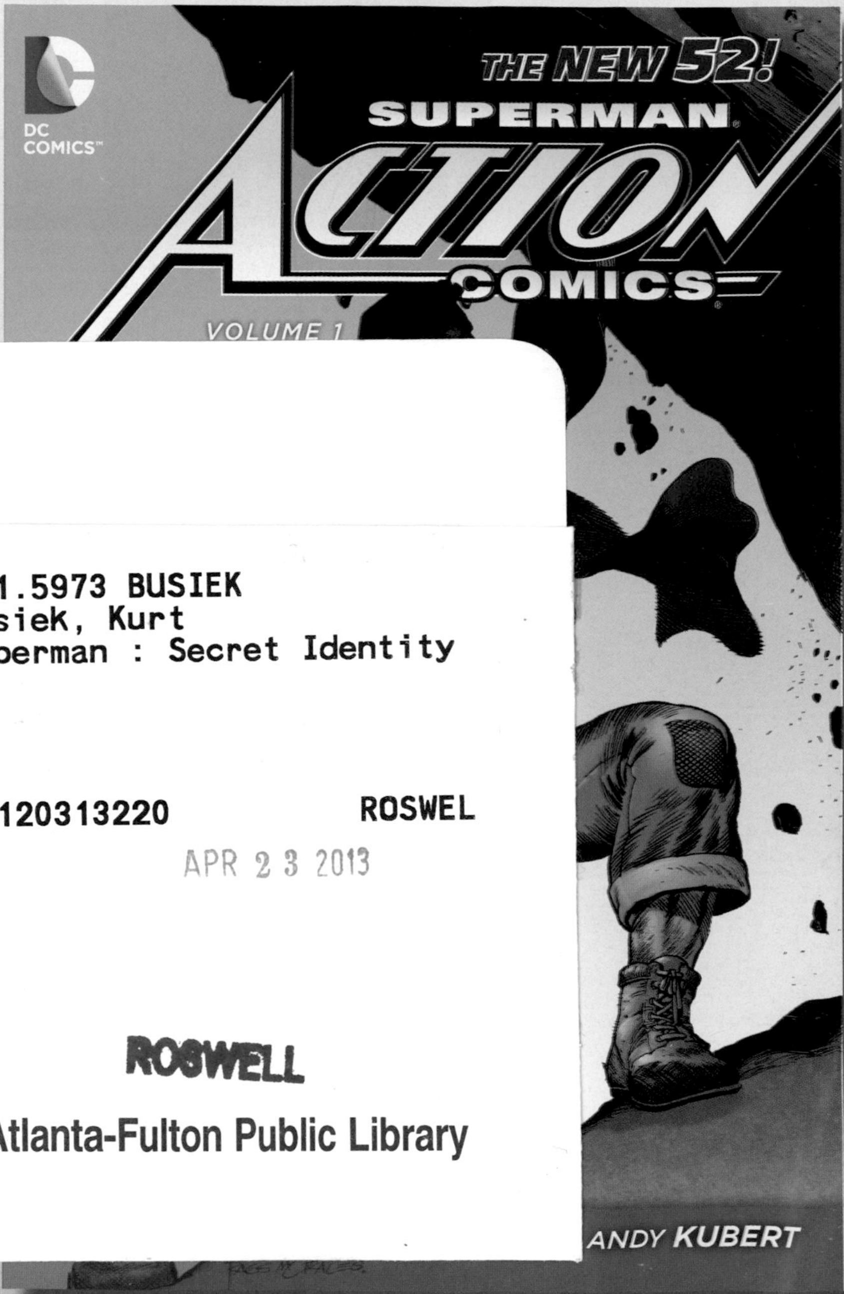
DC COMICS™
THE NEW 52!
SUPERMAN
ACTION COMICS
VOLUME 1
ANDY KUBERT

SUPERMAN VOLUME 1: WHAT PRICE TOMORROW?

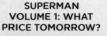

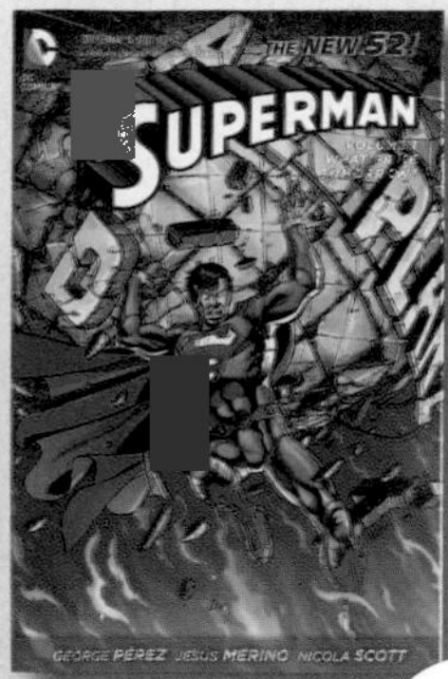
THE NEW 52!
SUPERMAN
GEORGE PÉREZ JESÚS MERINO NICOLA SCOTT

SUPERGIRL VOLUM
THE LAST DAUGHT
OF KRYPTON

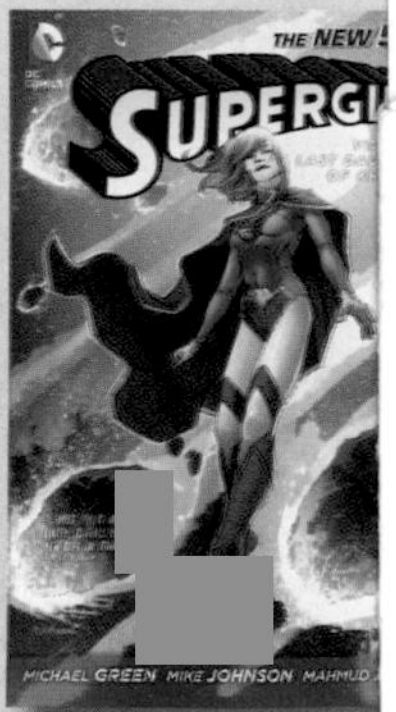
MICHAEL GREEN MIKE JOHNSON

SUPERBOY VOLUM
INCUBATION

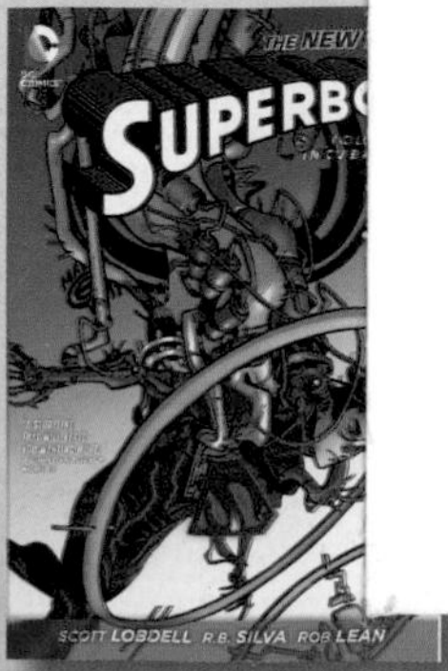
SCOTT LOBDELL R.B. SILVA ROB LEAN